A Celebration of Poets

Midwest
Grades 4-12
Spring 2012

creativeCOMMUNICATION
A CELEBRATION OF TODAY'S WRITERS

A Celebration of Poets
Midwest
Grades 4-12
Spring 2012

An anthology compiled by Creative Communication, Inc.

Published by:

creativeCOMMUNICATION
A CELEBRATION OF TODAY'S WRITERS

PO BOX 303 • SMITHFIELD, UTAH 84335
TEL. 435-713-4411 • WWW.POETICPOWER.COM

Authors are responsible for the originality of the writing submitted.

All rights reserved. No part of this book may be reproduced or transmitted in any form or by any means, electronic or mechanical without written permission of the author and publisher.

Copyright © 2012 by Creative Communication, Inc.
Printed in the United States of America

ISBN: 978-1-60050-511-9

FOREWORD

Dear Reader:

Is writing meaningful to your life? The greatest gift that my mother ever gave me was her writing. For over 70 years, she kept a record of every moment that was meaningful in her life. Taking these stories, she created several books which allow me to remember and relive moments in my childhood and the life my mother had as she grew up. She got into the habit of writing and has now left a great legacy.

As a parent, I know that my children bring home samples of their writing from school assignments each week. However, after a few days on the school bulletin board or fridge at home, these slices of their lives often get thrown away.

The books we publish create a legacy for each of these students. Their work is recorded to show friends, family and future generations. We are glad to be part of capturing their thoughts, hopes and dreams.

The students that are published have shared a bit of themselves with us. Thank you for being part of this process, as every writer needs a reader. We hope that by recognizing these students, writing will become a part of their life and bring meaning to others.

Sincerely,

Thomas Worthen, Ph.D.
Editor
Creative Communication

WRITING CONTESTS!

Enter our next POETRY contest!

Enter our next ESSAY contest!

Why should I enter?
Win prizes and get published! Each year thousands of dollars in prizes are awarded throughout North America. The top writers in each division receive a monetary award and a free book that includes their published poem or essay. Entries of merit are also selected to be published in our anthology.

Who may enter?
There are four divisions in the poetry contest. The poetry divisions are grades K-3, 4-6, 7-9, and 10-12. There are three divisions in the essay contest. The essay divisions are grades 3-6, 7-9, and 10-12.

What is needed to enter the contest?
To enter the poetry contest send in one original poem, 21 lines or less. To enter the essay contest send in one original non-fiction essay, 250 words or less, on any topic. Please submit each poem and essay with a title, and the following information clearly printed: the writer's name, current grade, home address (optional), school name, school address, teacher's name and teacher's email address (optional). Contact information will only be used to provide information about the contest. For complete contest information go to www.poeticpower.com.

How do I enter?

Enter a poem online at:
www.poeticpower.com
or
Mail your poem to:
 Poetry Contest
 PO Box 303
 Smithfield UT 84335

Enter an essay online at:
www.poeticpower.com
or
Mail your essay to:
 Essay Contest
 PO Box 303
 Smithfield UT 84335

When is the deadline?
Poetry contest deadlines are August 16th, December 6th and April 9th. Essay contest deadlines are July 19th, October 18th and February 19th. Students can enter one poem and one essay for each spring, summer, and fall contest deadline.

Are there benefits for my school?
Yes. We award $12,500 each year in grants to help with Language Arts programs. Schools qualify to apply for a grant by having 15 or more accepted entries.

Are there benefits for my teacher?
Yes. Teachers with five or more students published receive a free anthology that includes their students' writing.

For more information please go to our website at **www.poeticpower.com**, email us at editor@poeticpower.com or call 435-713-4411.

TABLE OF CONTENTS

POETIC ACHIEVEMENT HONOR SCHOOLS   1

LANGUAGE ARTS GRANT RECIPIENTS   5

GRADES 10-11-12 HIGH MERIT POEMS   7

GRADES 7-8-9 HIGH MERIT POEMS 39

GRADES 4-5-6 HIGH MERIT POEMS 133

INDEX 191

STATES INCLUDED IN THIS EDITION:

IOWA
KANSAS
NEBRASKA
NORTH DAKOTA
SOUTH DAKOTA

Spring 2012 Poetic Achievement Honor Schools

Teachers who had fifteen or more poets accepted to be published

The following schools are recognized as receiving a "Poetic Achievement Award." This award is given to schools who have a large number of entries of which over fifty percent are accepted for publication. With hundreds of schools entering our contest, only a small percent of these schools are honored with this award. The purpose of this award is to recognize schools with excellent Language Arts programs. This award qualifies these schools to receive a complimentary copy of this anthology. In addition, these schools are eligible to apply for a Creative Communication Language Arts Grant. Grants of two hundred and fifty dollars each are awarded to further develop writing in our schools.

Andrew Community School
Andrew, IA
Lisa Dursky*

Canistota Public School
Canistota, SD
Barb Spicer*

Cardinal Jr/Sr High School
Eldon, IA
Barbara Meyer*

Carroll Middle School
Carroll, IA
Jean Birks
Rachel Menken*

Central Kansas Christian Academy
Great Bend, KS
Lori McLeland*

Central Middle School
Grafton, ND
Tracy G. Forbord*

Chadron Middle School
Chadron, NE
Barbara Waugh*

Conway Springs High School
Conway Springs, KS
Kristy Martin*

Covington Elementary School
South Sioux City, NE
Mrs. Bossert
Jenny Mansfield
Kris Vondrak*
Diane Woodford

Dallas Center-Grimes Middle School
Dallas Center, IA
Brad Grout*
Mr. Jaspering
Steve Sales

East Mills Community School
Malvern, IA
Paula Singleton*

Ellinwood Grade School
Ellinwood, KS
Angela Petersen*

Falls City High School
Falls City, NE
Victoria Zoeller*

French Middle School
Topeka, KS
Mrs. Pamela DeFreis*

Frontenac High School
Frontenac, KS
Jan Becker*
Rosie Borchardt

Gilbert Middle School
Gilbert, IA
LisaJane Gildehaus*

Graettinger-Terril Middle School
Terril, IA
Joann Gano
Barb Larson

Hettinger Elementary School
Hettinger, ND
Sarah Morast*

Holton High School
Holton, KS
Karen Ford*

Holy Cross Catholic Elementary School
Omaha, NE
Heather Edinger
Carolyn Taylor

Humboldt Elementary Charter School
Humboldt, KS
Linda Rinehart*

Indian Hills Elementary School
Topeka, KS
Pam Slack*

Jefferson County North Elementary/Middle School
Nortonville, KS
Sherrie Wright*

Jefferson Middle School
Dubuque, IA
Mrs. Firzlaff*
Laura Lenz
Carol Schmitt*
Katherine Thimmesch

Lake Mills Elementary School
Lake Mills, IA
Angie Boehmer*
Mike Dugger

Lourdes Central Catholic School
Nebraska City, NE
Roxann Penfield*

Morton Magnet Middle School
Omaha, NE
Sharon Oakman*

Notre Dame Jr/Sr High School
Burlington, IA
Susan Veach*

O'Neill Elementary School
O'Neill, NE
Cindy Sellers*

Olpe Jr/Sr High School
Olpe, KS
Marilyn Stueve*

Patton Jr High School
Fort Leavenworth, KS
Rebecca Evans*

Perry Middle School
Perry, IA
Abbey Gerzema*

Poetic Achievement Honor Schools

Perry-Lecompton Middle School
Perry, KS
Pat Zimmerman*

Ponca Elementary School
Ponca, NE
Mary L. Husen*

Randolph High School
Randolph, NE
Peggy Lackas*

Roncalli Elementary School
Aberdeen, SD
Rose Kraft
Derek Larson
Marie Schumacher

South Tama County Elementary School
Tama, IA
Darla J. Cory
Deloris Ryan*

St Francis Middle/High School
St Francis, KS
Lisa Gibson*

St Mary's Immaculate Conception Catholic School
Guttenberg, IA
Peggy Rausch*

St Paul's Lutheran School
Norfolk, NE
Heidi Rixe*

Tonganoxie Middle School
Tonganoxie, KS
Kim L. Woodall*

Viborg Jr High School
Viborg, SD
Paige Zachariasen*

Westwood Elementary School
Junction City, KS
Donna Bond
Charli Chillers
Vallery Graham
Kathryn Locke
Jessica Nadal*

Whittier Middle School
Sioux Falls, SD
Emily Leitheiser*
Andrea Olson*
Angie Schlenker*

Wisner-Pilger Jr-Sr High School
Wisner, NE
Leigh Ann Glaubius*

Page 3

Language Arts Grant Recipients 2011-2012

After receiving a "Poetic Achievement Award" schools are encouraged to apply for a Creative Communication Language Arts Grant. The following is a list of schools who received a two hundred and fifty dollar grant for the 2011-2012 school year.

Annapolis Royal Regional Academy, Annapolis Royal, NS
Bear Creek Elementary School, Monument, CO
Bellarmine Preparatory School, Tacoma, WA
Birchwood School, Cleveland, OH
Bluffton Middle School, Bluffton, SC
Brookville Intermediate School, Brookville, OH
Butler High School, Augusta, GA
Carmi-White County High School, Carmi, IL
Classical Studies Academy, Bridgeport, CT
Coffee County Central High School, Manchester, TN
Country Hills Elementary School, Coral Springs, FL
Coyote Valley Elementary School, Middletown, CA
Emmanuel-St Michael Lutheran School, Fort Wayne, IN
Excelsior Academy, Tooele, UT
Great Meadows Middle School, Great Meadows, NJ
Holy Cross High School, Delran, NJ
Kootenay Christian Academy, Cranbrook, BC
LaBrae Middle School, Leavittsburg, OH
Ladoga Elementary School, Ladoga, IN
Mater Dei High School, Evansville, IN
Palmer Catholic Academy, Ponte Vedra Beach, FL
Pine View School, Osprey, FL
Plato High School, Plato, MO
Rivelon Elementary School, Orangeburg, SC
Round Lake High School, Round Lake, MN
Sacred Heart School, Oxford, PA
Shadowlawn Elementary School, Green Cove Springs, FL
Starmount High School, Boonville, NC
Stevensville Middle School, Stevensville, MD
Tadmore Elementary School, Gainesville, GA
Trask River High School, Tillamook, OR
Vacaville Christian Schools, Vacaville, CA
Wattsburg Area Middle School, Erie, PA
William Dunbar Public School, Pickering, ON
Woods Cross High School, Woods Cross, UT

Grades 10-11-12 Top Ten Winners

List of Top Ten Winners for Grades 10-12; listed alphabetically

Elisa Barguil, Grade 11
Townsend Harris High School, NY

Cailey Horn, Grade 11
Rabun County High School, GA

Kevin Maerten, Grade 11
Holy Cross High School, NJ

Garrett Massey, Grade 11
Animas High School, NM

Ryan Miller, Grade 12
Upper St Clair High School, PA

Miranda Paul, Grade 12
Menaul School, NM

Kimberly Paulsen, Grade 11
Viewmont High School, UT

Mia Tannoia, Grade 10
Bradshaw Christian High School, CA

Felicia Thornton, Grade 11
Science & Math Institute, WA

Emily Wiseberg, Grade 11
Collège catholique Franco-Ouest, ON

All Top Ten Poems can be read at www.poeticpower.com

Note: The Top Ten poems were finalized through an online voting system. Creative Communication's judges first picked out the top poems. These poems were then posted online. The final step involved thousands of students and teachers who registered as the online judges and voted for the Top Ten poems. We hope you enjoy these selections.

Ever-growing Distance

You are so self-righteous, it makes me ill
Your judgments set out to crush my free will
And you don't see how you've ruined my life
How your condescension cuts me like a knife
Your lack of sympathy has created a rift
Your cynicism has caused the two of us to drift
It's hard to believe that it hasn't always been this way
Do you remember how it felt before we wandered astray?
The secrets we never thought we would share?
The crazy way that we'd do each other's hair?
The late-night whispers when you spent the night?
The laughs shared upon each other's sight?
And the secret smiles we flashed across the room?
These beautiful things made our friendship bloom
But now it appears that it's all come to an end
And yet, I feel like the mistaken friend
I've given you reason to be bitter and hesitant
I've tried to hide it, but you've gotten the hint
And I realize you'll never feel the same as I do
Because I'm so completely in love with you

Kaitlyn Counter, Grade 10
Millard North High School, NE

What is Death

What is death?
Is it merely a passing from one world to another?
Is it to fade into oblivion?
Is it to return to the place where we once came from?
Is it to cause severe pain in the families that have lost
or is it to bring peace?
To end suffering upon those it falls upon?
Do the ones we lose look down upon us?
Peering through windows in the sky
resting on the clouds,
watching the world go by.
Does it bring forth a pair of wings?
Do they become an angel
or are they simply gone?
What is death?
Will we really ever know?
For anyone who has suffered
has yet to let us know.

Jocie Miser, Grade 10
Emporia High School, KS

Softball

BANG! I soar through the air
like a rocket racing to the moon.
But my ride is short-lived.
SMACK! Into a glove I go
and fly off again.
My ride is wild and I get sand in my eyes.
OH NO! I'm picked up to repeat the painful process.

Michelle Klein, Grade 10
Gehlen Catholic School, IA

Suicide Prevention

S uicide silences so many stories
U sing utensils to slip under
I nsomnia is driving me insane
C an't control the courage-crushing changes
I ndividuals in search of inner-peace
D epression deepens with every dream
E veryone else exists for something

P lease promise me that this pain will pass
R escue me, I really want to run
E verything tries to extinguish me
V iolence is no longer valiant
E nvy is everyone's emotion
N ever say nothing you do is not 'nough.
T eens that are troubled tend to feel trapped
I nside, include imaginary scenes of incredible freedom.
O utside, on ominous skies, awaits an oppressing force.
N eglect the never-ending lies, and the nerve-racking stares.

Siri Armitage, Grade 10
LaMoure High School, ND

Your Love

I held your love so dear to my heart
Until you stole it from me and ripped me apart
That was the day the first tear fell
And since that day it has yet to quell;
Constantly stabbing me like a dart.

I remember the times when you called me sweetheart,
All the countless hours we spent listening to Mozart.
I remember your distinctive, clean cut smell
I held your love so dear to my heart.

Our love was like a rare piece of art
The longer you stare the harder it is to part
And as much as I want to scream and yell
I think I'll just quietly say farewell
And finally I can begin my fresh start
I held your love so dear to my heart.

Mackenzie Clark, Grade 10
Olathe South Sr High School, KS

The Run

I run through the green grass
the calm blue sky surrounds me
as the blazing orange sun beats down on me
I feel my cheeks turning rosy red
my pale white legs begin to weaken
I take a break on a blue bench
I spot a grey water fountain so
I drink the clear water
I begin my journey back through the green grass
with the blazing orange sun beating down upon
my rosy cheeks

Nate Youde, Grade 11
Falls City High School, NE

High Merit Poems – Grades 10, 11, and 12

The Game of Life
Life is like a game
The rules are always the same
Someone is born, no one mourns
Someone dies, we all cry

It'll happen to all of us
That day will come
You'll see that light shining like the sun
Death finds us all
But in the end, God won't let the good fall
Some find the place where the devil hangs his hat
Some stand next to God, getting a pat on the back

One dies young because of a faulty lung
Another lasts forever
Disappearing into the wind, like a lost feather
That's the way it goes
For reasons no one knows
We try to understand, but no one can

It's just the game of life
Leah Ellensohn, Grade 10
Gehlen Catholic School, IA

Love
It's more than a feeling,
It's more than a thought,
It's much more than riches have ever bought.
It starts with two people,
With two lonely hearts
'Cus to make a whole being
You need two different parts.
You notice your pulsing: beginning to quicken
As when your love walks by
You become star stricken.
Then soon you remember
Since your love was so tender
That it couldn't last
And it's soon in the past.
You hold up your head
And pull back your shoulders
'Cus there's no looking back
When you only get older.
There'll be other chances to find the right person
But while you're still young
You'll just keep on searching.
Michelle Palafox, Grade 10
Rock Valley Jr/Sr High School, IA

Running Out
I am standing in an ever-changing room
Surrounded by clocks made from the hands of God himself
For idle hands are tools of the Devil
And Father Time desires to avoid a fiery embrace
Devlin Harris, Grade 11
Beatrice High School, NE

Monitor
I beep.
That is my job.
People watch intensely
seeing what will happen next.
I don't know what will happen next
or if what will happen next is
for the best.

Listening to my beeps
I see people weep
as my beeps become weak.

My job requires tears with a share of many fears.
There are good days and bad days which
keep me up all night. For those people
watching me, seeing what will
happen next, worrying their loved ones
never will wake from their
rest: do not fret
for heaven
is the
best.
Megan Livermore, Grade 10
Gehlen Catholic School, IA

The Dream
The moonlight on my bed keeps me awake;
I'm trying to sleep but I can't for Pete's sake
I try to shut the window then suddenly a quake
I run out to the porch and there's only a lake

Surely on this night it's a dream, it is fake
But I can't get out, I just can't wake
I then hear my good friend Jake
Saying, "Help, help, there's a very large snake"

I jump in the room and I do a hand shake
But quickly after, my hand starts to ache
I look down and my hand is a rake
I scrape up leaves and shake and bake
And at that time I did finally awake.
Justin Trisler, Grade 12
Burlington High School, KS

Darkness
There is a dark sadness
Deep down inside of my soul
It's just waiting
Doesn't make a noise not even a scream
He doesn't touch or speak to me
But he follows me at my heels
In the sunlight like a shadow
And all around my feet
Holding me down like the hot wax around a melting candle
Trelby Virus, Grade 10
Thayer Central High School, NE

Me

Madi
Determined, friendly, loving, witty
Sister of Steven, Richard, Susan, and Allie
Lover of chocolate, rainy days, and Shania Twain
Who feels that rewards come to people that work hard for them, Michael Jackson's legacy will forever live,
and there are far too many school days in a year
Who needs reassurance from time to time, at least 9 hours of sleep a night, and her dad's acceptance
Who gives her all in almost everything she does, trust to people who earn it, and sass to her mom
Who fears going to college, getting my heart broken, and the crazy, stupid things some people are going to do on December 21, 2012
Who would like to see the ball drop in New York on New Years Eve
Resident of Holton, Kansas
Iverson

Madison Iverson, Grade 11
Holton High School, KS

Me

Megan
Outgoing, funny, loving, and grateful
Sister of Drake and Lucas Lovvorn
Lover of food, dance and my family
Who feels happy when she's with friends, relief when school ends, and excitement for summer
Who needs air for survival, to find herself, and acceptance from others
Who gives friendship easily, her opinion even if it's not needed, and who gives up easily
Who fears tornados, not being in control, and losing her friends
Who would like to see her family in Alabama, world peace, her mom's birth parents, and herself become successful
Resident of Holton, Kansas
Lovvorn

Megan Lovvorn, Grade 11
Holton High School, KS

Me, Myself, and I

Megan
Daughter of Mark Clark
Funny, caring, intelligent, dedicated
Lover of softball, dogs, watching movies
Who feels she needs stability, love by her family, thankful for her friends,
Who needs her dog, family, friends
Who gives support, encouragement to others, advice to friends
Who fears spiders, the dark, creepy places
Who would like to see the world, KU win the national championship, her softball team win the state title
Resident of Holton, Kansas
Clark

Megan Clark, Grade 11
Holton High School, KS

Monsters Under My Bed

You're asleep. Dreaming. Of what I'm not sure, but I know it's your escape from the nightmare of your days. You wake the next day an ashen ghost. The sun no longer catches in your golden hair. The monster I have come to know as Cancer has stolen everything. Every morning you drew your sword in attempt to fight this beast. You put on your armor and entered into a continuing battle for life.

But through it all you remembered to smile. Two years, 730 days, but you lost the final fight. I climb into bed most nights thinking if you can fight off Cancer I can fight off the monsters from under my bed.

Rachel Johnson, Grade 10
Thayer Central High School, NE

High Merit Poems – Grades 10, 11, and 12

Reality

Sweet tender lies
I tell you it's a beautiful lie
Live by the rules of pretend
Feel the love
The guilt-free atmosphere
It's an illusion
You know this isn't right
What's to lose
Reality is inescapable
You can fall into your own web of lies
Live as you wish
But when you finally open the door to the real world
You will fall flat
You will be consumed
And your lies will fall apart

It is best to never lie to oneself

Reality is no illusion.
Patricia Anderson, Grade 10
Wyandotte High School, KS

Penguin

Deep in the frigid depths of the ocean
penguins twirl and plunge,
eluding infinite obstacles.

Out of the darkness, danger ensues.
Leopard seals full of latent speed and ferocity,
lurk in the background, unseen.

Eyes wary, muscles taut
as if they were a stretched rubber band.
Suddenly,   snap!

A game of agility and wits breaks out.
Which will win?
Eyes dart every which way, looking for escape.

Breaths of relief bubble skyward through the icy water,
as the pursued lays eyes upon a void in the ice
and bounds up onto dry land.
Katy Gerving, Grade 10
New Salem-Almont High School, ND

Sports

Concentration. Spirit. Pride. Sports.
The adrenaline pulses through your blood
With one thing bouncing around in your head like a ping-pong ball.
The win. You gotta be fast.
Speed. Endurance. Adrenaline.
The thrill of the race. With the win comes the Pride.
Courage. Faith. Strength.
From all these things comes the power within.
Alyssa Martin, Grade 10
Marcus-Meriden-Cleghorn High School, IA

Invisible Angel

Living for the moment, taking each day by day.
Not caring about the consequences,
That's what this high schooler used to say.
Her nightmare has become a reality, and now is growing inside.
She realizes it was a mistake, but her guilt will not subside.
She feels her stomach kicking, and her heart begins to race,
To start planning for the future.
Wishing she were in a different place.
All her friends have deserted her,
And her family has disowned.
She now feels isolated, and completely alone.
Placing her hand upon her unborn child,
She makes a plead to God.
To give her baby a better life,
To not dwell within the smog.
Now one year later, time has slipped between life's cracks.
It feels like just yesterday, and she vows to never turn back.
This hardshipped life that she has lead,
Is but a bleeding heart.
But she knows it was all worth it,
For her little angel and her were never far apart.
Rendi Den Burger, Grade 11
North Fayette High School, IA

The Stream

Slowly moving over the rocks, the
stream rolls and bubbles through the reeds
all the way to the foot of my favorite tree.
The cool liquid pulls on my toes
as I hold my nose —
Splash! —
off my swing and into the stream.
The darkness encloses me,
hugging me tight.
A fish swims by
making as much noise as a whisper in the night.
My body screams for air;
I'm forced to pull up.
The spring air fills my lungs
as I go down for one last plunge.
Madison Harpenau, Grade 10
Gehlen Catholic School, IA

The Race of a Champion

Standing in the track with the blue breeze arising
We wait to begin so we can start surprising
Sitting on the back of a black, anxious, mysterious ride
He stomps in place, his eyes full of pride
Finally the clock starts and the gates make a green open
We're off! Flying through the dirt, words unspoken
The white silence of the opponents is such bliss
Our time is now, we can do this
The yellow of the crowd yelled, "What a sight!"
We did it boy, we did all right.
Desiree Herling, Grade 11
Falls City High School, NE

Forever My Brother

When you are born into a family, there's something
you can never change, that's who your siblings are.
When you start growing they are some of the
first people you will meet. Throughout childhood
you fight over the silly little things. When I was a kid,
my brother and I would fight over the silliest things.
I would take something from him, say words that kids
should never say, and go at each other with fists.
Yell. Run. Run. Slip. Slide. Run. Run. Hide. Stay safe.
Like a broken record repeating until it becomes tedious.
You eventually learn that the fighting is unnecessary
and you start getting along, but some people actually
start off being friends then after something happens they
argue all the time & never want anything to do with each other.
Everyone says that siblings fight nonstop.
Some do all the time, but some get along perfectly.
Get along in the beginning. Fight in the end.
Fight in the beginning. Get along in the end.
Either way, when you are born with siblings, you
have a bond for a life of fighting and companionship
that only a sibling would understand.

Nicole Johnson, Grade 10
South Tama County High School, IA

Beautiful Confusion

The beautiful confusion,
Life spins out of control.
Where do I turn, to whom do I go?
What are we fighting for?
Who pulled the trigger?
The fighting words like glass piercing my skin.
Have we come so far to just let go?
I see the doubt written on your face.
Sad, apologetic eyes meet mine.
Silence envelops us like an overwhelming blanket.
Two hearts beat as one once again.
You wrap me up in your loving arms.
Our relief cuts the tension like a blade.
My life is a beautiful confusion,
But it's nothing without you.

Megan Buskirk, Grade 10
Alliance High School, NE

The Storm

The rain drums on the roof in grey
It trickles down the windowpane
The wind rattles the windows in blue
The tree branches scrape against the house
The thunder shakes the house in purple
Lightning fills the dark house with light
The cat shrieks in fear in silver
The whole house awakes in fear due to the commotion
The children tip toe to their parent's room in lavender
Warm and safe everyone is together

Mariah Stamper, Grade 11
Falls City High School, NE

Newton

Never thought you would go away
I miss you more than you know
You said that you would come back someday
Everyone tells me not to listen to what you say
They all knew you would go
Never thought you would lead me astray
Everyone says, you're so low
You said that you would come back someday
And I believe that you may
All the time is passing so slow
Never thought you would go away
You will come back to me I pray
People tell me to move on and I say no
You said that you would come back someday
All my blue skies are now gray
You were supposed to watch me grow
Never thought you would go away
You said that you would come back someday

Mary Ann Simpson, Grade 11
Falls City High School, NE

Don't Leave Me

The day your beauty leaves me,
I hope I can handle all of that pain.
'Cause your beauty makes me feel like I'm free,
If you ever left me, I would feel pain.
My days would never feel like they were bright,
Because you are the sun in my life.
And if you left it would all seem like night,
Without you my life would be full of strife.
My feelings for you compare to no one's,
You make me feel I can fly like a dove
And other people say things and make puns,
But there is nothing that can stop my love.
So as long as I have you to hold here,
your leaving is something I shall not fear.

Darrell Headrick, Grade 12
Superior Secondary School, NE

The People's Spring

A feeling of pride abides as the cowards hide,
A strong tide the people know the government lied,
People in the streets standing together fighting the heat,
Country in chaos unemployment and layoffs,
Oppression as if an obsession the people started to question,
Riots, the people will never be quiet,
The world is appalled watching as the innocent fall,
Rebels hear the call this isn't a fall but a spring,
This call is made for the people to unite and fight,
For the upper echelon the pressure is on,
They will fight for the right not to be gone,
As the rebels enclose to the capital's lawn,
All hope for the oppressor is gone,
For the people this is a new dawn

Ethan Esposti, Grade 10
Hill City High School, SD

High Merit Poems – Grades 10, 11, and 12

My Father's Saddle
Worn and experienced
You were a rookie long ago
Now you sit, perched on your rack
You were my father's saddle
For years you were there, hiding away, dust covered
I'll clean you off
Not supple anymore
I'll care for you
Oil your stiff leather
Making you young again
I'll ride on you
We will take you all over
Running through pastures
Walking through shallow water
Trotting on dusty field roads
I love your decoration of silver and leather strips
Though some strips sucked off by young calves
These are not flaws, but stories
If only you could talk…
If only…

Rachael Fangmeier, Grade 10
Thayer Central High School, NE

Change of Seasons
Winter tends to make me nervous.
Snow and cold do me no service.
Sunshine sounds much better than ice and sleet.
The gloominess convinces me to stay in bed beneath my sheets.
Spring brings lots of rain.
Which is good; it keeps the farmers sane.
School will be out for the year.
Then will come summer; have no fear.
Summer is a getaway.
No work; all play
The days are long and hot.
But then fall comes along and ruins the whole plot.
Back to school we go
And that's when we start hoping for snow.

Tacy Thelen, Grade 10
Randolph High School, NE

My Mom
She's always supporting my dreams and never screams.
She always seems so happy, full of dreams.
She and I are quite the team.
We love to go thrifty shopping till we're dropping.
It's exhausting, always talking, never stopping.
She's always trying and sometimes crying.
Her heart is always saving and blazing with love.
She is my angel sent from above.
When times are hard and life feels bad.
She saves the day in her special ways,
With her cheerful smiling face.
She always finds a special place, which is home.

Brianna Redmond, Grade 11
Villa Marie School, NE

A Road to Recovery
You're traveling down a gravel road
Gravel
The most dangerous surface to drive on.
You lose control
You roll once, twice, three times before the car comes to a stop
You don't remain in the car, now you're laying there in a ditch
Unresponsive and alone
Helpless in the middle of nowhere
Temperature
Cold but not freezing yet
Hours have passed
Still no one in sight to come to the rescue
Finally a farmer comes down the road
Sees a mangled and mashed car and comes across
Him, a boy covered in blood and dirt
My brother.
Rushed to the hospital
Doctors unknowing of what is going to come out of the tragedy
Leaving me to think of all the things I love and cherish about him
As he's rolled down the long white hallway.
To a road of recovery.

Bryanna Dudgeon, Grade 10
Thayer Central High School, NE

My Dreams
There is something I want you to see,
A world where there is only you and me.
A tear never falls down,
Not even rain falls to the ground.
I know that I'm safe and sound,
Now that I've been found.

Home of my dreams,
More lovely than it seems.
Flowers always grow,
And so, I'll always know where I'm supposed to go.
The sun will always shine,
Knowing that you are mine.
The man of my dreams,
My future, or so it seems.

Tamilyn Bauer, Grade 10
Sioux Falls New Technology High School, SD

The Bosendorfer Imperial Piano
Impossibly too much grenade-green angst,
The 96-keys roar grayly,
Heavy with black sharpness of hitting hammers,
As a broken body is thudded with shovels of surmounting dirt,
Chords darker than a black scream,
Low-pitched and deep with a fierce red,
After the hammers have left the yellow aura of darkness,
Light bleeds yellow through the heavens,
As Franz Liszt experiences a bright blue joy of white silence,
Unspoken love and soft blue resolution

David von Behren, Grade 11
Falls City High School, NE

Mother of Mine*
She has a heart so pure and kind.
She is my idol and my hero.
She is strong and so full of love and determination.
She has been there since the day I was born,
And she makes sure I do my best every single day.
She gives me words of encouragement,
Which make my life so much easier.
When I cry,
I cry to her.
She is my friend.
She loves me unconditionally,
For she would give her life for me.
She is my family,
And I would do the same for her.
She is my mommy,
For she has a heart so pure and kind,
And I love her with all my heart.

Kayla Henderson, Grade 12
Prairie View High School, KS
Dedicated to Amy Jean Ghareeb. I love you mommy.

Changing My Ways
I'm trying to change my ways but I guess not today.
Tomorrow is a different day.
I said the Lord's name in vain.
Tomorrow is a different day.
I swore at my mom.
Tomorrow is a different day.
I didn't do my homework.
Tomorrow is a different day.
I got fired from my job.
Tomorrow is a different day.
I got kicked out of school.
Tomorrow is a different day.
I robbed a grocery store.
Tomorrow is a different day.
I'm trying to change my ways I guess I start today.
Today's the day I get locked away.

Vincent Bennett, Grade 11
Falls City High School, NE

The Key
Once upon a time,
a little girl traveled far away
without saying goodbye
or even looking at what she was leaving behind.
She only carried with her
a tiny little key
that was in a warm coat
and as gold as a honeybee.
They key had written a word
that let her open everything.
It wasn't too hard, or too long:
just L-O-V-E.

Almudena Salmeron, Grade 10
Gehlen Catholic School, IA

Rain
The pitter patter of rain on my window
Beats like a drum in band class.

The rain on my windshield
Is like diamonds dangling from a necklace.

They glitter and sparkle
Like the first frost of winter.

It beats down upon my body
With tiny silver drops.

The feeling of rain on my bare skin
Sends tingles down my spine.

Rain is like camouflage to tears
It falls and splashes to make puddles.

At night the rain plays a sleep song on my rooftop
As I slip into a deep slumber.

Tanisha Fahrenholz, Grade 10
Stuart High School, NE

True Love…
For the true love you seek,
The true love you've always wanted to find,
Is just but a word, a picture in your mind,
A fairy tale you read in books.
Till that one day when all your dreams come true,
The one who makes you smile,
The one who warms your heart,
The one who is there for you,
Your one true love who makes your wildest dreams reality,
But till you find that one person,
Love is nothing but a word.
Love has no more of a meaning than any other word.
But when you find that one person,
Love will be the best feeling in the world.
There is nothing that compares with the feeling of being loved,
And that one person is you…

Rose Vesely, Grade 11
Palmer Jr/Sr High School, NE

A Word for the Lost
Tears roll down my eyes
as I think back to our final goodbyes.
In the ground you may lay,
but I know I will see you again someday.
I am happy the pain you went through is gone,
but the hurt of losing you lives on.
Even though with the angels I know you fly,
I still wonder why it was you who had to die.
Seeing your picture makes my mouth dry as if full of cotton
just remember though you may be gone, but you're never forgotten.

Leo Livingston, Grade 12
Waukon High School, IA

High Merit Poems – Grades 10, 11, and 12

Separate Lies

Two atoms splitting
Down the center at their core.
A heart that reeks forgiveness;
A soul without a cure.
I ache to feel the love of arms
Wrapped around my skin.
Instead I sit alone in this,
No time to settle in.
Another house, another car,
And still no home of mine
Has called to claim my lonesome heart
Or save me from my mind.
These separate lives
Break family ties
And lies keep spilling out your gut.
A wrinkled nose, a side-swept hit
Turn her tears to blood.
Out the door I watch you walk
Each step a long lost tune.
You wave goodbye like all is fine;
I yearn to see the truth.
Laura Whitmer, Grade 11
Atchison High School, KS

Lullaby

The rain whispers
me a lullaby.
The drops dancing
on the rooftop
as they sing me
to sleep.
Beat after steady beat.
Sing me a lullaby.
Dance to my song.
Heaven,
send your tears here
where they can dance
through the night.
Where they can
hold me close as I sleep,
welcome me as I wake.
Calm my fears
and whisper softly
into me ear.
"Don't worry," you sing.
"I am here."
Kirsten Hummel, Grade 11
Hamlin High School, SD

Sky

The sky is a river
One that is flowing quickly and rapidly
The sky is an ocean
Big and full of wonders
Tyler Edwards, Grade 10
Thayer Central High School, NE

Real, Live Color

Full of color displayed on your exterior,
Compared to any other model, you would make it look inferior.

I have watched you closely from a young age,
Figuring out your every attribute as I view and gauge.

In a way you are quite a good teacher,
Even better than soaking in a double feature.

On a weekend morning, what better is there to do?
Than spend a little alone time with you?

I can relax in your presence,
Yet at the same time you can take on the form of being so passionate or intense.

As the times change,
Your experience with valuable insight and news comes in a surprisingly large range.

Comprised of many different "channels" or phases,
I give you my utmost praises.

My father could be compared to a TV;
However, he means so much more than that to me.
Zach Frey, Grade 12
Cascade Jr/Sr High School, IA

Spring

Spring,
a time of year when life awakens from sleep.
Creatures of all kinds rise from their slumber.
Buds begin to bloom into an array of colorful flowers, bringing life to the scenery.
Nature starts to look vibrant again, giving us new hope and inspiration.
In spring, the fragrance smells of fallen rain; it invigorates our senses.
The rich earth thaws, revealing a glimpse of grass.
It provides the ground with a green blanket.
The air is light and frothy, combined with the sun as it shines and sparkles;
it creates and inspires a new attitude in the minds of the despairing and hopeless.

Life continues on in a circle:
it awakens in the spring,
grows and flourishes in the summer,
begins to wither in autumn,
and then is covered in a blanket of snow in winter.

Soon spring rolls around again.
You can just tell when it arrives.
All of a sudden the atmosphere changes,
you can smell it, taste it, breathe it in.
That is when you know it is
spring.
Sara Roder, Grade 10
Gehlen Catholic School, IA

Guardian Angel

My grandpa is an angel in heaven
My grandpa is an angel in heaven

The sorrow spreads like a plague through our family
My grandpa is an angel in heaven
Watching over our beautiful family
My grandpa is an angel in heaven
Walking around on the fluffy clouds
My grandpa is an angel in heaven

He lives in the hearts of our family
My grandpa is an angel in heaven
He is my own personal guardian angel
My grandpa is an angel in heaven
Spreading his love like angel wings
My grandpa is an angel in heaven

I see him in my uncle's face
My grandpa is an angel in heaven
Mourning the loss of my beloved grandpa
My grandpa is an angel in heaven
Waiting to see him once again by the gates of heaven
My grandpa is an angel in heaven.

Krisondra Smothers, Grade 12
Nebraska City High School, NE

The American Dream

Five years old, running through the sprinkler in the yard
Wild, Joyful, Free
An untamed spirit represented in youth,
Showing the idea of many in the vision of one.
Simply put, The American Dream

Buzz-cut hair, with eight weeks of training under his belt
Disciplined, Strong, Ready
Anxious for his shot to finally taste war
Waiting to defend all that he stands for.
Simply put, The American Dream

Twelve men dropped in the jungles of a foreign land
Scared, Nervous, Praying for Life
Shots are rattled off from either side,
All he wants is to save his hide
Simply put, The American Dream

Present day, the old man fights from bed,
Frail, Wrinkled, Weak
Tilling up the land he once defended
You can't believe what his eyes have seen.
Simply put, The American Dream

Trey Mogensen, Grade 11
Cedar Rapids Jr/Sr High School, NE

Change Within

Nothing was the same,
It was like the world was playing a whole new game.
I had once wished I could catch a shooting star on my tongue,
Now the idea could happen and be true.

I began to hold my life in my hands,
As I realized other people were letting my life slip through like sand.
With this new thought in mind,
I sank to the size of a pea.

Love became an open sky,
And loathing became a closed box.
Although I worried about this new look,
I knew I could handle the pressure.

The change for me was not the same,
And as for the world, it was not ashamed.

Melissa Huff, Grade 12
Cascade Jr/Sr High School, IA

Experience Life

Each and every day should be an adventure
Although you should watch what you say to others
And not let your friendships fray or fade
Enjoy the ray of sunshine beaming down
Soar like a blue jay or an eagle
Relax and play in the fallen leaves
Dance your way around the world
Frolic in the Georgia clay or even
Go to the Florida bay or the snowy mountains
Don't worry about the pay or any costs
Because regrets may later haunt you
So lay and experience life
Experience and stay close with God
He will always make a way for you
So enjoy the day and those to come
And may you always be thankful

Bethany Lampe, Grade 11
Falls City High School, NE

Love

Scratching at the surface
I find that I am not alone
I have an army, you see
And it includes just
You and Me.
With this army of mine
We can conquer the skies.
It never rains and it never shines
Without this lovingness of mine.
I know that you cannot leave me
I have my memories
Which cannot be replaced
So please don't forget me.

Kiley Klick, Grade 11
Chaparral High School, KS

High Merit Poems – Grades 10, 11, and 12

Lonely Beach

Engine sputters to life with a BANG, wheezing as it goes
The sun beams down on our sunscreen-painted faces
The boat wobbles, waves lick the sides

Our fuzzy-faced "Capitan" in Bermuda shorts
(And an unfortunate pairing of socks and sandals)
Tames waves as terrifying as kittens,
Directing us to a lonely patch of land

Engine cuts off
Moment of silence — hear the waves swish-swash
A gruff "Everybody off!" slices through
Boat wobbles as one-by-one we wade
To the solemn patch of sand and beach grass

Dripping wet feet seem to attract sand like flies to honey
Boat BANGs to life once more
A coughing engine and a nautical nod

The serenity of the ocean surrounds our private beach
A stoic lighthouse on the horizon
And a handful of footprints in the sizzling sand
Are the only traces of man left

I sigh and shut my eyes
It's gorgeous.

Caryn Friesen, Grade 10
Thayer Central High School, NE

The Bridge

I see a bridge that looks at loss
A bridge not many care to cross

Old and rickety, this bridge be
But the journey across does not scare me

I walked that bridge, not by ignorance, nor for pain
But because of the wisdom that I'll gain

You see I've crossed that bridge before
And there is nothing like it from shore to shore

It's the challenge I face every day
From those who don't do what they say

Or from those who do not mind
Who run around and are unkind

This bridge is a leader of few men
Who've died and been born again

This bridge takes those out on the range
And brings them in to make a change

This bridge is ready to lead
So come on by, my friends in need

Tyrel Baldridge, Grade 10
Lakin High School, KS

Hardwood — A Villanelle

The hardwood is a brilliant invention.
Echo does the gym of the bouncing ball;
A goal, a net, an unreal sensation.

Shots after shots, dreams of aspiration,
Watching others do, and waiting for the call;
The hardwood is a brilliant invention.

The game unchanging, the perfect creation.
My team in harmony as if in a music hall;
A goal, a net, an unreal sensation.

Officials blow their whistles, claiming the violation
Trying but failing, to prevent an all-out brawl.
The hardwood is a brilliant invention.

Teams staring down one another, provoking intimidation,
Tension builds up like bricks on a wall;
A goal, a net, an unreal sensation.

Always working toward the ultimate celebration,
Out of all sports, basketball is above all;
The hardwood is a brilliant invention
A goal, a net, an unreal sensation

Trent Tanking, Grade 11
Holton High School, KS

Shoeless Joe: A Villanelle

The man without shoes, his name was Shoeless Joe
The baseball player who just couldn't be bought
Always remembered on the south side of Chicago

When they came to his door he just had to say no
"I have to play the best games ever now," he thought
The man without shoes, his name was Shoeless Joe

During the Series, his batting average continued to grow
Every ball that came his way was always caught
Always remembered on the south side of Chicago

They lost and the players celebrated with their dough
But not Shoeless Joe, he was just sad and distraught
The man without shoes, his name was Shoeless Joe

He would never play another game in the Series though
He was banned from baseball, which he fought
Always remembered on the south side of Chicago

Because of the scandal he was no longer a pro
They thought that he was in on the plot
The man without shoes, his name was Shoeless Joe
Always remembered on the south side of Chicago

Zach Porter, Grade 11
Holton High School, KS

I Love You Like Butter on Popcorn

I love you like popcorn loves butter
Which is a wonderful snack
Which I like to eat while watching movies
Which I like to do with my friends on weekends
Which is my favorite time of the week
Which can be long or short, depending on homework
Which can make my head hurt
Which can make me not want to think
Which makes life uninteresting
Which makes me wish I would win the lottery
Which I only have a one in a billion chance to win
Which is saying that I most likely won't win, but that's okay
Which is saying that I can live without money, which is green
Which reminds me of grass
Which reminds me of summer
Which reminds me of fun memories
That I have with friends hanging out and watching movies
Which makes me think of snacks
Which I love to eat while watching movies
Just like popcorn loves butter.

Cheyanne Loeffler, Grade 10
Boone Central High School, NE

Beauty Within

When I say that she is truly beautiful
Why is it that she' won't believe me?
My affection for you is immortal
It is clear to me that you cannot see
From the start I was for sure that you were the one
Who would have thought our friendship would turn to love?
As the days go by one by one
You are the one that I think a lot of
Even when my day goes wrong
You always seem to make me happy
I know that you and I both belong
Together forever, you are the one for me,
Tiffany, you are the friend of my heart,
No matter what we will never fall apart.

Daniel Ansong, Grade 10
Lamoni High School, IA

Opuscule

In his heart,
he knew that his raw emotions
were the key to open up this world
into another dimension.
He welcomed a brand new kind of species
that spoke in nothing but riddles.

He called them his friends,
and with that,
he a wrote a three page opuscule of nothing but lullabies
that whispered in her ears
every night before she closed her eyes.

Anna Zheng, Grade 11
Blue Valley High School, KS

Sand Castle

Sunlight flashes from the highest tower,
throwing a shade of gold over all that are near

The spires stretch into the sky
breaking the canopy of clouds
that hovers lightly above

The grains, rough alone, but smooth as a whole
are perfectly shaped,
creating a choir of symmetry

Murmurs of wonder surround the structure
but soon
quiet down to a majestic calm

The world around goes on, but time is frozen here

The girl smoothes out a few rough edges
and stands back to admire
the treasure that she has created

Then the brine of the sea is left
to lick away the castle,
to take it piece by piece
back to an inky abode

And leave in its place
A memory

Matthew Collings, Grade 10
Red River High School, ND

Shadow Lady

She sits alone in the corner of a room
Covered in dark black shadows and gloom
The shadow seductress sits
Silent as a snake she's plotting her wits

Never drawing attention to her own
The Shadow Lady prefers to be alone
Maybe not favors but is accustomed to the quiet
Shy and afraid to do anything even just try it

Patiently she plots her place on the planet
Maybe move and change her name Jill, Ann, Janet?
The Shadow Lady always seen but never heard
Trying to figure why she's so absurd

The phantom woman plots vengeance on them all
Waiting for her shot at their total downfall
She plots upon the ones that made her a joke
Vengeance also to those that saw but never spoke

The female phantom is like a fly
Always seen but never a second thought why

Jordan Craig, Grade 11
Andover High School, KS

High Merit Poems – Grades 10, 11, and 12

Golf
It's very nice today.
Time to go to the course and play.
Golf is a great sport, Hooray!
Let's hope things go my way!

I'm on the first green.
I hope my ball doesn't be mean.
Sunny day, no wind, the perfect scene.
What a great shot I've just seen!

I've been shooting around par.
Things are going well so far.

I think my ball is under a tree!
Why does this always happen to me?!

It was a perfect day to play.
41, not bad, I must say.
Tony Thies, Grade 12
Randolph High School, NE

White Walls Collapse
"South Carolina
Oh-so-fine-a
Seaside tramps
And wheelchair ramps."
Hallucinating housewives quip
"Subjectivity
Does not exist."

DNE
My childhood friends.

The Chinese brother of Jesus Christ
Frowns upon the scene,
"39 steps towards Babylon
Will certainly cause paths
To never converge."

White walls collapse.
Tanner Boyle, Grade 10
Winfield High School, KS

Ghost
I walk through my life like a ghost.
I have no feelings;
I watch life pass me by
I just walk
Nobody sees me,
I am a ghost.
I am hollow,
For I have no heart.
My heart was shattered and stolen.
My feelings have turned to ice.
Ashlynne Roberts, Grade 11
Forest Ridge School, IA

Splattered Nonsense
Ink-splattered nonsense written across the page
Words are written in a scent of sage
We wage war on a single-sheeted note
Where is the point of what we wrote
Black lines and shapes and dots
I think I can feel my blood clot.
Ink-splattered nonsense spewn across the canvas,
Words create images with a bitter sense of hate,
What was I given, what was I handed?
Your words were all but genuinely too late!
I traveled through emotions for so long,
Just to have forgiven you for your wrongs,
This is the splattered song I sing,
This is the splattered portrait I paint,
This is the splattered poem I create...
Just to wind up with another ink-splattered nonsense written across the page,
Just to end up with another creation created too late.
So here I type up the date,
Where the ink-splattered nonsense written across the days,
Burns and lays
Where the dead fall ashen to their graves.
April Adams, Grade 12
Prairie View High School, KS

Where I'm From
I am from State Center, IA, where I go to West Marshall High School.
I am from the trailer house which then turned into a big house.
I am from family.
Dad – who has been with me my whole life.
Mom – who tells me what to do.
Rachel – who is my oldest sister, who is the nice one and is married, has a kid.
Brittany — the second oldest, the fun one, and a good sister.
Brandy — younger sister, annoying.
Mary — the youngest sister, gets me in trouble.
I am from varsity football, basketball, and track with all my best friends.
I am from a shy wimpy childhood, which was sheltered and small.
I'm from striving to work hard at life, live life to the fullest, have fun and do great things.
I am from a student, brother, uncle, and athlete.
I am from McDonald's, Culvers, Wendy's, and Applebee's.
I am from being there for friends.
I am from the 2000's, where technology has taken over with computers, iPods, and Xbox.
I am from here
Ronald Wilkey, Grade 12
West Marshall High School, IA

Fighting Beauty
The sun rises, but we are stubborn and sleep through it.
The birds are singing to us, but we shut the window.
The sun shines brightly for us, so that we can enjoy its light,
But everyone is annoyed, irritated by it, so we invented sunglasses.
Nature is so wonderful, but we close our eyes to it.
It's a shame really — we are given the gift of sunlight, the wind, and the Earth itself;
Then we build walls, roofs, and cities to block it out.
Is there a reason that we must fight nature?
Emily Maynard, Grade 12
CAM High School, IA

Watching

The pain of watching you walk out the door, not knowing when I'd see you again was unbearable.
I felt like a part of me was missing.
I was completely lost without you.
You taught me everything I know, from smiling to dancing, and even my attitude.
You helped make me who I am today. I looked up to you, I wanted to be just like you.
To me you could do no wrong. You couldn't disappoint me, you couldn't hurt me.
I believed that you would never hurt me.
I went to sleep that night hoping and praying that it was all just a mistake.
I woke up thinking it was just a normal day, then I remembered what happened last night.
I ran into your room to find it empty. I collapsed to my knees, crying, not understanding why you left.
Realizing I was wrong, because you did disappoint me, hurt me, and you did do wrong.
I didn't realize how much I depended on you.
Until the moment I was standing alone without someone to help me, to guide me.
I changed without you. We're different now.
I think we're too different, we grew apart. We fight more.
It always seems like we try to see who can hurt who more.
By doing that you've become someone I don't know…what happened to us?
Since the day you left, you said you were sorry, that you regretted the way you left.
But what you never said is that you regretted leaving.

Rebecca McIntire, Grade 11
Aplington-Parkersburg High School, IA

A Lost Heart

Someone special like you.
We are walking through a meadow with flowers of reds, blues, purples, and pinks.
I turn to see your face; first, I see your eyes.
A window to your soul shows that my heart is safe with you always.
Next, I see your smile, making me burst with devotion.
I turn and face forward then I look back; you're gone.
I don't understand?
Where did you go?
Why did you leave?
Where are those eyes where I felt safe?
Where are you my love? Where are you?
When you're not here with me I feel lost, scared, hurt, despair, but mostly angry.
Now I live in a world where you don't exist, life is more complicated, dark, gloomy, and more despair comes upon me.
It's scary enough to go through one day, knowing you're not here.
My heart was filled with life, now my soul is dark as night.
It's hard to know that you lost someone special.
Someone special like you.

Bailey Kelly, Grade 10
Marian High School, NE

Me

Lea
Tomboy, creative, artistic, loyal
Sister of Trint & Trevor
Lover of art, reading, and creative natures
Who feels anger at the sight of maltreatment, unnecessary misunderstandings, and mean people
Who needs the support of her friends, family, and pets to carry on
Who fears the act of falling, being forgotten, and not being cared about
Who would like to see Australia
Resident of Kansas
Bowers

Lea Bowers, Grade 11
Holton High School, KS

Moving On

They say that
kids grow up fast,
but you don't realize it
until you look at the past.
Now I hate to see my
childhood go
but that's what happens
as you grow.
I never thought that
the years would go by so fast
and I can't help but reminisce about the past.
I don't like the thought
of leaving everything behind,
but sometimes I realize a bright future
and then I don't mind.
Although I know I will
miss all my early years,
I know that I will have to move on
or else be left in tears.

Michelle Wolters, Grade 12
Enderlin Area High School, ND

How Wonderful You'll Always Be

It all started that one summer day.
From that moment that we first talked,
I knew you were meant to stay.
Also from that moment that our hands first locked.
Through all our relationship was full of doubt,
We still go on to prove them wrong
Proving that we will work out.
Through the misjudgments and gossip, we're still strong.
Now on together we go,
Do you see an end? I don't. Never.
Our love, boy how it glows.
We were meant to last. Forever.
You have found a place deep in my heart I thought I'd never see,
That only proves to me how wonderful you'll always be.

Laura Jaeger, Grade 10
Lamoni High School, IA

Interesting Animals

Very interesting animals
Including mammals
Like lions and bears
Or tigers and hares
Which can make a neat sound
But not like a basset hound
Who makes an annoying noise
When chomping on chew toys
Or when they bark
It's nothing like a beautiful western meadowlark
Which is Nebraska's state bird
Where Indians could spot a buffalo herd

Luke Andrew, Grade 10
Randolph High School, NE

Grandpa

As the sleek smooth boat
Drifts through the lake,
We wait until we are at the right spot to fish,
Numbly as being stung by a bee in Spring, but soothing,
Stopping now, the casting of lines begin,
With one cast I caught a 13-pound catfish.

He sits and guts our catch of fish,
Then my grandpa catches turtles with the guts,
With sleeves rolled up,
Wearing his chef hat and apron,
He is the best cook in the world,
By making the air smell like art.

One crooked finger holds the traps,
That we use for trapping more bait,
And for aquariums at our homes,
We watch them grow and reproduce,
So we can make millions,
My grandpa and I.

Dennis Stammer, Grade 11
South Page Community School, IA

Ode to Family

When family gather
And we all love,
It's a grand ole time with those who matter
Whether we are all here or some up above.
There are errors
There are trials,
But family does not sit in terror
The option of separation is of denial.
Through thick and thin
Together we will stick,
For we are brought together by blood, not skin
Family is something you can't quit, even if someone gets sick.
When problems do arise
We have family to lean on,
When we are troubled they hear our cries
The list could go on but I know that family is the strongest bond.

Callie Buske, Grade 12
Sioux Central High School, IA

Look Up and See What There Is to Find

Where I come from people do not rely on others
Where I come from people do not believe in trusting your brothers
So to change the lack of trust in others
You must show a love like no other
And a love like no other does not come from anywhere
But into the sky you must stare
And in the sky you will find
A love like no other kind

John McGivern, Grade 12
Goddard Academy, KS

Cutting Deep
Today was the day you said good-bye
And all we had was just a lie.
Why did you have to go?
Could it have waited for tomorrow?
Oh, can't you see?
Your words are cutting deep.
Oh, stay with me.
I need you to breathe.
Do you remember the nights?
We talked without the lights.
Will you remember me?
Will you remember our dreams?
Hopefully soon my days will get brighter.
But it's okay 'cause you were the liar.
I will move on,
Since you weren't the one.
It was nice that you broke my heart,
And left me here to sit in the dark.
You used to be so nice and sweet.
So why did you lie and cheat?
Shelby Powell, Grade 12
Southern High School, NE

Sleeper
If you will sleep, the world will cease
To chase you with its lies
If you will dream, the world will cease
To want for your demise
But when you wake, then you will find
You've lost yourself this time
Come to the trees, where I will wait
To wipe the tears you cry
Lie in peace, the world will cease
While stars light up the sky
Breathe deep, I'll rock you to sleep
Leave the past behind
Go back to sleep, the world will cease
With your hands wrapped in mine
Stay asleep, under the trees
Rest, you will finally find
Sydney Schwager, Grade 11
Home School, NE

Sleep in Peace
Sleep is just around the bend, beckoning
Close your eyes, let go of your worries
Temporary death will take you
Peace will fill your mind like lead
Life is a fleeting light
Dancing like teasing
flickering life
no more strife
Sleep and
See.
Nulee Kim, Grade 12
Dallas Center Grimes High School, IA

Spring
I watch the flowers open wide,
blooming for the spring.
For a moment I stand completely still,
to listen to all the birds sing.
I take in the smell of the freshly cut grass that awakens beneath my feet.
I lift my face up to the sun as my skin soaks up the heat.
The bright blue sky floats above my head.
The breeze is chasing the leaves.
And I fall to the ground with the forest as my bed.
Then I close my eyes and breathe.
Jena Nicholson, Grade 10
Winfield-Mount Union Jr/Sr High School, IA

The Child Artist
I've never seen a sky so blue
as the one colored on this page,
nor have I seen one quite so clear,
so pure, the eyes who filled this page.
In coloring books, lines are drawn;
These lines, I fear, I've disobeyed.
I think sometimes I know a way
that's better than The Creator's.
Though given endless color choice,
I confess, I choose gruesome gray
to match the skies I see inside,
which must suffer an endless rain.
I've completely clotted with clouds
the sky, which had not clouds drawn in,
to match the clouds within my eyes,
fogged by the cruel heart which has sinned.
Lord, clear my eyes to see your skies,
and not the ones which I have made.
Please, bless my heart with innocence
and color choice which shows no rain.
Mikka Mills, Grade 12
Wapello Sr High School, IA

Holding Preciousness
Life comes and goes.
It's a magical aspect to many.
Although, some are not aware
Others beware not to waste it.

An innocent distinguishes the secret
She lives by it each and every day.

With life one must hold it near,
Therefore you shall not fear.

Your life is yours.
No one can change it except you.
You decide the future past and present
For you hold your precious life
In your own hands.
Maggie Jo McElmeel, Grade 12
Cascade Jr/Sr High School, IA

Photograph
The sea stood still
For a glimpse in time,
Forever held
In a memory of mine.
A blue wave's crest
Forever paused,
A glistening reflection
Freshly caused.
A gull suspended
With feathery wings,
Brightly shined
Like silver rings.
The Sun shone down
With beating strength,
Each ray was cast
With exceeding length.
This memory held
In a photo of mine,
Forever will capture
This glimpse in time.
Anna Johnson, Grade 10
Clear Creek Amana High School, IA

Spring
Bring on the rain
Farmers go insane
Factors come into play
Tractors moving on the plain
Plants blooming
Rains looming
Grass growing
Farmers sowing
Taxes returned
Faxes sent
Mowers going
Kids throwing
People grilling
Kids chilling
Adam Thompson, Grade 10
Randolph High School, NE

Mallory Falconer

Mallory
Funny, loving, intelligent, independent
Sister of Matt
Lover of freedom, talking, California weather, and being nice
Who feels outrage when she gets blamed for other people's faults, happiness when with friends, and fright when alone
Who needs her mother's love, everyone's honesty, and her dad's intelligence
Who gives love easily, attitude to her parents, and laughs to her friends and family
Who fears getting yelled at, being alone, and getting punished for something she didn't do
Who would like to see the world, her parents in better health, and everyone getting along
Resident of Holton, Kansas
Falconer

Mallory Falconer, Grade 11
Holton High School, KS

Austin

Austin
Brave, intelligent, happy, loving
Brother of Mathew, Amy, Chris, and Mike
Lover of Apple, computers, and technology
Who feels anger when his siblings shout at him, happiness when he gets more technology, and fright on a dark Halloween night
Who needs faith from his elders, strength from his friends, and courage from his heart
Who gives friendship to the lonely, help to ones in need, and faith to the faithless
Who fears the presence of the Dark Side, Darth Vader, and Anakin Skywalker
Who would like to see all the kinds of birds in a cluster
Resident of Holton, Kansas
Watkins

Austin Watkins, Grade 11
Holton High School, KS

About Me

Hannah
Loving, caring, outgoing, and silly
Sister of Michael, Jonathan, and Joshua
Lover of the summer, sleeping, and being with friends
Who feels happy when she's with her friends and family, ecstatic when it's summer time, and relaxed when it's raining
Who needs water from Mother Earth, love from others, and contacts to see
Who gives advice to others, love to her cats, and help to children
Who fears losing the ones she loves, snakes, and getting in a wreck
Who would like to see everybody treated the same and World Peace
Resident of Holton, Kansas
Coverdale

Hannah Coverdale, Grade 11
Holton High School, KS

Shadows

I sit in the darkness. Afraid of the light. Everywhere I go, the shadows follow me. They speak to me as I walk. People tell me I'm insane, but I know what I hear and see. No matter where I look, shadows are following me. They scream my name, some cry out for help. Frightened I run towards the darkness. It's the only thing that saves me from the shadows. Sitting in the darkness, I tremble with fear. Scared the shadows will out smart the darkness and take me away.

Brianna Nawara, Grade 10
Cambridge Jr/Sr High School, NE

Sweet Dreams

Once upon a time
is a silly thing to say,
when fairy tales don't happen.
But for a tiny child
with hopes and dreams
to spare,
it takes a bit of time
to bid sweet fairy tales goodbye;
to let go the well-travelled sleepland,
to let go the things they wish to keep.
As searching,
and as hoping,
and as believing in sweet marvels —
like princesses and kings —
wave the childhood goodbye,
silly imaginations disappear into
nothing.
Here, children are no longer children, and
Here, teenagers do not just believe.
They let go the childhood fantastic
and realize their dreams.

Katerina Isom, Grade 12
Mediapolis High School, IA

Stitches

Open wound,
Bleeding and infected,
Sewn up tight
With seven
Surreptitious stitches:
One for denial,
To hide from the pain;
One for truth,
To know that it's real.
A stitch for the memories,
So they're never forgotten;
Another for dreams,
So hope can still remain.
Add a fifth for unbelieving faith
And a sixth for distempered fate.
Stitch number seven
Makes a pretty bow
That ties wound closed
And hides six other
Insane brother stitches
From probing worldly view.

Keely Higgins, Grade 10
Lincoln North Star High School, NE

Nature

The sun in your face
with the flowers on the ground
makes you feel special

Emily Wolf, Grade 10
Udall Jr/Sr High School, KS

Perfect World

People are trying and people are failing at making a perfect world
In order to change things and fix this mess, people must heed these words
No sticks, no stones, no broken bones, no words, no shattered souls
No glares, no lies, no impatient sighs, no stories filled with holes
No insults, no rumors, no cruel assumers, no more broken lives
No hassles, no teasing, nothing uneasy, no more cloudy skies
No stares, no tears, no hidden fears, no unstopping rain
No whispers, no secrets, no forgotten regrets, no never-ending pain
No stealing, no faking, no more heart breaking, no hiding behind the walls
No winning, no losing, no people-using, no waiting on phone calls
No ugly, no pretty, just in-between, please don't point and laugh
No lazy, no lying, no more tear-crying, and taking all that they have
No cruelty, no hitting, no anger-spitting, no more broken promises
People point and people laugh, we can't keep going on like this!
If I could change the world one step at a time, that is how it would go
The victims and loners and even the stoners are caught in an undertow
The bullies and fakers and all the heartbreakers have got to stop this mess
People are dying and people are crying and it will never stop unless
We help each other and stick together through every trial and storm
All of these things can change the world and keep us safe from harm

Alexis Alholinna, Grade 12
Hamlin High School, SD

Reflections on a Penny

Examining the profile: the stoic, copper gaze,
The motto "In God we trust,"
Hanging like a vulture overhead,
And liberty nagging at his right shoulder,
I wonder if the minted ghost of a man
Would appreciate the future's sentiment.
What cause is there for happiness after four years
Of crushing expectancy as a kindred spirit of
The punished Titan, who sees
Bloodstains everywhere, the telltale marks of murders he convicts himself of?
And then, to be the haunted miracle man
Overtaken in the home stretch by an unbeliever!
To become no more than a cold metal face with a birthdate not your own,
And an invisible statue in a pillared memorial, worth a single cent,
And an antique name in a thousand yellowed books,
And throaty, pedantic words on the lips of spectacled historians,
And a godlike figurehead in the minds of your people.
A dusty, American legend who never would reap the benefits in the flesh.
We all know those who would kill for the chance of such glory.
But they aren't the ones who end up on the penny.

Devany West, Grade 10
Lawrence Free State High School, KS

Tebow

There was once a man named Tim,
He put his fist to his chin,
Got on one knee,
Said his plea,
And then later he wins.

Dayton June, Grade 10
Udall Jr/Sr High School, KS

Rain

Rain,
Beautiful, peaceful,
Falling, splashing, soaking,
Rain is nature's magic —
Heaven's tears.

Jacob Sunderman, Grade 11
South Page Community School, IA

High Merit Poems – Grades 10, 11, and 12

A True Lack of Love
My cat's love for me is not quite right
Instead of eternal love, it is eternal fight
Her hissing and growling makes me sad
I feel her attitude is always bad
and it always puts me into a fright.

When she comes to sit on my lap at night
Her claws I always sight
It's like her growls are a new-found fad
Her love for me is not quite right.

No purrs and meows could overcome her mean might
Never a sweet face sees the light
I thought most cats were not this mad
My love for her only amounts to a tad
The worst thing about her is her bite
Our love is just not right.
Madison Kirch, Grade 10
Olathe South Sr High School, KS

The Color of Happiness
The color of happiness
Is yellow,
Like the sun on a beautiful day,
Or the yellow
Of popcorn on your first date.
The color of happiness is white,
Like the first snow,
Or the white
Of the diamond he puts on your left hand.
The color of happiness
Is pink,
Like the pink of a newborn piglet,
Or the pink of the receiving blanket.
That holds your crying happiness.
Justis Swartout, Grade 10
Volunteers of America-Turning Point South, SD

Nature Is Invincible
Nature is invincible —
The break of dawn rises in the east —
And a day's brightness pierces in from the beaming sun —
As the swift smell of flowers fills the nostrils —
The sensation is overpowering —
It won't let you escape —
The emotions freeze your body —
Nature is invincible —
The movement of unceasing clouds in the everlasting blue sky —
Then the day's darkness begins as the sun sets in the west —
The constellations peak through the blackness —
Man's day of work is completed —
Only One will know the rest of which is to come —
Nature is invincible —
Evey Choat, Grade 11
Cedar Rapids Jr/Sr High School, NE

Eyes Seen Clearly
Body so weak — but eyes so confident —
The path ahead — determined —
The gift of Life is something sent —
Yet something so broken and damaged —

One last day — to go out and play —
Explore and see the world —
Just a young boy —
Big blue eyes and hair tightly curled —

Yet the feeling shivered down his little limbs —
As the end was coming soon —
He had everything ahead of him —
Like the game that afternoon —

The determined path came just a little too early —
Those little blue eyes shut tight —
But everything was then seen clearly —
No matter who — You need to put up a fight —
Kaylee Penne, Grade 11
Cedar Rapids Jr/Sr High School, NE

Love
The past is the past the future is here
Don't dwell on what happened think about now
It's hard to get through it but don't you fear
It will be okay but I don't know how
You have to believe me when I say that
Times are hard but you have to get through it
Make your own path push that grass straight down flat
Join in my journey my candle has been lit
My love is a hard thing to give to you
But now it seems like the right thing to do
When I am with you I feel completed
I am speechless there are no words for this
As long as you're here I'm not defeated
Our embark will begin with the first kiss
Jacob Williams, Grade 10
Lamoni High School, IA

The Darkness and Light
The dark and the light, the black and the white;
Good versus evil while day faces night;
Immersed in pure holiness, to feel comfort and bliss;
Indulged in the demons, to taste death bringer's kiss;
Both sides keep calling, do I answer the call?
Or do I still keep to fading, too timid to fall;
I face a fork in the path, two choices, one fate;
The decision I make will determine the gate;
I envy the man, dressed in pure white;
But seduced by the woman, garbed blacker than night;
They turn to face each other, but what do they see?
No, it's the mirror...I'm looking at me
Brady Folkens, Grade 10
Volunteers of America-Turning Point South, SD

It's Time to Fly

A girl had a dream.
It was pretty BIG dream,
though she was a little, tiny kid.
Everyone said
she could not carry it
because it was too GRAND to her.

She said to them loudly
with confidence,
"I can achieve my dream.
I'm smart and clever.
Don't judge me like that."

But as she grew up more and more
her dream became smaller and smaller.
She made a wall which squeezed her.
She put herself in prison.
She didn't believe herself anymore.

Now, she knows
it's time to fly.

Daisy Choi, Grade 10
Gehlen Catholic School, IA

Alone

People swarm around me
I smile up at them
Though they cannot see
How I truly am
Even though I am well-known,
And they think I have a heart of gold
I am flawed
And disgusting
What they see is a fraud
Whom they should not be trusting
I am trapped
In a world that cannot understand
I will not adapt
Because they seem so bland
But I put on a smile
And they welcome me
Though they cannot see
I am truly alone
In a world
That I have outgrown
Alone

Arria Lakha, Grade 10
Norfolk Senior High School, NE

First Kiss

Why do my eyes mist
when I recall that first kiss
of youth's sharp longing?

Victoria Benvin, Grade 10
Udall Jr/Sr High School, KS

Unreal

My life is a book of dull, printed pages
My dreams seem far more real
Enormous doors bursting off of brass hinges
I don't know how to feel

All is gone; all has been taken
Held loosely with stitches, I smile
The sand on which I stand is shaken
Nothing's solid, all the while

I sit alone in this drawer of all the things that made me happy
Anger shakes these wooden walls and holds me closer than before
The sand comes through these openings and then it all falls through me
Rain is so much colder when it's covering your bedroom floor

Skin is fragile, red and white
Wiping the dirt on your sleeve
Everything we create in this life
Is the only mark that we leave

Savhannah Draper, Grade 11
Holton High School, KS

Remember That Day

Remember that day, I do
The one where I lost you
Remember that day, you said you'd always be there
The day I realized life isn't fair
Remember that day, the one I shed tears
On that day you confirmed my fears
Remember that day, the silence and sorrow
The reality that no one can promise tomorrow
Remember that day, they lowered you into the cold
Then the final words were told
Remember that day, the last one with you Dad
Took it for granted the things I had
Remember that day, I received that call
Still strange not seeing you front row when I play softball
Remember that day, a stone now marks your place
I miss the Pepsi you drank and signature cigarette protruding from your face
Remember that day, my life changed in a dramatic way
Now I just remember you, every day.

Nicole Romine, Grade 11
Falls City High School, NE

Trans Am

Cruising the highway,
My T-tops are off,
Turbo winding as I accelerate.
Wind rolls off my spoiler.
Wherever I go,
All eyes are on me.
Leaving my mark,
'81 Trans Am.

Sara Alexander, Grade 10
Gehlen Catholic School, IA

People

People are like snowflakes
Divine differences distinguish us
The elf-like girl, the mountain man
The scaly woman, the flawless baby
The wet sticky snowflake, the dry snowflake
Snowflakes are like people
All different but yet the same

Aaron Ammon, Grade 10
Stuart High School, NE

High Merit Poems – Grades 10, 11, and 12

Lead Poisoning

An eagle falls by a bullet
but it was not shot.
How can this be?
An eagle brought down by a bullet
but not shot?
Surely it must have been shot
and whoever the cruel evil man was
who would do such a terrible crime
should be punished!
But he isn't
He did fire a gun
but not at the bird.
A lead bullet escapes his gun
and lodges itself into the deer.
Hurt and dying,
the deer becomes lost
and knowing not of the death that awaits
the bird finds a meal out of its flesh.
An eagle falls by a bullet
but it was never shot.

Brittany Baumhover, Grade 10
Carroll High School, IA

Life Is

Life is a constant jumbled mess.
It is never fair and just.
It is always out to get you.
You can never just slide by.
You can never escape it.
It's always sitting at your stoop.
Waiting to come and get you.
But sometimes life is pleasant.
It will occasionally throw you a bone.
It may sometimes give you a break.
And let you have some fun.
But look out.
And watch your back.
Because Life is a crafty one.

Josh Ramos, Grade 10
Cardinal Jr/Sr High School, IA

Love

Love is the key to life,
To help us through the pain and strife,
Things may not go our way,
But love will try to make your day,
When you're destined to meet,
The person you will love,
You will start to hear,
the wings of doves,
Forever and always,
You will stay,
Together forever,
Forever and a day.

Devon Bishop-Martinez, Grade 12
Dell Rapids High School, SD

I Am Me

I am from a split family, I guess you could call it that.
I am from parents who were never together in my eyes.
I am from a teen mom — who suffered from judgment and denial.
I am from a shy father — who never knew his next action.
I am from questions that have never been answered…What happened? Who am I?
I am from stepparents, who showed me what a real family is, just never my own.
I am from an only child, to 5 siblings, none truly my own.
I am from heartbreak. Friends and boys, came and went.
As a child,
I am from skinned knees and backwards hats, I was spoiled and oblivious.
As a teen,
I am undefined. Troubled in finding my true self.
Prep, comedian, athlete, nerd. Random at day — I am in my own world.
I am me — forever.
I am from an unforgettable past.
I am from constant sorrows and what coulda been…
I am from "We miss you" and "Hope to see you soon"
I am hopeful for the future and eager for success.
I am undefined.
I am me.

Hailee Halverson, Grade 12
West Marshall High School, IA

Autonomous Glory

Computers are great, they never need to sleep
Always ready for calculations.
Computers are great, they are never wrong.
Unless if there is human interaction.
Computers are great, they never give up.
Always pushing through the trials.
Computers are great, when they aren't a fruit.
Because those are hardly computers.
Computers are great, never letting emotion cloud their judgment.
Just watch the movie War Games.
Computers are great, they never forget a thing.
Unless if there is a magnet next to it.
Computers are great, they can predict the future.
Like Sunny on I-Robot.
Computers are great because they have the properties of a Democrat.

Joseph Brightwell-Kelley, Grade 11
Falls City High School, NE

Just a Ball

A lethargic meteor on the horizon
Gradually proceeding across the sky
A majestic horse-drawn carriage of flames
Eating up darkness with each mile traveled
Within the first hour the darkness gives way
To the ultraviolet rays that implode every square foot of the world as we know it
Illuminating our planet as long as it retains its fuel
Only holding enough for eleven hours forty-two minutes and six seconds today
When finally exhausted the horses retire their chariot of fire to the end of the earth
Ready to teleport to the eastern sky the next morning
To start the flawless process all over again

Ben Hintz, Grade 10
Thayer Central High School, NE

True Love — Villanelle

As subtle as the wind when it wants to blow.
If it is meant for you, it will always return.
When true love is needed the most, it will show.

Looking close, you see it wherever you go.
It is around every corner and at every turn.
As subtle as the wind when it wants to blow.

It helps every person to mature and grow.
It is greatly desired and to which people yearn.
When true love is needed the most, it will show.

Through your heart, it likes to flow.
It will bring warmth like a fire will burn.
As subtle as the wind when it wants to blow.

A feeling that people of all ages can know.
Just like trust, it is something you earn.
When true love is needed the most, it will show.

No matter how old, you will never outgrow.
It is unconditional, and needs no concern.
As subtle as the wind when it wants to blow.
When true love is needed the most, it will show.

Rachelle Harman, Grade 12
Holton High School, KS

Shadows in the Light

There are shadows in the light tonight,
Their hollow eyes no more are bright,
I see them in the night's glow, dull,
A single glance can pierce the soul,

There are shadows in the light tonight,
In the darkness, cooled with fright,
The song in their hearts is no longer gay,
The hope in their hearts has flown away,

There are shadows in the light tonight,
They sit and hope everything will turn out right,
They have no happiness left inside,
Counting their miseries, time they bide,

There are shadows in the light tonight,
The joy of others is a savage sight,
They have not a tear left to cry,
It is their only wish, to die,

There are shadows in the light tonight,
Will you be the one to hold them tight?
Give them a reason to live, a hope like the breeze that blows,
Bring them into the light from out of the shadows.

Madelaine Colarossi, Grade 11
Colarossi Home School, KS

White Eyes

I glare into white eyes;
Searching for a stare in my gold pupils, but
Nothing stares back; my determination dies.

Investigating for dreaded lies;
Absent answers to my soul cut —
I glare into the white eyes.

I embark on a pointless journey with no supplies.
My purpose gone, I aimlessly stare at an abandoned hut.
Nothing stares back; my determination dies.

Everywhere I glare I see emptiness — a sight I despise —
An emptiness I can't escape; I continue to glare as if it were a rut,
I glare into the white eyes.

I try to ignore my instincts in an attempt to be wise,
My eyes, like my mouth, are a muzzle on a mutt,
nothing stares back; my determination dies.

My eyes' wants will be my demise,
My last defense will be to keep them shut, but,
I glare into the white eyes;
nothing stares back; my determination dies.

Conner Hampton, Grade 12
Holton High School, KS

A New Day

Awaken each morning with a smile so bright
Never pass up the chance of the day
Feel accomplished as day turns to night

Take the time to do things right
With a job well done you will receive your pay
Awaken each morning with a smile so bright

Take a chance and achieve a new height
Look at life from a new point of view as you lay
Feel accomplished as day turns to night

Stand your ground with all of your might
You'll be surprised how much one voice can say
Awaken each morning with a smile so bright

Be observant and broaden your sight
Look into others' hearts and see it their way
Feel accomplished as day turns to night

Open your mind and let your wings take flight
Soar among the warm sunrays
Awaken each morning with a smile so bright
Feel accomplished as day turns to night

Elizabeth Eickhoff, Grade 11
Falls City High School, NE

High Merit Poems – Grades 10, 11, and 12

D-End
I am the Hunter.
I sit at the line of scrimmage
Seeking my prey...waiting...watching.
The ball is snapped.
My prey hides in the thickets of the quarterback's arms.
He moves from player to player, thicket to thicket.
My prey ran away.
I set up for the next hunt.
I sit on the line...seeking the ball.
Then, he moves.
I am constantly stalking,
juking players and working through the field's grooves.
My prey, unaware, sits in the open field.
I dare to inch closer...then I dart forward.
SACK!
My prey, down. My prize, claimed. But,
The hunt is never over. I am never satisfied.
Always greedy and always hungry,
I set back up for the next play.
Patrick Livermore, Grade 10
Gehlen Catholic School, IA

Travel
To me travel is compared at a different rate.
Fast or slow travel has won me over.
Most tell me that travel is what they hate.
Travel gives me the chance to find the lucky 4-leaf clover.
You can travel fast or slow it's the journey that's important.
As long as it gets you to where you need to go.
When I travel I feel free and completely independent.
Nothing can compare to what travelers know.
In my dreams I travel far and wide.
One moment I can be at the highest mountain peak.
Then the next I can be watching the ocean tide.
Let your imagination run don't let it show if it is weak.
Don't be afraid of things you cannot bear.
When you travel you meet amazing people that are very rare.
Autum Jackson, Grade 11
Lamoni High School, IA

Books
Books, books, books
What's there to say about books?
There's big ones and small ones.
Blue ones and brown ones.
There's tall ones and short ones.
Funny ones and sad ones.
Happy ones and scary ones,
There are thrillers and naughty ones.
There are hang cliffs and bad ones.
There are my favorite ones and least favorite ones.
There are bug ones and there are life ones,
There are real ones and there are fake ones.
So pick up a book and find your favorite.
Sydnee Schnell, Grade 10
Randolph High School, NE

Gold
Thump, thump, thump that is the sound of my heart beating
Before the beginning of a big race
Muscles tighten in ready stance
Toes curled over the edge of the pool
Waiting for the gun to sound
BANG there's the gun
Push off the edge with all my might
Diving into water as cold as the Antarctic
Sucks the breath right out of my lungs
Right arm, left arm, right, left
Pulling with all my strength
Kicking my legs and pushing with all my might
With the fast beating of my heart
Breath, stroke, breath, stroke
I reach the edge take a breath, flip and turn
Under the water I see clear blue so quiet so peaceful
As I break the surface water splashing and people screaming
My arms are heavy as lead but I just have to keep going
Feels like forever breathing ever chance I can without slowing down
Slowly reaching out in front of the competitors
Pulling ahead realizing the gold is just two strokes away
3..2…1 SLAP my head hits the edge but the gold is mine
Ann Rush, Grade 11
Conway Springs High School, KS

Stop and Stare
Stop and stare as life goes by
There you go wasting precious time
Stop and stare as your comrades advance forward
While you're sitting they do not know what to do
Stop and stare as heavy artillery blows up around you
As your ears ring you try and come back to realization
Stop and stare as your friends fall around you
Bleeding so bad that there is no hope
Stop and stare as your life flashes before your eyes
Sitting there thinking about your family
Stop and stare at your sergeant telling you to press on
Telling you to fire your weapon and help the wounded
Stop and stare for that last second
As you advance boom
Stop and stare at your loves ones in the next life
Dakota Pentecost, Grade 11
Falls City High School, NE

Family Love
I love you after all the things you have done to me.
I cared about you while you never did.
I wished to be close when you just pushed me away.
I dreamed that you would be a part of my family,
When family was the last thing on your mind.
I wanted nothing more than a dad
and all ever got was…
nothing.
Kaitlyn Burton, Grade 10
Cardinal Jr/Sr High School, IA

Season for Warmth
Winter has gone, spring has come,
If only it was summer that has begun.
I sit inside alone and wonder,
Why is spring always full of rain and thunder?

The sun is out, but it is deceiving,
Because when I go outside it is freezing!
I always ponder nature's choices,
But I end with vague answers from hushed-toned voices.

If I had it my way, every season would be summer,
Because the cold is a real bummer.
It makes my aches and pains work hard,
When I should be sunbathing in my yard.

Global Warming and random weather,
75 degrees constantly sounds so much better!
With every flake and every drop,
My need for summer will ever stop!

Vanessa Gray, Grade 12
Chapman High School, KS

No Tears and No Cries
The rain falls like the tears, rolling down your cheek.
It's sad as a storm that seems dark and cold.
Full of sadness like the ocean, feeling lonely and ignored.
All you're trying to find is love and peaceful joy.
His hands like angels taking away your hurtful life.
Cleaning your tears that seems they'll never end.
But the more he's there for you, the more you fill accompanied.
Even though not physically, but emotionally.
His warmth like the sun.
His voice like the wind.
His accompany like a shadow,
going everywhere you go.
The rain falls like the tears
fading away little by little.
Your eyes sparkle like stars
showing their shining sparkle light.
Your tears, the tears, are gone away for now.
Now and forever,
No tears and no cries.

Beverly Santiago, Grade 11
Cardinal Jr/Sr High School, IA

Color Me Happy
Sunshine, smiley faces, yellow balloon
Looking at a smiling baboon
Happiness comes in different shapes and sizes
But yellow is the color that realizes
What the heart wants to see
A smiling image of you and me
Yellow is the color that makes me laugh
With a chick, banana, and a baby giraffe

Karlyn Stellingwerf, Grade 11
Volunteers of America-Turning Point South, SD

My Old Friend
The air outside whips me
with all its might.
It situates all around me until
I find my way back to my old friend.

My hands have hardened scars
and new cuts from my old friend.
It has arms, but never moves.

It will never leave
for the next season I am sad and solo
it will be there to comfort me.

Just like most friends
it's dangerous and can deal great disaster
but will be there until the world wastes away.

It guards me from the ground's grasp.
It keeps me safe and sound
from the dangers down below the dirt.

Kayla Bouska, Grade 10
Stuart High School, NE

The Trip
The plane arrives and carries you away.
Looking down on the distant world below,
You will not let anything cause delay.
Bracing yourself, you get ready to go.
As the plane lands at your destination,
You step onto unfamiliar soil.
The crowds of people in hectic motion,
The city seems as if in a toil.
The beach is the place your gaze does stare
With the waves, the sand, the breeze, you smile.
You can't help but smell the relaxing air.
This waiting and yearning was all worthwhile.
This, an experience never to fade.
Special times and treasured memories made.

Connor Strader, Grade 11
Holton High School, KS

Golf Ball
The smooth club brushed fresh cut grass.
The angry club came back around,
Smacked me.
I soared into the fresh air,
Stared at tiny people on the ground,
Rolled on the steep cliff next to the roaring river,
Hit a smooth rock,
Flew out,
Sailed towards the pin,
Went into the empty hole.
I thought I won,
But it was just a practice round.

Dustan Kneip, Grade 10
Gehlen Catholic School, IA

High Merit Poems – Grades 10, 11, and 12

Rain's Demise

Rain was in my heart,
Prior to its descent.
The sticky, hasty air,
I relished the scent.

I breathed the drops,
When suddenly I realized,
That our home, Mother Earth,
Is rain's demise.

Demise, demise.
The flow of it, acquired.
For the roses, the thorn,
Steady sunrises, the tired.

Dry oaks, the blaze,
The inception, the finale.
Blue sky lake, the drought,
Peak's runoff, the valley.

Never despair your closure,
Nor the unstoppable disease.
After the rain has met with Earth,
It shall retreat to the breeze.
Connor Birzer, Grade 12
Ellinwood High School, KS

Goodbye — A Villanelle

The leaves fly through the autumn sky
I was at school that tragic day
Why did I have to say goodbye?

My mouth now is ever so dry
They all said it would be okay
The leaves fly through the autumn sky

My mother called to tell me why,
My dad's life was taken this way
Why did I have to say goodbye?

My father was such a great guy
His life is what he had to pay
The leaves fly through the autumn sky

He was not able to get by,
The car that hit him gone astray
Why did I have to say goodbye?

I stand over you now and cry
I will see you again someday
The leaves fly through the autumn sky
Why did I have to say goodbye?
Ryan Haefke, Grade 11
Holton High School, KS

Keira Jade

You're a blessing from above
So precious you are
I give you nothing but love

Your eyes like wings of a dove
Our love will grow far
You're a blessing from above

Levi liking you we couldn't shove
Leo's love was right on par
I give you nothing but love

You fit in my arms like a hand in a glove
My heart flutters like fireflies in a jar
You're a blessing from above

You're everything I dreamed of
Every day you're raising the bar
I give you nothing but love

Keira, you're beautiful like a dove
You're embedded in my heart like tar
You're a blessing from above
I give you nothing but love
Kelsey Hayes, Grade 11
Falls City High School, NE

My Greatest Fear

Please don't leave me here lonely
Astray from the light
Don't sing the "Amazing Grace" song
Don't leave out my life.

I whisper I love you so much
For all the things you do
I need your motherly touch
Because forever is ending too soon.

I look at her body
Crying my acid-like tears
There's this emptiness
When the doctor yells "Clear."

She's gone to be with her maker
And with all the others
My eyes get even wetter
I can't live without my mother.

There's no getting better
I'll forever cry these tears
I don't wanna lose her
This is my greatest fear.
Tavia Carter, Grade 10
Highland Park High School, KS

Within the Blink of an Eye

Within the blink of an eye
Something can change fate
With seconds saying goodbye

It happens fast and seems to fly
With rage and hate
Within the blink of an eye

People watch and cry
Waiting for their mate
With seconds saying goodbye

It's strange that a friend could cry
But it's way too late
Within the blink of an eye

I think about it and sigh
that you were taken out of hate
With seconds saying goodbye

I don't want to imply
But you were my friend and it was hate
Within the blink of an eye
With seconds saying goodbye
Clayton Hardenberger, Grade 11
Falls City High School, NE

Tomboy

hike your skirt up a little higher
wading through the water and
getting the hem wet anyway.

I don't even wear skirts.
too much vigor in this girlish frame
too bold for fabric
with open ends.

sinking feet in mud
that is what this is, isn't it?
and getting
stuck.

my shoes were lost long ago
deep in the underwater gunk
and I do not even begin
to care.

away from normal
I have always been
not quite fitting in
with the girls who ride in boats.
Hanna Carter, Grade 12
Marshalltown High School, IA

H.A.T.E.

H.A.T.E. is only a word
Yet I can not pronounce it
It's stuck in my throat
I think I'm gonna choke
My world used to revolve around it
Like it's my god
No more! No more!
I'll throw some rocks at the shore
Gotta get my anger out
Cause I dislike that word
It's in my mouth!
It's in my mind!
Get out! Get out!
I'll scream and shout!
You make me cry
You killer word
Push, push down to my lungs
I won't speak of you
H.A.T.E. We won't ever meet again!

Tori Bruggeman, Grade 10
Forest Ridge School, IA

Misfit Island

I am the island of misfit toys,
Cast away by all the girls and boys.

Isn't it just such a pity,
That I was the doll that wasn't made pretty?
That's why I must live in constant fear,
Of walking past even the smallest mirror,
Knowing I won't like what I see,
Maybe that's why they don't like me,
I know I'm missing a few parts and screws,
But why does that mean that I have to lose?

I am the island of misfit toys,
Forgotten by all the girls and boys.

Brittany Charboneau, Grade 11
Lebo High School, KS

Molly

Molly is my dog
She likes to jump off this log
She is energetic and loads of fun
All she does is run
She brings me lots of joy
But she will bite me like a toy
This dog is kind of crazy
She's the opposite of lazy
If she were to ever die
I would sit in my room and cry
She'll always be my little Molly
My crazy Border Collie

Kayla Backer, Grade 10
Randolph High School, NE

Where I'm From

I am from where words don't speak.
Where notes on the page say more than what we think.
Your fingers slide across the keys, pouring your soul into the unknown.
It guides your short journey of getting away for the time being.

I am from an art.
Where limbs move gracefully to diminish the power against you.
To meet the requirements of what you want to become.
When giving it your all and setting the example is exactly the stipulation.

I am from the greatest power of the earth.
When your goal is to give it to each person you meet.
To be like the one who gave you the chance
To breathe.
To live.
To love.

I am from a place foreign to mankind.
It is a place of which you can only dream…until He says your being is complete.
It is a place of complete comfort and peace.
It is a place that someday I will be once again.

Kayla Nuese, Grade 11
Deubrook Jr/Sr High School, SD

Farming

There are a large variety of jobs to do on a farm
Some people thing that in order to have success one has to have a lucky charm
Some people raise chickens that act as an alarm
If you're not careful you will lose your arm

You can grow all kind of crops
To grow some crops you need props
Some crops are used in pops
There can be a drought and your production rate drops

You can raise livestock
Sometimes the market is a crock
To be raised some need a dock
Some of them live or travel in a flock

If you're not careful you can end up in a body cast
Your life will change fast

Rodger Haselhorst, Grade 12
Randolph High School, NE

Perfectly Pink

Life is a pink lotus
Surrounded by water, struggling to stay afloat,
Gliding through, until a lily pad gets in the way,
Battling to move, and then building up power from within to travel around,
Starting with white tips and ending with deep pink,
And in the middle a yellow bunch, almost like a brain,
Yes, life is a pink lotus

Maddie McGrew, Grade 10
Clear Creek Amana High School, IA

A Love Story

Blood splatter on crisp white sheet
Purity in paradise marred in defeat
Marriage for king and his bride
Sacrificed in love he died
Evil temptress blowing kisses of sweet suckle scents
But the tortured perfection laments
Begging for perfume to be spilled in red
Safety to these others the living dead
Reflections revelations flow in tears
Lived in love with this man who stole their fears
Silence stillness nothing shakes
Twisted thorns misshapen wood laced with stakes
My heart breaks
Breath of finality a chasm of darkness invades
Clouds bubble with the cries of every debt paid
Bodies burst from your chambers below!
Joining the somber celebrated show
One being shatters the stranglehold
Fabric so strong impossible to unfold
Conquer the impossible just a word
Love is this story to be forever heard

Maggi Abbas, Grade 12
Aplington-Parkersburg High School, IA

You've Been Remade

Leaving everything I ever knew,
Only because I want to stay true,
The lies that have been said cannot be undone,
But can be unfolded and shown to everyone,
I used to be afraid of believing in myself,
But that's when things changed and now I'm by myself,
Although it may be a lonely road for me,
I know I've correctly chosen out of those three,
I could have turned away and possibly been dead,
But that's when my friend created a thread,
Now I freely wander with wise thoughts in my head,
Praying thanking God that I'm not dead,
This life that I now live is more than I could ask for,
There are no words or actions that can hurt me like before,
All the tears that I've shed are all dried away,
And the memories with them so they won't ruin my day,
Between him and I we worked things through,
Only to go back and review,
I will always wonder where I would be,
If I hadn't put trust before the feelings inside me.

Laura Russell, Grade 12
Valley City High School, ND

Goodbye Barathrum

Sinking, swaying, out of focus — and fading
Floating, and falling, into a blue daze
Relaxed, released, very appeased
A distant drone — whoosh, whoosh
Of wings

Vanessa Kelly, Grade 10
Forest Ridge School, IA

To Whom I Can Only Remember

My love for you pleads, nay, refuses
To become a ghost of past tense.
It lingers here in my
Beaten and beating chamber,
Holding through the days and nights
And months and years so numerous
I wish to have not counted them.
Always am I yearning for you as you once were,
For how am I to know you as you are now
When my letters are rewarded no responses?
Your hair, be it still bright?
Be your lips still soft and
Do they still tremble
When brushed by those of another?
And be mine the last others to make
Your lips tremble so?
Or be you loved by a man aside from I?
Fearing these questions shall retain
The status of my letters; unheard and uncared for,
I sign this, regardless, with my heart as seal,
Tears as ink, and postmarked with hope.

Peter Swanson, Grade 11
Bonner Springs High School, KS

Garden of Love

How much do I love you?
I love you much like a wide rose, a sweet token of symbolism;
and an appearance of beauty and peace.
I love you much like a sunflower, a sign of brightness;
as it develops into a vast character.
I love you much like a lily, an indication of fragility;
when it produces uniqueness into an individual.
I love you much like an iris, a sea of colors;
once shaped to form a rainbow.
I love you much like a tulip, a greeting to typify emotions;
while we are joined.
I love you much like a lilac, a representation of flawless passion;
after it creates happiness from a crisp sense.
I love you much like a garden, no matter how many there are —
You will always be my flower.

Annika Eckholm, Grade 12
Wing High School, ND

Night to Remember

This was supposed to be their time
Their night
An unalienable right
A night that was theirs for their taking
Part of the future they were making
But they followed the crowd
And drank the poison
Later that night their car crashed
A few weeks later their mothers wore shrouds
And remembered the night where their lives were smashed.

Jeremiah Anthony, Grade 10
West Sr High School, IA

Who Am I?

Who am I?
Am I a girl or am I a guy?
Am I straight, lesbian, or bi?
Am I another to the list of cast-outs?
Am I the target to hate without doubt?
Am I yours or am I alone?
Am I your love, left unknown?

Who am I?
Am I strong or am I weak?
Am I the one that you still seek?
Am I rich or am I poor?
Am I another to be kicked out your door?
Am I skilled or am I useless?
Am I still the girl you miss?

Who am I?
Am I light or am I dark?
Am I your end or am I your start?
Am I sensitive or am I reckless?
Am I the cause of all your stress?
Am I still your beautiful dove?
Am I nothing more than your dead love?

Stephanie Wickham, Grade 10
Alliance High School, NE

My Grandfather

M ysterious
Y et unpredictable

G enerous and
R eady to help
A lways there for me
N o matter what
D ad's best
F riend
A nswers any questions
T eacher of many things
H e may not always be well liked by
E veryone, but he
R eally is one of the
   strongest men I know

David Frederick, Grade 11
Falls City High School, NE

Ghost

I make it hard to sleep at night
I am the spirit of the dead
I haunt you wearing ghastly white
I make it hard to sleep at night
I'm here when you turn out the light
A ghost that haunts you in your bed
I make it hard to sleep at night
I am the spirit of the dead

Matt King, Grade 12
Nebraska City High School, NE

Addiction

Hear no evil, speak no evil, and see no evil.
Tragic misconception;
My friends gathered around me,
To them, they see themselves in the life of luxury,
A place they can never be harmed;
They see no evil.
To them, they keep secrets, finding ways to lengthen their ultimate supremacy;
They speak no evil.
To them, what I describe as destruction,
They see it as a way to ease their lust for power,
While they babble on about a way to make it through the next day.
They hear no evil.
To them, they see minutes turn to hours,
Hours turn to days,
And days turn to weeks.
Suddenly, it's all running together,
Day after day, month after month,
And year after year, I watch them wither away, into nothingness.
Utmost and utter destruction.
Evil found them…

Austin Prescott, Grade 12
Burlingame Jr/Sr High School, KS

Friday Night

Click, clack, click, clack everyone's cleats scrape against the cement
in an orange spark of friction
Game time on Friday night is the best feeling a teenager can have
Boom! The kicker's toe collides with the ball in a brown embrace
Nerves go crazy as the first play of the game is about to begin
Then all of the sudden the quarterback yells HUT with red fiery intensity
Two players crash into each other at full speed
The ref blows the whistle with a high-pitched, yellow shriek
This process is repeated over and over again until one team emerges victorious
as the clock counts down to zero
The winning team lets out pink claps and hollers of joy
Football is mentally and physically challenging, but it has great rewards

Wade Maddox, Grade 11
Falls City High School, NE

Chase Wilson

Chase
Friendly, caring, hard-working, lovable
Brother of Colby
Lover of good food, friends and family, relaxing
Who feels happiness when not at school, focused at practice, and mad after a loss
Who needs friends and family, money, free-time
Who gives help, love, and friendship
Who fears death, spiders, the dark
Who would like to see movies, the Super Bowl, and the future
Resident of Holton, KS
Wilson

Chase Wilson, Grade 11
Holton High School, KS

High Merit Poems – Grades 10, 11, and 12

That Kid
That kid who given the chance
would run far, far beyond where the eyes can see
That kid who yearns to be free
yet endures the pain of being encaged
That kid who dreams about the day
when he can escape
His problems left in the past
with his troubled family at last
That kid who stands up for himself
and fights for change in his life
That kid who will rise up and break away
who is inspirational
unforgettable
That kid who is the rising sun for so many people
If just given the chance,
that one kid could change the world
Allison Owen, Grade 11
Blue Valley North High School, KS

The Ride of My Life
The minute I hear the seat belt click
I know I better hang on for dear life.
As the roller coaster makes its way to the top,
I am thinking in my head, "Don't look down!"
Finally, when I reach the top,
the roller coaster goes soaring downhill.
My hands get sweaty as I hang onto the bar.
All you can hear is SCREAMING!
I can't see anything, for my eyes are closed.
I am hoping it will make me feel safer.
I feel the wind taking in my breath.
My throat hurts from laughing and screaming at the same time.
Then the roller coaster comes to a halt,
and I let out a HUGE sigh of relief.
Hannah Kessenich, Grade 10
Gehlen Catholic School, IA

No One Else
You're not just another face,
But together we were quite a disgrace.
The key to any relationship is trust,
Even though the feeling inside of me was just lust.
On my knee I fall.
I thought you could see this after all.
The size of a pea my common sense was,
Well gee, I guess just because.
You used to be my best friend,
Together we were starting to mend.
Maybe it was just me imagining things,
But the worlds she spoke hurt more than a bee sting.
There is no other "he" like you seem to think,
This is your chance to flee, like a boat that's about to sink.
Tressa Chandler, Grade 11
Falls City High School, NE

My Best Friend
Music is the rhythm to reality
It is organized through and through
Music has always been there for me

Music can accelerate or stay steady
There is nothing music can't do
Music is the rhythm to reality

Music is more than it's known to be
It's not just something for you to dance to
Music has always been there for me

It can help a blind man to see
It can match any mood felt by you
Music is the rhythm to reality

It's used at ceremonies whether sad or happy
It is an emotional breakthrough
Music has always been there for me

It can intimidate and make the scared flee
It can assist in your ability to woo
Music is the rhythm to reality
Music has always been there for me
Jessup White, Grade 11
Holton High School, KS

Hope, Not Ignorance
Let's get one thing straight,
I am a boy, and you are a man.
The definition of time makes you more,
But hark, and digress.

I bear the scars in this equation,
I'm a pest.
With my abstract thoughts of love and life,
Things you gave up on.

Add the ways, and subtract the fear,
Divide your tears as they multiply ore' the years.

Listen,
Hear,
Here.

As old men sit and talk,
Let me be forever remembered as the boy who stood and fought.

"I'm doing it all wrong."
They say,
They breathe.
I'd just have them believe.
Colten Quigley, Grade 12
South Tama County High School, IA

I Love You

I love you
You were there all along
I love you
You stood by me when I wasn't strong
I love you
You told me where I belong
I love you
You make me feel so strong now
I love you
You have my heart and soul
I love you
You have never acted like a tool
I love you
You have never told me I was ugly
I love you
In your eyes I am beautiful no matter what
I love you
Brittanie Dixon, Grade 11
Falls City High School, NE

True Friends

So many memories to gather
It's hard to write them all
We've been friends such a short time
But still it feels as though it's been forever

There is never a dull moment with you
We always make the best of things
We have our moments of disagreement
But in the end we work things out

Every word that we type
Every day that we talk
Every hour we spend
Only makes our friendship stronger

If I could know what I did to deserve you
To deserve your grace presence in my life
I would do it all over again
'Cause you are the greatest friend
Krystal Hanson, Grade 11
Kee High School, IA

Seasons

The autumn leaves fall
And onto the ground they lay
Life will start again

Fire burns down the trees
They will grow back soon enough
Until next season
Morgan Hack, Grade 10
Udall Jr/Sr High School, KS

Art

Softly shade or shadow,
Any medium will do,
Lasting impression to lasting impression,
Priceless to worthless
To worth more than priceless.

Stroke, stroke is a color's rhythm,
Set in vivid pools of vibrant nature,
Stretched until
Something is born or freed,
For nature calls and creative minds answer.

Wet, slick, and smooth like silk to the touch,
Molded and folded,
While mashed and formed,
Fired and glazed,
Now dry and smooth to the touch,
Impression made, impression left,
Creative mind gone.
William Pokojski, Grade 12
Lincoln Pius X High School, NE

Before the Storm

An overcast sky.
A gust of wind.
Two tables fly.
Two trees pinned,
Down.

A cryin' pup.
A car to stow.
Two kids rounded up.
Two flights to go,
Down.

The hail's a-comin',
Down.
Genevieve Jesse, Grade 10
Mercy High School, NE

School

School is what we all have to go through
Even if we don't know what to do.
We listen to the teachers
While they give us lectures.
Sometimes, we get to watch movies
And bring each other goodies.
We all think school lasts forever,
And we can't wait 'till summer.
We talk with our friends,
Until the day ends.
At the end of the day,
Everyone goes their separate ways.
Michaela Strathman, Grade 10
Randolph High School, NE

Shelter

I find no shelter in this place
No one will understand
How hard this life can be
Without the upper hand
And though you may have fooled them
With tricks, lies, and deceit
No longer shall I stumble
Into my defeat
And as long as we hate
Or bring each other down
Slowly everything
Will burn to the ground
This part we play
Is more important than you know
The souls we destroy
Will finally begin to show
So as I say this
Listen well
For hatred
Is the worst place to dwell
Tara Hurt, Grade 11
Holton High School, KS

Picture

Picture life, etched in stone
Life, sketched in poems
On sidewalks with dry chalk, next to homes
Picture life, on the main streets
Frame it, it's all of you
Everything you've ever felt
Try to name it
It's called you
Picture, in the space between breaths
It's the race between steps
And the message in this make-believe text
Picture
Gabriel Bates, Grade 10
Frontenac High School, KS

Here I Am

Here I am,
desperate and broken.
My mind gone astray,
tendrils of darkness intertwine.
Scarlet satin hits the floor,
the sound millions of miles away.
Pain, eager and willing,
trying to break through the silence.
Tears, falling and quenching,
my thirst still begs for more.
Caitlin Peter, Grade 10
Clear Creek Amana High School, IA

The Call of Death
Red curdling scream sounding from my throat.
A blue noise echoes around me.
I heard a clap of murky gray thunder.
The wolves sound off a silver howl at the moon.
A doorbell rings a golden tune.
Purple footsteps approach behind me.
My old brown stairs squeak as the creature creeps.
My yellow hairs scream the loudest of all.
A bright pink thump pounds in my chest.
This white clank is my unforgiving chain.
Courtney Hamilton, Grade 11
Falls City High School, NE

Grades 7-8-9 Top Ten Winners

List of Top Ten Winners for Grades 7-9; listed alphabetically

Keelan Apthorpe, Grade 8
St Anne Catholic School, TX

Kelly Brown, Grade 8
Fairbanks Middle School, OH

Natalie Ciepiela, Grade 7
Landisville Middle School, PA

Golda Dopp, Grade 9
Davis High School, UT

Madeline Elliott, Grade 7
Holly Middle School, MI

Lydia Heydlauff, Grade 8
Gilbert Middle School, IA

Mariella Jorge, Grade 8
Madrona Middle School, CA

Kaitlin Kilby, Grade 8
North Kirkwood Middle School, MO

Maryann Mathai, Grade 8
Windy Ridge School, FL

Jacob Nelson, Grade 8
Leesville Road Middle School, NC

All Top Ten Poems can be read at www.poeticpower.com

Note: The Top Ten poems were finalized through an online voting system. Creative Communication's judges first picked out the top poems. These poems were then posted online. The final step involved thousands of students and teachers who registered as the online judges and voted for the Top Ten poems. We hope you enjoy these selections.

The Ocean

The ocean
Blue ocean, yellow boat,
Man rowing, woman staring,
Houses sitting, ocean waves,
Boat rocking, wonderful waves.

Kaleb Johnson, Grade 7
Whittier Middle School, SD

Spring Play

I want to go outside today
Because I want to run and play
Tossing the ball around
Without hitting the ground
That is how I imagine my day.

Travis Rogers, Grade 8
St Francis Middle/High School, KS

My Dad, a Rock

My dad, a rock.
Always there for me.
Now he is a feather, far away…
I try to catch it,
But it just floats away…

Jarrett Jarecke, Grade 7
Blessed Sacrament School, NE

Troubles

Men
Lazy and messy
You remind me of big babies
Crying every day
I wish you would mature

Makenzie Barnard, Grade 7
Olpe Jr/Sr High School, KS

Mule

Mule,
Bray and snort
Running, kicking, stomping
Not wanting to listen
Peaceful

Faith Talent, Grade 7
Frontenac High School, KS

Who's There?

I heard voices outside my window
To whom they belonged I didn't know
I saw my hands shake
As I looked at his face
I can't tell. Who is this so and so?

Hannah Wolff, Grade 8
St Francis Middle/High School, KS

You Never Really Know

I never really knew how quickly things could leave your life
Until that day when something I truly loved disappeared from my sight
The doctors said she wouldn't make it
That there was nothing they could do
They told me over and over again that they were sorry for the loved one I was going to lose
As I walked into that little room and saw the scared look in her eyes
I knew instantly that I wouldn't be able to live without her in my life
I took her little hand and held it tight inside of mine
I told her I wouldn't let her go and held her real close for that little bit of time
I knew I was losing more and more of her as the seconds ticked by
She kept telling me the angels were coming to carry her up to God's side
A few moments later she said Mama I Love You and softly died
That day I lost something I can never replace
Something I will never get to see again another day
So take this to mind always hold your close ones real tight
Because once they're gone they can't come back
No matter how much you wish, pray, or ask
I hope this left a lasting impression on how short life can be
You never really know how quickly things can disappear, or leave

Tamara Drinkard, Grade 9
Valley Falls High School, KS

Ice Cream Shop

Today I am going to the ice cream shop.
I'm going to buy a big Sundae with cherries on top.
I'm going to have them pour pop all over until it over flows and drips and makes a big glop.

I can't wait till I get there.
I have been waiting for this moment all year!
It's a bummer it's only open once a year, but I'll enjoy it while it's here.

I finally reached my destination
the ice cream shop is a wonderful sensation!
They have all kind of flavors, from vanilla to birthday cake creations.

I can't seem to make up my mind
so maybe I'll just get a scoop of each kind.
Vanilla, chocolate, any kind I can find.

I enjoyed every bite.
It seemed to satisfy me just right.
But my pants are feeling a bit too tight!

Kailey Hansen, Grade 8
Jefferson Middle School, IA

Reading

Travel into a world you have created
Take every word off the page and put them into your own perspective
The characters dance in your head as they go from page to page
Create beautiful landscapes and a world of make-believe
Escape your life and live someone else's
Find new ways to look at things
Time flies out the window with each turning page
This is your world

Maddie Bruha, Grade 7
Gretna Middle School, NE

High Merit Poems – Grades 7, 8, and 9

Just Because
Just because I'm Native American
Doesn't mean I'm a bad person.
Doesn't mean I drink,
And doesn't mean I do drugs.
Just because I'm Native American
Doesn't mean I'm not smart.
Doesn't mean I'm responsible for all the white people that died.
Doesn't mean I don't know about my culture.
Just because I'm Native American
Doesn't mean I'm like Billy Mills
Doesn't mean I'm not athletic
Doesn't mean I'm poor.
Just because I'm Native American
Are all people prejudiced?
Do all Native Americans live on reservations?
Are all Native Americans poor?
I don't think so.

Kevin Catches, Grade 8
Chadron Middle School, NE

Hunting
Taking a hunting class that ends late at night
Having homework that you can't even believe
Oh how stressful homework can be, all right
So passing the class means I can leave.

I'm there in the field, cold, wet, and scared
You can't talk or move, but must sit still
The tree stand is smaller than I had dared
Then a deer comes and we take a kill.

Oh how hard it is to watch the deer die
It is now time to field dress the deer
The smell of blood makes me want to cry
Now we can go home with a new kind of cheer.

Once I get the deer meat,
It is nothing you can beat!

Jenna Schoettger, Grade 7
Faith Christian School of Kearney, NE

Friendship
Friendship is…
Support when you feel down.
A laugh when you start to frown.
An outstretched hand when you are about to drown.
Friendship is…
A shining light that will guide the way.
Something that will always stay.
A person staying by your side all day.
Friendship is…
Building up lots of trust.
But most of all, friendship is…
Always a must.

Mikaela Hastings, Grade 8
Chadron Middle School, NE

Close Encounters of the Principal Kind
I pulled into the parking lot; I backed into the space.
I got out with my two feet first
And smacked my pretty face.

The window wasn't open; I really thought it was —
I got out with my forehead sore,
And made a giant fuss.

The school bus was approaching — the great big yellow kind —
And when I hit the side of it,
I fell on my behind.

My brain felt very scrambled; my eyes rolled in my head.
I stumbled towards the building,
And wished that I was dead.

I crawled up to the entrance and opened up the door,
And promptly saw the principal,
Then fell upon the floor.

He dragged me to his office, and said, "You're quite a mess!
But, at least you're entertaining, that part I must confess."
And then he started laughing like jolly old Saint Nick.
My cheeks became tomatoes; I exited real quick.

As I bolted down the hallway, he yelled, "Are you all right?!"
I couldn't even face him, and scooted out of sight.

Riley Walker, Grade 8
Gilbert Middle School, IA

Bench Warmers
My warrior cries screaming, my thoughts and anger's steaming
Bow to the coach with my silent reproach
Crowds yelling are just a foretelling's body armor
Telling all to my fellow bench warmer
Don't give up

Never going in, never giving up
Going to play my hardest no matter what
Bench warmers forever, never getting cut
Why do I fill my teammate's cup
Don't give up

My teammates are telling me I suck
Their last name is giving them luck
Repel them like magnets
I get called a loser because I never get to play
Don't give up

Red and white, ready to fight
Bursting out my warrior cry
Buzz! 41 to 34
Looking for the dawn after the storm
Don't give up

Joshua Lingo and Tyler Novotney, Grade 8
Tonganoxie Middle School, KS

Page 41

Every Word Means Something
The young kids of this modern world
Think it's funny to insult and tease
In most cases it is, but believe my word,
It can reach certain degrees

They think that they're not hurting you
Since they're friends, it means nothing
But put these thoughts into view
Because every word means something

I know that they don't mean it
They're my best friends; they're only playing
But sometimes it feels like they mean it
These harsh words that they're saying.

They think their snappy remarks
Are funny and make them seem cool
But for me, it only causes sparks
And makes me feel like a fool
Anna Gates, Grade 8
Jefferson Middle School, IA

The Battle of Birmingham
Suddenly I heard a loud crash
And glass went in my eyes
I thought the church would be the safest place to be
Not where everybody dies

Suddenly I heard a loud crash
I remember calling Addie
Then I was hospitalized
And cried out "Daddy"

Suddenly I heard a loud crash
I just thought this isn't fair
How could they take her life
Ms. Denise McNair

Suddenly I heard a loud crash
But it helped the civil right acts
We would be the country we are today
Because we are all equal, even the blacks
Blake Lansing, Grade 8
Perry Middle School, IA

Cooper
My dog is really fast
Every time he gets a chance to get out
Zoom, he speeds out like a streak of lightning
Sometimes he can run faster than me which is kind of frightening
Sometimes he heels but that's not always the case
He only has one pace
Cooper
Kylea Hintz, Grade 8
Thayer Central Junior High School, NE

Stillness
The lifeless branches stand still
Without the gust of wind,
On their own will
Leaves that once were green have fallen from the sky
And hit the brown dirt with a sigh.

The sun shines for just a bit
Making the trees and grass glow
But then the clouds come in and cover the sun with a hit
Making them glow no more.

Now the winds howl even stronger
And the clouds turn to gray
The tree branches stand still no longer
And the trees are covered with rain.
Kendra Gonzalez, Grade 9
Boone Central High School, NE

Now or Never
5, 6, 7, 8
I count in my head as the music starts
The pressure is on
My nerves disappear like water vapor
I lose myself in the music and choreography
Every leg extension and reach is precise
A mistake as simple as not pointing my toes is
Fatal
My legs slice the air when I do my ala secondes
My toes smack my head on my firebird
We finish
The crowd is roaring lions
The judges look at us in amazement
They know we came here to
Win
Shaela Tiefenthaler, Grade 8
Carroll Middle School, IA

A Riotous Rainy Day
On a gloomy day
Inside a house
Near death of boredom
Above the clouds are heavy
Down the rain pours
Across the lawn the road is filled with puddles
Behind me my dog sleeps
Down is the way I feel
Instead of fun there is nothing to do
Between me and you I don't like rainy days
Outside the rain stops
Around the corner is the forest waiting
Until 3 p.m. I wait
In the forest I run as fast as I can
Like a canopy of green, it is a pleasant relief
Katie Braaton, Grade 8
Newell Middle School, SD

High Merit Poems – Grades 7, 8, and 9

Meeting an Angel

Sometimes life gets hard,
Sometimes it knocks you down,
We have all gone through it,
But not everyone chooses to get back up,
They think happiness walked away and won't come back,
But some people are lucky,
Because they meet someone like you,
Who helps them through it,
And makes them stronger,
You helped me when I was down,
You brought me back up,
And now I have a reason to fight back,
You have changed who I am.
For the best, not the worst,
Sometimes life gets hard,
But at least you're by my side,
Like an angel, you have healed my pain.

Bladimir Roldan, Grade 8
Perry Middle School, IA

Butterflies

Butterflies swarm in me when you are near,
Eyes locked in with mine
We tried to speak but can't hear.
The way we intertwine

Makes my heart skip a beat.
Sneaking a smile
Hoping to meet
Makes it all worthwhile.

Not wanting to leave your side
My hands linger in yours.
Your touch will abide
You're the one I truly adore.

You're the key to my heart
We shall never grow apart.

Reilly Dvorak, Grade 9
Palmer Jr/Sr High School, NE

The Magic of Teamwork

Waiting for the gun to fire
I look at the other runners I'm against
I look at my teammates, and the gun fires
Runner number one is off, running fast in 2nd place.
She reaches the next runner and hands her the baton
Running fast and proud, she runs to the next runner.
She gets to her and hands the baton off
She sprints off, heading straight towards me!

She gets close to me and I turn my head and count to three.
"Baton, good luck!" I hear her say, and I'm off.
I'm in 4th place, running as fast as I can
My heart beating faster, beating harder.
Almost to the finish line and I run as hard as possible
I pass one girl, my heart beating faster, beating harder.
And my heart jumps and adrenaline kicks in
I hear people cheering my name as I finish in 3rd place.

Taylor Lathrum, Grade 8
Perry Middle School, IA

The Final Game

Sweat, hard work, repetition
Is what it takes to be a basketball player
Running up and down the court…
Sweat, hard work, repetition
Peripheral vision is required
To play this game of skill
If you make it big, you'll be admired
And play till your old, like Grant Hill
Driving in the paint
Trying to get people in foul trouble
Draw the foul, count the shot, now I've got a double-double
Make the foul shot, now we're ahead by 1
The clock ticks down. 5…4…3…2…1
Throw the ball up
It whistles through the air
Smile for the cameras
Proud to represent the jersey that I wear

JR McCord, Grade 8
Perry Middle School, IA

Drip Drop

As the rain went down drip drop, drip drop
The even harder plop, plop, plop, plop
I sat there watching in a daze
As raindrops went by, I was so amazed
I sat there saying my oh my
How do they come from up in the sky
In the sky they frolicked and flew all through the day
They were blown to the ground with a sway
They were so little, so light
Then all of a sudden the sun burst out, it was so bright
Away went the rain
And on the town it made a wet stain

Jacia Christiansen, Grade 7
Viborg Jr High School, SD

Violet

Violet looks like a gemstone, a rhinestone
The color of people's birthstone
Violet sounds like the sunset's dim glow
Violet smells like a garden tulip
Violet tastes like sweet tangy grapes biting at my tongue
Violet feels like sad, left out, and generous
Violet looks like a graceful peacock chirping on the prairie
The color of moonlight in the sunset
Violet is the sound of a big juicy plum in my mouth
Violet smells like a newly sharpened colored pencil
Violet tastes like the fresh dew in the morning
Violet feels like loving and caring friends

Alexis Huettl, Grade 7
Newell Middle School, SD

Just Because…

Just because I'm half African American
Doesn't mean that I get into gang fights
Doesn't mean that my family is poor
And doesn't mean that I'm different
Just because I'm half African American
Doesn't mean I like being called a Negro
Doesn't mean that I like to sing
Doesn't mean that I work for white people
Just because I'm half African American
Doesn't mean I only have African American friends
I don't hate white people
I do sports just like you do
I play basketball and do dance
Just because I'm half African American
Does it mean I have to be treated differently?
Don't I have feelings too?
Can't I be just like you?
Can I be accepted?
I think I can.

Tiffani Pile, Grade 8
Chadron Middle School, NE

The Ballad of Death

It'll happen to everybody, it's inevitable
What you do before it happens is up to you
When it comes, it can be a surprise
But just remember, what you do before it happens is up to you

Some choose to waste it
Some choose to savor
Some don't deserve to die, some really need to
And some choose to worship a so-called savior

But what you do before is entirely up to you
Some believe there's an afterlife
A place commonly referred to as heaven or hell
But a savior wouldn't tell you how to live

So live your life to the fullest
Die with no regrets
Strive to be the best
Be happy, because one day you fate will be met

Sebastian Ramirez, Grade 8
Perry Middle School, IA

Malcolm X

Malcolm X
was a black man
who lead civil rights movements
in the mid 1900's.
He traveled all over the world
giving his famous speeches.
He wanted complete and total segregation
because of the torture whites had given his race.

Ben Garvis, Grade 8
Morton Magnet Middle School, NE

Volleyball

I come into the gym unaware of what to do next
I decide to stretch, so I point and flex
I wait for the other girls to arrive
I am scared, practice is going to be hard, and I will not survive

Our coach tells us to do laps
When we are done, I feel like I am going to collapse
I practice my serving
The people on the other side try to reach it by swerving

I had as much energy as a little kid
The ball came in front of me, so I slid
We are undefeated as a team
If we win our last game, we are all going to beam

We have worked so hard,
That we are never off guard
We will be there for each other whenever
We will be a team and friends forever!

Madie Conrad, Grade 8
Perry Middle School, IA

All Eyes on Me

My name is called;
My body goes numb.
All eyes are on me;
I get up there and wait.

Standing still and stunned,
I know they're waiting for me to start.
My voice and hands are shaking
As if I've had a lot of sugar.

I don't know where to look.
I mess up; my face turns red.
I just want this to be over.
I just want this to be over.

It's a fear that's near to be done and dealt with,
So I don't have to be afraid anymore.
I'm done with my speech and sit back down;
The worst part is over.

Natalie Gammon, Grade 8
Gilbert Middle School, IA

White

White is the light of the day shining on our backs
White is the snow under our feet
White is the taste of a marshmallow sticking to your teeth
White is the feeling of serenity
White is the smell of a crisp winter's day
White is the sound of a baby's laugh
White is the color of the clouds on a clear day
White is the quietness that keeps us strong

Kayla Myers, Grade 8
East Mills Community School, IA

High Merit Poems – Grades 7, 8, and 9

Super Bowl Sunday
It was Sunday
But not any Sunday
It was Super Bowl Sunday
My favorite team, the Packers, were playing
They were playing the Steelers
By the end of this game I would learn a lot
I would learn that anything can happen
That the last seed can still win
Even if most of their team was hurt
But they still won
They won because they never gave up
This showed me I can do whatever I want
Even if I am the underdog
Jake Brickell, Grade 8
Jefferson County North Elementary/Middle School, KS

Jared Barth
Jared
Tall, athletic, caring, respectful
Son of Craig and Brenda
Lover of dogs
Who feels tired, mad and crazy
Who finds happiness in surprises
Who needs help
Who fears bears
Who would like to see me
Who enjoys playing baseball, football and hunting
Who likes to wear shorts
Resident of Sherrill
Barth
Jared Barth, Grade 8
Jefferson Middle School, IA

My Backwards Day!!
I brushed my hair and scrubbed my teeth,
I sat on my cereal and ate the bus,

I bit my book and read my tongue,
I sat on the floor with my feet on the chair,

I painted the floor and jumped on the wall,
I chopped my water and drank my wood.
Today was a backwards day,
I hope tomorrow is a better day that's all I have to say.
Austin Noah, Grade 7
Whittier Middle School, SD

First Time
When I first saw, I was scared to meet you
When I first met you, I was scared to talk to you
When I first talked to you, I was scared we would become friends
When we first became friends, I was scared I would love you
And now that I love you, I'm scared to lose you
Abby Kinney, Grade 8
Dallas Center-Grimes Middle School, IA

Football
As all the players gather in a huddle
The quarterback will say their next play
BREAK
We run up to the line
Down, set, hut!
We bolt from our stances
With chances of getting a touchdown
We push forward with full aggression
With an obsession of protecting the ball carrier
But then as the ball is passing through the air
Everyone's eyes are on the guys down field
Touchdown
Broderick Harms, Grade 8
Thayer Central Junior High School, NE

The Gift Greater Than Gold
What is it most people seek;
What do we want to find and keep?
Things made of shining gold and silver;
Even if just a tiny sliver.
All of us have human greed;
We take, we meddle, we want, we need.
A man I know, he gives more than silver and gold.
He gives a gift of knowledge, powerful and old.
His wisdom makes the world seem small;
And to me, riches then matter not at all.
Come and listen to what he will say;
Now, with your gold, will you stay?
Grant Rheinschmidt, Grade 7
Notre Dame Jr/Sr High School, IA

Crazy Snow
Snow, you bring mixed feelings,
Sometimes bad, sometimes cheery
Snow you bring bitter cold,
For that you'll always be known,
To wake us up half past seven,
To make sure the sidewalks are cleared of your flurry from Heaven.
You make Christmas bright and merry,
But you ruin the chances of snow after February.
Occasionally I enjoy watching you blizzard,
But I'd make you disappear if I had the power of a wizard.
For when you come you make me lazy,
And my feelings for you remain forever crazy.
Haiden Sullivan, Grade 8
St Paul's Lutheran School, NE

My Grandfather
The wonderful Manson Jones
An old man who loved to garden
During the long, hot summer days
In his garden up in heaven
He loved to be outside with the lovely nature
Dallas Reed, Grade 9
St Francis Middle/High School, KS

I Am

I am different and unique.
I wonder how many people care about the world's problems.
I hear the silent cries of broken hearts.
I see the tears that want to fall out.
I want the broken hearts healed and the environment's issues solved.
I am different and unique.

I pretend to smile so no one knows I hurt deep inside.
I feel the shattered pieces of her heart.
I touch the night sky to escape the pain.
I worry that I'll always feel this way.
I cry knowing I was used to get to her.
I am different and unique.

I always say, "Smile, never frown, because you can't give anybody the ability to tear you down."
I try to forget all the pain I was put through.
I hope life for everyone will go easier down the road.
I am different and unique.

Ajia Nguyen, Grade 8
Perry Middle School, IA

Just Because…

Just because I'm Muslim
Doesn't mean I walk around wearing a head scarf in the heat of Saudi Arabia during my leisure time.
It doesn't mean I'm somehow related to Osama Bin Laden.
It doesn't mean 9/11 was my fault.
Just because my last name is Rahman
Doesn't mean airport security needs to be suspicious.
It doesn't mean my religion is hateful.
It doesn't mean I believe in everything Al Qaeda believes in.
Just because I'm a Muslim girl
Doesn't mean I don't have rights.
It doesn't mean I have to dress a certain way.
It doesn't mean I can't have the life most girls my age have.
Just because I'm Muslim
What is religion?
Aren't there good and bad people in every race and religion?
Can't I be judged based upon my personality rather than my religion?
I think so.

Shoilee Rahman, Grade 8
Chadron Middle School, NE

My Sister

Harley
kind, respectful, loving, responsible
daughter of Stacy and Tad Patridge
who cares deeply for her family, her pets, her brother and sisters
who feels sad knowing her grandpa is going to die, happy when around her family, angry when something does not go her way.
who needs to have more freedom, to have a cell phone, to get a car.
who give time to her family, to her pets, time to sit down and have a family dinner.
who fears spiders, bees, and snakes
who would like to see Hawaii, her name on her diploma, her having a Lamborghini
resident of Sioux Falls SD
Glammeier

Kassie Glammeier, Grade 7
Whittier Middle School, SD

High Merit Poems – Grades 7, 8, and 9

One Word
One word said and tears were shed
One mistake
That made your world shake
Time goes by and still you cry
Words will never die
No matter how hard you try
Anger tries to hide
But lingers its way to find
And swallows you deep inside
You know you've done wrong
To one of the weak
That has no time to see
You truly are sorry
It's just a word
Like the one you said before
That doesn't take back
The hatred you put toward
Love has never found
Its way to peek around
The one word said
Will never be dead
Cheyenne Rupard, Grade 8
Tonganoxie Middle School, KS

Pollution
I believe pollution is wrong.
Pollution is aerosol cans.
Pollution is Sonic wrappers.
Pollution is trash.
Pollution is always
on Earth.

I believe pollution is
Earth hurting.
Pollution is hairspray.
Pollution is plastic bags.
Pollution is toxic.
Pollution is gasses.

I believe pollution
is horrible.
Pollution causes
global warming.
All in all pollution
is killing our Earth.
Willow Jensen, Grade 7
Gretna Middle School, NE

Football
Football
Exhilarating, thrilling
Run, pass, kick
Go for the win
Touchdown!
Tyler Albert, Grade 9
Cardinal Jr/Sr High School, IA

Football Is the Game of My Life
Football is the game of my life
From the practice to the field
The instant sound
The cheering crowd

Football is the game of my life
Learning different plays
Things that you can improve on
And things you already know

Football is the game of my life
From the coach to the players
To the last whistle
To the last touchdown

Football is the game of my life
Everything that matters
Comes down to the final play
Football is the game of my life
Joe Olvera, Grade 8
Perry Middle School, IA

Navy SEALS
I see a gun
I hear bullets ricocheting off stuff
I smell gunpowder in the air
I feel bad that my friend got shot

I smell the sweat in the air
I see my American eagle patch on my arm
I hear cries of people
I taste the dripping sweat

I hear bombs exploding
I see blood
I smell the blood
The emotions are high

I hear people screaming
I see shells on the ground
I feel my legs aching
I taste the blood
Dakotah Bailey, Grade 8
Perry Middle School, IA

Rosa Parks
Rosa Parks
Born to be someone in 1913
Fought against segregation
Inspired the bus boycott in Montgomery
To be treated as equals everywhere
Refused to give up her seat
Got arrested
Just to get individual rights
Megan Niederle, Grade 8
Morton Magnet Middle School, NE

My Grandma
Grandma, I miss you
I love you so much,
Wish you were here
I dream that a bunch.

It was four years ago,
That cancer took you away,
God saw your tired face
And you left our family that day.

She was a farmhouse wife,
A mother of four,
Was involved in her church,
It was always quite a chore.

I have many great memories
I'll remember them forever,
You brought my life happiness, but
Family was your greatest endeavor.

You're the greatest guardian angel
A girl could ever receive,
I know you'll always be with me
All I have to do is believe.
Maddie Iben, Grade 8
Perry Middle School, IA

When the Lark Returns
I went searching for it
At the end of the cold time,
Through the tender green fields,
Refreshingly sublime.

It would come this day
So I new in my heart,
For the happy waves of wind
Bore the song of the lark.

And other friends from the south
Melodious martins on wing,
Joined the lark's chorus
To herald glorious spring.

Blissful were we
In those fields so fair
I whistled with them
We caressed the warm air.

We sang and we sang
And happy we three,
To shed the bonds of winter
We're free!
Bernadette Williams, Grade 7
St Mary's Academy & College, KS

Twin Towers Go Down

On September 11th, 2001,
The people in New York didn't know what was yet to come.
The people thought it was a normal day,
Until they saw an airplane zooming their way.

Crash! They hear one tower go down.
Then things started falling straight to the ground.
And then they heard another coming,
People started screaming and running.

Boom! Crash! Another hit.
People lost lives because of it.
This was a terrible, sad, awful day,
The image in people's minds will never go away.
This day won't be forgotten,
This work has been done by Osama bin Laden.

Laura Koley, Grade 8
Holy Cross Catholic Elementary School, NE

Just Because I Live in Nebraska

Just because I'm from Nebraska
Doesn't mean I'm hillbilly
Doesn't mean I'm a redneck
And doesn't mean I'm inbred
Doesn't mean I have bad grammar
Doesn't mean I chew
Doesn't mean I wear overalls
Just because I'm from Nebraska
Doesn't mean I was born in a barn
Doesn't mean I live on a farm
Doesn't mean I'm in the KKK and for the Confederates
Just because I'm from Nebraska
Why do people just assume things?
Why do they look at us different than they do people from big towns?
Why do they think these things?
Well that's not how all of us are!

Jarrod Briggs, Grade 8
Chadron Middle School, NE

The Last Play

I look down and see the green grass
This last play is all on my back
Tick Tock, Tick Tock. The clock runs down
The quarterback sounds like a dog as he barks the count
The quarterback screams hut one
I'm off
The ball is pigskin
I run the ball to the outside in a dash
I have two yards to go
The goal line is right in front of my eyes
I reach with all my might
I look up and see I'm in the end zone
I get mobbed by my glorified teammates
We have won the State Championship
The music is ringing and dinging in my head
The title is coming home.

Nathan Simmons, Grade 8
Carroll Middle School, IA

Nature

Walking by a lake
It's so real, it's almost fake
Playing under the sun
It's always so fun
Bunnies hopping by
I smile and sigh
There is nothing anyone can say
To stop making this the perfect day
All of this nature, there is no pain
Like taking bad memories and putting them down a drain
I watch the birds chirp and play
I wonder what they say
Kicking pebbles down the road
I feel so bad hitting a toad
I open my door and want to cry
One day, this nature will die

Emily Lenox, Grade 7
Wisner-Pilger Jr-Sr High School, NE

Once in a Blue Moon

Once in a blue moon,
I looked out on the water and saw a loon.

It was such a mystical creature,
With a few wonderful features.

I told my story and made his-story,
Then I realized we shared the glory.

With his white, speckled back,
We both agreed that his name was Jack.

And from that day on,
He'd sing his song at the break of dawn.

Jonah Montgomery and Alec Kirwan, Grade 8
Sabetha Middle School, KS

Path of Trees

Trees help me by giving me shelter
trees shade me from the sun

When I'm feeling down I climb
a tree so I can stop and look around

Even though the pollen makes me sneeze,
the growth of a sapling amazes the world

When I see a tree being cut down it makes me think,
trees keep me alive so why don't we keep them alive?

Walking through a path of trees the sights
of colorful foliage awed me.

Alex Gress, Grade 7
Lourdes Central Catholic School, NE

I AM an Indian

I am an Indian,
A poor selfless Indian.
I was treated like an immigrant,
Even though they were the different ones.
I was taken away from my home,
And was treated like an animal.
I wanted to go back home,
But I was alone.
I was scared,
I did not know the white man's ways.
They took my faith away from me.
I was left empty handed.
They cut my hair,
They stripped me from my clothes.
I was still left with nothing.
I tried not to let the white men get inside my head,
But they killed my faiths and my beliefs.
I was lost and I was lonely.
I was left to die in the darkness of humans who were just like me.
I died empty handed.

Clarice Bartek-Miller, Grade 9
Mercy High School, NE

Nature

Nature comes in many forms.
From mountain ranges to the sun that warms.

Every vast valley presents its vegetation.
While the brilliant night stars reveal their locations.

The tall oak trees show beauty, its trunk nice and brown
but the flowers show more that's why they take the crown.

The deep dark ocean whispers its mystery.
For it has been there throughout history.

The mighty sun beats down its strong rays,
so the ocean can be warmed as people swim in its bays.

Nature shows us all how beautiful it can be,
and with help nature will get even more beautiful, you'll see.

There is so much more that nature can express.
Just go outside and you'll find the rest.

Samantha Starsnic, Grade 8
Patton Jr High School, KS

Life like a Rodeo

You get an awesome sight,
until you bite the dust.
You ride the bull many times in your career,
but at some time or another you will get the horns.
You only get 8 seconds to show your skill.
You have to get off at some point.

Joe McCance, Grade 8
Chadron Middle School, NE

Do You Know the Feeling?

When your heart stops beating,
When the Earth is crashing down on you,
When you're thinking is this really happening to me,
Do you know the feeling?

When you start to fall apart,
When you think you can't possibly cry anymore,
When you can't take it anymore,
Do you know the feeling?

When you feel so alone,
When you feel no one understands,
When you don't know what's going on,
Do you know the feeling?

When you think no one cares,
When you feel lost inside,
When you can't breath any longer,
Do you know the feeling?

I know that feeling,
I felt it time and time again.
When the last thought in my head was…
Is my dad going to be ok again?

Don't worry you're not alone…I know the feeling

Mackenzie Thomas, Grade 7
Charles City Middle School, IA

Never by My Side

You were the one that was supposed to be there for me
And never leave my side
There were all these things you were supposed to be
But you just let it die

Some days I hope you never find me
I'm sorry I wasn't good enough for you
It's not like you'll ever see
The pain you put me through

It's not supposed to be this way
This dark despair I feel
Without you in my day
But maybe someday I'll heal

Everyday I wonder about you
I try to imagine where you are
I hope you think of me, too
But I know that's way too far

There are all these crushed hopes and dreams
And it makes me want to cry
But that's not the way it seems
And it's all because you let it die

Delaney Schwarte, Grade 8
Carroll Middle School, IA

I Am a Puzzle Piece

I used to be a radio playing your favorite songs…
but now I am the wind, freely flowing

I used to think the world revolved around me!
but now I know that I revolve around the world as another infinitesimal piece of life's puzzle,
but in the end with every unique piece to make a beautiful picture

I used to be a sponge soaking in all the sweetness of the world…
but now I am a sprinkler shooting out all the lessons to be learned to all the fathomable

My hands were once smaller than my pinky-finger but they grew…and grew
and before I know it they have grown more than five times the size that I can remember.

God gave me these carpenter's hands so I can carve out just a fragment of wood in the shape of a seed
the seed will grow rapidly or slowly but ever so surely
but when it sprouts it will grow like a weed

It will grow…grow…and ever so much more
till it reaches the canopy and it will be seen from every door
when even such the most nugatory of creatures comes scurrying around
many big, small, important or not important at all
when they look up they won't want to look down
for the most priceless and beautiful of gifts was given to us for free
all you have to do is accept and obey

We are all a little Insignificant little puzzle piece Alone
but Together with all in one we will form a picture more Beautiful than the Sun

Daniel Nakazono, Grade 8
Patton Jr High School, KS

The World as It Is Will Not Do

As the world spins around, the screams are a deafening sound.
The screams of people caught in wars of all types.
World war, gang war, war on terror, race wars, war against hunger, war against the people of this world
who strive to make it the most terrifying place that you can't even imagine.
I hear the screams of the people caught between the walls of hate.
Unfortunately, those walls are closing in, ready to trap the guilty and innocent alike.
Because pain does not discriminate.
It devours anyone it feels worthy of acceptance,
especially the people who are naive enough to think that nothing bad can ever happen to them.
The horrific truth is that it can and it will.
Unless, for instance, a miracle were to take place.
This miracle can be achieved, although so far has been proven to be an opponent of gargantuan stature.
Would you like to know what this miracle happens to be?
It can be transformed into a simple acronym.
ELE: everybody love everybody.
If everyone were to live by that golden rule, the world would be as majestic as it once was.
In a time before you or me, or anybody who inhabits this war-torn wasteland we now call home.
Extraordinary miracles have been performed, not by an act of God but an act of man.
Our generation could change the world with great audacity.
If only that day were to come in my lifetime. If only…

Dominic Cote, Grade 8
Rugby High School, ND

High Merit Poems – Grades 7, 8, and 9

Only Me
When I was small you held me close
But I'm getting older
And you're getting colder
I clung to you like a child with its blanket

Your hand is supposed to guide
But it takes control
All this frustration is taking a toll
You're starting to take my sanity

You were strong
My love will be forever
But it's starting to sever
I'm starting to rise above you

You used to be a tower
Towering so tall
But I'm no longer as small
Now I'm tall and you're so small

I am tall; I'm no longer small
I am strong; I'm no longer weak
I am not yours; I'm no longer meek
I am only me.
Alexandria Springer, Grade 8
Carroll Middle School, IA

Frustration
This feeling,
Fills my body
Time after time
It comes and goes.

I try to brush past it,
Calm myself down
It comes from everything around,
The uncontrollable beyond.

It enters so quickly
But is hard to clear out
It's an overwhelming emotion.
This balance between me and my mind.

It feels like a firecracker
Trying to hold back, but
Exploding in front of everyone.
There's no turning back.

The feeling of frustration
And anger for perfection
Is felt rushing through my body
Time after time.
Brenna Lehmann, Grade 8
Carroll Middle School, IA

Depression
As I stare up at the sky
I look at clouds rolling by
As I stare at the sky
I immediately start to cry

As I lay face down in bed
There is a throbbing in my head
As I lay in my bed
My body feels like it is lead

As I'm hunting in the woods
I think about my childhood
As I'm in the woods
I think that I'm no good
As I'm dreaming quietly at night
It seems I've taken flight
As I fly through the night
I see hope's flickering light
Devon Siess, Grade 7
B & B Jr/Sr High School, KS

Pawn
I am not a piece in your games
I choose my own fate
I only want to live MY life

My mom and my sister
Are not part of this
I only want to live MY life

A pawn
A piece
A chip
A player

I will not
I refuse

I am my own person
I only want to live MY life
Ashton Stuart, Grade 9
Palmer Jr/Sr High School, NE

Unique Name
McKenzie
It means funny, athletic, and strong
It is the number 1
It is like the falling sunset
It is going dancing all night with friends
It is the memory of Mercedes Ritchy
Who taught me faith and courage
When she is at my side
My name is McKenzie
It means I stand up for what I love.
McKenzie Taylor, Grade 8
St Francis Middle/High School, KS

Nature
Weeds growing on the side
They came on their own
Tall buildings hide
But nature stands alone

As butterflies play
Cars drive by
Where dandelions lay
Wire is strung high

Where ants crawl
Concrete is laid out
Trees stand tall
Fence is scattered about

Nature is pleasant beauty
Keeping it here is our duty
Rylee Simon, Grade 8
Mulvane Middle School 7-8, KS

Howl
I heard a howl; I heard pain.
I heard a whisper; I heard secrets.
I heard a scream; I heard anger.
I heard a voice that spoke my thoughts.
The wind spoke many languages at once.

I looked outside; I saw fury.
I looked outside; I saw torment.
I looked outside; I saw disruption.
I saw the air that resembled my being.
The wind looked like many people at once.

I walked around; I felt hurt.
I walked around; I felt vengeance.
I walked around; I felt anguish.
I felt the chill that mirrored my feelings.
The wind inflicted many pains at once.
Rachel Hulme, Grade 9
Columbus High School, IA

The Holocaust
Many things come to mind.
Pain   Suffering

Death

Some things go unnoticed
In the black world of despair

Hope   Love
We will be counted upon
To never forget the tragedy that was
The Holocaust
Sam Vinogradov, Grade 8
Morton Magnet Middle School, NE

The Description of a Wedding...
A wedding is said to be the happiest day of a woman's life...
A wedding is when her father is in a puddle of tears because he has to give his little girl away...
A wedding is a day full of happiness and festivities...
A wedding is when two people decided to make a commitment together...
A wedding is when everybody is as happy as they can possibly be...
A wedding is when you forget about the future and start enjoying the present...
A wedding means you will have more than enough good and bad memories together...
A wedding is considered the perfect day...
It depends on how you look at it...

Lane Tegarden, Grade 8
NE

My Family
My family is a collection of birds.
My dad is an American bald eagle, as he is the leader of my family and a leader at work.
My mom is a peaceful peacock, she makes me happy when I am sad.
My sister is a white cockatoo, she thinks she is pretty, she is sociable and she is not an early riser!
My dog Mia is a chicken hawk because she thinks she is big and chases after things bigger than her.
And I am the shy pheasant who is always hiding, yet ready to take flight!

Noah Salter, Grade 7
Whittier Middle School, SD

What My Future Holds
I'm scared of what I won't become, you're scared of what I could become.
What my future holds.
I won't let myself end where I started. I won't let myself finish where I began.
I know what is within me, even if you can't see it yet. What does my future hold?
I have something more important than courage, I have patience. I will become, What I know I am.

Terence Stephens Jr., Grade 8
Patton Jr High School, KS

Truth Is...
Truth is, you know you are in love when you can't fall asleep at night,
'cause life is finally better than your dreams,
everyone may say love hurts, but truth is, loneliness hurts, rejection hurts, and losing someone hurts,
but love can help you find your way back and make you happy again, love is the key to everything.

Megan Jacobs, Grade 7
Dallas Center-Grimes Middle School, IA

Feelings Are...
Feelings are...
tears dropping to the floor,
smiles creeping across bright faces,
emotions tearing you apart,
an unexplainable roller coaster,
a disaster,
a blessing,
what ruins a good day,
the sunshine that warms your day,
the moral piece that tears your mind from your body,
driving your world into the dark depths of sorrow,
the reason you keep yourself going every day,
the heart that pushes you to wake up and embrace life.
Feelings are the heart and soul of the world.

Murphy Churchill, Grade 8
Chadron Middle School, NE

The Everlasting Art
It hits your ears and makes you feel like you've never felt before.
No matter how much is made, someone will keep creating more.
The music beats in your ears and changes the mood.
And some music can leave one feeling wooed.

Close your eyes and let the musician's voice take over.
And soon your mind will become a true rover.
A note lasts a second, but leaves an impression over a lifetime.
The beauty of music throughout the world will forever shine.

Music will endure and will continue to have an effect that will move.
Until the end of time people will sing to help it improve.
The rules of music people will continue to defy.
That only makes it better and proves that music will never die.

Vivian Parr, Grade 8
Holy Cross Catholic Elementary School, NE

High Merit Poems – Grades 7, 8, and 9

Wretched Rhyming

My mother has always liked any words that rhyme;
She drives me crazy with rhyming all the time.
Making suggestions about things she wants me to do,
Commenting on things *she* thinks are funny or new.
And sometimes she does this without even trying;
This habit usually makes me feel like crying.

Teachers who assign writing poems also make me sad,
Because this is something at which I am very bad.
Word pairs that rhyme don't just pop right into my head;
Trying to rhyme makes me wish I was already dead.

When I find out it's for a contest with prizes,
That's what really makes me hate these writing surprises.
At least we're not limited to only one topic;
If that happens I'll want to escape to the tropics.
Having my poem published is not a goal for me,
I would rather hide it away where no one could see.

Since on this assignment I am not really that keen,
I'm going to stop now that I've reached line eighteen.

Kaleb Waters, Grade 8
Colome High School, SD

Spring

Everything is waking up
Everything is restless
As if it got no sleep
As if it only sat there
Waiting for spring to come around again

Irises shake off their coats
And show their skin
Flowers bloom colorfully
And pop against the landscape

Trees say hello to the warmth
And let it warm them
Trees show what they've been hiding all winter long
Bushes say hi to the rain
And drink it 'til they're full
Bushes show us their prettiness
Hidden under the ugliness

Everything is waking up again
Everything is restless

Virginia Staton, Grade 7
McMillan Middle School, NE

Winter

Winter creeps in with sorrow
On an icy road
Skulking in the night
Crawling snail-like from death toward change

Marc Bluestone, Jr., Grade 8
New Town Middle School, ND

Basketball

Kyla
Determined, smart, athletic, caring
Sibling of a wonderful girl named Karly
Lover of the sport called basketball
Who feels basketball is the most amazing sport ever
Who needs more height so she can dunk it
Who wishes she could play for Kansas State
Who loves to play basketball with her teammates
Who would like to see Brittney Griner play basketball
Resident of Saint Francis, Kansas
Bandel

Kyla Bandel, Grade 9
St Francis Middle/High School, KS

The Crazy Backwards

I straightened my toast and ate my hair,
I sat on my binder and worked with my chair.

I slept on my homework and worked on my bed,
I slapped my quiz and ripped my head.

I ate my story and read my cake,
I cooked in the shower and washed as I baked.

I know this is a backwards day,
I hope tomorrow will be better, so that's all I can say.

Alexandra Rote, Grade 7
Whittier Middle School, SD

My Life

Ashlee
Faithful, loyal, trustworthy, hardworking
Sibling of one caring, amazing sister
Lover of being crazy and having fun
Who feels I have a very loving family
Who needs to always keep in touch with friends
Who wishes all my dreams could come true
Who loves to watch exciting football games
Who would like to see everybody being themselves
Resident of Saint Francis, Kansas
Orth

Ashlee Orth, Grade 9
St Francis Middle/High School, KS

Our Blue Eyes

He has saved many lives,
But his job sometimes takes him out of mine.
Last night he came home safe.
I felt the tears stream down my face.
For I worry about him often,
And miss him as well.
I glanced up,
Saw my eyes reflected in his own.
Daddy is home.

Brianna Mullen, Grade 8
Eisenhower Middle School, KS

Page 53

Basketball
He drives
He shoots
he dribbles left,
right,
fakes out,
goes middle
He puts it up and is fouled hard,
pressure's on,
if he makes his free throws
they win
swish
makes the first
his eyes are burning from sweat
he hears his heart beat time slows
all he hears is the crowd
he feels his hand release the ball
it rolls around the rim and drops…in!
the crowd goes wild
Nate Steele, Grade 9
Cardinal Jr/Sr High School, IA

Finding You
Wind, rain, snow, or hail
Nothing can keep me away
Branches broken, ship crashed
Lost, stuck, stranded on an island
With only a view of land
But don't you worry my love because
Wind, rain, snow, or hail
Nothing can keep me away.

Houses, fields, people, you
All so far away
To loosen my pain
I decide to paint
Beautiful, heart stopping, lovely, amazing
I painted a picture of you
Just remember darling
Wind, rain, snow, or hail
Nothing can keep me away!
Emma Hockenberry, Grade 7
Whittier Middle School, SD

Rosa Parks
Refused to give up her seat
On a bus in Montgomery Alabama
So that blacks didn't have to sit in the back
A woman who changed the world

Prayed at church
African American leader
Real strong woman
Kind hearted person
Segregation is what she fought for
Kim Boyes, Grade 8
Morton Magnet Middle School, NE

A Natural Performance
Branches of light
grow across the sky.
Though it's song not in sight
you can hear it sigh.

The beauty burns bright
with a flash everywhere.
It shows everyone in sight
to those who stare.

Drums are played
they beat the sky.
Though they made,
a tune and hold themselves high.

The thunder keeps playing,
the lighting keeps dancing.
They leave behind
a natural performance.
Kara Torster, Grade 8
Patton Jr High School, KS

My Role Model
Standing tall cap and gown,
I look upon you without a frown.
So happy, carefree
I hope someday that will be me.

Never stressed
Loves to impress
Day in, day out
Fearless fighter, without a doubt

Strong, smart as well.
No burdens to tell.
Hardworking,
Striving, consistently learning

Standing tall cap and gown,
I look upon you without a frown.
So happy, carefree
I hope someday that will be me.
Ashley Siegner, Grade 8
Carroll Middle School, IA

Home
Country, calm
Watch television with my family
Late in the day
Birds chirping, cows mooing
Tractors plowing, combines harvesting
Hunting, playing
Today, after school
Happy and excited
Jesse Jenkins, Grade 8
St. Francis Middle/High School, KS

Friends
Best friends are like family
They help you through tough times
Know you better than anyone
Love the same songs as you
Do the same things
We sing like superstars
Get in fights
But never split like a peel of a banana.

My best times have gone
from laughter to memories
My best friends have gone
from friends to family

You know someone
is a true friend when,
you are about to
break down and cry, but
they will say the stupidest,
most random thing
just to see you smile.
LeAnna Wolverton, Grade 7
Wisner-Pilger Jr-Sr High School, NE

Dancing in the Dark
We all love dancing,
in the dark,
we love to frolic,
in the cool, crisp night,
We love to walk,
on a sandy beach,
Among the things we love to do,
in the dark,
dancing is the most favorite,
of all,
We can dance in the dark,
From dusk till dawn,
anytime, anywhere,
we can go dancing,
in the dark,
The very dark of night,
So let us go,
Dancing in the dark,
It will be the most memorable,
night of your life,
Come dance in the dark with me.
Bonnie Hansen, Grade 8
Leyton Elementary School, NE

In the Hoop It Goes
On the court
among the people screaming
over the opponent's head
inside the hoop it goes.
Wendy Rosales, Grade 7
Whittier Middle School, SD

Pompeii

Run.

No.
Is his answer every time.
He doesn't get it.
I know what happened in 79 A.D. I was there.

I know he doesn't understand why.
I don't care how long the volcano has been inactive.
It WILL kill again.
I tell him every morning.
It's exhausting to hear him reject me every time I warn him.
I want him to listen.

Run.
He tells me every day.
No.

He doesn't get it.

He wants me to leave all I've ever worked for. I'm fine.

The volcano has been inactive since 1944.
I know . . .

It WON'T kill again.

It's exhausting.
I want him to listen.

Caroline Groesbeck, Grade 7
Charles City Middle School, IA

Mirror

I look in the mirror and what do I see?
I see a distorted face, no distinct shape, no exact form, no true person that I want to be.
I see someone who has been through so much, everything she loves taken away.
I see someone with bruises and scars from her past, no chance of recovery because they refuse to go back to their previous ways.
I look in the mirror and do you know what I see?
I see shattered hope and faded dreams staring back at me.
But there is one feature about the person I see in that mirror that makes me think.
This person, so discouraged, so put down and feeling so useless, knows how strong she has been even when sanity is at the brink.
As I look at my reflection, silent tears stream down my face.
I see someone who has transformed into something worth fighting for, waiting at the end of the race.
Someone that knows how beautiful she really is, how strong, how brave.
Someone who no longer needs to be saved.
Someone who has shed the world around her and is truly free.
Someone who lets go of the hurt and smiles back at me.

Mary Briganti, Grade 9
Mercy High School, NE

The Vivid Songs I Hear

I hear American singing, the vivid songs I hear,
Those of workers who work all day keeping their family in what they need.
The mailman singing his country song, putting our mail where it belongs.
The house woman working in the yard planting many flowers with many vivid colors,
Which reminds her of the beautiful song.
The carpenter singing his melodious native song, reminding himself where he really belongs.
The children playing in the sun making up any song that reminds them of
What's around them "I hear birds chirping chirp, chirp, chirp."
The friends hanging out with the ones they love the most,
The best to their friends singing their hip hop beat.
The couple getting married ready to hear those bells go "Ding, dong, ding,"
Making their life turn around hearing that beautiful sound.
Everyone sings what their heart wants to hear,
By singing together we can make a beautiful melodious song.

Yaretzi Villa, Grade 7
French Middle School, KS

Never

Never leave
Don't go
Never cry
Please no,
Never change
Forever stay the same
Don't abandon me,
Always be my friend,
Always, never

Katie Thompson, Grade 7
Dallas Center-Grimes Middle School, IA

Not So Far Away

My death may be soon
If I can not help it
For I see in my dreams
Behind the nightmare wall
A great sort of happiness
For when I leave
I may not return
For the happiness I seek
Is not so far away

Sydney Morton, Grade 7
Roncalli Jr/Sr High School, SD

October

October
Slowly walks in
With a yawn.
It crawls around
Spreading fall.
Then it just waits
Staying still.
Then it runs away
While showing November the way.

Cameron Wilkinson, Grade 7
Kansas City Christian School, KS

Teeth

Teeth
White and straight
You remind me of a pearl necklace
Brushing with all my might
I wish it was easy to care for my teeth.

Josh Coble, Grade 7
Olpe Jr/Sr High School, KS

My Teachers Disgusting Meal

Spider sandwich
Bot-fly stew
Vulture salad, EW
Brain milkshake
Organ pie
And maybe a slice of moldy rye

Quintin Robertson, Grade 7
Whittier Middle School, SD

Boys of Fall

There they are, who once were boys dreaming of the chance
To be on the field under the bright lights, now young men.
Hearing the roar of the crowd, sweat starts to roll down their rough skin
Symbolizing their hard work and dedication to get to where they are now.

The smell of the fresh-cut grass and hot dogs is intoxicating.
Looking up at the sky, feeling the cool, calm, crisp wind brush their arms
The crack of pads echo as they begin to warm up.

Then comes the time for the starters to be announced.
The team lines up in an organized fashion,
Looking to see what they are up against.
Their opponent is rowdy and wild, but this only amuses them.
Our men are relaxed, focused like a sniper in the midst of war.
One by one they are announced, running to the middle of the field,
They pray to the one who gave them this chance.

Once on the sideline the crowd settles down,
Our country's national anthem is sung; like a sonic boom, the crowd erupts,
Coaches talk over the game plan one last time…it's time for kickoff.

They are ready, have been ready for this moment their whole lives.
Will they succeed? It's all up to them to achieve their dreams —
No one can stop them, it's their time.
Once again, silence surrounds the young men, and the whistle blows.

Wyatt Mazour, Grade 9
Boone Central High School, NE

The Tear That Fell

How did you sleep that night,
knowing that you had made me cry?
What gave you the right? I still don't understand why.

Why'd you treat me the way you did?
the pain in my heart that I hid,
It never really goes away,
But I'll never again see you in the same way.

I cried for hours that night and everything in me, lost its fight.
I didn't want to see your face, or even see the light of day.

You got off free,
All the humiliation and pain, left for me.
You don't understand what it's like,
to hold back your tears and try to fight,

Every instinct says to cry,
Because everything I had thought, was a lie.
But slowly, I found myself again.
I understand I'm better off now than I was then.

I'm actually happy and alive and well, even though I went through hell.
I still hope someday you'll regret,
The day that I will never forget.

Angela Wright, Grade 8
Carroll Middle School, IA

Clouded Skies

When the sun fades away,
And the dark storm clouds appear,
That is gray.

Gray is an early morning on a gravel country road,
Surrounded by shadowed fog.
It is the soft touch of a husky's fluffy fur.

Gray is the gentle pitter-patter of rain that is fiercely falling forward
Onto the cold, dark ground
On a bleak spring afternoon.
It is a sad music being played on a gloomy day.

Gray is the smoke I smell
Rising up from an immense fire.
As the flames grow brighter,
The smoke rises higher.

A swift silky ribbon
Gently floating through the pale blue sky:
That is gray.

Old black and white photographs
Containing memories
And once happy times:
They are gray.

Caitlin Mander, Grade 8
Gilbert Middle School, IA

The Color of War

Olive drab green is conflict.
Olive drab is Sherman tanks rolling —
Wheels squeaking and gears grinding —
To meet the Panzers in open warfare.

Marching towards death or victory,
Olive drab is the clack of military boots.
All of the men will be affected by the coming time;
None of them will forget.

Bombs bursting, the air permeated by the smell of gunpowder.
Smoke and blood fill the air while darkness fills the hearts of men
Who still reside there.

Olive drab is salty, tangy, and sharp: the smell of gasoline burning.
Olive drab is soft worn leather,
Yet a sharp knife.

The warmth of a bullet cartridge freshly discharged,
Scattered haphazardly across the littered ground,
It is the silence of an empty battlefield.

The only sound that is heard is the call of a mournful bird;
After all is said and done, olive drab is the color of war:
The color of deeds no man should do,
And yet they have been done.

Isaac Stahr, Grade 8
Gilbert Middle School, IA

Celebration of Poets

Rhyming or not
As long as you want
With a backbone or as flimsy as rubber
It's just expressing your thoughts

About anything from A-Z
Ideas come from anywhere
As serious as black or as light as white
You can write it and so can I

With titles sitting proud at the top
Words small and big, straight or not
As quick as a hare or as slow as a snail
Some enjoy it, some do not

Poetry is anything
It can be found in everything
None is the same of that before
Mine is mine and yours is yours

Some is old and some is new
Be proud of your work, because it's all you!
Make it choppy, just make it flow
It's a celebration of poets, where it takes us, who knows?

Emily Dvorak, Grade 8
Carroll Middle School, IA

The Morning of the Rising Sun

In the early morning.
The Rising Sun came out of the west.
It went over the hills and through the valleys.
It went past the towns and around detection.

The Rising Sun came down from the sky.
And light up the harbor.
Then it made the sea turn black.
And the sky turn dark.

The Rising Sun made the harbor burn.
For the sea, there was no escape.
It tried to fight back.
But the sea was overwhelmed.

The sea sent waves that could escape
At the Rising Sun.
The waves chased it off.
But they were too late.

The Rising Sun had won the battle.
The sea was no more.
The Rising Sun thought it was all over.
But it would not win the war.

Beau Briles, Grade 8
Perry Middle School, IA

Broken Butterfly
I was stuck
She said so many hurtful things
She stepped on my delicate wings
And they shattered along with my pride
She took so many tears
I was her friend
I was broken and hurt
Now my heart was stained with anger

It was the worst
She expected me to let her win
To give him up to her
Like my wings
My anger was like a raging fire that doesn't die

My wings were fixed
And I was aiming for her
I didn't let her walk on me again
She didn't like it
He chose me
She cried
I laughed
My wings weren't broken anymore
Jamie Stanwix, Grade 8
Tonganoxie Middle School, KS

Only One Truly Sees
Seeing a different view,
With eyes open,
Personality stretched,
Into the blue,
Speechless, I still try,
But it's a lost cause,
'Cause they don't hear me,
Like lotus bugs in a small room.

I'm too bland, too simple,
Yet so unique,
Like a spider's web,
But I don't catch their eyes,
Spin them and suck them dry,
They don't even look my way,
I'm nobody.

From nobody's view,
You think I see nothing,
But my sight stretches yonder,
And they don't know,
I sit here, and see everything,
The loner, with no friends, but they will never know what I see.
Nicklas Stanley, Grade 9
Valley Southwood Freshman High School, IA

Dark and Cold
Deep and dark and cold at night
The crow caws and the stars give light
Help me find what I'm looking for
Is it you I hear knocking at the door?

Why are you at the door?
I hear a noise and I drop something on the floor.
I open the door just to see
That the doorway is empty

I lock the door
I drop to the floor
I wait there
As I hear the footsteps come near
Alyssa Howe, Grade 7
Dallas Center-Grimes Middle School, IA

Pencil
This pencil is my life
When I'm smart, I'm sharp
When I feel duped, I'm dull
I make mistakes with no eraser
So I shed off another graphite layer
To welcome another filled with life anew
And balanced feelings that I recruit.

When I'm stressed, sometimes I snap
And it takes time to grow again
Hard work and a friendly smile will build me up
And I don't know when my lead will run out
But when it does, I'll know I left a mark
Not on papers, but on hearts
Carissa McAfee, Grade 8
Jefferson County North Elementary/Middle School, KS

Life
The ocean is a blue abyss
the sunset a blur of neon colors
sand and seaweed caught between my toes
sinking my feet in the little grains of sand
it is slowly covering my ankles
it is everywhere
now on my face and hands,
brought by the waves, onto my clothes
the water is making designs as the wind blows.
As the sky gets dark the blue ocean darkens
now as I'm feeling the sharp grains,
wondering if somebody will feel them someday,
as I let go, the grains fall, like an hourglass
my life was ticking on.
Mikayla Bertels, Grade 7
Jefferson County North Elementary/Middle School, KS

High Merit Poems – Grades 7, 8, and 9

Rainbow
Rainbow
Colorful and bright
You remind me of happiness
Streaming across the sky
I wish your pot of gold wasn't so far away.
Maranda Scheller, Grade 7
Olpe Jr/Sr High School, KS

Cowboy
Cowboy
They ride horses
Cowboys work on the ranch
They round up their cattle and herd
Yee haw!
Jacob Heineken, Grade 7
Olpe Jr/Sr High School, KS

Roses
Stuck in soil, sitting up and down
Nowhere to go, stares at the ground
Oh, so red and shiny
Magical and tiny
Best smell in the world yet to be found
Kayla Reed, Grade 8
St Francis Middle/High School, KS

Storms
The weather is horrible at this time
The wind is moving the wind chime
The rain hasn't stopped yet
My clothes are soaking wet
The sun's color is like a lime.
Carol Eve Harris, Grade 8
St Francis Middle/High School, KS

Cancer
Faith, hope, and love make you a fighter,
In your own world the sky is brighter,
With your head held high,
You can reach for the sky,
Cancer cannot win if you are stronger.
Emily Elfers, Grade 8
St Francis Middle/High School, KS

Birthday Party
Birthday
Cake and ice cream
Ribbons, bows on presents
Friends, family to celebrate
Enjoy
Kyler True, Grade 7
Olpe Jr/Sr High School, KS

How Many More Will Die?
We are calling for our freedom, we beg to the moon.
We howl in unison, and the wind carries our tune.
Man hears the call, by hundred they come.
They wipe out my kind, and then call it fun.

Your ancestors weep, and our souls will remain.
You'll find out when I'm the last one to kill, you had nothing to gain.
Nature doesn't need your help, she'll control the disease.
Have you ever stopped and wondered, that next she'll hear you scream?

You invade our land, and then you call it preservation.
The only thing you're worried about is next year's hunting reservations.
You hold our bodies out in display, like you have won a prize.
Little do you know, that you're the only wolf in disguise.

We aren't meant to be owned, or stuffed for display.
We're meant to be free, how many more will have to pay?
When will we be protected, and free like the eagle flies?
And how the wild mustangs run through the grassy plains?
How many more will you slaughter in "preservation,"
How many more will die? (Wolves)
Stepheny Jensen, Grade 7
Viborg Jr High School, SD

The First Day of School
Over the summer I was a hibernating bear
it was the first time in three months for me to hear "ring ring."
Same old doors, but new school year…
Super studly superstar: my reflection in the door.

The freshly waxed floor shines like a diamond ring in a jewelry shop.
Hallways smell like I've jumped into a huge bottle of 409.

When I carry my brand new supplies from class to class,
It makes me feel like I am a king in his castle.
It's a shame that it's all going to be wrecked and thrown in the trash at the end of the year.

Everyone looks as if they just got back from a huge shopping spree at the mall.
One day down; one hundred seventy-nine to go!
Jordan Cole, Grade 8
Gilbert Middle School, IA

Livin' the Life
Cade
Adventurous, funny, athletic, driven
Sibling of Hanna
Lover of any type of sport
Who feels that the world won't end in 2012
Who needs a new 2012 450 motorcycle
Who wishes it was summer already
Who loves to do anything active
Who would like to see myself doing something at the professional level someday
Resident of St. Francis
Bracelin
Cade Bracelin, Grade 9
St Francis Middle/High School, KS

Our Last Night

Close your eyes
Help me hide
Through the night
We will survive

Please don't cry
Just hold on tight
This is our last night
You and I

Salem Owens, Grade 8
Morton Magnet Middle School, NE

The Holocaust

Till the Holocaust is over people hide
Beneath the house
Under the stairs
Into the house the Nazis go
Off to the concentration camps
Within the fence they work
Across the camp they carry rocks
For all that time they were brave
From that day on we honor them!

Taylor Lazio, Grade 8
Morton Magnet Middle School, NE

Minecraftia

Wonderful, imaginary
First day of April
Right after sunset
Cows mooing, wolves howling
Animals feeding, people building
Sleeping during night, hunting during day
When birds chirp and school is out
Exhausted after working

Zach White, Grade 8
St Francis Middle/High School, KS

Spring

S ome people like to
P lay outside when it is warm
R ing out the towel
I ntroduce the pool to yourself
N ot getting sick today
G reen plants everywhere you look

Quinton Cravens, Grade 7
St Francis Middle/High School, KS

NYC

Honk, crash, they scream and yell,
Ring-a-ling, they talk and tell.
Flip, flop down the street,
NYC is pretty neat.

Sydney Steinlage, Grade 7
Olpe Jr/Sr High School, KS

Four Inches Wide

Chalk splitter-splattered all over the beam
The rhythm of my heart beating crazily
Like the tick-tock of a clock times ten
A smile keeps peeking from the corners of my mouth.

My hands are ice cubes in the sun;
Blinking, I salute the judges and begin.
Hundreds of pairs of eyes are like spotlights zeroing in on my every move;
Teammates smile at me with looks of confidence in their eyes.

Like water flowing from the tap,
Or notes streaming from a piano,
Or words being sung while performed,
My routine is the back of my chalky, beat-up hands.

All the hours of hard work and passion...
The pain and struggles only make us stronger.
As the public appears, our bodies and minds seem to shut down, and forget,
The 30-40 hours a week in the sticky-like syrup gym.

At times, the beam pulled me down, but I got right back up where I belong.

Gillian Klein, Grade 8
Gilbert Middle School, IA

Canton

The glossy floors, the shining busts
They are crowded with roars, and rumbles
The eternal graveyard for players, coaches, and sports writers
Canton Ohio known only for one thing
The Hall of Fame opened their doors back in 1963
The first stars Sammy Baugh he was like a cannon passing the football
And Ernie Nevers quick as lightning, he scored six touchdowns in one game
To get your name enshrined forever
Footballs top honor
It is the best feeling in the world
History speaks for itself
Behind every wall
Millions come to see the faces of the men who changed the game
Every August the pop, and piping of the teams playing in the Hall of Fame Game
This is the Hall of Fame

Hunter Schaal, Grade 8
Carroll Middle School, IA

My Family's Songs

I hear my family singing the many different hymns I hear,
With music and melody, I hear their whispers in my ear,
I hear my father singing, while he works all day and night,
I hear my mother singing, as she cares for her kids and makes sure they're alright,
I hear my older brothers singing, songs of literature, writing and reading,
I hear my older sister singing, while she plays her favorite sport,
I hear my little brother singing, while he also dribbles down the court,
I hear my little sister singing, her melodic voice so soft, steady and sweet,
I hear my even younger sister singing, she joyously hums along,
I hear all my family singing, their own special song.

Lindsay Braun, Grade 7
French Middle School, KS

High Merit Poems – Grades 7, 8, and 9

A Solitary Journey
Stepping to the blocks
For an intimate journey
I reach deep into my soul
I feel so alone
Relying only on myself
I kneel behind the line as if in prayer
I lift my weight
The pistol pops

The crowd roars, but I perceive only silence
My shoes are in flames
Leaving a trail of tar on the track
Perfect form, like poetry in motion
Triumph closer with every stride
The finish line, my journey ends
I am alone again, energy drained
Victory
Elisabeth Culek, Grade 8
Gilbert Middle School, IA

Trees
Trees are fun
until you run

You can climb
as long as you have time

Like clothes you can wear
the leaves they bear

Some are old
but not cold

Go look
but not in a book

Trees are fun
unless you run
Rachel Meyer, Grade 7
Graettinger-Terril Middle School, IA

Cafe
Ka-ching
Goes the cash register
Sizzle Sizzle
Goes the bacon
Ding Ding
Goes the bell
Grumble Grumble
Go their stomachs
Ba Bink
Go their plates
Mmm Mmm
Go the customers
Zack Mauch, Grade 7
Wisner-Pilger Jr-Sr High School, NE

My Starbright Starlight
You are my star bright,
A star I see at night,
I wish you here by day,
And at night when I lay,
My friends I do not tell,
But shall I wish them farewell?

It is only my starlight,
Whom I see every night,
My one and only true friend,
Will I know you till the end?

I'll tell you a story now,
I hope I won't get a frown,
But my star bright I know now,
Lives once upon a crown,
In heaven belongs that crown,
So bold and glorious now.
Emily Ferris, Grade 7
Wall Middle School, SD

Invisible
It's shown through the eyes.
the soul,
their underlying actions

most can't see it,
some don't care,
some take advantage,
it remains unsaid

unappreciated, it worsens
until they become,
so fragile,
they can't risk confrontation

they retreat within,
and just like that…

they're gone
Andrea Spencer, Grade 8
Patton Jr High School, KS

Trust
Trust is like a tree that grows with truth
Over time it can be broken
Responsibility is key
Mend it with care
Love
And be truthful
Return
You will be gifted as well
Freedom is a gift
Trust will blossom
Zane DeVlaminck, Grade 8
Patton Jr. High School, KS

Sun
The sun,
a bright, shiny,
ball of helium and
hydrogen, but more than
just that to me.

Let's start over.

Sun a bright, shining
ball of light.

You give everyone
and I mean everyone
an exultant feeling.
Your piercing gold rays
of warmth
make me want to
lay out on a blanket
to warm my whole body.

But we'd better whisper
when we talk about you.
or you might slither
behind the dark,
ominous clouds…
Meghan Koenigsfeld, Grade 8
Charles City Middle School, IA

I Am Sad as Can Be
I am sad as can be
I wonder why you left me
I see red, puffy eyes
I want you home with me
I am sad as can be

I pretend you are here
I feel you are there
I touch the air
I worry you're there
I am sad as can be

I understand you were sick
I say you're not, my Grandpa Rick
I dream you're here with me
I try to be happy
I hope you are somewhere within me
I am sad as can be

I wipe these tears from my eyes
I try not to cry, when I say goodbye
I know I'll see you later
I say goodbye one last time
I remember all our memories
Sara Weir, Grade 8
Perry Middle School, IA

Stop to Listen
I'm reaching out to you
With open arms.
You don't care about
What I'm going through.

I've been calling
For your help
But you never even stopped
To listen.

I've been crying
For a long time…
Tears of just a simple girl.

So do you stop
To hear a poor girl's
Cries? Or do
You ignore them?

You pushed and
Strived for power,
But in your struggle,
You've lost it all.

I've been crying, been bleeding
For you.
Heaven Lorenz, Grade 9
Montezuma High School, IA

The World of Forest Green
Green is the forest,
The flow of the leaves.
Green is a lime,
That makes me pucker.
Mold is the green fuzz,
That makes you want to barf.

Green is what makes salad taste good.
Green is the sound of a mower.
Cutting the giant green grass.
Green is the color,
Of my favorite car.

Green is money neatly stacked.
The sound of green is,
Sirens warning you of tornadoes.
Green is spring when,
The grass starts to turn.
Green is my favorite color.

Green is the nature.
Green is very bright.
Green is a color,
That is just right.
Josh Crum, Grade 8
Gilbert Middle School, IA

My Monster
Teetering over the edge
of the tall terrifying tower,
I have no triumph to tell.
There would be no one
to help if I fell.

They say the sky's the limit;
well, I prefer the ground
to look at all the scenery,
and hear the wind with its whistling sound.

The roller coaster is a swiveling snake;
when we got to the top, I began to shake.
I searched for good thoughts,
but none could be found,
for if I looked down
I could not see the ground.

My fear is a monster:
it scares, startles, and stirs.
It always seems to appear
when an edge is near.
I will try my best to calm my breath
and conquer this fear.
Ciara Morgan, Grade 8
Gilbert Middle School, IA

A Young Lass's Secret
Should thou be told?
Would I be *too* bold
If I gave thee my Love,
Or would thy heart be cold?

Be thee my Love
And bring me above
The fair clouds of sweet Heaven,
Renouncing all *courtly* Love.

I glorify thy face
Where there's not a trace
Of a blemish or flaw
— Only radiance in Vice's place.

Thy Love is lucid bliss;
All I ask for is one kiss:
A singular token
Of knowing naught is amiss.

Thy name is pure gold
And thy family extolled.
Thy affection is far better
Than any Love ever told.
Madeline Salyers, Grade 9
Red River High School, ND

This World Is Mine
When I hear the beat,
I get up on my feet.
I lose myself in time,
Oh, this world is mine.

When I hear the beat,
I just go wild,
I give it all I've got,
And I'll go hard, not just mild.

Dancing is in my blood,
My emotions just flood.
I find the beat and just
Stick to it, it is a must.

I move my body in time to the music,
Nobody can stop me,
For this is my passion,
And I will not flee.

Because when I hear the beat,
I get up on my feet,
And I just lose myself in time!
Oh, this, this world is mine.
Daniella Soto, Grade 8
Perry Middle School, IA

Fire Within a Gem
Ruby is fire
that blazes within a gem.
It's the heat from the sun
at a cold winter's end.
It's the smooth feeling of hot chocolate
as it slides down my throat.
Ruby is warmth.

Ruby is a lion's roar on the savannah
and a breeze that rattles the forests' leaves.
It's our apples and a spicy pepper,
yet as sweet as strawberries.
It's a severe thunderstorm in midsummer
and the flowers that bloom.
Ruby is strength.

Ruby is companionship
when no one is at your side;
It is a good friend
when life is rough and harsh.
it's a hug from a parent
when no one understand you.
Ruby is caring.
Quinn Vandenberg, Grade 8
Gilbert Middle School, IA

High Merit Poems – Grades 7, 8, and 9

I Am

I am something different…
I wonder what the world is like in places unknown.
I hear a bomb going off,
I see people yelling and crying.
I want to explore the world in a different perspective,
I am something different…

I pretend to be a small fish in a big pond,
I feel like I'm drowning,
I touch the hands of those trying to save me,
I worry no one will be there for me,
I cry because I know I can't be saved,
I am something different…

I understand that we don't always get what we want.
I say there is no god to believe in.
I dream I will grow old with someone I love.
I try to be a good person, to make good decisions.
I hope to die at the age of 105 on February 25.
I am something different…

Sabrina Nicolaisen, Grade 8
Perry Middle School, IA

I Am Beautiful, But Different

I am beautiful, but different.
I wonder why people care so much.
I hear the chatter of people behind me.
I see the clenching of fists.
I want to be loved for who I am.
I am beautiful, but different.

I pretend to not care so much.
I feel like the weight of the world is on my shoulders.
I touch the sky and dream of a different life.
I worry about my future.
I cry when I see you hurt.
I am beautiful, but different.

I understand that you are your own person.
I say that you just need to shake it off.
I dream of a better day.
I try to be the person you want me to be.
I hope you can accept me for who I am.
I am beautiful, but different.

Kalyn Cooklin, Grade 8
Perry Middle School, IA

School to Teachers

Teachers wake up with confidence,
ready to take on the day,
but when they get to school,
the kids come in to play,
at first the kids are grumpy,
and they never listen,
they act all innocent
even though their assignment's missin',
by the end of fourth period
and they're done with P.E.,
it's like someone gave them sugar
or diagnosed them with ADHD;
lunchtime is teacher's only break,
it's their time to eat and relax,
but when the bell rings
they brace for the children's attacks,
it's now the end of the day
and all the assignments have been made,
but school's not done for the teachers,
they have papers to grade.

Alex Simon, Grade 8
St Mary's Immaculate Conception Catholic School, IA

I Am

I am lovable, but complicated
I wonder why people are so mean
I hear the ticking of a clock
I see a butterfly flying around
I want to be successful in everything I do
I am lovable, but complicated

I pretend to be happy, even when I'm not
I feel happy to have a family that cares about me
I touch people's hearths, not their hands
I worry I'm not good enough
I cry when someone I care about gets hurt
I am lovable, but complicated

I understand not everyone is going to like me
I say "Whatever is meant to be will work out perfectly"
I dream that I'm falling into the darkness
I try to do good in school
I hope someday I'll see my brother
I am lovable, but complicated

Cinthia Perez, Grade 8
Perry Middle School, IA

Garden

G reen lawn of life and beauty,
A place to dream and just be you;
R est, eyes open, smell the earth around,
D ress a plant with water and the soft dirt ground;
E very plant and delicate flower,
N ever die, through sun and shower.

Genevieve Lowery, Grade 7
Olpe Jr/Sr High School, KS

Easter

E ggs are hiding in the grass
A fter the first full moon of spring
S pring is a time of green grass and new leaves
T he white lilies are symbols of purity
E very day we celebrate Easter
R abbits are symbols of new life

Josh Koger, Grade 7
St Francis Middle/High School, KS

American Childhood
I knew it would be fun
We wanted to play and run
Soon we learned words
We had to think
We played a game
It dealt with our name
I thought this day would fade away
But I will always remember the day
Allison Hughes, Grade 7
St Philip Neri School, NE

Grandma's House
Warm, bright
First day of spring
After lunch
Birds chirping, dogs barking
Birds eating, ducks running around
Planting, walking
During Spring Break
Happy and tired
Chris Hoard, Grade 8
St Francis Middle/High School, KS

One Shot
Onto the court
Into my hands
In my mind was fear
Behind the 3-point line
Near the basket
Through the basket
Toward me the team came running
Victory!
Trevor Schultz, Grade 7
Whittier Middle School, SD

Softball
S trikes
O uts
F ielding
T ies
B ases
A ccidents
L ove to play
L ong season
Madison Snyder, Grade 7
Graettinger-Terril Middle School, IA

Bridges
Bridges
The river stretches
It blocks the paths

Find a way across
Build a bridge
Sydney Wagner, Grade 7
Dallas Center-Grimes Middle School, IA

Amusement Parks
I am ecstatic when I am at an amusement park.
People everywhere, walking in a frenzy.
There is something fun for everyone.
The bright colors of the attractions make you notice them.
There are many refreshing snacks like corn dogs, cotton candy, slushies, and lemonade.
Ice cream is a delectable treat that comes in many delicious flavors.
Enormous roller coasters with twists, turns, and drops.
You get an adrenaline rush on roller coasters.
Some rides can make your stomach lurch.
Bumper cars collide with each other.
Massive Ferris wheels have many seats to hold passengers.
The tilt-a-whirl turns rapidly.
You get squished against the edge.
A water ride is wonderful on a hot day.
You can get drenched from head to toe.
If you play carnival games, you could win a prize.
You can take a break and play some games in the arcade.
Gift shops have amazing souvenirs.
Time flies by when you're having fun.
Going to an amusement park is a gratifying experience.
Brianna Doser, Grade 8
Jefferson Middle School, IA

Fire!!!
Blackness, blackness as far as the eye can see.
Oh, why must this happen and happen to me?
I'd log onto Facebook to see what I missed,
But being burnt to a crisp is not on my list.

All my possessions, all I adore —
All of it gone, except what I wore.
A terrible plague inside my house:
Nothing could stay here, not even a mouse.

My house is a sauna; that's over the line.
Of all the houses, it had to be mine.
It's up in my nostrils, my mouth, and my eyes;
Sooner or later it settles and dies.

The sirens are wailing and coming to me;
The dangers Smokey talks about, I can now see.
It struck me hard and came like a hit
And all that is needed to start this monsoon was keeping a lamp light lit.
Timothy Gallus, Grade 8
Gilbert Middle School, IA

The Sweet Songs
I hear America singing, sorrow words for the soldiers who have lost their lives.
I hear the janitor whistle, as he sweeps the hallways.
I hear the teacher sing an unforgettable song as she grades papers.
I hear the doctor sings a nice rhythm song wile he checks on recovering patient.
I hear the firefighter hum an amazing song as he slides down a shiny pole to save lives.
Singing with their happiness, singing loud and proud.
Lindsay Tilton, Grade 7
French Middle School, KS

Awful Things

What awful things could be living here
Stinky, hot fumes rose from the swamp
I was peeking around the trees when I heard a loud bonk
Yellow, horrible eyes were upon me
I felt something slide past my knee
My thoughts were swimming with fear
What awful things could be living here
Mean crocodiles or poisonous snakes
I hope I get out of here before anything wakes
Then I heard a growl, a gurgle, a sneer
What awful things could be living here
Around the next bend I go
This surely can't be the end of the road
Then a splash came from the bog
That's when I was attacked by a tree frog
We tussled and tumbled
Until I mumbled, "I'm done. Quit!"
From there, the story ends well
I found my way out of the terrible spell
Never to go back to where the awful things dwell!

Kiya Passero, Grade 8
Chadron Middle School, NE

I Am

I am very boisterous and energetic
I wonder if I will still be here years from now
I hear all the cries of people in pain
I see the world as I wish it to be, not as it is now
I want people to stop hurting
I am very boisterous and energetic

I pretend that I can live forever
I feel that everything is possible
I touch all the hearts I meet
I worry about all the people in need
I cry when people are treated badly
I am very boisterous and energetic

I understand that bad things have to happen sometimes
I say that everyone deserves to be happy
I dream that someday everyone will be equal
I try to always be very positive
I hope that someday, I'll be remembered
I am very boisterous and energetic

Haileigh Kenyon, Grade 8
Perry Middle School, IA

I Am a Barbie

I am a Barbie
I know that I am better than an ordinary doll
I touch my face and it is plastic
I worry because my eyelashes are too short
I hope I am always tan
I am a Barbie

Abbie Moody, Grade 7
Frontenac High School, KS

I Remember

Not many people stop to remember,
The loved ones they've lost.
But I remember!

There was once a time, when my great-grandma lived.
She has been gone almost seven years now,
Even though it feels like it was yesterday
I still remember!

I think about her every day,
and Mae,
was her middle name.
I still remember!

Many people forget those people who have touched their hearts.
But I remember!

No matter how much I want her back,
I try to remember that she is in a better place.
I know that we will all go someday too.
But I remember!

Someday we will all be together again,
So when you get there, fly as high as a lost bird.
Till we are joined together again.

Kyle Neuhalfen, Grade 8
Perry Middle School, IA

The Quilt

"Time to get up…" mom says.
My room is as dark as midnight
and I think,
"Why do I have to get up so early?"

We get into the car
And drive to a place
That is so scary
I just want to stay home.

After we talk about what I am about to go through,
I get separated and go into a room
ALONE!
People push me into my final destination.
There are more people in the room.

They put a mask on my face.
The smell is horrible — like nothing I've smelled before!
Then…the real horror begins.
I don't experience it, but I know it is going on.

All around me machines breathe loudly.
The people by my bed stick needles in my body
And leave behind narrow stitches.
I am a human quilt.

Sean Timberland, Grade 8
Gilbert Middle School, IA

Rider

There was a BMX rider.
He rode his bike like a glider.
Then he got fired from the team.
He was so mad, he wanted to scream.
The rider was the worst fighter.
Kason Guinn, Grade 7
Graettinger-Terril Middle School, IA

Sidewalk

Sidewalk
Hard cement path
With cracks and bumps and holes
Daring my skateboard to throw me
Face plant
Alex Ausdemore, Grade 7
Wisner-Pilger Jr-Sr High School, NE

Brother Against Brother

Young men turned into soldiers
The American Civil War
Our nation's darkest days
The United and Confederate states
To defend their nations and families
Erik Nelson, Grade 9
St Francis Middle/High School, KS

Summer

My dad and me
We love to fish
On a calm, still day
Out on the endless water
To get away and to be alone
Nick Easter, Grade 9
St Francis High School, KS

Rhino Cake

would you make some rhino cake?
every piece, I will take
until I got blueberry pie
rhino cake: Facebook friendship denied
I still love rhino cake; I lied.
Joshua Petrich, Grade 7
Graettinger-Terril Middle School, IA

Walls

Colorless and boring.
You remind me of a blank sheet of paper.
Sitting there doing nothing.
I wish that you were more colorful.
Tagan Webb, Grade 7
Olpe Jr/Sr High School, KS

Fear

I lay there silently.
I feel a slight cool breeze.
I smell sweat and dirt.
I only remember the top closing.
I was as scared as a rabbit in a lion's den.

I never thought I would be in this situation.
One second I'm walking and the next I see this box closing.
I pass out from fright and a headache.
My headache was a car accident gone crazy.

I search my pocket hoping to find something useful.
I find my cellphone and turn it on.
I look to see if there is service and just my luck, none.
I couldn't take the tight space any longer. I started to shake and breathe heavily.
I passed out after about a minute or so.

I wake up for the second time to check my phone for a signal.
I finally have one;
I called 911 as fast as possible.
Finally after a few minutes I heard a hurricane of helicopters hurrying my way.
Noah Hardy, Grade 8
Gilbert Middle School, IA

Pigs

Pigs are cool and very messy.
They like to eat, sleep and plop around in the mud all day.
They are all sorts of colors.
They can be white, black, red, orange, black and white, and orange with spots.
They eat anything they can get their teeth around.
They once ate my dad's straw hat when he left it in the pig lot!
They can be tame, or they can be wild.
They can get stuck in the mud very easily because they lay in it all day.
Baby pigs are very boisterous.
They are full of energy and play all day and are also shy.
They are also troublemakers when they get out of their pens.
They root up everything and eat everything.
Pigs are my life!
Avery Noll, Grade 8
Jefferson County North Elementary/Middle School, KS

Sara

Sara
Smart, funny, nice and athletic
Sister of Zach and Kyle
Lover of pets, friends, and family
Who feels sad when left out by friends, happy when I am with true friends,
And angry when I get blamed for something I didn't do
Who gives help, comfort, and support
Who fears tornadoes, snakes and bats
Who would like to see my uncle Rusty, Grandpa Grady,
And my brother, Kyle.
Who lives in the small town of Graettinger, IA.
Harris
Sara Harris, Grade 8
Graettinger-Terril Middle School, IA

High Merit Poems – Grades 7, 8, and 9

Darkness
Ready to creep on me unexpected,
coming towards me like a lion to its prey:
It may ruin one's life,
But hopefully not mine.
I want, I need light.

The sun is its enemy
that fights for the day.
I fight for the light.
I want, I need light.

I lie awake wanting it to stop,
but it may never end
until the next sunrise
I want, I need light.

As it stops, I thank God;
I give Him a nod
for the work he has done.
I have, I'm glad for light.
Nathan Lund, Grade 8
Gilbert Middle School, IA

Blindly
I fear the unavoidable
The inevitable, sadistic abomination
It is as ruthless as a hurricane
It is as fast as a fox
It takes who it pleases

I'm afraid of how it could come about
Or how it might happen
I can only walk blindly
Until I am with our God

I must not live in fear
But live life to the fullest
I can't afford to waste
The one life I have to live

I cannot see what lies ahead
Yet I still enjoy what time I have
I can only walk blindly
Until I am with our God
Josh Pierce, Grade 8
Gilbert Middle School, IA

Touchdown
Across the football field
Before you get there
Towards your goal
Beside your teammates
Into action, the quarterback throws
Touchdown!
Chris Trujillo, Grade 7
Whittier Middle School, SD

Calving
Waking up in the night,
Making my rounds through the heifers.
I like going out,
Even when it is dark and cold.

A heifer is calving,
But not doing good.
I go and get Dad,
We get the heifer in,
He gets the puller and pulls the calf out.
The calf is healthy and doing well.

Two seasons from now,
That calf will be a heifer,
And it will have a calf of its own.
Jacob Linn, Grade 7
Elm Springs Elementary School, SD

Fantastic Flurries
Falling down so gracefully,
Floating everywhere.
You drift with great beauty,
And you are full of fine flair.
I adore how you descend,
Onto my tongue to melt.
You've been an excellent friend,
I'm full of love that's heartfelt.
It's heartbreaking to think:
Spring's just around the corner.
Your giant piles will shrink.
The weather will be much nicer,
But the snow will not be here.
I guess that this will be,
Goodbye, until next year.
Mandy Abernathy, Grade 7
St Paul's Lutheran School, NE

My God
God blesses me with His love.
When I am in pain He carries me,
He protects me from up above.
Jesus loves me and you, can't you see?

He died on the cross for us all.
Christ died for you too!
He loves you whether you're short or tall,
Trust me, Jesus loves you!

God has plans for me I do not know.
He loves me even when I sin.
I trust He'll lead me where I need to go.
When you accept Him as your Savior,
Your everlasting life begins!
Hannah Schelling, Grade 8
Faith Christian School of Kearney, NE

Messed Up
This place is crowded;
my head's getting clouded.
The people are like bees in a hive;
the air is beginning to feel alive.

Maybe this time won't be the same —
maybe this time won't be so lame.
But I don't feel comfortable up here,
Like I've been stabbed by a spear.

I almost start swearing,
so people start staring.
My face starts getting red:
Right now, I'd rather be dead.

Slowly, slowly at first,
I swallow and forget my thirst.
My mouth begins to gush,
words in a gale-force rush.

And then, I stumble'
words become messy: a jumble.
Now I talk in a grumble,
and finish in a mumble
Paul Weaver, Grade 8
Gilbert Middle School, IA

Goodbye
I tried to wake you up,
You didn't answer.
My mom walked in,
and said you died of cancer.

I miss you so much,
"Why, why!"
You were my favorite,
I didn't want you to die.

You were a great grandpa,
"Why, why!"
I miss you the most;
you made us all cry.

"Why, why!"
I was too late.
You were awesome.
You were great.

"Why, why!"
My mom was with you,
beside you when you died.
I wish I was with you too.
Justin Hay, Grade 8
Perry Middle School, IA

The Meeting

I see a figure in the distance
I think nothing of it at first
I hear the door open, squeak!
Everyone one looks that way
They don't think anything of it
But my eyes won't turn away
I see the most beautiful girl in the world
She glances in the room
She looks my way and smiles
I want to smile back but all I can do is stare
I feel my feet leave the ground
I slam against my best friend, thwack!
I say sorry and steady myself
I feel like a fool, I see her still looking at me
I feel as if my face is right by the sun
I make a goofy smile towards her, she giggles
I can't help but smile when I see her, I walk towards her
I start talking to her, after a while she has to leave
She gives me a hug and I feel like the luckiest man in the world
I have never felt that way for one girl and I never have since.

Brandon Denney, Grade 8
Carroll Middle School, IA

Don't Be Afraid

Don't be afraid of love because
You won't know what it is until you feel it.
Don't be afraid of night,
For it is a friend of the morning.
Don't be afraid of living,
You only live once.
Don't be afraid to take a chance,
It might be the only chance you get.
Don't be afraid to be alone,
You are never alone.
Don't be afraid to speak,
But don't be afraid to listen.
Don't be afraid to fall,
The bruises will be a reminder for next time.
Don't be afraid to be 'uncool',
Cool is overrated.
Don't be afraid to listen to your heart,
It will help you out at the end.
But most important,
Don't be afraid to be yourself.

Maddy Bollinger, Grade 8
Rugby High School, ND

Myself Portrait

My hair is a river of carmel chocolate.
My eyes are as brown as the Berenstain bears.
My fingers are like slow working snails.
My mouth is like a runner's shoe.
My heart beats like bass from my car.
My skin is as smooth as peanut butter.

Abbigail Henry, Grade 7
Whittier Middle School, SD

Why, Daddy, Why?

There was a little girl who was misunderstood.
She always tried fitting in
But she just couldn't hide the cuts, scars, and bruises
That were upon her arms, legs, and chin

Every night she's sit and wonder
"Why, Daddy, why!?"
She'd sit on her bed, saying
"When you hit me it makes me cry!"

So you see, the little girl was abused
Every night he'd kick open her door
And kick, punch, slap, and throw things
It's a habit he's had since she was only four

All she wants is to be happy
A place to play
A place where everyone likes her
A safe home, a place to stay

Cindy Mejia, Grade 8
Perry Middle School, IA

The Four Seasons

Spring! Spring is the time for walks or picking flowers.
It's when one can see the beauty of God's powers.
Spring comes once a year to provide time for weaning.
It's the time for burning pasture or deep cleaning.

Summer! Summer is the time trees start their shading.
It's when one can sit and watch the sunset fading.
Summer comes and goes but it is thought to be the best.
It's time for picnics, barbecues, and no tests.

Fall! Fall is the time for jumping on the hay bales.
It's when boys can hunt, trap, or collect raccoon tails.
Fall stays for three months so the harvest is just right.
It's the time for fishing while the moon is so bright.

Winter! Winter is the time for adoring Jesus Christ.
It's when one can go sledding as their feet get so iced.
Winter comes last in the year, but have no fears;
It's the time for Christmas trees, family, and no tears.

Madison Brackenbury, Grade 7
St Mary's Academy & College, KS

Love

The phone, it rang, he called to say goodbye.
My heart it broke, how could this be the end?
The walks, long talks, hours spent with him now ceased.
Will I find love once more or not, please tell.
The sun, it rose next morn and shined on me.
Its warm, the rays, I knew right then God's near.
I'm fine, I live, I'm strong, moving on with friends.

Hannah Jamison, Grade 8
Chadron Middle School, NE

High Merit Poems – Grades 7, 8, and 9

Fly Away
Fly away on that day
when you feel the pain,
the pain you know —
that pain that only
you know that came;
sometimes you just
need to fly away,
and when you fly away,
the pain is yesterday;
don't they say
'Put the past away'?

Collin Krapfl, Grade 7
St Mary's Immaculate Conception Catholic School, IA

Snapped!
Snap! Crack! Pop!
In the middle of a math test.
It is pointless.
My beautiful #2 lead is gone.
The point in life, my inspiration has snapped.
A dull, pointless end surrounded by yellow paint.
The beauty has left my Ticonderoga.
The paint is chipping off.
The eraser is dead,
Someone please, take my head!
My pencil is pointless.

Emma Koestner, Grade 7
Dallas Center-Grimes Middle School, IA

My Heart
My heart is a fragile
but tough thing,
when I see your face
I hear it ring;
my heart belongs
to you only,
please don't ever leave me lonely;
my heart is a wonderful song,
and I promise
always my heart
will go on.

Rachel Anderegg, Grade 7
St Mary's Immaculate Conception Catholic School, IA

Life Is a Wrestling Match
Life is a wrestling match,
You have to step up to the challenge and take control,
Sometimes you score,
Sometimes you get scored on,
sometimes you win,
Sometimes you lose,
And whether you win or lose,
You have to pick yourself up,
And move on to the next.

Sammie Schmidt, Grade 9
Cardinal Jr/Sr High School, IA

The Last Spark
Everyday I shrink back
And fall down into a crippled crack

I shudder and shiver in disgust
This is beginning to rust

The further I go down
The deeper I frown

I don't know what I've become
Or how I could have been so dumb

I am alone and I don't belong
I am no longer strong

I cry out for hope
For someone to save me, help me cope

I don't show anger or pain
And trust me, I'm not sane

My heart and mind is a bomb, waiting to go boom!
Somewhere, somehow I'm trapped in a room

In this room, it's completely dark
Nothing, not even a small spark

In this room, there is nothing to see
Except that there is no hope for me

Haley Clinton, Grade 8
Carroll Middle School, IA

You and I Have a Fear
You and I have a fear that makes us shiver and quiver;
It sometimes sends chills up our spines —
It's not something I want to face,
But something I should embrace.

When I am forced to face it, I am extremely scared,
But once it's over, I am relaxed and eased
Like a lazy cat waking up from a nap.
When I successfully face it,
I feel like a weight is off my shoulders.

Facing my fear is the hardest part:
So many people staring and glaring
And listening to what I have to say;
It makes me shy, shaky, and shiver.

Even though it is scary,
Even though it is unwanted,
It is a skill we need to master
And a fear we need to overcome.
You and I have a fear.

Julianna Battles, Grade 8
Gilbert Middle School, IA

Life as a Mountain Man
We are on our search through the mountains
With hope to come across some water fountains
We have our food ready in sight
With no partner to share with

Morning sky has peeked in
As winds blow into my den
The magnificent smell of morning flowers
I must keep moving on

As I stare at a mountain's white-tipped peak
A bear appears hungry, in search of his sheep,
So tired of climbing these mountains
I rest on a rock for a snack

The day is ending with cheer
Because of the upcoming elk I hear
I got my chance with the elk
It looks like I got my dinner

Brooke Roes, Grade 8
Chadron Middle School, NE

Baseball Problems
One game the weather can be cold and rainy
The next game will be 90 degrees and humid
Baseball problems

You make one error in a game
And the whole team runs poles
Baseball problems

Being burnt on one arm but not the other
Is like only putting in half an effort
Baseball problems

Pitcher blowing a fast ball by you
Making you look slower than a turtle
Baseball problems

Baseball can be a very downing game
But being mentally tough
Is the best way to play

Tyler Williams, Grade 8
Carroll Middle School, IA

Don't Leave
Please, don't leave me so soon.
Please, don't rise as if you are the moon.
I will be a shipwreck sinking down if you leave me like this.
You, I would always miss.

It wouldn't matter if you were a plane flying high.
If you died, I would surely cry.
You are my best and truest friend.
Even when you die, our friendship will never end.

As your body sits six feet under,
Your possessions would quickly be plundered.
I want things to remain the same.
To be without you, I would rather be maimed.

The only comfort I would truly have.
Is knowing the great life you already had.
I love him so much, and I hope that he knows,
That I will always love my bro.

Christopher McGuire, Grade 8
Gilbert Middle School, IA

The Birmingham Bombing
On September 15, 1963
I went to church that day
Thinking I'd come home today
Talking with my friends, thinking of what to say

On September 15, 1963
In a church on 16th street
A man laid a box outside the church
Drove off, waiting for the clock and zero to meet

On September 15, 1963
We were skipping to the basement
"Sara go away!" I said, she followed us anyway
Down, down, down, to the basement

On September 15, 1963
A bomb went off by the tree
Five, four, three, two, one
Killing my friends and me

Hannah Nelson, Grade 8
Perry Middle School, IA

The Music Capital
Drizzly, friendly
Early in summer before the crowds
Late at night in the refreshing air
Groups yelling in amusement, roller coasters humming
Families enjoying each other, restaurants as far as the eye can see
Viewing, hiking
End of May
Rejuvenated, relaxed

Jakob Church, Grade 8
St Francis Middle/High School, KS

Sailing Away
Far away in the deep ocean blue,
There is an old boat coming, it's true.
It will come in the night and take you away,
To this new foreign place where you will now stay.
Your old familiar life will be left behind,
It will never; not once, re-enter your mind.
Turning back? That you won't do
Once that little old boat comes to take you.

Madison Elliott, Grade 9
Olathe Northwest High School, KS

Home

On nights like this,
When the moon is high and the sky is full of stars...
All your worries fade away.

When the light sheets are pulled to your chin,
Slide open the window,
And let the gentle breeze come rushing in.

And as the smell of sweet hay fills your lungs with joy,
You just simply let go of all the stress and noise.

As the lace curtains begin to blow,
You get that feeling because you know,
This is the country.

Not a peep, nor a creek in the quiet farmhouse
Just the peaceful song of a cricket in the distance.

And as prayers go up,
And heads come down,
You feel safe and secure knowing you're home.

This is the best part of the day,
You want it to last, because pretty fast
You'll see the sun shining and hear the birds singing their songs.

Kennedi Rowlands, Grade 7
Charles City Middle School, IA

The Big Sea

All around me I see hatred. All around me I see black.
All around me I see nothing. All around me, I'm being attacked.

All around me, I see darkness, never any lights
I look out towards the open and all I see are fights
Everyone acts so sacred
But all I see is hatred

All around me, but now inside, I can't find anything
The big fish overtake me, like they are queen and king
All I want is me back
But all I see is black

All around me, I see their faces, they tell me what to do
I want to speak out, but I'm too afraid too
I swim away till I'm puffing
But all I see is nothing

All around me, I hear their voices, they swarm inside my head
And sometimes I get dizzy from all the secrets that they spread
Loyalty and trust is something that they lack
But all I see is me; I'm being attacked

These big fish are sharks, but they think they're really great
Someday they'll wake up. By then though, it will be too late.

Rose Eischeid, Grade 8
Carroll Middle School, IA

My Room

A room is a young child's mother,
A mother whose child comes to her to take the child under her wing
To listen and not speak, judge, or worry
She is someone you can never fight with
She is there night and day for you
She is filled with the things that keep you strong
And her words are true.

Her walls are straight and sturdy,
Ready for any words you throw at her.
Hurtful (to help lift off the hurt from others)
Or words that the boy at school will never hear about
And that is why I love my room.

A room is a young child's mother,
A mother whose child comes to her to take the child under her wing
To listen not speak, judge, or worry.
That is what a room is.

Jasmine Morrow, Grade 7
Rugby High School, ND

Winter

From the ashes of last fall
Arises the white
This white has bite, and blocks all sun.
It brings promise to those inside
Children press their faces up against the window to feel the cold.
It gives life and takes it away
To those up north, it is a time of bitterness.
Sometimes in the morning, after first light
The lonely trees freeze, and are empty.
A time of cute couples cuddling, and
The way the snow muffles.
But in this time of cold there is celebration
And stories by the fire.
With new years and new fears
Everyone starts over
This is the season of love.
Until the ashes of last fall
Rise again.

Holden Terpstra, Grade 8
Perry Middle School, IA

Basketball

B asketball, an incredible sport
A thletes everywhere play the sport
S kill is what it takes
K nown all around world
E asy to play, hard to master
T wo people, that's all you need
B ounce the ball, that's what you need to do
A lways played with a ball and a hoop
L eagues like the NBA, WNBA, NCAA, and so many more
L ittle kids to grown men show their skills on the court

Bryce Riniker, Grade 7
Notre Dame Jr/Sr High School, IA

Teenager

On your laptop when you should be doing homework
Just checking your inbox for the email that never comes
Hearing about all the parties where you are never invited to come
Seeing girls with boyfriends and wishing you had one

But maybe

You're at the party but you're feelin' all alone
You have lots of friends but you don't really have one
You have a boyfriend but he treats you like trash
You have two parents but on their agenda you're last

And even

That girl that tries to get noticed at least once
She'll do what ever it takes, even never having lunch
The drugs she will try you can't even imagine
But how could you when you never take time to see it happen

All these things happen but we dismiss them as if they're not there
We see stuff happen but act like we don't care
If we helped out more and helped carry others pain
There would be less there and fewer tears would be made

Chelsea Klahr, Grade 9
Holton High School, KS

The Joy of Youth

Have you heard what they say?
About the night,
about the day.
About when you're up
they tear you down.
About happiness
that is a frown.

Do you know that it's not true?
What they say,
about me and you.
That sometimes people
feel so strong.
When what they're doing
is entirely wrong.

Can you see what is out there?
Way down deep,
what is fair.
We are strong
and we speak truth.
They can not deprive us
from the joy of youth.

Hannah Dade, Grade 7
Jefferson County North Elementary/Middle School, KS

Hard Work Pays Off

Seven seconds left on the clock,
We're down by one.
We have the ball getting ready to throw it in,
We pass it in to our point guard,
She passes it up to me.
I go up for the lay-up and get fouled.
I'm on the free-throw line getting ready to shoot,
The first shot goes in.
My heart was pounding, muscles aching, and adrenaline rushing.
I shoot the second shot,
It bounces on the rim and my heart sinks,
Then it falls in, "swoosh," the crowd cheers.
We won the game and my muscles relaxed.
I knew that the hard work to get here paid off.

Amanda Wistuba, Grade 8
Jefferson County North Elementary/Middle School, KS

Fears

Why can't you see this is who I am?
I won't change, don't you understand?
All the fears cloaked in darkness
Suppressing my thoughts trying my best
Wanting to expose, afraid of the loss.
Everything's so far the road I can't cross.
Tomorrow's so far away, yesterday has disappeared.
The present seems so confused, darkness confirms my fears.
I can't walk away. I can't stay here.
Will you take my hand and chase away my fears?
Something I can't grasp my tears stopped falling,
But they continue to crash not needing the warning.
Desperate to find myself, afraid to walk away,
Leaving you behind should I decide to stay.

Kylie Debus, Grade 8
Colome High School, SD

Today

I walk outside to smell the fresh air
I feel the nice slight breeze go through my hair

So much as one squirrel runs across my lawn
While the sun shines down I start to yawn

And then I dream of this day
To never drift away

My life is perfect today
In the most lovely of ways

My life will have some wonderful days
Today is a good day in all ways!

Alexandra Fischer, Grade 7
Viborg Jr High School, SD

Unavoidable

The thing about being a fear is that:
It creeps toward us, ever near.
It can attack quickly or slowly,
Yet it seems so quiet and lowly.

It cannot be avoided by anything,
Nor can the pains it may bring.
It continues executing its quiet theft;
We just wonder how much time we have left.

Slowly its victims fade away:
For it, there are no shades of gray.
You are one way, or you are the other:
Mother, Father, Sister, Brother;

However, when I think about it now,
I am not quite as afraid somehow
Because this Monster is still quite far away,
At least that is what we hope to say…
Andrew Cannon, Grade 8
Gilbert Middle School, IA

Rhythm of Love

When does love exist
When is love ever missed
Do you ever see me glancing at you
Watching everything you say and do

Should I move on with my life
Or should I stay and bear all this strife
Can I love you any longer
Or will this make me stronger

If I move on and stay away
How do I know I'll be okay
I'll stay strong and take it with all my might
My head is up high as I walk from this sight

No I know this longing in my heart
I won't let this tear me apart
I can wait forever for you
If you say you love me too
Sarah Steffen, Grade 8
Carroll Middle School, IA

Ours

From eyes I cry and cuts I bleed
Some wounds and scars aren't easy to see
Everything seems different when you are gone
I shake my head like everything is wrong
There's too many towers for me to fall
It's easier here behind this wall
You're encouraging for me to end up on my own
But nothing seems to kick me off my throne
I'm standing my ground
And singing my sound
You're hurting yourself with what you say
But I'll move on and forgive you today
The past is the past and it's over and done
And what happened for me has just begun
Everything won't matter in the end
People die and I'll see you again
Over and over you repeat in my mind
So in my life is where I stay, knowing we're one of a kind
Kavi Wilson, Grade 8
Dallas Center-Grimes Middle School, IA

Life In Betrayal

You take one step back,
You chose to walk away.
No reason behind your betrayal,
I still look the other way.

Lend me a smile, or at least let mine recover its shape,
Under my conditions, I still tend to fix my smile.
Knowing you're still the same, you will never change,
I convince myself you have for a while.

Past, present, and future, you promised me you'd be here,
I thought I went insane, but it just isn't me.
Thinking that I'm broken,
Realizing that's something I could never be.

Cherish each moment for better or worse,
Because nobody can live forever.
You only live once, so make the positive memories,
The ones you always remember.
Natasha McCoy, Grade 8
Perry Middle School, IA

To Play Piano

I've played piano since I was four.
I have played many songs out of the piano books.
I went from practice books to song books.
Since I don't play sports, piano is everything to me!
I enjoy piano, and the keys are challenging,
But that's what makes it fun!
Once you really get accomplished,
You start moving your fingers all over the keyboard.
This really makes piano playing exciting!
Kassandra Linn, Grade 7
Elm Springs Elementary School, SD

Military

M y mom's husband is a firefighter in the air force.
I n England, I played outside all the time.
L eaving England was sad to me 'cause it was so fun.
I learned a lot of new stuff when I was there.
T o go to London, we had to fly.
A nyone in my family thought it was good for me to go.
R andomly, we are going to Whitman, Missouri.
Y elling at my brother to stay close when we went to Paris.
Spencer Matthews, Grade 7
Graettinger-Terril Middle School, IA

Sky Treasure

When I, the sun,
Come out to shine,
The clear blue waters,
Catch my jewels so fine,

When I, a girl,
Swim in the sea,
I reach out to grasp the jewels,
Yet they slip away from me,

When I, the sea,
Possess her jewels so rare,
Nothing but the night,
Can pluck them from my watery lair.
Amalia Seppanen, Grade 7
Hamlin Middle School, SD

Blizzards

Fluffy, white flakes, soft as a Kleenex,
With no visibility whatsoever.
Beautiful snows, outside my window,
And lot's of cold in the weather.
Struggling to get warm, with freezing air.
Snow as white as a marshmallow.

The wind rustling the treetops,
Snow plastered on the windows.
Is that Jack Frost??
BAM! The tree hits the house!
Snowed in, now what?
Snow falling, no louder than a mouse.
Madison Mumm, Grade 8
Thayer Central Junior High School, NE

Beautiful Snow

Oh snow, you are so bright,
You always glisten in the sunlight.
You are so white and puffy,
You are so very fluffy.
You fall down from the sky,
Carelessly you descend.
You have many sizes and shapes,
And many wonderful flakes.
Snow, you are so nice,
Until you turn to ice.
You look so light,
When you are in flight.
Oh snow, I love you,
Oh, you bet I do!
Tyson Price, Grade 7
St Paul's Lutheran School, NE

My Soul

The darkness surrounds me,
It's getting dark and cold.
I'm all alone,
With no one to hold.

My world is so empty,
All what is left is pain.
No sunshine to lighten my way,
Just never-ending rain.

I drown in tears,
My heart is crying.
No one seems to notice,
My soul is dying.

No hope. No faith,
No one can brighten my day.
It's cold, dark, lonesome, and scary,
"My soul is dying" I say.
Jordan Bane, Grade 8
Perry Middle School, IA

Snowflake

I am one of a kind
falling out of the sky,
out of a cloud
I say "Goodbye"

I am one of a kind
because I'm the only one
I fall softy out of the sky
but I know my time is almost done

I am one of a kind
because nothing can stop snow
it falls out of the sky
like a one-of-a-kind show

I am one of a kind
cold and shy
and now my life comes
to the end, and I say "Goodbye"
Brody Kimrey, Grade 8
Perry Middle School, IA

Football

F ield goals
O nside kicks
O ffense
T ouchdowns
B ig hits
A merica's game
L eave everything on the field
L ose some, win some
Ben Christensen, Grade 8
East Mills Community School, IA

Fall

Leaves upon leaves are changing,
To colors from red to gold,
Everywhere I turn
They are all around.

It's time to pick pumpkins
To carve with funny faces,
Or bake them till soft
For Thanksgiving pies.

Chilly winds whistling
Blowing and scattering leaves,
Here comes the frosted windows
Beckoning on the winter chill.
Emily Erlendson, Grade 7
St Mary's Academy & College, KS

Dirt Bikes

Dirt bikes are really fun!
I have one of my own,
It's a red and white Honda,
And I ride it all of the time.

I chase coyotes and antelope
And whatever is in the way;
I chase them around the field,
Until they get away!

I ride it all around the country
I use it all the time,
My Honda will take me anywhere.
I do everything with my dirt bike.
Carter Elshere, Grade 7
Elm Springs Elementary School, SD

Basketball Is...

A way to be myself
Determination and commitment
Finding faith and believing in yourself
Sweat, blood, and bruises

Memories that will last forever
Pushing yourself to always be better
The feeling of victory or defeat
A family in your team

A rush of adrenaline
Trusting yourself and your team
The sound of a buzzer
Living life to the fullest
Jayden Garrett, Grade 8
Chadron Middle School, NE

High Merit Poems – Grades 7, 8, and 9

Choices
I spend all my time at a studio.
Where my dance instructor tells me
to Battement and Pas de chat,
to a piano tune of adagio.

While others are at school sport occasions,
I'm taking technique classes far away.
I try to improve my floor combinations,
and do the same, the very next day.

Sometimes I wonder,

Is it really worth it?
To turn down opportunities to spend time with a friend,
so I can take dance classes
and practice Fouettés beyond no end.

But as I think about it more and more,
I realize that dance is not a bore.
To express my feelings, as I gracefully move
there is always something to improve.
Kassie Kent, Grade 8
Thayer Central Junior High School, NE

It's Yours
My fear is not a common fear;
It's not losing anything I hold dear.
My fear is not being left behind;
It's keeping my life stuck on rewind.

My fear is the only thing helping me;
It keeps everything sealed tightly.
My fear is bottled up like shaken up pop:
It's darkening; I want it to stop!

My fear is not how you treat me;
It's not what you say to me.
My fear is more about how you treat them;
It's your fault my rage has awakened.

My fear is something so scary it can't be halted.
It's not sweet; it's over-salted.
You should think before you act and speak.
It's no my problem that my fury has reached its peak,

It's yours.
Lucas Keigley, Grade 8
Gilbert Middle School, IA

Rights
Feet are walking down the road,
fighting for a right to vote.
The grass is green the clouds are grey,
but they know they will have the same rights one day.
Triana Tilden, Grade 7
Whittier Middle School, SD

Child Abuse
I met this kid who is very shy.
He's always nervous, like a fly;
he never says "Hey" or goes outside to play.
He has different bruises every day.
I knocked on the door to see if he was home.
I looked through the window, and there he was, all alone.
I heard a car pull up; I hid from the lights.
I saw a happy couple walk inside.
I looked through the window again,
and saw an evil man prepare to hit him.
He tried and tried to move fast,
but the belt hit the end of his back.
He ran outside and sat on his porch.
I told him, "I'm callin' the police."
He said, "No, please."
He grabbed my phone and shoved it down.
As I watched his teardrops hit the ground.
It was the saddest thing I have ever seen.
Watching this average teen
being abused like that.
He walked away with slashes on his back.
Taviar Lucas, Grade 8
Perry Middle School, IA

Men of Poverty
There are men out there who have nothing but their family.
These men have to have multiple jobs just to feed their family.
To these men, we have one thing to tell them.
Don't give up.
No matter what the world throws at you,
Stay strong, and keep working hard.
Even if it seems like you will never make it,
And your goal seems millions of miles away,
The last thing you should ever do is give up.
Don't give up.
If people won't lend you a hand or give you land,
Or if your boss is a snooty pig that loves money,
But won't give you enough for even a jar of honey,
You might turn to drinking, rather than keep thinking.
Do not let anything bring you down.
Don't give up.
While you may be hard working,
your coworkers can be very lazy,
And yet they may get more pay than you.
Don't let them affect your abilities
Don't give up.
Zachary Calovich and Marcus Barnes, Grade 8
Tonganoxie Middle School, KS

Let's Play War
Let's play war, it'll be nothing more
Families will be torn
While Old Glory soars!
Many will pay for a game politicians call war!
Zach Tilton, Grade 8
Jefferson Middle School, IA

Fun Days

I sat on my ice cream and licked my couch
Drank my cereal and poured out my juice box

Kicked my pencil and wrote with my ball,
I walked in the shower and washed in the hall

I picked my clothes and wore my nose
I sprayed my pool and swam in my house

I drank waffles and ate my Coke
I ate my brother and hit my artichoke

I blow-dried my windows and closed my hair
I sat on my book and read my chair

What a backwards day I can say
But it was really a fun day!

Sabrina Lickiss, Grade 7
Whittier Middle School, SD

Death

Death is an unavoidable thing,
That all must come to.
When the bells start to ring,
You realize what time can do.

It can be painful, or gentle.
You can slowly drift away,
With a death that is uneventful.
Or for hours you could lay.

But we all know what will occur,
And in time we come to understand.
For there is no cure,
To a short life span.

So as you take your last breath,
Remember it's only natural, to submit to death.

Taylor Goldring, Grade 8
Mulvane Middle School 7-8, KS

My Family

My family may be crazy,
my family may be strange,
but I'll always fit in with them
and that will never change;
I will always love them,
they will always love me,
we will always stick together
even if sometimes we disagree;
to my mom, dad, and sister,
grandma and grandpa, too,
my uncles, aunts, and cousins,
I will always love you!

Molly Andersen, Grade 7
St Mary's Immaculate Conception Catholic School, IA

Footprints on the Moon

It was once said,
"That the sky is the limit,"
But I do not believe this.
The Wright Brothers worked hard
To create the first plane,
But do not worry, because it did not end in vain.
As technology got better,
So did our airplanes.

Nowadays we have airplanes that
Can go faster than the speed of sound,
But with the airplanes came the rockets.

It was once said,
"That the sky is the limit,"
But I do not believe this.
Then came the day,
The day when Neil Armstrong stepped on the moon,
And till this day, his footprint is still there.
So how can one tell me, "The sky is the limit,"
When there are footprints on the moon?

Cassie Felts, Grade 8
Perry Middle School, IA

Ode to Pencils

Pencil, oh, how you save me from reality,
You take me away, into a whole new world,
You help me in school and during my free time,
You make lines, shapes, points, and marks of reason.

You come in many shades and multiple colors.
You are sharp until I use you.
So then, I make you shorter and shorter,
When I sharpen you.

When you're gone, I'm lost and confused,
Not making those marks on the paper.
Lonely I am, until you come back to me.
Stay with me. Please, and thank you.

Kyleigh Kalcevic, Grade 8
Graettinger-Terril Middle School, IA

Blanket

A blanket is a safe haven
They're always there to save you.
A blanket is a monster-repellent
You always feel safe under them,
No matter the vastness of the problem.
A blanket is a time line.
They will continue to keep all of the
Generations to come safe from worries.
A blanket is that extra hug before you fall asleep
If you fall asleep before your parents come up,
That blanket will surround you.

Rylee Hawk, Grade 7
Wisner-Pilger Jr-Sr High School, NE

High Merit Poems – Grades 7, 8, and 9

Vacation
aboard the plane
to Egypt
at the Valley of the Kings
as we took a tour of King Tut's tomb
after we entered, the tour guide spoke
beyond this point
underneath the floor are various traps
around the traps successfully
to the exit, the tour is over
across the desert
toward the airport
off to home
Trevor Moller, Grade 7
Whittier Middle School, SD

Someday
Roses are red,
Violets are blue,
I may not know you,
But I want to,
Your laugh is sweet,
Your smile is pretty,
I want to meet,
Though you live in New York City,
I know right now,
My life isn't great,
But if you come into my life,
Maybe we can go on a date.
Christina Hunter, Grade 7
Notre Dame Jr/Sr High School, IA

Sunsets
The sun is so bright
like a very big light
It fades through the night
But it's all right
Just go fly a kite
For quite a little or not so long
While you sing, sing, sing a song
Sitting, swinging, or standing tall
It doesn't really matter at all
Where you are, when the sun is setting
In your heart, the light you will be letting
Duana Lee, Grade 8
Viborg Jr High School, SD

Won!
SWOOOOSH! And the ball goes in the net
We celebrate the few points we get
We're going to win, I bet
I have hope in us!
We can do it, yes we can
If we can do it, anybody can
…We have beaten the New York Nets
Misty Shaw, Grade 8
Thayer Central Junior High School, NE

Hard Helmets
Each time I strap those pads to my chest,
They grab tight to give me strength and protect.
The rivalry throbs in your brain.
Every minute reminding you of how much you hate the opposition.

When you step on the field, it is like a newborn baby.
The grass, so soft and freshly cut.
The pressure always crawls into my gut and plants butterflies.
But as soon as I see the other guys, the pressure runs away.

That stupid little pigskin has a mind of its own.
It rolls and ducks between my legs like it's frightened to be taken away.
I throw to Ryan and the ball screams the whole way there.
He catches it and the grass reaches for his feet but he jumps out of the way.
He scores and the crowd cheers us on.

During a time-out, the other players bring us water.
The water bottles flow water into our mouths like waterfalls.
The bench taunts us to sit down and rest, but we don't give up.
The field lights turn on and give us energy, like a new life.
We fight like heavyweights until that final whistle.

I put the game ball away and say, "Goodbye."

The ball always taunts back, "Until next time."
Hunter Hager, Grade 8
Rugby High School, ND

Goodbye Papa
I see you lying in the bed,
Asking God why you're so sick,
All the family crying,
Wondering if this is some sort of trick.

My mom says "Honey, he is almost gone."
I want to cry, but I have to be strong,
I try to keep my tears in,
Hoping you won't have to suffer for long

I lean in close to you,
You say "I love you, please don't cry."
I try to hold you forever, but Momma pulls me off
As you slowly die.

I see you one last time in a white box.
You are very cold and dry, so I lay my blanket and lotion down with you,
And try not to cry.

We walk away
As I say goodbye,
Momma says you're watching me
So as I look up in the sky, I see you waving and lying up there in the sky.
Cleanna Castro, Grade 8
Perry Middle School, IA

Outsiders

Come all of you Outsiders.
Don't let them poison you,
Like spiteful spiders.
Don't let them give you the shoe.
Stand up for yourself.
Just be you.
Ignore their insult.
For it is not your fault.
You are wonderful, you are significant.
You are not an imbecile ant.
You are awesome.
So all you Outsiders stand,
Up and ignore those who make you glum.
Emmalea Bush, Grade 7
Potter Dix Middle School, NE

Timber Wolves

T he best team
I dolize Kevin Love
M innesota Timberwolves
B eat the clippers
E njoyable to watch
R icky Rubio

W esley Johnson
O ffense is good
L uke Ridnour
V ery good
E xcellent team
S uper exciting to watch.
Nate Harris, Grade 7
Graettinger-Terril Middle School, IA

Set Free

I see it in the sky
Ready to pass by
I see it in the wind

I see it attached to a string
Ready to be in the breeze
I see it soar high in the sky
Ready to go on its own

I see it go higher than ever
Ready to be let go
I see it fly away attached no longer
Ready to be free
Austin Fleener, Grade 8
Carroll Middle School, IA

Friends

They make me happy
They are always there for me
I love all my friends
Kara Mueller, Grade 8
Andrew Community School, IA

Soft and Sweet

Lavender is the beautiful summer days all around the world.
The savory sweet smell of a lilac,
Holding memories of summer.
It is the tempting tangy taste of freshly picked berries at my farm.
Lavender is the sunset at dusk,
With streaks of vibrant colors.
It's the color of the smooth ocean at sunset.

Lavender is royalty.
The color of Jesus' robe,
The Prince of Peace our Savior.
It's the smell of a warm breeze when you step outside in the summer,
That rustles the grass and flowers.
The beautiful rainbow after a storm,
Giving one peace and happiness.

It is a grand piano with soft ivory colored keys,
A beautiful, smooth, and flawless Mozart piece.
Lavender is the touch of a silky prom dress,
The texture of creamy melted chocolate.
Lavender is the softest and sweetest shade.
Lizzy Johnston, Grade 8
Gilbert Middle School, IA

Do You Feel Good?

Do you feel good?
Are you proud of what you've done?
Maybe it's just a little thing that will go away,
or you're just another monster.
You step on everyone like you're the boss,
but in reality you're just another insecure person.

Are you happy when you manipulate multiple people just so you can have it all?
And when you meet people, you turn into a two-faced Godzilla,
munching and chewing on everyone's hopes and dreams.
Well, let me tell you,
you may have a crappy secret life,
but hurting and ignoring me doesn't make you taller in the pyramid of life.
You're with the rest of us—scrambling and scraping to the top!
So, let me ask you,
Do you feel good?
Selina Call, Grade 8
Gilbert Middle School, IA

A True Musician

I see the beautiful strings of the Bass guitar over there…
I see the beautiful lining of that piece of paper…
The secret language that only a musician's eyes can read and understand…
I hear the soft gentle sound of the French horn playing near…
I picture Louis Armstrong playing a shiny silver trumpet…
The sound so bold and meaningful…
Only a true musician notices the small sounds in the music…
And the true inspirations that started music
Alexandra Weir, Grade 9
Van Meter Jr/Sr High School, IA

The Wind
The crowd goes silent and the pain in my stomach is violent
Everything is shrouded by the sights of the night, it is dark
as I wait for the man to say, "Runners, to your mark"
I can't help but feel some sort of pain in my heart
just as he is about to yell, "START!"

The gun is fired, BANG, and the adrenaline is highered
my legs burn as I break away from the pack
I guess it's from all the practice I have, and the practice they lack
Then I cross the finish line like the wind, the race is won
the glory is mine

I take a rest because it is known I am the best
and the others cower at the sight of a true athlete's sheer raw power
and with records broke, which they all were a joke,
I go home a winner, because my strength was inner
I had more heart, this was established from the start, I am the wind
Hunter Guerra, Grade 8
Carroll Middle School, IA

Another Day in Paradise
It's just the second hour of the day,
Students are griping and groaning.
We come trudging through the door on our way
To our desks which also seem to be moaning.

We all look up to the board,
To see our daily "Caught Ya."
My computer is dead, where is my cord?
Oh! It's in my bag, duh!

Time for a team-builder,
Because our team skills are poor.
I overheard "I could have killed her!"
I think we need to work on this some more.

"Let's get started class!"
Hey, can I get a bathroom pass?
Kassidy Kucera, Grade 9
Palmer Jr/Sr High School, NE

Gymnastics
You might fall down,
you might fall short,
gymnastics takes strength,
it's not just any sport;
every day you practice,
every day you train,
gymnastics is hard work,
where you suffer through the pain;
stretching is important,
flexibility is the key,
gymnastics is fun,
and you can win a trophy.
Amanda Auer, Grade 8
St Mary's Immaculate Conception Catholic School, IA

Spark
It all starts as a spark,
one great day to change it all
a new light brought upon the world
to flip your world upside down
to spin your emotions to and fro

The spark intensifies growing greater by the second
your feelings get stronger also growing
you know what is best but don't want to accept it
feelings change others arise
leaving you helpless, envying more

The light dies dead to the touch
all that is left is but a small kindle
the light at the end of the tunnel dying
leaving me hoping for more
leaving me wanting the light back again.
Zachary Macke, Grade 8
Carroll Middle School, IA

There Is Something Hiding Under My Bed
There is something hiding under my bed
Its fingers are long and thin…
I can feel it grasping my head!
It has a rather pointy chin.

It comes out at night.
It sits in my chair.
It gives me quite a fright
And quite a scare.

It runs up the halls laughing.
It has long sharp teeth,
Jumping and bouncing
With very small feet.

Under my bed you see his white teeth…
Do I dare pick up my sheet?
Isaac Brodrick, Grade 8
Chadron Middle School, NE

Green
What color do I feel today?
I don't know…
It's hard to say
White, blue, pink, or gray
I'm going to say…
Green

Green makes me think of —
Flowers, grass, trees, and fun
How it all glistens in the morning sun
How the grass flattens under your feet when you run
Green…It's the sign of spring!
Alexia Jensen, Grade 7
Viborg Jr High School, SD

Never Alone

Knowing that you will always be there,
I will never cry alone,
knowing that you will always be there,
I will never laugh alone,
knowing that you will always be there,
I will never face fear alone,
knowing that you will always be there,
I will never dance alone,
and when you reach heaven,
I will do great things,
knowing you will always be there.

Sydney Froehle, Grade 8
St Mary's Immaculate Conception Catholic School, IA

The Life I Live

McKayla
Fun, athletic, ambitious, adventurous
Sibling of two brothers, one sister
Lover of the ones who earn it and not expect it
Who feels life should be lived to the fullest
Who needs the little things in life just as much as the hard ones
Who wishes life could have an easy button
Who loves to do the things which make me happy
Who would like to see the wonders of the world
Resident of the home of the brave and the land of the free
Taylor

McKayla Taylor, Grade 9
St Francis Middle/High School, KS

Music

Gil
Fun, funny, loud, and energetic
Relative of Jerry Garcia
Lover of music
Who feels the need for music
Who needs music
Who fears the death of an iPod battery
Who gives this poem to a contest
Who would like to see his fingers on a drum machine
Resident of this music-filled world
Garcia

Gil Garcia, Grade 8
Perry Middle School, IA

Lightning

L ightning is Mother Nature's light bulb
I t is very hot
G ood source of energy
H ow do you save yourself from it
T here is lightning every time there is thunder
N othing is quite the same
I t can cause mass destruction
N ot very many people have lived once struck
G ood thing to do, stay indoors

Tommy Hoffman, Grade 7
Notre Dame Jr/Sr High School, IA

A Beautiful Painting

I stare at the blankness in front of me
With the relieving wood gripped in my fingers.
Dip
Ideas sprint into my mind
And dance the salsa.
      the waltz.
      the disco.
Dip
Dripping blankets of color begin to unravel
like a beautiful meadow.
like a festival across the world.
like a deep sea adventure.
Before me,
Once a canvas screaming to be clothed,
Has been transformed into
A beautiful painting.

Jenny Huang, Grade 8
Leawood Middle School, KS

Track

Always nervous before a race,
And hoping you can keep the leader's pace.
Standing in your lane you hear the gun.
Startled, you must begin to run.
Doesn't matter whether you're in the sun or rain,
You have to deal with the aches and pain.
Some find it as torture, but I think it's fun!
No, this is not a pun,
When you're running the feeling is indescribable,
But it is very recognizable.
Coaches always trying to push you.
I'm so very glad they do!
Sadly, the season is short.
This isn't the best sort.
Some girls would rather be at the mall,
But not me, because track is the best thing of all!

Mariah Kinzer, Grade 8
Colome High School, SD

Missing You

I woke up around dawn
To find out you were gone
You cannot be replaced
And our heavy hearts are left with an empty space

We couldn't help but cry
When we said our final goodbyes
You had lost a battle you fought for years
Even though you may be gone, you are still very near

I think of you everyday
I shed a tear or two
Then I look up to the sky
And know the brightest star is you

Macie Bock, Grade 8
Carroll Middle School, IA

High Merit Poems – Grades 7, 8, and 9

Controlled with Strings
I've done terrible, thoughtless things;
a feeling in my stomach it always brings.
In my memory it stings
as if the devil is controlling me with strings.

I knew it was wrong.
I try to be strong,
but it sits in my head for so long;
My heart sings a sad song.

Inside I feel as if I'm hollow.
In my sadness I wallow
over the rules I didn't follow.
What I have done I must swallow.

It was wrong, I know,
but something in my head said, "Go, go, go."
I want someone to tell me it isn't so,
but I did it, no, no, no!

Moving on is never fast,
but finally I get peace at last.
Remembering it's in the past,
far from here the devil I cast.
Audrey Nelson, Grade 8
Gilbert Middle School, IA

Summer's Hue
I believe that sky blue is the color of lazy summer days
and the memories of summer that will last a lifetime.
Family barbecues are sky blue
with the smoky smell of hamburgers grilling and the sight
of my younger cousins running barefoot through the grass.
It is memories of sweltering July mornings
spent dribbling, passing, and shooting goals at soccer practice.

Sky blue is the sweet taste of
chocolate ice cream on a humid August night.
Watching my cousins catch fireflies for the very first time
and hearing their excited voices;
these sights and sounds are sky blue in my mind.

The strong chemical smell of chlorine emanating
from the sapphire waves of the pool is sky blue.
Sky blue is a piece of sea glass found on a pristine white beach:
smooth and flawless to the touch.

The color sky blue is the sharp smell of sunscreen used to
protect my fragile skin from the fiery and golden summer sun.
On one of the last days of summer,
sky blue is the beautiful setting sun that grimly reminds me
that summer is over and of the school year to come.
Kristen Kemp, Grade 8
Gilbert Middle School, IA

Baseball Is…
America's past time.
Not caring what's going on around you.
Letting loose and having fun.
Bats, gloves, hats, and uniforms.
Determination and the love of the game.
Heart breakers and walk-off winners.
The Chicago Cubs and the Minnesota Twins.
Sore muscles from getting hit by pitches.
Embarrassing errors and stunning web gems.
Playing for one sole reason.
Jayden Stack, Grade 8
Chadron Middle School, NE

He Is a Mountain Man
He is a mountain man
living on the grizzly land.
Where he lays on the mountainside
waiting for the spring sun to arrive.
For when hunger comes around,
hunting for beaver is very smart.
Buckskin pants and moccasins,
play a very big part.
Sharing adventures that guide,
he is a mountain living along the mountainsides.
Lorraina Fraser, Grade 8
Chadron Middle School, NE

Lost Flag
There once was
a flag with
beauty and grace;
this flag was sent
to a loving friend,
yet never received;
to this day the
flag is lost,
but the memory
will forever stay.
Logan Bries, Grade 8
St Mary's Immaculate Conception Catholic School, IA

Sisters Are
The annoying fly buzzing in your head
The youngest in the family who gets everything
The happy-go-lucky one
The one who doesn't get caught for starting the fight
Sisters are…
Also the ones who bring entertainment
Who help take care of you when you need something
Who do things with you when your friends are gone
Sisters are…
The gift God gave us.
Chandler Hageman, Grade 8
Chadron Middle School, NE

Katie and Michael

You don't know my name.
You don't know anything about me.
You don't know how it feels to lose a brother.
You don't know how it feels to lose a sister.
And you definitely don't know how it feels to lose
Katie and Michael.

Katie was sweet, nice, pretty,
Talented, and good with kids.
Michael was nice, talented, family oriented,
and religious.
Both had so much going for them,
but they had to loose their lives
when Michael was sixteen,
and Katie seventeen.

You still don't know my name.
You do know a little more about me now.
And you may know how it feels to lose a brother.
And you may know how it feels to lose a sister.
But you still don't know how it feels to lose
Katie and Michael.

Amanda Reichert, Grade 8
Grant Elementary/Jr High School, NE

Love

Love is like a rose,
it comes and goes,
it will be pretty one day,
and fade away another,
the colors of love may be full,
but then they will turn dull;
love is like a miracle,
and it can be experimental,
love can bring you sorrow
but my love you don't have to borrow,
love will make your heart break
and sometimes love is fake,
but my love for you
will forever be true.

Jaderial Staebler, Grade 7
St Mary's Immaculate Conception Catholic School, IA

The End of the World

If the world ended tomorrow,
Would we hide ourselves in sorrow?
Or would we spend the last day together
Through the windy, rainy, and snowy weather
If the world was going to cease
Would we stand together in peace?
Or would we sit upon a couch
Doing nothing but being a slouch
There is only one thing I must do
It is spend my last day with you

Carey Schave, Grade 7
Whittier Middle School, SD

Shooting Star

I cannot fall asleep tonight, I lay with my eyes open wide
I've tried counting to one hundred, and I've tried lying on my side
I peer through my curtains, and beyond the darkness I see
A small bright crescent of moonlight, shining back at me
I think I must be dreaming, for it's so bright tonight
Numerous stars twinkle way above, they're giddy with delight

I throw back my covers, and pull a sweatshirt on over my head
I silently creep down the stairs, as quiet as if I were dead
I slowly open our front door, and stealthily slip outside
I lie down in the grass, as the moon and stars coincide
I lie with my hands behind my head, for just a little while
It seems so clear out here tonight, I can see in every way for a mile
And as I lay there in the yard, a miracle took place
A shooting star streaked 'cross the sky, as if running in a race

I've never seen a miracle, and so I gasped in awe
There are no sufficient words, to describe just what I saw
Later on in bed that night, I wondered what I'd seen
Was it magic? Science? A plane? Or the moon's heavenly queen?
I decided it was an angel, what I had seen from afar
Yes, of course! That's it. An angel in a shooting star.

Mariah Hintz, Grade 8
Thayer Central Junior High School, NE

The Last Race

With the lane at my feet
I can feel my hearts ever-steady beat
The journey is almost done
But not before one last moment of freestyle fun

The world grows dangerously distant
As I slip into my mind for an instant
The time seems to freeze
As I'm getting ready to bend my knees

My body tenses
As I feel all my senses
I hear the buzzer sound
And instantly I'm off the ground

Jack Fordyce, Grade 8
Carroll Middle School, IA

On the Streets of Down Town

Different people I see.
All sad and tired of how their living their lives.

On the streets of down town.
Mothers and Fathers afraid that their children will follow their ways.

Oh how I wish I could stop, they say.
Stray cats wandering the town watching and hearing them beg.

Oh how I wish I could stop my terrible ways.

Whitney Grush-Wolf, Grade 7
Whittier Middle School, SD

The Orchestra of Nature

I poke my head out the window of our car and smell the sweet air.
I feel the mist collide with my face from the small sea of blue.
I look up and see a pelican flying over the lake, its reflection bouncing off the water, singing its sweet song.
As the wind picks up, my blond hair flies and flips.
The trees whisper to me telling me of all the wonders in nature.
Suddenly, out of the corner of my eye I see a goose and her little goslings waddling behind her.
As we drive a little further I see two pheasants pass along the winding creek.
The clouds roll in bringing the smell of rain with them.
Soon a soft mist kisses my cheeks as we drive on.
Suddenly I realize something…something life-changing.
I listen, smell, feel the world around me, and let out a deep sigh.
Ahhh! I understand now! I have finally understood.
Nature is all one big orchestra…
the birds singing their sweet song, the soft pitter-patter of the rain falling and draining off the trees,
the distant rolling of thunder, the rustling and swaying of the trees, and the wind whispering to you a sweet, sweet lullaby.
All of these things leave me awestruck and speechless.
But, perhaps the most important thing of these is the conductor, the leader.
YOU!
You are the one that opens your heart to the music, that is…
The orchestra of nature.

Alyssa Peterson, Grade 7
Viborg Jr High School, SD

Why?

Why did the teasing continue on? Why didn't they see till she was gone?
Why didn't someone say, that's not the right way?
Why do they find such pleasure, in hurting people to this measure?

Can't you see the hurt? Don't you see the tears? Can't you tell she longs for someone to be near?
Can't you be her friend, true to the end?
Can't you see how you tear her apart and break her heart?

If only they would have left her alone, instead of breaking her bones.
If only someone would have had the strength to tell them NO, push them away.
If only someone would have taken the time to say, That's not okay!

Can't you see the hurt? Don't you see the tears? Can't you tell she longs for someone to be near?
Can't you be her friend, true to the end?
Couldn't you see how you tore her apart and broke her heart?

Why did the teasing continue on? How didn't they see till she was gone?
If only they could have been her friend. Only it's too late…It's the end.

Mikaela Reth, Grade 9
Maquoketa Valley Sr High School, IA

Kith and Kin

I hear America singing the many songs they love.
The hot pan singing while it crackles, steams, and pops with grease as the grandmother watches.
The cards singing as they shuffle, slide, and land into adults' hands.
The sweet lullaby singing with its sleepy tune putting the little ones to sleep.
As their harmonies of fondness beauteously flows from dawn to dusk.
The delicious singing of a grandmother, or the beloved song from a mother, to the song of an antic daughter.
Each singing what sets to them and to no other.
The sun's soprano to the dark bellow of the moon, each voice singing their own song just like you.

Carah Crooms, Grade 7
French Middle School, KS

Walking in the Night

The lights illuminate our path
As we walk through the puddles.
The pitter-patter of our feet
Echoes through the night.
The cold, crisp fall air
Stings our cheeks.
The headlights moving in the distance
Light up the leaves above our heads;
Making them look like a kaleidoscope
Dancing above our heads.
The lake illuminated by the light
Making it look like an iridescent ice rink.
The lights show our way.
Not knowing where we are going.
Yet, we walk on.

Spencer Alefteras, Grade 8
Rugby High School, ND

Flying Flames

Frightened fire fighters
Ignore the smoke
Run in to save
Everyone with hope
A building is burning
People are turning
Clouds of smoke fill the room
While people are sitting in gloom
People waiting to see friends
They left back home
Guessing everyone got out safely
But not everyone gets that lucky
Off to heaven she goes
My new baby sister
Never got the chance to grow

Belle Breitbach, Grade 8
Jefferson Middle School, IA

I Should Be

Someday I should be a food critic
Going to fancy restaurants
Eating delicious food
Or I could be a vet
Going to different places like zoos
And taking care of sick tigers
Or perhaps I could be a good pilot
Fly planes everywhere
Also flying lots of private jets
It would be fun to travel to exotic places
Learn a new language or religion
Eat some type of exotic food
What should I be or do?
How will I do something or be something?
I don't know…

Noni Nowlan, Grade 8
Chadron Middle School, NE

Lest We Forget: A Memoriam

Blazing fires rupture as
The planes hit in two
Innocent lives were lost
And I instantly think of you

It was another ordinary day
As I said goodbye
But never did I realize
It was the last time

To all of you who lost the family member
I am deeply sorry for you
But all of those who still have them
Thank God that he blessed you

And to the 2,752
People that died
You didn't die in vain
But instead raised America's pride

And now 10 years later
I still rejoice
Because if I had to do it all over again
I would have made the same choice

Morgan Holmstrom, Grade 8
Perry Middle School, IA

April 9, 2011

The tornado came in April,
on a warm spring day.
The air was damp, the sky went dark,
thunder and lightning lead the way.

The warning sirens bellowed,
the tornado was already here.
Sending all for cover,
filling all with fear.

The seconds felt like hours,
as glass sliced the air.
Maple trees came inside,
as if playing truth or dare.

Pushing open the broken door,
left an unforgettable sight.
So much was damaged and gone,
so much was just not right.

But family members were okay,
God had heard our cries.
The tornado didn't break us,
and determination filled our eyes.

Shayla Brown, Grade 8
Anthon Oto Maple Valley Middle School, IA

The Beautiful Color of Earth

Brown is the earth upon which life lives,
and upon which life spawns.
Brown is the color of my eyes which
I use to gaze at the skies.
Brown is life:
sharp as a knife.
Brown is ever so beautiful.

The fresh earthy smell
of all the animals who dwell
in the deep dark dank caves
or near the crashing waves.
The colorful look of earth.
The secret of nature; birth.
Brown is ever so beautiful.

The taste of chocolate—oh, so sweet—
not salty; that's the taste of meat.
To the touch, brown is hollow.
Providing homes for swallows.
A moor, incredibly expansive and big.
Brown is the color of a twig.
Brown is ever so beautiful.

Omair Ijaz, Grade 8
Gilbert Middle School, IA

You

You are you.
You do what you do.

You grew. You are new.
Someday you will break through.

Don't be blue.
You will pursue. You will make do.

You will outdo
Everyone who has hurt you.

Don't argue.
You will be rescued.

You may be with people who
Want to boo you.

But that's okay because you
Are almost perfect too.

Always be true
Because you are you.

Molly Schultz, Grade 7
Wisner-Pilger Jr-Sr High School, NE

High Merit Poems – Grades 7, 8, and 9

The Holocaust

My love goes out to all.
The ones that suffered,
Lived and died, they had
To live a horror that
None of us shall feel
They are the bravest
Ones, the unfortunates
Who were targets for
A person that killed
Them for differences.

Ashlynn Stoysich, Grade 8
Morton Magnet Middle School, NE

Against the Urge

Along with the sick and weak
Into the changing room we go
Between thousands of others to get clean
Beneath the pipes where I stand
Comes out not water but gas
In our mouths and
On our skin it eats us away
Towards our airways
In spite of our attempts to keep alive
Against the urge…to die

Stephanie Andrews, Grade 8
Morton Magnet Middle School, NE

Friendship Is…

spending every weekend together.
laughing so hard you cry.
sharing your deepest secrets.
having the greatest memories.
eating Daylight Donuts every Saturday.
doing everything as a pair.
dressing the same.
having trust in one another.
crying together on our worst days.
always being there on every beckoning call.

Toni Doescher, Grade 8
Chadron Middle School, NE

The Holocaust

In the 1940's
Under the command of Hitler
Into the ghettos they went
Until they were taken
To camps of horrible kinds
In spite of their misery
Ahead they looked in hope
Around the corner help awaited
About 6 millions Jews were killed
For the rest to live

Hannah Lazio, Grade 8
Morton Magnet Middle School, NE

My Favorite Things

A pples so red and juicy.
B rilliant and sunny days with my family.
C hocolate-coated raisins.
D oing things to help others.
E lephants playing in the mud.
F antasizing in school.
G rape juice with ice on the deck.
H uskies black, red or silver.
I guanas changing color.
J aguars free in Africa.
K icking back and relaxing.
L aughing with friends
M anatee happy in Florida.
N arwhal swimming free.
O ctopus that are all contrasting.
P enguins in Antarctica.
Q uoting someone brilliant.
R eading a good book.
S leeping late.
T urtles that are really big.
U nicorns in my imagination.
V ampires in Twilight.
W eddings that are fun.
X -ray vision would be a cool super power.
Y ogurt that is frozen.
Z ebras running independently.

Gabrielle J. Manders, Grade 8
Jefferson Middle School, IA

While Emotions Make a Song

I hear America singing the various songs I hear.
The parents singing prayers for their young.
The teenagers rapping their emotions to the world.
The doctors singing for a cure.
The coaches singing for a win.
The rapper telling their story.
Those suffering singing for help.
Each song they sing belongs to them, their heart, no one else.
The adventures belong to the day, while the wonders roam through the night.
Singing with open emotions, a pure tone, the various songs I hear.

Hannah Watson, Grade 7
French Middle School, KS

People of the World

I hear America singing, the varied carols I hear, the poets of different cultures singing.
 The artist singing as she paints on her canvas.
The dancer singing as he makes wonderful movements.
 The poet singing as she writes away her feelings.
The violinist sings as he plays and makes uplifting music.
 The costume designer singing as she cuts away fabric.
The swimmer singing as he swims like a fish.
 Everyone singing what he or she is destined to do.
All singing with minds free and bright futures
 This is America

Destiny Williams, Grade 7
French Middle School, KS

A Goal

A goal is something that takes determination,
It's keeping your head up even when people fill your head with rude thoughts,
waking up every day and never thinking of something negative,
fighting the whole way up even if the goal is steep,
focusing on your objective and taking it down,
never backing down and taking on your task with all your heart,
standing toe-to-toe and face-to-face with your goal ahead.
Now that goal doesn't stand a chance.

Naleka Sayaloune, Grade 8
Chadron Middle School, NE

Rainy Days
Sometimes there can be days
when you think you may
not make it through the storm.
The clouds blow up and block
your beautiful sunshine.
The lightning and thunder
drown you in dreary dreams.
Desperately, you try to fight through it,
but it seems like the storm won't pass.
Just remember, it can't rain forever.
Soon the storm will surrender and the sun
will return, everyone will try to forget it.
But we all look back, and now
because of the storm, a beautiful
rainbow has come from it.
It blocks you from that terrible storm, so
never again can it drown you.
Victoria Hegstrom, Grade 8
Perry Middle School, IA

Denzel Washington
Daring
Entertaining
Noble
Zest
Elegant
Leader

Winner
Actor
Strong willed
High spirited
Intelligent
Never stops believing
Gifted
Talented
Open minded
Never gives up
Ben Hinsley, Grade 8
Morton Magnet Middle School, NE

Holocaust
They talk about survivors
But what about the ones
Whose names are numbers on a list?
The bodies with burned faces
Never to be known
People shot and gassed
Laying in a ditch
Mass graves unmarked
People unknown
Never to return
What took them
The Holocaust
Kelsey Jones, Grade 8
Morton Magnet Middle School, NE

Anger
Anger
everyone knows how it feels
it picks and pulls and peels
it reaches in for the tears
and pulls them out without fear

anger, it's one of a kind
and it has many signs
like the lump in your throat
or your bulging eyes

it rarely ends there
you grind your teeth
and you pull your hair
it's hard to hide the feelings beneath

Now it's all over
and you've become stronger
because you have overcome
this feeling called anger
Jaugger Thomas, Grade 9
Seaman High School, KS

Always Be Yourself
I try to be a person
That I'm not
I want to be myself   Always
But it never works out.
To be defined and
Pushed around. I'm not
The person I want to   Be
I try to be calm and
Be different. But
I noticed I'm not normal
I'll never be normal.
Just follow   Your
Heart.
I thought to myself
I am who I am
That will never change.
I don't want to change.
I just need
To put my head to it and
Find my inner   Self.
Tasia Rae Two Bulls, Grade 7
American Horse School, SD

Music
Music, relieves the stress.
Music, only the best.
Music, my release.
Music, smoothes out many a crease.
Music, screams for me.
Music, what I want to be.
McKayla Hellyer, Grade 7
Graettinger-Terril Middle School, IA

Mask
Why do you hide yourself
Behind the mask you wear?
You rearrange your face
So no one knows you're there.
Not quite the old
You used to be.
It's under but
Not quite seen.
Just holding back
Not letting go.
Is it some secret
That you hold?
Some desire
Not quite told?
Free yourself.
Let fear go.
Mark McLaughlin, Grade 9
Home School, SD

Bandit
At the dead of night,
Bark! Bark!
The sound of the dog, yet again!
Bark! Bark!
He runs about the outside of the house.
Bark! Bark!
"Quiet!" a voice yells.
Bark! Bark!
Midnight…
Bark! Bark!
Two…
Bark! Bark!
Five…
Silence.
Curl up and sleep, but wake up…
At seven o'clock for school.
Macey Starman, Grade 7
Wisner-Pilger Jr-Sr High School, NE

Those Nights Worth Fighting For
Gazing upon the stars each night
fighting for our country till the end
their pressure was on way too tight
he took a gunshot that he couldn't mend

Fighting for our country till the end
it began as a simple vision
he took a gunshot that he couldn't mend
a life-taking decision

It began as a simple vision
gazing upon the stars each night
a life-taking decision
their pressure was on way too tight
Karissa Jacobsen, Grade 7
Bellevue Mission Middle School, NE

High Merit Poems – Grades 7, 8, and 9

Colors
The world is of a million colors,
Reaching out to you,
Soft candle flame yellow,
Cool dark blue,
Burnt gray ashes,
Bright green eye,
Old black night,
Smooth cool white,
Harsh orange light,
Sad silver tears,
Rough smooth brown,
Light cool purple,
All for you.
Emma Hajek-Jones, Grade 9
Mercy High School, NE

Love
My heart is pumping
To the beat it is thumping
Of something called love
From way up above
Whoosh! It's ablaze
As I gaze
Into the sky
To see an angel fly
God is looking down
Yet not to see me frown
To see me smile up above
Of something called love
Layne Bormann, Grade 7
Dallas Center-Grimes Middle School, IA

Rosa Parks
Rosa Parks was an everyday woman,
Who fought for what she believed in.
Which was to stop the segregation,
And begin a prejudice free generation.
This carried on for some ten long years,
Before she was successful.
Her journey began in segregated Alabama,
And ended in a judge free Alabama.
Peoples' wish to not be judged by,
Racism, was her command.
Making people feel equal and,
Proud was her mission in life.
Shaundra Shepherd, Grade 8
Morton Magnet Middle School, NE

Ants
One by one the ants align
In rows as straight as a pine
Back to work they go
But one is way too slow
Now where will he be going?
Journey Lee, Grade 8
St Francis Middle/High School, KS

Life Is a Long Story
There are times when I'm disappointed in myself.
There are times when I can't even tell what I feel.
Times in which life has no meaning, and
The only thing I wish for is to disappear.
There are times when I feel hopeless and frustrated,
Especially when life doesn't go the way I want.

There are times when life pushes me down, and
The only thing left to do is stand up.
Life doesn't go the way I want, but
In life, not everything looks dark and dull.
There are also happy times that I just don't want to end.

There are moments that I really enjoy with friends and a great family,
Moments that I always try to make the best of, and
Leave behind each mistake.
Life is a long story.
Samuel Juarez, Grade 8
Perry Middle School, IA

Another Great Saturday
Buzz buzz buzz, waking up, buzz buzz, at 5:00 a.m. shut
Off my alarm. Every Saturday morning a different time to
Wake up and feed the animals, never ending. Finding warm
Clothes to stand in the cold spring gusts. Never getting to eat,
Until arrival, to the shoot. Might need to take a comforter. Never
Knowing what to take. Except a gun, 50 to 100 Shells, and ear plugs,
For when the guns start to go bang!!! And they don't stop until the
Awards ceremony and all needs to be quiet. Not a noise, except the
Distant rush, of a car that is late for a job, or the cheer of a team who
Has a winner in their midst, or a family that is happy for their shooter.
Now time to depart, to go back to that happy comfortable place that
We all call home. To feed the animals that are hungry again. To eat
Supper and go to bed, and get up to start Another Great Day.
Colton Fangmeier, Grade 8
Thayer Central Junior High School, NE

Love
What is love that everyone desires?
Is it true? Or fake like liars?
Love is when you want to be with someone constantly and forever.
It's when a feeling is so strong that it will end never.
As I gaze into your deep blue eyes, my stomach turns, I get butterflies.
I can't control it, my heart beats fast.
It makes me forget all the hard times from our past.
I think about you all day long.
I sit and stare as I play our song.
Now I know for sure that this feeling isn't fake.
Because my heart, with you, will never break.
I know this love we have is real and true.
Because I'm only me when I'm with you.
Annie Kessler, Grade 8
Holy Cross Catholic Elementary School, NE

I Follow My Dreams
I get laughed at,
I get ignored,
I often feel trapped,
and keep my thoughts stored.
People can be cruel and very mean,
but no matter what,
I follow my dreams.

Life has waves,
I know that.
But I stand brave,
and I just take it all.
I may feel exhausted and totally creamed,
but no matter what,
I follow my dreams.

I know what I want,
and I won't stop trying.
Quitting? I can't,
for now I am flying.
It's impossible, it seems,
but no matter what,
I follow my dreams.
Winter Godfrey, Grade 7
Wall Middle School, SD

I Love You
I loved you
you told me you loved me,
you didn't mean it.

You said we would never be apart,
look at us now!
I can't get over you,
you're with her.

You love her now,
not me anymore.
I am nothing to you,
but you're everything to me!

Why can't you see?
I love you,
But all you see is her love
not me, I don't matter!

I will always love you
forever and ever!
I hope you will see,
so we will be back together!
Stephanie Lawrence, Grade 7
Charles City Middle School, IA

Mae Jemison
Motto is "purpose"
Astronaut
Endeavor spacecraft

Joined Nasa in 1987
Eight days in space
Makes the most of every opportunity
Inspired by her uncle
Star Trek fanatic
October 17, 1956 was her birthday
Never gives up
Hannah Lazio, Grade 8
Morton Magnet Middle School, NE

Scars Forever
Scars forever left on hearts
Living with the regret and pain
Closing eyes seem like an impossible task
Memories slowly creep back
Making history once again a reality
These memories are all we have
Keys to the past
Little wisps of information
That will soon be gone from the world
We must learn from the past
To protect the future
Rachel Pistello, Grade 8
Morton Magnet Middle School, NE

Paradise
I love to run in the sun
On the beach
Just me
Before the sun comes up
The nice cool water
Keeps me refreshed
My footprints leaving a trail in the sand
It's absolute happiness,
Perfection
A stunning sight…
It is paradise
AnnMarie Anderson, Grade 8
Isaac Newton Christian Academy, IA

To the Raspberries
Through the bush,
Past the log,
Over the river,
To the house,
In the backyard,
Near the flowers,
Past the peppers,
Over my foot,
Yum, raspberries!
Brandon Wilson, Grade 7
Whittier Middle School, SD

Summer
it is a hot summer day
let's go play
in the pool
where we can be cool
cause it's so hot
like a big, boiling pot
we get a snack
in the shack
it tastes funny
a little bit like honey
we go down the slide
into the tide
now that sun has set
I bet
tomorrow
we will be in sorrow
'cause we forgot sunscreen
Sydney Rants, Grade 7
Dallas Center-Grimes Middle School, IA

Broken Life
The worst part about this life
Is waking up, forlorn
Having to know what I had
Has now gone out the door

The lovely life that used to be
Is now painfully broken
Maybe, Just Maybe
That life I shouldn't have been breaking

It's now
Just the sorrow
In my feelings, haunting my soul

Changes
So quickly
I could maybe try for a second chance
Dan Buck, Grade 8
Carroll Middle School, IA

My iPod
My iPod gives me music.
I play games on it all the time.
It calms me when I'm overwhelmed
And most of the songs rhyme.
My iPod is hot pink.
It goes with me everywhere.
Sometimes I'll fall asleep
And wake with it in my hair!
The ear plugs are jet black.
I lose them a lot.
That's why I have a second pair,
But they're in a knot!
Allissa Meyer, Grade 7
Wisner-Pilger Jr-Sr High School, NE

High Merit Poems – Grades 7, 8, and 9

Rosa Parks
Rosa Parks
Born in 1913
Was African American
Who was born in Tuskegee, Alabama
Refused to give up her seat
Was arrested
Known as the "mother of civil rights movement"
Helped African Americans fight for their rights
Believed in equal rights for all people.
Maddie Arandus, Grade 8
Morton Magnet Middle School, NE

Spaceship
S paceships stay on launch pads until take off
P repare all the boosters to fire up
A ll systems have to be ready to lift off
C ool inside the spaceships and the space station
E xplores the Moon or Mars
S pace has no oxygen for astronauts
H elmets are used in space
I n the space station they have a lot of computers
P reparing for launch is the hardest part of taking off
Trey Van Allen, Grade 7
St Francis Middle/High School, KS

Author
G reat author of my time
R ating his book no less than eight
I ncredible intense action that keeps pages turning
S elf-determination is what Grisham has
H as had movies made from his books
A uthor of the famous book "The Pelican Brief"
M ystery books are his best
Taylor Rogers, Grade 7
St Francis Middle/High School, KS

What I Would Feed My Teacher
Dried cricket and moldy cheese salad
Armpit sweat stew with finger crackers
Dolphin Steak with crushed cockroaches and worm sauce
Eyeball juice and tear latte
Bear claw and maggot flavored ice cream
Joseph Blankartz, Grade 7
Whittier Middle School, SD

Drown
Submerged in water.
Plunged into the sea.
Fighting against the current.
Fighting against the urge to breathe.
Exhilaration and peace become one.
Staying under water until you are none.
Shelby Freestone, Grade 7
Dallas Center-Grimes Middle School, IA

Final Words
My father was going to Afghanistan on a suicide mission.
It was optional, but he signed up for it.
He told me that he only had one life and he wanted to live it right.
What he considered right was to serve his country.
He gave me his dog tags,
And told me to wear them when he came home.
Those were the last words he ever said to me.
Zachary Caraccilo, Grade 8
Patton Jr High School, KS

Amazing Season of Spring
Spring is very nice,
The air smells much like nature,
Spring is here at last.

Weather is pleasant,
The sun is always shining,
Nights aren't cold but cool.

Some storms rage outside,
Come and go as they happen,
Weather is okay.

Go fishing at lakes,
Pools are open for swimming,
Water cools us off.

Birds sing far and wide,
Different varieties,
Fly and come back soon.

You can go to parks,
Or family gatherings,
Just celebrate.

Trees are full of leaves,
Flowers blooming everywhere,
Spring is here again.
Crystal Hefel, Grade 8
Jefferson Middle School, IA

Goodbye
The sun has lost its shine
The sky has lost its blue
There is grey in the clouds
When I think of you
There's something I never
Wanted to do
And that was say goodbye to you
But I guess nothing can stay
Not even if you want it to
I wish wishing was true
Because you don't have a clue
How much I miss you.
Angela Houtcooper, Grade 8
Viborg Jr High School, SD

Autumn Nights
The sky turns gold
When the sun sets
In the autumn sky
All the birds sing their songs
To put the kids to bed
While the moon is red
The calf goes to its mom
While people sleep
The coyotes come out
The night has arrived
While the fireflies dance
And light up the night
Soon they will go to bed
And a new day starts.
Angel Welu, Grade 8
Jefferson Middle School, IA

In
In my bed
(I sleep)
In the kitchen
(I make breakfast)
In my bedroom
(I get dressed)
In the bus
(I get driven to school)
In the cafeteria
(I eat lunch)
In the classroom
(I learn things)
In my imagination
(I pretend I'm things that I'm not)
Korbin Savick, Grade 7
Wisner-Pilger Jr-Sr High School, NE

The War
Fighting an endless battle
You'll never keep me bound
Easy to deceive, easy to read
Strong enough to defeat you
To bring you to your knees
No longer do I hide in fear
Loving every second of your shame
I take glory that you've lost your own game.
In a world where oceans bleed to the sky,
Take the pain of you and I
Holding you close in a heap of scarlet
No longer will the lies fill your lips
And here I sit, taking in,
Complete bliss.
Bailey Howard, Grade 9
Boone Central High School, NE

So Different…
Sometimes I wonder;
Why am I so different?

Is it good or is it bad?
Does it make a difference?

When the world changes,
I change.
We're all really bright stars in the sky.
I'm so different.

Living a loud, lovely, life.
That's how I am; what about you?

You're really unique, and I am too.
Can't you tell?
How we walk and talk.
How you write and how you laugh.

We're so different.
But many don't know it.
You're you, and I'm me;
So don't be afraid to show it.
Neyda Alfaro, Grade 8
Perry Middle School, IA

The Utopia
White is a chorus of colorful voices,
A rainbow with compromise,
Or a team without tension;
White is peace in its purest form.

White has colder ice,
harder steel, and sharper glass
Than all of man's most deadly weapons.
It is a tool of great power
That fights in silence.

White is all rainbow —
All race, all religion
All people, all life —
In one piece of art.

White is peace: peace fit for utopia.
White is nonexistent: a dream.
Life is a rainbow filled with conflicts.

One sees color as beauty;
I see it as hatred.
White is peace, joy, and beauty.
Andrew Metzger, Grade 8
Gilbert Middle School, IA

Fur Trade
There was a man named Chartran.
He was a mountain man.
He trapped the rivers and stream
All 'cause he had a dream.

He came to a land of Sioux
So his dreams could come true.
He set up camp on Bordeaux,
Livin' through the winter snow.

Buffalo robes and hides too,
He traded with the Sioux.
Guns and whiskey for their fur,
Tradin' in the timber.

That's how he made his livin'
He was trappin' and tradin'.
And so that is why they say
How Chadron found its name.
Clay Madsen, Grade 8
Chadron Middle School, NE

Second Chances
Second chances
Are not always deserved
Just free my soul from my mistakes
That I seem to make
Second chances
Build a bridge and get over it.
All we need are
Second chances
To make it
Through this
Life together.
Second chances
Help me break
The chains that
Have been holding
Me back from
Pursuing my goals
Second chances
Please just save me.
Kristan Soukup, Grade 7
Wagner Jr High School, SD

The Underground Railroad
No track to see
No tracks to feel
For escaped slaves from the 60's
No choice but to run
A choice which cannot be undone
Slaves from the south
Running to be free
Freedom alone, is all they can see
Tyler Zimmerman, Grade 8
Morton Magnet Middle School, NE

Sitting Bull the Prophet
On the prairie vast
Oh the grasses sway
The great prophet Sitting Bull
Looking far, far away.

He cries, "We will prevail
Against Custer we'll win
He knows not our strength
Swift arrows pierce pale skin."

Brash Custer failed the fight
The cloud of battle fades
Sitting now a prophet true
And a leader in epic raids.

After the battle, by Natives won
Enraged soldiers to capture their prey
Sitting Bull the primary goal
Vanished already far, far away.

In his South Dakota cabin he sits
Thinking of that fateful day
A prophet foreseeing his own death
Looking far, far away.
Josh Hyer, Grade 8
Chadron Middle School, NE

Longboarding
What's brown and sticky?
A stick.
Yes, a stick.

Sticks come from trees.
Trees are made of wood.
Wood makes the deck that is my retreat.

I retreat from the annoyances
that come with the world.
All the stress, and the sorrow,
and everything else.

The wind flowing through my hair
as I go down a hill.
Blowing it back,
so relaxing.

What's brown and sticky?
A stick.
That comes from a tree.
That is made from wood.
The wood that makes my board.
The board that is my freedom.
Cole Whitney, Grade 8
Perry Middle School, IA

Skiing Adventure
I love skiing
Skiing is fast and fun
To get your adrenaline to run
Jumping and grinding rails
Too much skiing never fails
If you're like me and like to fly
The fears in skiing are so high
Like the clouds in the sky
Skiing so fast like a flash
Keep hope you will never crash
As we go down the steep hills
Our bodies get the winter chills
All we can see is the winter glow
When we go skiing in the snow
All of you should try to ski
You'll love the feeling of being so free
Darien Smothers, Grade 8
Jefferson Middle School, IA

My Smurf
Thank you, friend, for all the things
That mean so much to me
For concern and understanding
You give abundantly
Thanks for listening with your heart
For cheering me up when I'm blue
For bringing out the best in me
And for just being you
Thanks for in-depth conversations
That stimulate my brain
For silly times we laughed out loud
For things I can't explain
For looking past my flaws and faults
For all the times we shared
For all the kind things you do
Thank you friend, I love you.
Gracely Benitez, Grade 8
Perry Middle School, IA

The Lost Boy
Living in shame
Is the story of my life
It's my mother's fault to blame
Knowing I will not be rescued

Wearing the same clothes for years
Bruises and burns appear on my skin
All I can do is hold back the tears
Knowing I will not be rescued

Escaping my mother's games
No more sleeping on the cold hard floor
I have a new family to claim
Knowing I am rescued
Emily Mills, Grade 8
Chadron Middle School, NE

My Ocean Stroll
As I strolled down by the ocean
Where waves beat upon the shore,
And glisten in the burning sun;
Where in still water, shells grow more.

Where in the ocean deep the coral grow
There also live many different creatures,
And below the boats which the men row
Are fish and plants with strange features.

Looking out over sparkling waves
I see a colorful boat,
The daring surfers that ride waves
On surfboards that float.

Then I remember home I must go,
Where I can in my bed dream;
For in my mind I know
How beautiful God made this scene.
Mary-Elizabeth Carl, Grade 7
St Mary's Academy & College, KS

A Country Girl Like Me
I live in the country,
That's where I like to be,
For the city life will never suit
A country girl like me.

I drift asleep with a sigh.
Listening to nature's sweet lullaby.
The wolf howls, the owl hoots —
The gentle wind sounds like flutes.

Living so happily and free —
Oh, how I wish you could see
What it is like to be
A country girl like me.

There are many treasures in the world
But from them I would hurl,
For my greatest pearl
Is to be a little country girl.
Therese Kaiser, Grade 7
St Mary's Academy & College, KS

Maya Angelou
Maya Angelou,
A renaissance woman,
Never let
Fear
In her way
Only great
Success
Came her way
Isabelle Knight, Grade 8
Morton Magnet Middle School, NE

Winter Fun
Oh, snow, you are so bright,
Making everything merry and white!
Snow is a sign of winter and cold,
You can be soft or unsightly bold!
When you fall it makes me a little sad,
But you are not always necessarily bad.
You are the reason for lots of winter fun,
It is quite sad when the sledding is done!
When the sun comes out and melts you away,
It always makes me want to go out and play!
But until next winter when you shall fall again,
I would rate this winter a perfect ten.
Molly Meysenburg, Grade 8
St Paul's Lutheran School, NE

I Thought You'd
I thought you'd never forgive me,
But you did.
I thought you'd leave me forever,
But you won't.
I thought you'd never love me again,
But you do.
And every time, before I did something,
You knew what I was going to do.
You know me better than anyone in the world,
Because…
You're my God,
And I will follow your ways.
Maddie Calease, Grade 7
Dallas Center-Grimes Middle School, IA

What a Backward Day!
This morning was backward
And I thought it was awkward.
I made my hair and straightened my bed,
I called my homework and worked on Uncle Ted.
I ate my friends and texted my food,
I talked to my cereal and ate some dude.
I walked in the shower and bathed out the door,
I convinced my Pop tart, and ate my mom, saying, "I want more!"
I sat on the car and drove my seat,
This morning was long and I'm already beat!
This morning was weird, can't you see?
I bet no one can be as stupid as me.
Lyric Lott, Grade 7
Whittier Middle School, SD

One Family
The blacks, the whites, Hispanics and Asians
Meet as one large family
Near the end of our lives
On our planet Earth
To show that race doesn't matter.
Aby Fernandez, Grade 9
St Francis Middle/High School, KS

Jackie Robinson
J ackie Robinson
A n amazing African American
C ould never be forgotten
K ind to every person
I nspires many children
E lected Hall of Fame in 1962

R espect for what he loved
O utstanding baseball player
B roke the color barrier
I n 1982, first African American to play Major League baseball
N CAA champion in 1940
S emi-professional football for Honolulu Bears
O utside of baseball he enjoyed football, basketball and track
N ational League in 1949
Angelina Adrian, Grade 8
Morton Magnet Middle School, NE

Blue Eyes
You, me
We are just perfect together you see
There's nothing that I would change.

I love the way you brush my hair out of my face,
I love the way you say you love me and act like you care,
all because you want to see my so-called beautiful blue eyes.

Your hand feels warm against my own,
You've made my heart explode,
I would not wish today any better.

I love the way you brush my hair our of my face.
I love the way you say you love me and act like you care,
And all because you want to see my so-called beautiful blue eyes.
Olivia Young, Grade 7
R J Barr Middle School, NE

Keep on Tryin'!
You whine like a newborn puppy,
and speak hundreds of languages, most of them ineligible.
Keep on tryin'!

You scream and you yell at the top of your lungs,
but all that flies out if gibberish and cryin'.
Keep on tryin'!

Desperate to be understood, you'd do everything you could,
try as you might and put up a fight and still no one comprehends.
Keep on tryin'!

They think you're in La-la-land that you've gone crazy,
but you know what you're talking about and someday they will too!
Keep on tryin'!
McKinna Shelton and Leah Bartels, Grade 8
Tonganoxie Middle School, KS

Rosa Parks

She was born in 1913 in Tuskegee, Alabama.
She refused to give up her seat and move to the back of the bus.
Arrested for what she believed in.
She started the bus boycott.

African American.
Believed that whites and blacks should be equal.
African American leader
Rosa Parks got what she always believed in and that was
FREEDOM!

Adrianna Gould, Grade 8
Morton Magnet Middle School, NE

Slaves

Slaves
Looked for freedom
For many years (up to the Civil War)
On the underground railroad.

Abolitionists
Helped slaves
In their time of need
Everywhere they were needed
Because they believed everybody deserved their freedom.

Andres Willis, Grade 8
Morton Magnet Middle School, NE

Basketball

Basketball is my favorite sport,
I like to dribble up the court.
When I shoot I always score,
then I come back and shoot some more.
When I play for awhile,
that is when I start to smile.
When the crowd goes wild,
I feel as happy as a small child.
When we score again and again,
that is when we always win.

Jenna Kramer, Grade 8
Jefferson County North Elementary/Middle School, KS

You

You are you,
no one else is you,
you decide whom
you want to be;
don't listen to
the people who
tell you that you
have to be this or that;
you be who
you want to be

Tyler Bolsinger, Grade 8
St Mary's Immaculate Conception Catholic School, IA

Take It on Today!

We shall take on the world today
We shall win over the difficulties
We need to live fully everyday
Thinking about the battles needing to be won

Always alter all of the bad of the world
And think about all of the good
All that is given to you as a gift
And all that is needed

Remember the past and learn from it
So that life can be lived to the fullest
Find fullness and happiness in your future
And always know your strengths and struggles in the present!
Also grow stronger each day and never fade away!

Justin Thooft, Grade 8
Carroll Middle School, IA

What Mattered

At first I hated the way you made me feel
I hated it, because I knew it would never happen
Then I found out you felt the same way
And someone told you how I felt about you

You were so happy
We were so happy
We were already great friends
But we both knew there was more there

Everyone said we were great together
We really didn't care what others thought
It didn't really matter
We both knew how we felt about the other
That's what mattered

Jackie Willenborg, Grade 8
Carroll Middle School, IA

Ups and Downs

You open your doors to let them inside
They bring you up, then leave you behind
You slide back down until you're needed again
Elevators can't have a permanent friend

You go to all levels to give them a ride
Then they disappear, they seem to hide
You see new faces everyday
The old ones seeming to drift away

No one appreciates what you do
They'd have to take the steep stairs without you
Your routine runs the same everyday
Up then down and back the same way

Brett Snyder, Grade 8
Carroll Middle School, IA

Music Is...
loud and exciting.
quiet and calm.
soft and sleepy.
fast and energetic.
slow and boring.
monotonous and annoying.
unexpected and surprising.

many things.
Seth Sloan, Grade 8
Chadron Middle School, NE

Airplane Rides
Aboard the airplane,
Across the sky,
Alongside the breeze,
Around the clouds,
But down I go,
Towards the ground,
Past the other planes,
On the ground,
Safe!
Brenda Lethcoe, Grade 7
Whittier Middle School, SD

Wrestling Room
Warm, soft
First day of the wrestling session
In the afternoon
Grunting, moans, screams
Great coaches, amazing wrestlers
Determined athletes
Running, wrestling
Next practice we have
Refreshed, relieved
Clayton Cassaw, Grade 8
St Francis Middle/High School, KS

Not Normal
Simply put I'm not normal
I'm weird I'm strange I'm eccentric
I'm everything else which is pathetic
The odd ball out
You singled me out
Not normal is just who I am.
Ashley Reuter, Grade 8
Jefferson Middle School, IA

Gun
Gun
Loud and powerful
You remind me of the crack of lightning
Pouring out with bullets
I wish you weren't so dangerous
Andrew Emo, Grade 7
Olpe Jr/Sr High School, KS

Strong-Hearted Women
The struggle these women
go through   Fighting for
their lives   Hoping to survive
Praying to God   they'll be alright
Wishing no one   could see them like this
Looking to   find a cure. Thinking
about things   they would rather be
doing, Playing,   Laughing and Enjoying
the life they love   Not laying in a bed
Crying to their   families Hoping it
will be okay   These women are the
Strongest women   I   have ever seen. They
don't give up.   They won't be fragile.
They are   determined to
find a solution to this horrible
disease. Whoever survives
can survive anything.
We have   to honor
these women.   The ones that
fight and won   Also the ones
That fight and   lose. We have
to remember the   struggles and
the pain the agony   the heartbreak
They have been   through. We cannot
Triumph until we find   what we need and
Want the one thing that   We are desperate for
We need a cure   Won't   You help us
Jordan Smith, Grade 9
Cardinal Jr/Sr High School, IA

Looking into the Future
Will I be alone? When my life is done, where will I go?
Will I see my family again? Will I hear anyone, a voice...anybody?
Not even birds chirping, or wind swerving, is anybody there...anyone?

Will I be alone? What is my plan for life?
Will my fairy tale dream come true...or will it fade away?

Will I be alone? Left at this aisle, my dreams will fade away,
And I will never know, the real respectable reason.

Will I be alone? No one is by my side,
And everyone fades away slowly, then, I will be alone.

Will I be alone? What will happen to me in 50 years?
Will I still be able to hear? Will I live by myself, or with a family?
What is my fairy tale dream, and will it ever come true...?

Will I be alone? Do I ever want to see a fortune teller?
Or do I want the future to be a mystery,
My life is different every day, I feel like every day is a new me.

Will I be alone? Is being a different person
A good thing. Will I be alone?
Abby Rioux, Grade 8
Gilbert Middle School, IA

Growth of Life

It grows stronger and stronger every day
Learning, believing, and achieving in every way
But there comes a time when it must go
For it is not here to stay forever
It's the growth of life
It takes years to mature
But then comes challenges that it must endure
There are those storms, those sunny days, those days of drought
But it manages to grow older, yet stronger everyday
It's the growth of life
It may feel chopped up or burned
Or it may even give off new life
Next time, it won't be so lucky
You've just got to remember
This life won't live forever, but
It's the growth of life

Henry Melendrez, Grade 8
Perry Middle School, IA

Fenway Park

Fenway Park gives fans a spark.
It is the only place for my heart.
When I'm not there,
I sit daydreaming about it in a stare.
The Green Monster in left,
Robbed many home runs. Some people call it theft.
Then you have Pesky's Pole,
Wrapping the ball around it is a goal.
It is said to be the most beloved ballpark.
To Red Sox fans it is a historic landmark.
The park is on the street of Yawkey Way.
When you walk down it, you know it is game day.
In right field you can see The Lone Red Seat
That is marked by Ted Williams' home run exactly 502 feet.
It hasn't seen a World Series since '07.
Every Red Sox fan knows that Fenway is heaven.

Reed Harter, Grade 8
Colome High School, SD

Muscles

Fully stretched and ready
Fill with power
Ripple as we flex

Boom! Power being drained
Working as hard as a motor, pedal to the metal

Being torn down
We are machines, but yet we collapse
Knowing we will come back stronger

Working until withered
Down for the count with nothing left
We will be back stronger and ready next time

Levi Shield, Grade 8
Carroll Middle School, IA

Running from My Feelings

Wind blowing through my hair,
Getting in my face, but I really don't care.
Running, as fast as a crazed fan.
In my way, nothing will stand.
Nothing going through my mind. I'm free!
Understood by the whispers of the wind, no one can break me!
Running. It's a passion,
Well, for me. I'm not one for fashion!
If I feel worried, or misunderstood.
I go for a run, out by the woods.
I sit, for just a moment or two
To catch my breath, and think, of the people I just never knew.
When I think back, my past wasn't that great.
I will go along with God's desire, without debate.
He has a plan for me, and I trust in Him
To save me from the deathly threats of sin.

Miranda Bendig, Grade 7
Atkinson Elementary/Jr High School, NE

Baking Cookies

Taste from the smell through your nose
The burning sensation, just want to taste them!
Sharp pain of the hot pan
Dull pain on your hand after your mom hits you
The best smell throughout your house
Different kinds have different flavors
Savor the flavor as long as you can
Then swallow and have the temptation to eat another
Finally do, and feel the hotness
But after it cools, taste the tanginess
If you drop one, it'll make everyone say, "Oh no!"
The best cookie is made with love by my mom
Don't eat a burnt one, or it'll be like coal
The soft, doughy cookie is good in everything
I think the chocolate M&M's are the best
Oh yeah, I forgot about them in the oven!

Cody Shanno, Grade 9
Boone Central High School, NE

My Crackly Nails

My crackly nails are like chipping paint,
My nails are the walls the paint goes on.
When the paint gets old and starts to crack,
My parents would've thought about that.
The paint cans come out and so does the nail polish,
Every coat of paint is like a new car they wanted.
Every coat of polish that goes on my nails,
Is like a new fashion statement waiting to be unveiled.
When the painting is all done and the looking is over,
We expect everything to go back to normal.
After a few weeks and years later,
This happens all over again.
We repeat history over again even if we don't know it,
Just like my crackly nails are like chipping paint.

Jessica Young, Grade 8
Jefferson Middle School, IA

Sitting in Your Lap
You had a chair
That only you could sit
And would sometimes hold us
In your lap…
I called you Grandpa
Like every grandchild should.
For a Grandpa is a Pa who is very, very Grand…
That chair you had
Is now so empty
But that does not hold back
The memories of sitting in your lap…
You are very far away now
And even though that cannot change,
You will always be my Grandpa…
Forever and ever.
Felicia Borslien, Grade 9
Sheyenne 9th Grade Center, ND

Acts of Nature
I walk through the shimmering rain, feeling its icy pain
But still I keep on going, walking down the street
Not truly knowing, what lies under my curious feet
I listen to the sounds surrounding me
I think about the things I see
To hear nature's voices, singing furiously aloud
To see its exquisite beauty, a bright luscious cloud
The thunder roars, a sweet melody
The lightning flashes, together in harmony
I don't know where I'm heading, but I'm traveling pretty fast
Life is like this walk, so many things already in the past
I'll feel the pain when things don't go right
But I'll feel the joy, when things are alright
I'm thankful for this life I'm leading
Stay true to yourself, and keep on proceeding
Katelyn Wachendorf, Grade 9
Central High School, SD

Sorry Mom
Sorry Mom
Sorry for the pain
Sorry for worries
Sorry for bringing tears to your eyes
Sorry for the heartbreak
I am really sorry Mom
If I could take it all back I would take the pain away
Make the worries go away
I'd wipe the tears from your eyes
I'll glue your heart back together the best I could
I'd do everything different
Just to prove the love I have for you
I just hope someday you'll FORGIVE me…

I LOVE YOU MOMMY
Kim Fool Bull, Grade 9
Volunteers of America-Turning Point South, SD

Wonderful Blue
Blue is the sky on a sunny day
It is the water of a crystal clear ocean
Blue is the best part of the rainbow
A giant iceberg in the South Pole is blue

Berries dangling off a bush are blue
Blue is sweet and smooth
It is the whisper of a secret being told
Blue is a snowcone just made for you

Blue is the pitter patter of rain falling from the sky
Blue is a nice summer breeze in the middle of May
It is soft and cool to the touch
A soda straight from the fridge is blue

Blue is water rolling down a stream
It is the tropics on a beautiful vacation
The cold in the middle of December is blue
Blue is a balloon floating through the air

Blue is a blanket wrapped around a newborn baby boy
Blue is the chirping of a little Blue Jay
It is cotton candy melting in your mouth
Blue is a flower blooming in the spring
Sadness in a person's misty eyes is blue
Adam Baker, Grade 8
Gilbert Middle School, IA

Up Down, and All Around
Clickity clack, clickity clack
I could feel my nerves kicking in.
I walked into the park, and knew I was near
The sound that caused my greatest fear.

"Hey Mom look at that!" my sister screamed.
"Oh my, that's the super scary snake!
All of us should go on that ride."
"But, Mom, I'm scared," I said with tears.
The whoosh, the sway, the crack and whip,
It all caused my stomach to do a flip.

"I promise, you'll be fine,"
She said as I got in.
But it still scared me greatly
And was as curvy as cooked spaghetti.
It's the Eiffel Tower to my eye;
I really thought I was going to die.

"Ahhh!" I scream; "Ahhh!" I shout.
We went up, down, and all around.
Wait a minute; that was fun!
"Again!" I say. "Again!" I say.
Five hundred more times, and that was the day.
Ryan Blum, Grade 8
Gilbert Middle School, IA

In the End Zone
Beside the quarterback
Through the line
Between the defenders
Beyond the safeties
Down the field
Along the sidelines
Onto the pylon
Touchdown!
Bradley Struck, Grade 7
Whittier Middle School, SD

The Ocean
It reaches for the heavens,
but is only led astray.
It climbs up the shore,
and slowly drifts away.
It runs along the dunes,
and harbors ships at bay.
Lapping calm or rolling fury,
a mariner can never say.
Tristyn Stokes, Grade 8
Patton Jr High School, KS

The Sphere of Hope
It brings warmth to the world
Like the smile of a friend,
Its golden beams shine as a spotlight
Of reflection in our creation of corruption,
Its glowing form like the halo of an angel
Keeping the darkness at bay,
It remains a constant in the heavens
As an unrelenting source of hope.
Samantha Schroeder, Grade 7
Olpe Jr/Sr High School, KS

Hawaii
Windy, sunny
First day of Spring Break
Early in the morning
Birds chirping, waves crashing
People surfing, children playing
Swimming, surfing
Next Spring Break
Happy and replenished
Justin Pacheco, Grade 8
St Francis Middle/High School, KS

Basketball
On the court
Over to the player
To the top of the court
Near the hoop
Above the hoop
Slam dunk!
Kristine Zellmer, Grade 7
Whittier Middle School, SD

Close Your Eyes
Through my eyes, you can see,
Exactly how cruel our world can be.

I stand alone, shut off the phone. I don't want to go home.
As cruel as it may seem to me, Peace is still around, you'll see.
Take a second, close your eyes, Open them up and see the surprise.

Get rid of all the evil, Take away those terrible people,
Watch the sun, watch the sky. Beauty isn't something to buy.

Listen to the wind blowing. Hear water softly flowing.
The best part is knowing, Knowing, there's quiet somewhere,
Calm in the air, No battle over there.

Peace and serenity, Take away the enemy, No honor to its identity.
The enemy will stand alone, break a bone, destroy every home.

But if you close your eyes, you can sleep and not weep,
You won't hear a peep. Just sit and count sheep.

Almost like a time stop, No gun pop, Freeze frame, the world is tame.

Close your eyes, Forget the lies, Yes, I despise, those wild guys.
Take the time to breath it in, this is a win.

Silence of the world's destruction, this is part of the movie production,
Free the world, Take hold of what you've been told,
Now go ahead and close your eyes. Let your mind be up in the skies.
Cheyenne Vasquez, Grade 8
Carroll Middle School, IA

Nebraska Life
The work is done, dusk is near —
The smell of freshly cut grass hangs in the air,
The cattle are bustling about, for they know what is coming
It's a storm, I can feel it in my bones.

A crack of thunder lurks in the distance
Heavy, dark clouds roll in the west,
Complimenting the amazing sunset that glistens off the bright red barn
A bright, shimmering bolt fills the sky,
BOOM! A clap of thunder blares in the west, even closer than before
Making the hair on my neck stand up on end —
A slight breeze now lifts the leaves
They wave to the oncoming storm;
One by one, drops hit the ground, making the dust stir around.

Then comes the smell,
The scent of sweet, soft, summer rain hangs in the air
By now the wind is up to a dull roar,
Thick heavy drops fall all around,
Two quick flashes blind my eyes — BANG!
Livestock is running, birds stop chirping, the dog runs for cover,
An old farm is chaos.
Joseph Brugger, Grade 9
Boone Central High School, NE

That Day*
We rented a car for the week. It was a red Ford with a gray interior. I remember it perfectly. I liked the new car, even though we couldn't keep it.

It was the day that we had to take it back. We had to take two cars, the truck and the rental. My mother was in the rental, while my father, sister, and I were in the truck. We met at the local gas station. I begged my mom to let me ride with her, but she refused.

My mom went the "new" way, and my dad took the "old." Our father was taking his time going to town. Suddenly a foreign number called. My father quickly turned around and jetted back the way we came. Eighty, then ninety, almost a hundred miles per hour. It was as if we flew over the hilly, country roads.

We stopped at a car accident. There was fire everywhere. I saw a semi on the side of the road and a red-looking car on fire in the ditch. I was terrified while we ran up a hill, my shoes falling off, towards an ambulance. My mother had broken bones, there was no more blood. Me relieved. My mother, safe.

Athena Russell, Grade 8
Jefferson County North Elementary/Middle School, KS
**Dedicated to Dawn M. Russell*

The Day That Will Never Be Forgotten
The sunny day on the 11th of September,
was a day that everyone will remember.
A plane crashed into the North Twin Tower,
the great impact from the aircraft was filled with power.
Bam! Another plane hit the towers, but this time it was the South.
When trying to escape from the crumbling buildings, the smoke and dust would fill your mouth.
The sunny skies turned black from debris and dust.
Ever since this day the United States has lost all trust.
These terrible acts of terrorists changed our nation forever.
Hopefully someday we will overcome it, as long as we never say never.

Katie Buckley, Grade 8
Holy Cross Catholic Elementary School, NE

Ballads of Freedom
I hear America singing, the varied carols I hear,
I hear the immigrant's melodic singing, their ballads of freedom I hear,
The lively mother cooing to comfort her teary-eyed, terrified children,
The relieved brothers and sisters singing as the Statue of Liberty comes into view,
The homesick grandparents singing of being broken,
The sobbing children's deafening shrieks as the boat rocks back and forth,
The uncle's song, the handsome father studying from dawn to dusk,
The cheerful singing of the grandma, or of the young mother taking care of her children, or of
the teenager whispering and purring her unknown secrets,
The open-mouth immigrants, singing their ballads of freedom.

Linda Deng, Grade 7
French Middle School, KS

I Hear the Sadness of America Singing
I hear America moaning, the varied melodies of depression.
The girl that hates her life sings as she cuts herself in every direction as she wakes up to the morning sunlight.
The boy who is bullied sings as he does drugs trying to kill himself at dusk fall of the night.
The "fat" girl sings as she starves herself during the middle of the day hoping she gets skinnier.
The therapist sings as he searches for a cure to treat the depression of children worldwide.
Singing with their eyes full of tears and their mouths barely opened as they try to moan the varied melodies
Of depression while the sun rises all the way until it is now dusk.

Tomi Francis-Ramirez, Grade 7
French Middle School, KS

High Merit Poems – Grades 7, 8, and 9

The River Ride
Rowing a bright yellow boat.
Holding a small little toddler.
Houses in the background above the water.
Happy along the ride.
Relax and soothing.
A bright blue sea
Clear blue sky.
Selena Hall, Grade 7
Whittier Middle School, SD

Country Life
Olden days.
Country boys.
Hard working.
Dangerous tools.
Hot blistering sun.
Long days, short nights.
Work, work, work, repeat.
Lezlie Walters, Grade 7
Whittier Middle School, SD

Graveyard
At a graveyard
Complete silence
Sight of tombstones from dead relatives
Kneeling
Praying
Crying
All alone, with souls of loved ones.
Nathanael Lehr, Grade 7
Blessed Sacrament School, NE

Black n' White
Black
Hot, dark,
Burning, alone, silent,
Inside, bad, good, outside,
Crisp, alive, loud,
Cool, bright,
White
Madison Mahlmeister, Grade 7
Whittier Middle School, SD

Friends
F aithfully
R ealistic
I n
E very
N oble and
D elightful
S mile
Jessica Klumpe, Grade 7
Olpe Jr/Sr High School, KS

Dazzling Dreams of Spring
Spring, oh spring, what a delight,
Fields of grains shining so beautifully in the light.

Dandelion seeds float though the air,
Like sparkling pixie dust sprinkling everywhere.

Let the breeze tickle you,
As it picks up the scent of sweet, sizzling barbecues.

The sound of birds tweeting is in the air,
Like music to the ear.

Rain drops fall lightly,
Drop, drip, drizzle, mizzle — rain splashing.

Flowers are blooming —
Tulips, lilacs, daffodils, roses, and sweat peas.

Full sunsets are so beautifully bright.
They are the evening sky's last light.

Evening storms, thunder crashing, pelting rain, bolts of lightning.
Birds are singing, eggs are hatching, snow is melting, and grass is greening.

Spring is splashes of color. Squirrels are dashing everywhere.
Spring is near, almost here.

Smells of fresh new flowers, so nice, oh, how I love springtime.
Alissa Bridges, Grade 8
Howar Jr High School, IA

Undefined
Tickling the early bird's feathers,
blue is the sparkling morning dew.
It is a flopping fish,
struggling to take a breath.
Blue is the bug skittering up the wall;
it's the small swallow's simple chirping call.

When my health is under the weather,
blue is the cough that breaks the silence.
Blue is the speckle on an expensive dish
that exclaims an artist's craftsmanship
in a language of twists and curls.
To fall into bed, when exhaustion overcomes me
and I wish that I were dead,
for blue is the undying worry hanging over my head.

Blue is the hot fudge sundae's warmth that fills my soul with contentment,
It is a practical car and the sigh that's uttered every drive,
wishing for better things to come.
Blue is when I have patience.
Blue is when the feeling is solemn.
Blue is mine to define.
Grant Peterson, Grade 8
Gilbert Middle School, IA

I, Dylan Warwick
My hair is like a curly fry
My eyes are a black hole
My fingers are faster than Mohammad Ali's
My mouth is like a magnet to girls
My heart beats like a quick African drum
My skin is as colorful as caramel
Dylan Warwick, Grade 7
Whittier Middle School, SD

100% Muhammad Ali
20% African American
10% Riding a bike
30% Boxing
2% Education
8% Working at home
30% Family
Brian Garcia, Grade 8
Morton Magnet Middle School, NE

Life
Life
Short and long
You remind me of family
Whose time has come and gone
Coming and going
I wish you would never end
Paul-Michael Johnson, Grade 7
Olpe Jr/Sr High School, KS

Why?
Why do there
always have to be
check marks
on my papers?!?
Why can't there
be correct marks?!?
Devin Rasmussen, Grade 7
Wisner-Pilger Jr-Sr High School, NE

Shoes
Shoes in the store
Sitting by the door
Lying on the shelves
All by themselves
By tomorrow
There won't be anymore
Beau Schany, Grade 7
Graettinger-Terril Middle School, IA

Crown
Bright and beautiful,
You remind me of the sun,
Sparkling like diamonds.
I wish I was a king.
Dylan Redeker, Grade 7
Olpe Jr/Sr High School, KS

Gone
You finally got your wish; I finally gave up on you.
I hope you're happy. You used to be my idol.
Abandonment.

I stuck up for my loving idol, but you refused.
I wanted to happily help. I was by your side through thick and thin.
Pain.

I spoke through my heart, but all you did was lie.
I can't take this anymore, why can't you stick to your word?
Broken.

Your lying was like sticking a sword through my heart.
I wish every night at 11:11, but I never receive that wish. All I want is you to stop.
Begging.

Every night I watch the clock. Tick tock, tick tock. You are as heartless as a fish.
Why can't you care for once?
Believing.

Finally, you come to your word.
You stopped doing what broke me, you now are my loving idol.
Happy.

That pain went away,
A ray of sunshine appeared. I knew you would come back; I love you, my idol.
Rylie Riesberg, Grade 8
Carroll Middle School, IA

Shining Knight
Silver is a shining knight
wielding his sword into a fight.
He reflects all with his shiny shield
while covered in armor from head to heel.

Silver is a new car zooming on the highway and tearing up the tar.
Exhaust is also this color's smell as is the odor of acrid gunpowder in a cell.

Silver is the breathless sigh of the wind,
the clickety-clack of a nighttime train,
the clashing, clanging, and clinking of loose change.

Rain on the ocean gives one the notion
that the whole world is made of steel.
Silver is a cool icy curtain that makes light uncertain
and everything it touches unreal.

It is icicles dripping from the roof's eaves,
hard water droplets exploding on my sleeve,
the metallic taste of blood in my mouth,
the white bellies of geese at dawn flying south.

Silver is glimmering moonlight
and the stars shining bright!
Liam Dougherty, Grade 8
Gilbert Middle School, IA

I Am

I am hard to love
I wonder if anybody can handle me
I hear people saying nobody will
I see you leaving me behind
I want you to say you can handle me
I am hard to love

I pretend that I'm okay
I feel that nobody will care
I touch the necklace you gave me
I worry that you won't come back
I cry because you left me alone
I am hard to love

I understand I can be a pain
I say I will try my best
I dream about finding someone who loves me for me
I try to be perfect
I hope someday I will be loved
I am hard to love

Maryha Rosas-Kirkman, Grade 8
Perry Middle School, IA

I Am

I am frustrated and confused
I wonder if anybody else can see it
I hear people judging and not even knowing a fact
I see the choices people make and their effects
I want to change it, but don't know where to start
I am frustrated

I pretend to not even notice
I feel the world coming down on me
I touch the thick coat of lies that are left behind
I worry that it will never go away
I cry at the sight of the mistreatment
I am frustrated

I understand why they do it
I say "Who cares?" but I already know
I dream of everything just changing
I try to speak up, but my voice just fades away
I hope that I work up the courage to scream from the mountains
I am frustrated and confused

Richie Paz, Grade 8
Perry Middle School, IA

Wild and Free

I am wild and free
I wonder how my day is gonna be
I hear the tweeting birds out my window
I see the orange cool sun over the hill
I want to run nonstop in the fresh morning breeze
I am wild and free

I pretend that I am a wild animal on my own
I feel like a predator when I am alone
I touch the land underneath my paws
I worry about being captured where I should belong
I cry when I lose the one I truly love
I am wild and free

I understand the meaning of life
I say stick to what is true to you
I dream of being with my brothers with faith
I try to stay true to who I am
I hope for life to be happy and joyful everyday
I am wild and free

Katelynn Humpal, Grade 8
Perry Middle School, IA

Still Dream Big

Even if they say you'll never make it
Still dream big
Even when people hate on you
Still dream big

If life gets rough and the road stays tough
Still dream big
If something stops you from making it
Still dream big

Sometimes it will feel as if you've failed
Still dream big
If you make a mistake, get up and
Still dream big

Once you've made it, and your dream comes true
Still dream big
The people that claimed you wouldn't make it, and
The things that tried to stop you, only made it possible for you…
To dream big.

Gage Welch, Grade 8
Perry Middle School, IA

Friend

Friend,
 You are a bright sunrise, gentle and calm,
  You bring warmth and light into my life and the day,
   Your vibrant golden glow is a light to the world.
    Your vibrance recites the joy and encouragement
     You bring to the dark sky and to life.

Adeline Vanderpool, Grade 7
Frontenac High School, KS

About Me

my hair is like an elegant sunflower
my fingers are like a ghost passing while texting
my mouth is like a drum beating back and forth
my heart beats like a snake would devour a rat
my eyes are like the deep blue sea
my skin is as white as a marshmallow being roasted on a campfire

Brooke Wegener, Grade 7
Whittier Middle School, SD

A Plane Home
Between two strangers
Through the air
Under the clouds
Toward the ground
Above the tarmac
On solid ground
Past the doors
Off on a car ride
"HOME!"
Ethan Masching, Grade 7
Whittier Middle School, SD

Life
When you weather the storm
It's not just something they say
But a legacy to live up to
For you don't count what you lost
But you'll feel what you gained
That pounding in your chest
Must never be strained
The strength within, you will always feel
For what lives inside, now that is real
Madeline Vanderfeen, Grade 7
Whittier Middle School, SD

Dreams
Dreams are like heaven.
Where we can do what we want.
Walking is like flying on a cloud.
You can't feel the ground under you.
You can walk right over the world.
With nothing left behind.
You take chances.
They can leave messes.
But you're strong enough to pick it up.
Shelby Vesely, Grade 7
Wisner-Pilger Jr-Sr High School, NE

Myself
M an
Y oung
S elf-confident
E qual to others
L eader
F riendly
Steven Martin, Grade 7
Olpe Jr/Sr High School, KS

Deer
Deer
Majestic, fast
Running, jumping, fighting
Animal that lives in the wild
Mammal
Joel Hill, Grade 7
St Francis Middle/High School, KS

The Winning Game
It's the last game of the season.
We are undefeated.
The net is a huge mouth,
Waiting for the ball to go tumbling in.
I am a forward.
It's my turn.
I sprint towards the ball, KICK!
It bounds towards the other end of the field.
I run.
My teammates follow, THUD!
I look back, and someone fell on the opponent's team,
Trying to stop me.
I grin.
My teammate passes the ball to me.
I am close to the goal.
I kick the ball.
It goes straight through the goalie's legs.
I am as excited as a kid at Chuck E. Cheese's.
My teammates run to me and give me high fives and slaps on the back.
I won the final game of the season.
Heather Vonnahme, Grade 8
Carroll Middle School, IA

That One Flower
I sit there staring at a flower not expecting much from petals and a stem.
The little bugs that crawl out from under each petal lie in the center covered in pollen.
The drips of water run down the stem as if it was a child going down a waterslide.
The sweet smell lingers around the flower like a honeybee and its hive.
On windy days the flower sways and on rainy days the petals wilt.
As I continue sitting in this meadow I'm comforted by the silence of each individual flower.
When I feel the flower, the stem has a roughness, but yet it's soft like velvet.
The soft suede-like petals overlap each other like an incoming tide.
Sitting alone in this field makes my senses come alive.
The honey-like scent can almost be tasted and the insects can be heard across the meadow.
One thing I noticed about this flower is it's different.
The colors, the shapes, the personality is vibrant.
The pinkness and ripples lie on each narrow petal.
The yellow pollen lays under the apricot-colored ruffles.
The dark forest-colored stem has thin thorns circling it.
The rest of the meadow contains white flowers like a daisy.
The centers are brown with orange seed like spots.
This one flower sitting in this meadow of millions is the one that caught my eye.
It doesn't care what the other flowers look like or how it's supposed to look.
It's one of a kind.
Madeline Cunningham, Grade 9
Mercy High School, NE

What Spring Is
Spring is the pitter-patter of rain as the ice is thawing,
The soft green of the flowers blooming,
The grass growing in the mud that rain leaves behind,
The sweet smells of the lilacs and daffodils you will find,
But it is also the singing songs of the flashy birds in the treetops above,
Their colors of yellow, blue, and flashy red and the duller, softer colors of the dove.
Talia Cunningham, Grade 7
Howar Jr High School, IA

The Crow
I am mad, that is all I feel
When I'm mad I see black like a crow so I kill.
Feathers falling everywhere, it soars high
I capture the crow I tell it no, but it keeps flying
So I put it in the cage where I cannot hurt

I feed it pain, it drinks the anger.
I try to kill it, but it grows stronger
Everywhere I go it crows loud to shut it up
I cover it up. Nobody knows the crow.

When the crow grows old it struggles for life
I must kill to keep it young so I go to my foe
I show my foe the crow he is scared.
I put the crow on his head as I watch it attack
Him then I realize he is dead.

Isacc Nickel, Grade 8
Tonganoxie Middle School, KS

Ode to Books
They whisper my name every time I am near
Calling for me to read them.
One glance at a book puts me in a trance
As if I am hypnotized.
Books take me to a place that no one dares to go
My own vacation away from home.
Their words so vivid and dear
Makes me want to never let go.
They make me feel many emotions
That can not be explained.
They are a part of me that no one understands.
Every flip of paper I flip
Tells me that my book is almost gone.
It is hard to let go
When it is time to go back to the real world
Where I belong.

Cameron Hart, Grade 8
Graettinger-Terril Middle School, IA

Beautiful Trees
The trees of summer big and green
Like the evergreen trees at Christmas time.
Housing for the animal families.
Big and small.
Chimps and squirrels.
Shade for all the things that need it.
Kids playing football in the warm summer day.
Trees tall, tall, tall. Way up in the sky.
Landing pads for sparrows and robins that tire in the blue sky.
Trees hardy and strong. Stand up to the powerful winds.
Of the mighty storm.
Trees of variety everywhere
In all places of the world.
Beautiful are the trees.

Jack Bakula, Grade 7
Lourdes Central Catholic School, NE

Closer and Closer They Come
Deep dreadful darkness surrounds me;
I stand paralyzed in the blackness,
And the walls start to close.
Closer and closer they come;
I feel my heart begin to race!

The walls reach out for me:
A newborn child reaching for its mother.
I want to move;
I want to scream,
But I feel as if a vacuum has sucked the air from the room.

Standing alone in the sea of black,
I start to panic:
Images of horrors and hauntings fill my mind.
I see myself being crushed by the enclosing walls —
The walls are still moving;
Their fingers grab for me…

Closer and closer they come.
I brace my hands against the walls.
It is all I can do to keep from falling,
And being swallowed by the darkness.

Kristy Ihle, Grade 8
Gilbert Middle School, IA

Evan Greenhorn
Simple as could be, but with a dark past, you see,
That golden hair swishing in the wind.
Hazel eyes stare you down, with both good and evil to be found,
In the moss where you lie.
His mother is shunned, his father condemned,
And only a girl can save him.
Great magical power, that grows by the hour,
For evil it may be used.
Half of his heart knows what to do, the other is pain enough for two,
And he ruins the one that may save him.
So old his child is gone, to hurt the child he was wrong,
She needed him so completely.
But his heart sees the light, his revelation is bright,
And he finally turns to good.

Hailey Neidig, Grade 8
Patton Jr High School, KS

Our Proud U.S. Flag
I hear America sing aloud,
   Loud and so proud
Standing on the mountain top,
   Watching the stars shine so bright
How proud I am for our U.S. flag,
   Red, white, and blue will always shine through
Together we stand our nation so proud,
   We honor those who sacrifice their lives
     To keep our freedom and our flag flying so high…

Kassidy Whitt, Grade 7
French Middle School, KS

Make-up
Why do you cover it up?
Why do you use that stuff called make-up?
Why don't you show who you really are?
Are you afraid to go too far?

Just show me who you are,
Without the powder and glitter.
Don't let the glitz and glam define you.

Why do we use it?
Is it to enhance our natural beauty?
Or to reassure us of ourselves?

It's tiring on the brain always
Trying to make those permanent scars go away.
I don't get it; you're the only one who sees it.
For it's within you, the damage that deceives you.

You're perfect just the way you are
So don't cover it up,
Or dare wear that stuff called make-up.

Cameo Rector, Grade 8
Wauneta Palisade Jr High School, NE

My Backwards Day
I blew my teeth and brushed my nose,
I wiggled my waffles and ate my toes.

I turned on the ice cream and licked the bathroom sink,
I sipped my book and read my drink.

I made the pool and swam in the bed,
I scratched my iPod and turned on my head.

I sat on the table and set the chair,
I braided my homework and finished my hair.

All in all, it was a backwards day,
I hope tomorrow is better, that's all I have to say!

Emera Gurath, Grade 7
Whittier Middle School, SD

Muggy
The lively sun beats down from above,
Soaking the lush green grass with its rays,
Putting the grass and trees in a daze.

The green grass glistens with the morning dew,
Just as the great ball of fire is about to rise,
And the darkness of the muggy night dies.

As a humid day is about to start,
You can sense the thick rain coming up fast,
And long sticky hours that sure will last.

Marie Wolf, Grade 8
Holy Cross Catholic Elementary School, NE

The Unknown
The moon will illuminate my room;
I'm no longer consumed by doom.
The night crawls up on me;
It's the time where my fear comes to be.

It's like the monster
Living under my bed.
My fear is a cave.
It's a fast, open nothingness that swallows the light.
Closing my eyes could never work.
It frequently follows me for light's not its friend.

Can I get rid of it?
To be rid of it is what I want.
But when nightfall comes,
It takes me under once again.

I can be surrounded in pillows
Or wrapped in blankets,
But as soon as the light turns off,
It takes me under once again.

Natasha Widdowson, Grade 8
Gilbert Middle School, IA

When the Wind Blows
When the wind blows,
Butterflies in the sky fly,
They flutter and play,
In the bittersweet wind.
When the wind blows,
Children play in the distance,
The echoes of laughter resonate in my heart,
It is ever so quiet and peaceful when the wind blows.
When the wind blows,
The light sound of traffic is distant,
The cars moan when they have to stop,
Only to get where the wind blows.
When the wind blows,
You can hear the ocean waves crashing,
The waves fear the thought of being alone,
So they ever play when the wind blows.
When the wind blows,
It is ever so silent,
I rest upon the grass,
Waiting for the moment when the wind blows.

Allyssa Williams, Grade 8
Patton Jr High School, KS

The Election
Red white and blue in the air
Houses and signs with an election filled care
A Saint Louis art museum is filled for a poll
George Cable Bingham is sure to win
It is a good day for a smile above the chin

Sam Haddican, Grade 7
Whittier Middle School, SD

High Merit Poems – Grades 7, 8, and 9

On Top of the World
On top of the world
Where the grass is always green
The weather is always perfect

On top of the world
Where you can think about anything, everything
Where you can see the birds soar

On top of the world
Where you can live like a princess
The houses are heaven above

On top of the world
Where there is no death, despair
You will have no worry, no doubt

On top of the world
Where you can love and be loved
No fear of being left alone

On top of the world
Where there are no drugs
No one is drinking, smoking

On top of the world
Where you can be yourself; you will never be judged.
Micaela Bretey, Grade 8
Carroll Middle School, IA

Vibrant
Mint green is the vibrant color
  of grass in June,
    and the savory smell
      of stew simmering away in the pot.
        It is the herbs in the garden
          and the rough texture of carpet.

    This color is the smell
      of the soil we tread on,
      and the relief brought
    by a crisp, cool wind
on a hot, sunny summer day.

Mint green is the smell we all know
  of freshly cut grass
    strewn across the lawn.
      It has the texture
        of melting ice cream, fresh
          from the freezer on a humid
            day of blistering hot temperatures.
          It is the heat of a
        spicy habanero in a world of
      bland, mild cheese and salads.
    Mint green is a vibrant color.
Spencer Carlson, Grade 8
Gilbert Middle School, IA

Little Fireflies
The fireflies are dancing into the starry night.
They act like deer prancing, flying with all their might.

The moon goes down and the sun comes up,
The specked light drowns except for the light in my cup.

I put it in my room where it is dark in there.
Keeping the light out of its doom because it's all I have to spare.

The dark appears and I look out my door
To see little bugs near, but there aren't more.

The fireflies aren't dancing into the starry night.
They don't act like deer prancing and they seem to have some fright.

I think I am the creep; I stole all their friends.
I want to cry and weep because it's time for this to end.

So, I go back into my room and find my little cup.
The light is in its doom, but its future is looking up.

I let the light go and the little light flies,
I won't say no, instead I will say goodbye, goodbye, goodbye.

My secret is out; I can see it in their eyes.
My secret is traveling about like little fireflies.
Kourtney Mead, Grade 8
Carroll Middle School, IA

Belly Gunner
The smell of the exhaust from the engine starting
This certain smell makes me nervous
As I know that soon we will take off
I will be doing my service.

Now I see our target
Our bombers are flying so low
I start shooting at the German troops
As the bombs start to flow.

Now German fighters come
I become filled with energy
I twist the turret towards them
And a bullet whizzes through me.

It's nothing much, it just hit my legs
But it also hits the suspension bar
Now I am terrified
The ground is so far.

By now I see our base
I can barely feel my feet
My crew mate opens the hatch to rescue me
When I hear Captain say "Mission complete."
Sean Riley, Grade 8
Perry Middle School, IA

Worry, Hope, Pray
Every time I hear a phone ring
I worry about her
Every time I talk to her
I hope I will talk to her for a while and she makes me laugh

Every time I listen to her
I worry about her health
Every time I think of her
I hope she is doing well

When the phone rings and it is
Not about her
I feel relieved

Every time I listen to her
I try to understand
Every time she comes to mind
I pray everything will be fine

Every time I look at her art
I admire her
Every time I hear her name no matter how hard I try
I can't stop thinking of her

I worry that it won't
I hope and pray that it will
Emma Mockler, Grade 8
Mazzuchelli Catholic Middle School, IA

Freedom
With 50 stars and 13 stripes
Standing proud of what I am
Staring down at children in schools,
Waving back at all the veterans who wave at me,
And flowing in the wind as the eagle passes.

I stand proud as soldiers march
Into the battle of blood and tears.

I am a symbol of Freedom,
As president after president passes
Through my home, I stand proud,
To show how honored I am
To be red, white and blue.

I get remembered all the time,
Especially on the fourth of July
Boom, the color and light
Explode, as everybody looks like me.

I get appreciated every day
In schools, homes, and offices.
People love me. I'm a star.
I am the incredible, respectable, irreplaceable American Flag.
Taylor Wangerin, Grade 8
Rugby High School, ND

The Circuit
Within a heart
There lies a circuit.

That circuit is what we rely on for life, for energy,
For blood.

What tells us when we are dead? Gone? Alone?
How do we tell where we end when we barely know where we start?
Questioning reality is only bound to bring biased opinions,
Based on the facts,

But never anything else.

Behold the hand,
The merciless grasp of hate
Leads us to the depths —
Where we are bound to only see darkness.

But in those depths we hear a musicians' play
Of a dulcet harp,
Fingers plucking the strings,

The sounds do not fade…and we listen…

All at once, we rise,
We break free of our dangers and our self loathing
And surface again into the circuit that was initially left open.

Mending the transparent tear in our broken hearts.
Dani Lipman, Grade 9
Valley Southwood Freshman High School, IA

Bullies/Victims
They believe that they have to
They are always hiding something
They never think to stop into someone else's shoes
They are scared of changing

We are always scared
They are a foot
Us like a bug being squashed
We're always paired
We're scared of changing

They are mainly older
They can't stand up to us
We smash and mash them like fodder
To us, it is a must.
They are scared of changing.

It seems like a million years before we get away
We are the mouse
They are like the cat
We are scared of changing
Sophia Wetta and Sammi Bates, Grade 8
Tonganoxie Middle School, KS

Forgotten Light
Shining so bright,
But always being covered
Never getting to move,
And never choosing the position
Expected to work,
At the whim of someone else,
So they can enjoy the shine
Attached to a greater power
That controls almost everything
It may seem unimportant
Forgetting its importance
All that it does
How it brings light to dark
Showing the way of what's needed to see
In the most fashionable way
And when it dies,
No one cries
It would just be replaced
Not even caring
All the beautiful light it brought
Just for everyone else
Margaret Lamphier-Meier, Grade 8
Perry Middle School, IA

Because of You
No words I write can ever say,
How much I miss you every day.
As time goes by, the loneliness grows,
How I miss you…nobody knows.
I think of you in silence,
I often speak your name.
But all I have are memories,
And a photograph in a frame.
No one knows my sorrow,
No one sees me weep.
But the love I have for you,
Is in my heart and mine to keep.
I never stopped loving you,
And I don't think I ever will.
Deep inside my heart,
You are with me still.
Heartaches in this world are many,
But mine is worse than any.
My heart still aches as I whisper low,
"I need you…and miss you so.
I love YOU."
Aubrey Foster, Grade 9
Palmer Jr/Sr High School, NE

Snowmobiling
Snowmobiling is fun.
It's fun to jump a drift.
It's not fun when you get stuck.
It's fun to ride the ditch with friends.
Carter Anderson, Grade 7
Graettinger-Terril Middle School, IA

Pearl Harbor
On the 7th of December,
is when we remember.
The chaos of that tragic day,
that took so many lives away.
The bombs flew overhead,
and left so many people dead.
The Earth stood still,
not a word was said.

Japan had us believe,
but we were deceived.
Bombs fly in the air,
the beginning of warfare.
Now we're in a ward,
and only the Lord,
can get us back together in one accord.
Now when the soldiers put on their armor,
it's all because of Pearl Harbor.
William Danze, Grade 8
Holy Cross Catholic Elementary School, NE

Girl Football Star
G ame at Jefferson
I mpossible they say
R eady to tackle
L ead the team

F air and responsible
O pportunity to score a touchdown
O pponent is scared
T each my players to respect
B elieve we will win
A wesome team
L isten to the coach
L ive young wild and free

S erious tackles
T eam appreciation
A ppreciate your team
R espect the other players
Megan Kohn, Grade 8
Jefferson Middle School, IA

Basketball
B uzzer Beater
A ssist
S core
K nockout
E astern All-Stars
T eam spirit
B etween the legs
A mazing
L ayup
L os Angeles Lakers
Weston Copperstone, Grade 7
East Mills Community School, IA

A Good Beat
Whenever you hear a good beat,
Two people will meet.
They might fall in love,
It just needs a shove.
For two people to feel complete.

It might be a small shock to see,
How this music can make people be,
So in love and without care,
Because of the smiles that they share.
It is music that made them so happy.

It's the music that got them on their feet.
The dance got them up to meet.
So now you know what to do.
In order to find a match for you?
All it will take is a good beat.
Sarah Jones, Grade 9
Chapman High School, KS

Music to My Ears
Fingers fluttering, flying, soaring.
Dancing on the keys.
Down and up, quickly, slowly.
Did you know your hands can sing?

They speak with anger,
They speak with joy;
It doesn't matter who you are.
The piano is their voice.

The notes carry themselves
Off of the music, onto the keys,
From the piano to inside of you.
Hear the melody's story.

It's music to my ears.
Hannah Thompson, Grade 8
Central Lutheran School, IA

Touchdown
At hut
To the ball
Past the scrimmage line
Through the lineman
round the linebackers
Near the corner
Down the field
To the end zone
Inside the 20
Against the wind
Near the end zone
Across the goal line
Touchdown
Jacob Koelzer, Grade 7
B & B Jr/Sr High School, KS

Shooting Star

As I hopped upon the gray and yellow car,
The ride attendant spoke, "You're on the Shooting Star."
My heart is a big bass drum,
duh-dun duh-dun duh-dun duh-dum.

The ride took off; I started to panic.
A strange man beside me says, "Why are you so frantic?"
Then he says to let it all out,
So I scream and shout all about.

As I screamed some people started to stare.
I think to myself, this isn't a typical county fair.
My magnificent mind is a mushy mangled mess.
I am still very very scared I must confess.

The brakes lock up and become stiff.
My stomach drops like a boulder off a cliff.
As the day comes to an end and I get in the car,
I say to myself, I rode the Shooting Star!

Garret Jensen, Grade 8
Gilbert Middle School, IA

Touch of Silver

Silver is soft starlight, singing sweetly in the night.
It is the spray of rainbows, thrown up by the sea.

Silver is the cold wind, that ushers winter in.
It is the shining snow, spinning to touch the ground below.

Silver is a reptiles skin, to cold, uncaring scales akin.
It is the night's full moon, peeking into every room,
Finding all hidden secrets.

Silver is a ceremonial blade,
Hollow dagger filed with poison,
Beautiful, yet so deadly.

Silver is the coldness, of ice that has yet to melt,
Binding the river's waters, to join it with the thaw.

Silver is the light, that illuminates the night,
Until the rise of the sun in the morning.

Bryleigh Janvrin, Grade 8
Gilbert Middle School, IA

Rosa Parks

Rosa Parks
Was thrown in jail
For standing up for what she believed in.
Inspiring a bus boycott
In Montgomery, Alabama
Around the year 1955.
Because she knew treating blacks with such disrespect was wrong.
Leading to a community of equal rights!

Skyelar Taylor, Grade 8
Morton Magnet Middle School, NE

Present Day

You are my history?
You are my future?
I have no answers.
The only answer I have is that you are my present.
My everything.
The only one that matters.
I do not worry about my future or history all that matters is now.
What happens now is because of the past.
What happens in the future is because of now.
The present is the most important time.
Thanks to you.

Alxis Peil, Grade 8
Jefferson Middle School, IA

Titanic

The giant monster floating through the icy water
Her enemy was an iceberg that fought her
Slowly, slowly sinking down

Screaming people scrambling for their lives
Few people jumped off into their demise
Slowly, slowly sinking down

So many peoples' lives were lost
This was such a tragic cost
Slowly, oh so slowly sinking down

Isaac Clark, Grade 8
Newell Middle School, SD

Syvia Perlmutter

Syvia
Brave, patient, young, survivor
Daughter of Isaac Perlmutter
Lover of family, safety, and home
Who feels hunger, hatred, and lost freedom
Who needs a real home, food, and freedom
Who gives love, food, and help
Who fears dying, losing family, Holocaust never ending
Who would like to not hide, eat a real meal, have life back
Resident of Lodz, Poland
Perlmutter

Isabelle Knight, Grade 8
Morton Magnet Middle School, NE

The Truth

COURAGE isn't asking a guy out.
BEAUTY isn't made with makeup.
INTELLIGENCE isn't knowing the latest trend.
LOVE isn't for shoes.

COURAGE is standing up for your beliefs.
BEAUTY is on the inside.
INTELLIGENCE is knowing what's right.
LOVE is for your family.

Emma Carper, Grade 7
Notre Dame Jr/Sr High School, IA

High Merit Poems – Grades 7, 8, and 9

Caught on Camera
My heart is pounding
I'm running through my dance
Making sure my technique is spot on
When I count and listen to the music
Then I walk onto the stage, with all eyes on me
My music begins so I can start my dance
Everything is going perfect
Then it is time to do my firebird
I jump up like a kangaroo then whack!
My foot hits my head, but I don't care
Since that means it had to be good
The dance is over
All of my hours of hard work, poof!
Gone in less then three minutes
I walk over to where our pictures are from our dance, and there it is
Toes pointed
Arms up and long
And back arched
My perfect firebird
Caught on camera

Katelyn Ryan, Grade 8
Carroll Middle School, IA

Never Return
Underneath the stars and the dark sky
When light fades from your hazel eyes,
Only then will I realize that words will not come to mind,
Now that I'm gone, I will never return for you
Never will you be mine, but my love will stay true,
I can do nothing but watch you cry,
Do nothing as you ask yourself why
Why you are now all alone and why I'll never return home,
I cannot return to hold you close and get rid of your fears,
But you know that I still love you,
I'll shelter you from your worst fears
Show my love to you in any way,
I wish I could love you every day
And stand exposed, out in the rain,
As I feel it eases away your pain,
We had the feeling that we finally cared,
About the ones you had affection for,
And finally, I can say that you swear,
That we had once achieved perfection,
But not anymore

Rebecca Dobson, Grade 8
Perry Middle School, IA

Dreamer's Dream
There is a dream, and there is a dreamer
A dream can end, and a dreamer can continue
A dream can last, and a dreamer can live
A dream can be there, and a dreamer can stay
A dream can succeed some, and a dreamer can succeed many
A dreamer can dream

Georgia Morse, Grade 7
Gretna Middle School, NE

For You, for Me
When I think of you,
What do I do I cry,
For you, for me.

When I don't think of you.
What do I do I laugh,
For you, for me.

When I see a dragonfly.
What do I do I smile,
For you, for me.

When I see a picture of you.
What do I do I wish,
For you, for me.

I cry because I miss you.
I laugh because I remember the times I had with you.
I smile because I love you.
I wish because I wish you were still with me.

Sarah Mockler, Grade 8
Mazzuchelli Catholic Middle School, IA

I Wish
I wish I could live forever and fly away.
I wish I could be a star in basketball.
Dribble better than anyone else.
I wish I could live in a castle with
Knights, queens, kings, and princes and to live there forever.
I wish I was a little kid again playing kid games.
I wish nothing mattered;
No drama, no nothing.
Everything would be great
I wish I had a ship,
To sail everywhere and see magnificent things,
Sail the world and have no worries.
I wish for peace and food for everyone, no poverty.
I wish to be strong.
At the top or bottom of my life like a mountain or a trench.
I wish to see those special people,
Who have gone to a better place.
One day I will…
So maybe I don't want to live forever
I wish the world to be just the way it is.

Shea Heidlebaugh, Grade 8
Rugby High School, ND

Family
F amily, people that we care about
A lways and forever, they will never leave you
M om, Dad, and little brother
I n a family, you are always one of a kind
L ove, is what a family is made of
Y our family, is your support in life

Meghan Riley, Grade 8
Notre Dame Jr/Sr High School, IA

Easy Days
Some people say their day was easy
Some people say it was hard
To me, there is no easy or hard
There are only challenging days
Every day you make choices
Those choices may not seem to matter
But to me, every choice is a big decision
Because what is ahead relies on that decision
You are challenged by every choice you make
You may not notice you are challenged
But you are
So the next time you think you are having an easy or hard day
Say to yourself…the only easy day was yesterday…
Ian Terry, Grade 8
Dallas Center-Grimes Middle School, IA

Friends
A lways are there for you

G o through everything with you
O ver and
O ver again
D o nothing to hurt you

F ight your battles with you
R emember all the good times
I nvite you to events
E ven when they're mad
N ever
D o you wrong
Logan Donald Wilson, Grade 7
Jefferson County North Elementary/Middle School, KS

Undefined
The most important thing
about this person
is that she cares about her family.
She is also a mother,
a sister, a friend, an advisor, and a giver.
But the most incredible thing about this person is —
Undefined
for all the great things she has done…
and will do…
This person is my mom.
Mykal Drosdal, Grade 8
New Town Middle School, ND

My Twin
Total opposites, yet the same in every way.
Dark to Light
Fire on Ice
Opposed yet unified
Sometimes my total opposite, but we are just the same.
Kieran, Yang to my Yin, always my twin.
Bralyn Wilson, Grade 7
Frontenac High School, KS

My Backwards Day
I ate my shower and washed my cereal.
I combed my clothes and put on my hair.

I pet my video games and play my dogs.
I read my water and drank my book.

I threw the chair and sat on my football.
I peddled my flag and waved my bike.

I typed my door and shut my laptop.
My day was backwards, I hope tomorrow is forwards.
Kacey Kubik, Grade 7
Whittier Middle School, SD

What Earth Is Made Of
The ocean is the tears God shed
The land is the bones of our ancestors
The wind is God's breath
The clouds, angels' gowns
The thunder is the voice of the Lord
The sun's as bright and beautiful as Mary
The birds of the sky are the flowers of heaven
The animals of the land are made of clay from the Earth
And we?
We are made from dust
And to dust we shall return
Molly McGuire, Grade 7
Blessed Sacrament School, NE

When I See You
When I see you I see everything
sometimes I want to go and hide
but sometimes I just smile
sometimes I laugh
I see that you are nice and caring
you are so hilarious
you are strong and when needed serious
you aren't immature like all the other guys
you are fun and outgoing
you are generous and sweet
I see that you are the perfect guy for me.
Grace Kramer, Grade 7
Jefferson County North Elementary/Middle School, KS

Freedom
It was the word.
The word Harriet Tubman lived by.
The Deep South.
Many slaves boarded one station there but never returned.
They escaped to the north.
Back in the 1800's
She led the train of slaves to freedom.
She was the conductor.
Harriet Tubman.
Trae Sampson, Grade 8
Morton Magnet Middle School, NE

Linsanity

The disappointing Knicks of New York were in a free fall.
Their record was 8-15 and they could not play solid basketball.
When 'Melo and Amare, the stars of New York, got hurt and couldn't play,
The city of New York needed a star to save the day.

Then out of nowhere came an Asian from Harvard called Jeremy Lin.
He was inserted into the lineup, and all the Knicks did was win.
They walloped the Nets of New Jersey and then thumped Utah,
Lin was a spectacular sight to behold, and many people came and saw.

Lin hung 38 on Kobe's Lakers and the Knickerbockers easily won.
After barely beating the T-Wolves, against Toronto, Lin hit the game winning three at the gun.
Nicknames sprang up: LINsanity, LINsational, unbeLINable!
Even players like Lebron and Kobe agreed he was legit and lovable.

After dropping a close game to the Hornets, they beat the NBA champs, the Mav's.
Now, Lin was a household name and a fantasy-basketball must-have.
The Knicks murdered the helpless Hawks by seventeen.
Lin is now New York's new basketball king.

After being added to the Rising Star All-Star Event,
We all know that Lin is meant,
To be the savior of New York. He raised the Knicks from inanity,
Thanks to a little bit of luck and a lot of Linsanity.

Nico Verdoni, Grade 8
Holy Cross Catholic Elementary School, NE

Whispering of the Trees

The sound of swaying and rocking of the light, almost white weeping willow surrounds my circumference.
The high-up and strong trees keep me hidden from the cold world and bring light into my world.
Trees allow me to be free from words of people and let my ears open to the words of life around me.
Leaning against a sturdy tree while I gaze at a beautiful never-ending forest before me
Trees support us when we need a roof over our heads and a place to hide
The circle of trees gives a reason to be inspired and a reason to love the Earth and take care of it
The taste of life takes me to another world where there is no judgment and there is freedom
The whispering of the wind through the branches gives new and bright ideas to the world
Lost, but not afraid of the proud standing forest before me brings great memories
The sound of a cardinal, then a flash of red, is all I see before the bird takes flight into the never-ending trees
No matter how small or tall the trees stand strong

MacKenize Stueck, Grade 7
Lourdes Central Catholic School, NE

My Bio

Hailey
Pretty, stylish, energetic, charismatic.
Sibling of Mason, Hayden, Grayer, Ryder, Weston, Easton.
Who cares deeply for friends, family and money.
Who feels sorrow when someone is hurt, rich when paid, and happiness when others are happy.
Who needs friends, love, and chocolate.
Who gives love, care, and a listening ear.
Who fears heights, fights, and robbers.
Who would like to see Mount Everest, Washington D.C. and the pyramids of Giza.
Resident of Sioux Falls.
Van Hull

Hailey Van Hull, Grade 7
Whittier Middle School, SD

The Crazy Color Crimson

Crimson is the ruby on a millionaire's ring
glistening majestically in the light.
It is the smell of ladybugs as they reach their demise:
a stench so strong it burns my eyes.

Crimson is the cardinal tweeting a beat
on the branch of a big green tree.

Crimson is the nose of a clown at the home of a young boy.
It's the boy's expression
when he gets a glimpse of the clown's face.

Crimson is the brick, rough to the touch,
which causes blood to trickle down my finger.
It is the sweet taste of Coke —
refreshing on a warm summer's day.

Crimson is the fire
whose dangerous flares burn down the forest.
It's the fire truck that saves the day.

Crimson: the tomato that is fresh,
similar to the sweet succulent scent of a citrus fruit,
eaten early on the breakfast table.
Crimson is the rose presented on Valentine's Day
which heats up the room with happiness.

Humza Firoz, Grade 8
Gilbert Middle School, IA

Fear Is a Scenario

Fear of the worst-case scenario
Goes through my head day and night.
Waking up and knowing you might not be here,
Seeing you every day relieves the worry.

Fear of falling with no one to catch you
Knowing that you may never rise again.
But there is that one person there to help,
To reach out to help you get back to your feet.

Fear of the worst-case scenario.
It bothers everyone in the world.
Some can conquer it, other perish.
Love is just one of those scenarios.

Fear of falling is like breakups,
Breakups make people fall but climb right back up.
Some take it harder and need help.
Some get it…others do not.

Fear of falling goes through my head,
Like veins in all of our bodies.
The fear rushes through like blood every second,
Every time you fall, get back up and lose that fear.

Trevor Longie, Grade 8
Rugby High School, ND

Tebow

Standing on top of Mile High
Breathing in the cool breezy air I give a sigh
Just remembering that one night
Where I did give up the fight

The team that everyone expected to show
Went home early in the winter snow
But going against Brady
Makes me feel almost shady

Praying on my knees
I hope someone will find me
I swear I can stand out
Trust me I will shout

I will succeed, please trust me
The hope I bring will set you to your knees
But I did meet that one set
The set that trust me, because now I am a Jet!

Chance Sturgeon, Grade 8
Carroll Middle School, IA

Nephew

I never thought I could feel so much love.
He is my little bundle, sent from above.
He is only one; he is only one year old.
There are so many stories, so many stories to be told.

He has smooth, pale, white skin, and lots of blonde hair.
He is such a brave little boy; he'd do anything you dare.
When I tell him I love him, his smile's the biggest you could see.
He doesn't understand words, but I know he understands me.

He went from sitting, to crawling, and now he walks a lot.
He'll do anything we teach, he's done everything we've taught.
When he walks, he trips, he truly trips a lot.
You'd think it would hurt, but I guess not.

This little guy has affected my heart.
I hate it, but, we always must part.
When we do, he kicks, he screams, always the same cycle.
But I really love this guy, Roman Michael.

Ashtyn Gilmore, Grade 8
Perry Middle School, IA

Swimming

Swoosh, swash, swoosh,
through the water I sail,
with others trailing behind,
I'm in the front with no way to lose,
But what should I do, if others try to pass me,
So I look behind and see no one behind me,
And realize,
There was no one else but me, so I can't lose this race.

Travis Steffens, Grade 8
Jefferson Middle School, IA

Summer

Summer is time for fun,
Just time to lay in the sun,
Time to hang out with friends,
Go shopping and enjoy an awesome trend.

Molly Wingert, Grade 7
Shelby County Catholic Schools, IA

Eagles

They fly and soar
They're symbols of us
Watch them feed their baby birdies
Love them

Reece Garriott, Grade 7
Olpe Jr/Sr High School, KS

Horse

Fast and elegant,
You remind me of a jet,
Moving with precision,
I wish you would live forever.

Joel Miller, Grade 7
Olpe Jr/Sr High School, KS

Snowman

Cold, white
Swirling, moving, molding
Forming to a person
Snowman

JR Landenberger, Grade 7
St Francis Middle/High School, KS

Night Time

Bright, big
Gleaming, shimmering, shining
Fills the sky with light
Stars

Danielle Frink, Grade 7
St Francis Middle/High School, KS

Clouds of a Rainy Day

The clouds are heavy
The look of darker colors
Hoping it will rain

Makayla Rogers, Grade 7
St Francis Middle/High School, KS

Lion

Stalks the tasty prey
Chasing the prey all around
Roars for victory

Carl Fabre, Grade 8
St Francis Middle/High School, KS

Leaf Life

I started out as a bud
By Summer I'm a healthy green leaf
Once in a while it gets really windy and my brothers and sisters fall off
But I hang in tight
Months go by, and I don't change
Not till September comes around
My brothers and sisters turn red and yellow, It must be fall
By mid-September I start to change
I change to a really pretty yellow
It's Halloween and I'm still on the tree
Its November now, and I'm on the ground
A little girl sees me, She thinks I'm beautiful
She takes me to her home and leaves me on her table
Where her mom finds me and throws me outside
A big gust of wind blows me away
Far away...From my home...The little girl
There's this white fluffy stuff falling from the sky
It buries me
Its Dark...
Cold
Where am I?

Rachel Sullivan, Grade 8
Charles City Middle School, IA

Being the Best!

Someone will pick the best,
And that will be you!
You will be the lucky guy, narrowing the gap between people who do nothing
And those who go off the road.
It's time to get smart and pull more than just your own weight —
Heads will turn when you strive to be your best.
Introducing the new guy, who decided to be a part of history.
Isn't it time you stepped up?
Be fantastic!
When shooting for gold, kicking butt is mandatory,
Taking names is optional.
And remember,
You can't have too much glory.

James Reiners, Grade 9
Boone Central High School, NE

Discovery

It's an innovation the innovation of moving forward to new heights.
The movement of progress that keeps our minds moving forward.
Ever since this man has soared to new ground tamed the wild with the iron beast.
Those not moving forward will fall behind.
But it has been used for terrible innovations.
It's a disgrace that man must live in fear because of the fission of an atom.
Or the vaporization of terrible agents or vicious microscopic soldiers that pick no side.
Because of this man is pulled apart because of different ideals values and beliefs.
This is madness when will the slaughter end!
It's also given us the miracle of curing the deaf dumb and blind.
It's stopped the hand of nature from smiting us down.
What will discovery do next.

Virgil Warren, Grade 8
Jefferson Middle School, IA

To Be

Talk, but not too much.
Listen, but let your voice be heard.

Learn, but be content with what you know.
Strive, but don't push yourself too hard.

Know, but always seek more wisdom.
Be patient, but don't let others control you.

Be independent, but know your limits.
Be amazing, but know that you're not perfect.

Cry, but don't let it define you.
Fear, but laugh in the face of death.

Be incredible, strong, caring, sensitive, careful, gentle.
And above all, be yourself.

No strings attached.

Kristin Sheridan, Grade 8
St Gerald Catholic School, NE

The Beautiful Rain

Let it pour, all of the rain
Give me more, don't let it drain
Please forget, all of the anger
While I regret, most of the wager.

All I ask, is let me go play
And mask all of the pain
I need hope, and I hope it starts raining
But nature says nope, and it starts hailing.

As the ice falls, I run inside
And wish for silent walls, I hide
Hiding does not help, as my eyes close
Falling into a deep sleep, as I sleep, I have a rose.

The rose grows, as I snore
The rose flies, asking for more
The great calm, how I wish you would show
Waking in the palm, now I know.

Devyn Olnes, Grade 9
Boone Central High School, NE

Sarah

It's the end of the day
and all is calm
some have forgotten
but you still live on
in the lives you have touched
in your own special way
those people will remember you every single day

Sonya Harwood, Grade 8
Dallas Center - Grimes Middle School, IA

Trees

I hold up my arms to get shade.
I wave to all my friends in the wind.
Trees, birds, squirrels are my best friends!
Squirrel and I love to have lumber parties!
I shiver when the wind hits my skin. Brr!
All year round I wear a brown dress.
In the fall I like to shed my fingernails.
Before I shed them I love to paint them bright orange and red!
My favorite drink is Sunny D.
I may make scary sounds at night,
but it is probably just me and squirrel
having fun!

Krista Ott, Grade 7
Wisner-Pilger Jr-Sr High School, NE

Maya Angelou

Maya Angelou is her name
Always being creative
Youth role model
Arch in my back and the sun in my smile—Phenomenal Woman

A dream within a dream
Never doubts anything she does
God given talents, a blessing to many
Encourager she is
Loving and courageous her poems express
Optimistic believes in everything she does
Understanding to society and its problems

LaTeya Broadway, Grade 8
Morton Magnet Middle School, NE

World's Wonders

I stop and listen, it is all around.
The movement of the Earth, vibrant colors and sounds.
Every breath I breathe, is brilliant fresh air,
And I see all the great things, as I try hard not to stare.
And leaves on the trees rustle, and the birds chirp proud.
Some pretty little quiet things, but some very loud,
Like the roar of the thunder, in a frightful storm,
Or the crackle of the fire, soft, soothing, and warm.
The cool chilly breeze flows through my hair.
The moon and the Earth dance, the loveliest of any pair.
This is a beautiful world, but not everyone can see
All of its wonders as well as they may be.

Josie Noll, Grade 8
Jefferson County North Elementary/Middle School, KS

Questions

Who wishes and hopes for straight A's
What is life like after high school
When do the aspects in one's life begin to change
Where will I end my path in life
Why are the questions always endless

Mariah Beikman, Grade 9
St Francis Middle/High School, KS

Lifting the Black Veil

I wander along, lost among the trees
When a mirage of light looms indistinctly,
But all too soon the light fades and leaves me alone —
Alone, alone in the dark,
Somberly swaying in the wind.
I look and listen; I see and hear nothing.

The obscurity of the place welcomed me,
So secret and isolated that not even the crickets chirped.

I carefully place my steps on the rough land, wary of the tree roots;
Despite my care, I stumble and fall,
Scraping my knees on the dirt.

Returning to my feet, I trek onward.
Coming to the glade, opening to the sea,
The murky water gloomily glowing without the moon,
Silently, I sit and stare.

Amazed at my insolence, I realize everything:
The waves gently lapping the cliff,
The moon and stars shining like bright shining light bulbs.

I look and listen; I see and hear everything.
Nick Greiner, Grade 8
Gilbert Middle School, IA

The Social Court

All of my decisions
I try to make on my own,
But it's hard when there are people
Staring, glaring, and caring,
Like it's their own life and they know what's best.

I see my friends;
They don't have a care in the world,
But I wonder if they worry
That people think badly of what they do,
And we all know that people will find our imperfections,
But how can we ignore those people?

Some people gossip for fun;
Some people gossip when they're jealous.
When they run out of things to say,
They sit around like flies on the wall
Waiting for something to happen
So they can go gossip more.

People think it's hard to ignore them,
But it's really easy if we try;
And when we accept ourselves,
Everyone else seems to disappear.
Kiersten Carter, Grade 8
Gilbert Middle School, IA

Coming Up Short

Gold is what I strive for, yet all I get is this.
It is the color of second place.
No one wants to be around it;
It's the weird kid in school.
This is what I get, even though I try my best: silver.

If I don't want to succeed, silver is great.
Average and sub-par are silver.
Extreme eminent excellence is what I want.
Why would I want to be minimal when I can be outstanding?
Silver is a homeless person.
Who wants to be in their sopping substandard shoes?

The color of jealousy: when I receive it, I cringe.
I want to be like the golden kids;
I don't want to be silver:
The color of "could have been and done."
I could have done better, but I didn't.
People who do better than silver, I envy.

Silver can also be improvement;
I know I can do better than silver.
Silver is telling me that I am almost there.
Motivation is silver; who tries for second?
Austin Graber, Grade 8
Gilbert Middle School, IA

Battle Colors

Red is the color of a battle raging,
and the sound of drums blaring
to show the strength of the Republic —
Its red-striped flag so gallantly streaming
And the bloodstained ground
on which the soldiers march.

The way they clash and batter is a ship crashing,
but only one will be the victor.
This is the sound of gunfire
and bodies striking the ground.
Red is the color of death.

But red is also sacrifice —
and a battle can't be won without sacrifice.
While the war rages,
red brings the battle to an end.
Red is a nation's sacrifice to bring about something new —
something greater and better.

Red is the taste of victory
with all that has been spent.
And with the thoughts of the taste of sweet apple pie,
red is the color waiting for the soldiers back home.
Jonathan Mennecke, Grade 8
Gilbert Middle School, IA

All Him
All him
His warm sweet laugh
His warm perfect green eyes
Too bad he has to go away
Why him?

Kylee Smith, Grade 7
Olpe Jr/Sr High School, KS

Free
If I were a bird
I'd fly so not a soul heard
Lift off, ever so gracefully
Flying wherever my wings will take me
Free

Jenna Williams, Grade 8
New Town Middle School, ND

Finding Treasure
After lots of digging
Under the sand
Inside the box is the gold
From more digging, we find the key
Money!

Zac Dial, Grade 7
Whittier Middle School, SD

Track
Track
Sorrow, victory
Competing, sprinting, jumping
Trying hard to come out on top
Running

Sophie White, Grade 7
St Francis Middle/High School, KS

Rain
When it rains,
it is like a whole
bunch of random words
falling from the
Sky.

Helena Schulz, Grade 7
Wisner-Pilger Jr-Sr High School, NE

Rain
Rain
Pouring everywhere
It won't stop till it's done
Watch out, a flood will be coming
I run

Kristy Tift, Grade 7
Wisner-Pilger Jr-Sr High School, NE

Flowers
Tulips and daisies, roses and orchids
Flowers blooming all around
They open their petals to the bright morning sun
Stretching like athletes before a big game
Flowers are springtime happiness and love
They say the words we keep in our hearts
A perfect gift, a pretty sight
Flowers awaken the soul, show it the morning light
Colors that remind me of a better time, full of people all unique
Flowers are my childhood garden, growing beside my house
They are the gift for Mommy
My favorite thing about flowers is the petals, scent and sympathy.
Flowers open a window and let out the gloom.
They release the sorrow in our hearts and make room for more memories.
Flowers always accept you, always remember too
And even though they wilt and die,
You can still remember their happiest time
Flowers are people, in a sense
They show a time of growth, a time of perfection, a time of fading away.
Flowers still have dignity and all things they were, in the beginning…
Flowers will always remain true and real to me.

Aly Crow, Grade 8
Chadron Middle School, NE

A Lifesaving Creature
massive and superior
continually shining above the world
every shape and color, every size and scent

giving hope and delight, never harmful or foul
always making me at ease and giving me endless bliss
in no way the same, always natural, strong, and proud

a forest mystical and hidden, keeping secrets yet to be discovered
trees are lifesaving, letting one expand their imagination to new levels
thanking mother nature for giving such magnificent creatures

giving a canopy, shelter from the outside world
supplying sweet, delicious fruit
always sprouting anew
full of peace to the world and keeping it calm

Maggie Funke, Grade 7
Lourdes Central Catholic School, NE

I Hear the People Singing
I hear the people singing, the different voices I hear,
Those of fathers singing over their baby girls' heads,
The pastor singing in his church as he praises his Lord on high,
The mothers singing bright and rue as she cares for her little children,
The policemen singing as they stand by their cars after working hard,
The teachers singing as they spread their knowledge throughout the classroom,
The children singing as they play and dance and shriek,
The firemen singing as they hose down terrifying fires,
Each person singing loud and clear for themselves and only themselves.

Grace Cole, Grade 7
French Middle School, KS

High Merit Poems – Grades 7, 8, and 9

Down in the Deep
Down in the deep where the coral grow,
Where sharks come out and say hello,
Where the angler fish uses his light
To attract fish, so he may have a bite.

Down in the deep where jellyfish swim
In light that is only but dim,
Where dolphins play and dance about
And are never tired to show off tricks, no doubt.

Down in the deep where starfish cling
To rocks either dirty or clean,
Where schools of fish hurry around
Busy as cities on solid ground.

Down in the deep where oil spills,
Where trash and pollution builds,
Where fish have lives (like me)
And where only we can save the sea.
Sophia Tompkins, Grade 7
St Mary's Academy & College, KS

Untitled
Nothing's real in this blank boring building
The only reality in this place is conformity
When you're different, you're an outcast
And friendships never last

When you walk in this building everyone wears a mask
Most are painted on to hide nothing more then insecurities
Very few are actually hiding pain
Pain that is so bad that there is nothing to gain

In this place everyone is fake
The only viewpoint most people have are the ones of their masters
Not an original thought in this place
The only goal here is to win the popularity race

I wish people would be real here in this dark dank place
But the only people that are considered real are the fakes
No one ever challenges the status quo here
Maybe it's because of fear
Sierra McCullough, Grade 8
Carroll Middle School, IA

Music
The one thing that gets me through everything
the thing that brings people together
that thing that separates us
the one thing that is able to narrate my life
it has no color it has no scent
people make it, people buy it
like air you cannot see it, but you hear it.
Heather Zaccardi, Grade 8
Chadron Middle School, NE

The Sounds of American
I hear America singing, the varied sounds I hear.
The bouncing of the basketballs on the rough wooden floor,
The swooshing of the net after a made basket.
The cheering of the crowd after a touchdown, whoooh!
The smashing of the football onto the ground after a touchdown.
The blowing of the vuvuzelas during the World Cup
The booting of the soccer ball into the net.
The clinging of the bat after a home run,
The happiness of the fan after catching a home run ball.
Each sound is what it means to you and no one else.
The sounds of American will continue to go on and on forever.
I hear America singing, the varied sounds I hear.
Kyle Rice, Grade 7
French Middle School, KS

Summer Days
Birds chirp and the leaves sway
Flowers bloom and cars honk
Newspaper boys cruise down the drive
Bumblebees buzz working hard all day long
The Sun burns hot, fighting gravity
The wind whispers softly and the parties blare loud
A child's laughter rings out clear
Bangs and booms blast out almost deafening
Clean crisp cotton sheets wave gracefully in the breeze
The pool offers a refreshing break from the blazing heat
Campfires smoke and marshmallows turn golden
Then the world sleeps and all is still
Ashley Florer, Grade 9
Norris High School, NE

Grandparents
G reat
R esponsible
A lways helpful
N ice
D ear to all
P olite
A mbitious
R eady to help
E ager
N ever say no
T hankful
S miles for everyone
Trevor Friedlein, Grade 8
St Mary's Immaculate Conception Catholic School, IA

Life Won't Wait on You
Who is going to save you?
What can they even do?
When are you going to leave?
Where are you going to stay?
Why are you waiting for life to happen to you?
Echo Jones, Grade 9
St. Francis Middle/High School, KS

Egg

An egg is like a heart.
Can crack at anytime.
You don't know what will come out.
It could be good or bad.
The stuff inside is like Jello.
Solid and slimy
Never moves
An egg is like a heart.
It can easily fall apart.

Jayda Oligmueller, Grade 7
Wisner-Pilger Jr-Sr High School, NE

Harriet Tubman

A slave that escaped
An old black woman
Conducted the Underground Railroad
A secret slave trail
Hidden from the eyes of racism
In the days of segregation
Risking life and limb
To save other slaves
Her brothers and sisters

Sam Vinogradov, Grade 8
Morton Magnet Middle School, NE

Greene Field

Open, green
Game day
Late in the afternoon
Crowd cheering, pads crashing
Quarterback throwing,
Defensive lineman tackling
Running, catching
Next fall
Tired and exhausted

Lane Hobrock, Grade 8
St Francis Middle/High School, KS

Insect

Insect
Peaceful, beautiful
Fluttering, landing, rising
Climbing high into the big blue sky
Butterfly

Katie Schmid, Grade 7
St Francis Middle/High School, KS

Earth

Birds chirping,
Plants blooming,
Just as spring sets in.
As the weather is changing,
The clouds sinking,
Silently into the sky.

Joshua Gormley, Grade 7
Blessed Sacrament School, NE

She

She made everyone smile all the time.
Whenever you saw her, she would have a smile on her face.
Her smile could make anyone smile;
It was a beautiful, genuine smile that had the ability to instantly light up a room.

She was a joy to everyone.
She had such a positive outlook on life.
No matter what, she could always cheer you up.

She was amazing at basketball; her defense was the best I've ever seen.
It is because of her that defense is my favorite part of basketball.

She was the nicest person you could meet.
Nobody could have hated her; there was no possible reason to.

She was a blessing to her family and they always came first in her life.
They loved her so dearly and will continue to their whole lives.

Her name is Mariya Tate Bernhardt.
She may not have known me personally, just only my name.
But that doesn't matter.

She passed away due to a terrible tragedy.
She has and continues to inspire me in so many ways.
She lives on in our hearts today, and always will.
She will never be forgotten.

Ashley Schmaltz, Grade 8
Rugby High School, ND

The Sea of Faces

Staring, watching, staring, watching.
I look up only to see hundreds of eyes burning through me like red hot spikes.
They're waiting for me to do something, waiting for me to say something.
I stare down at the pillar in front of me, the crumpled piece of paper giving me little comfort.
What do I say; what do I do?
I look back down, but the words are just a scribble on the paper.

I start to speak, but the words mean nothing.
They are meaningless sounds droning on and on.
I am going, struggling to remain calm, the sea of faces never looking away.
Panic shrouding what is happening, I look down at the paper, but I've lost my place.
What do I do now; what do I say?

I desperately scan the pages slowly, trying to find my place.
I'm trying not to drown in the pressure;
I'm trying not to drown in the sea of faces.
Soon I find my place and keep pushing on.
Now I'm constantly checking my paper for help when I get stuck.

Finally, I look down at the paper only to see that I just finished my last point.
When I look back up, the crowd starts yelling and clapping.
I realize then that they're cheering and whistling for me.
At last I step off the stage; I'm finally done and I survived.

Simon Taylor, Grade 8
Gilbert Middle School, IA

High Merit Poems – Grades 7, 8, and 9

The Sunset

The sunset is a glorious sight
A rainbow of colors in the sky
Soon we will be without light
The sunset is a glorious sight
Before we know it will turn into night
The day has gone by in the blink of an eye
The sunset is a glorious sight
A rainbow of colors in the sky

Margaret Kratz, Grade 8
Jefferson Middle School, IA

Softball

S liding to home base
O uts
F ield the ball
T eam
B ats and balls
A nother team
L eft field catches the ball
L et's go to home base

Hailey Derrickson, Grade 7
Graettinger-Terril Middle School, IA

Harvest

H aving fun in the field
A marillo sunset
R otary combines
V ery busy time of the year
E astern sunrise
S itting in the cab
T aking the combine another round

Kort Von Ehwegen, Grade 7
Graettinger-Terril Middle School, IA

Kids

Kids run and play
They scream and yell
Kids are sweet and innocent
They get mad and throw tantrums
Kids learn and grow
They think they are the center of the world
Kids are kids and you will always love them

Meggan Pfeiler, Grade 8
Jefferson Middle School, IA

Underground Railroad

Slaves only escape
Follow the drinking gourd
Kept the North Star in sight
Hid during the day
Walked at night
Ran for their lives
Don't let them catch you

Corey Gepson, Grade 8
Morton Magnet Middle School, NE

Love

Love is a special thing,
It is a very powerful thing,
It is the most strongest feelings you can have for another person,
You can't help the feeling,
Once you love them, it's hard to stop,
Love can make you do things that even make you wonder why you did them,
Love can really hurt at times,
But yet it can be the best thing that ever happened to you,
Love doesn't always last forever,
Love is a natural thing, you can't put it together,
It has to come naturally for it to be true love,
Love is the most beautiful, precious thing in the world,
It can make you go crazy, love will always be there for you whenever, wherever,
You should love someone for what they are like on the inside not by what they look like.
So, you can find someone to love you, but there is only one person, your soul mate,
Who honestly, truly loves you for who you are.
If they truly do love you they will always be there for you.

Macy Grannes, Grade 7
Dallas Center-Grimes Middle School, IA

Just Because

Just because I'm short
Doesn't mean I'm inferior,
Doesn't mean I'm not feisty,
I am not a midget.
I am not a dwarf.
Just because I'm short,
Doesn't mean I won't find a way to reach the top shelf.
Just because I'm short,
Doesn't mean I'm small in heart,
I dream big.
I am strong.
I am a Limbo champion.
Has it ever been proven that short people were of less heart than the tall?
Did David not slay Goliath?
I am David.
I may be short,
But there is nothing I can't do!

Allie Johnson, Grade 8
Chadron Middle School, NE

The Beauty I Have Come to Know

In 1872, J. Sterling Morton had a brilliant suggestion for us to pursue.
To plant trees for beauty, shelter, food, and O2.
He will never know the lasting effects which generations from now will come to enjoy
Years go by and the trees seem to touch the sky.
I lean back and take in the beauty with a sigh.
Families gather for a day of fun,
Hide-and-go-seek through the trees as they run.
Under the oak trees we find shelter from the wind, and stand close to it like an old friend.
Nothing can compare to nature's way,
Forests, green, and tall
Free entertainment is there for all

Victoria Gress, Grade 7
Lourdes Central Catholic School, NE

Face to Face
Six legs slowly scuttle across the floor.
Shivers slink down my back.
It stops in its tracks;
I do the same.

We seem to sense each other:
We are like the prey and the hunter.
We turn face to face;
Neither one will blink.

So small a shoe could squash it,
But I am too afraid.
We are like the prey and the hunter:
If I kill it, I would be the hunter.
At the moment, though, I feel like the prey.

My throat feels dry:
I'm too afraid to scream.
It seems to realize my fear;
It seems to know I won't hurt it.
The small creature turns and leaves.
I stand still, frozen with fear.
Emily Koenig, Grade 8
Gilbert Middle School, IA

Writer's Block
I cannot think.
I cannot write.
No poetry will come to mind.
What should I do?
What should I say?
Must I work on this all day?
No poetry is coming.
No thoughts are coming through.
This is not good.
This is not grand.
This writing's starting to hurt my hand.
When can I stop?
Should I give in?
No words are flowing from my pen.
But then...what's that?
It cannot be.
I think I'm writing poetry!
Here I go.
It's coming fast!
Thank goodness, I'm done.
At last!
Natalie Jabben, Grade 7
Pioneer Trail Middle School, KS

Basketball
Racing down the court
Looking for the open shot
Feels great scoring two
Kylie Sherlock, Grade 8
St Francis Middle/High School, KS

A Mountain Man
My life is being a mountain man.
Living day by day,
Huntin', trappin', fishin' and ridin'.
Being with nature.
The smell of the air makes you wonder,
What might be around that corner.

It gets lonely sometimes,
with only a horse to talk to.
It gets hard to stay sane.
You hear things all the time.

My life is being a mountain man,
I sure hope I can.
Matthew Kerner, Grade 8
Chadron Middle School, NE

Am I Found?
In your eyes I get lost.
In those seas turned and tossed.
I see the sun far above,
Calling me to my true love.
I see you ship clean and bright,
Throw me a line and I'll hang on tight.
Save me from this ocean's lair,
Before I sink to my despair.
Don't save me because I love thee.
But save me of thy love for me.
Tides are turning, winds are shifting.
In that sea still I am drifting.
Darkness creeping, billows roll.
What I have said bespeaks my soul.
Jonathan Ansley, Grade 8
Home School, IA

Set Free
Trying to hide my tears
Wondering if I can face my fears
I don't know what I'm supposed to do
Do I have to go up to you

I'm done trying to be somebody I'm not
Trying to get through the foughts
You try to tear me down
I'm not going to frown

Just step aside and let me be
Because I'm setting free
I'm ready to take on this flight
To a greater height
Hannah Patterson, Grade 8
Carroll Middle School, IA

Let Her Go
We walked down the aisle,
But not the good kind.
She won't ever leave my mind.
She didn't deserve this.

I want her back, but I can't.
I just have to face the fact,
That she is gone, and I'm alone.
She didn't deserve this.

Why did you take her?
She is a good friend, always will be.
She was all I had.
She didn't deserve this.

I'm a crying baby.
I don't want her to go.
I just wish it were us.
She didn't deserve this.
Brittany Behrens, Grade 8
Carroll Middle School, IA

War
War is never a spectacular thing
War is dread in my eyes
You may hear people bawling
Or maybe waving goodbye

When you hear the gun shot
It is ringing in your ears
But then you get to the spot
That is filled with fears

You know you are risking your life
For those who look at you
When you say goodbye to your wife
She won't know what to do

When you see the white flag waving
The war is now done
But then your body is aching
Even though you have won
Brianna Sigler, Grade 8
Newell Middle School, SD

Canyon
Scorching, breezy
During Spring Break, when it's raining
Late afternoon
Rattlesnakes hissing, motorcycles racing
Windmills, cows, ponds
Jogging, walking
Fourth of July
Tired and lazy
Philip White, Grade 8
St Francis Middle/High School, KS

High Merit Poems – Grades 7, 8, and 9

Wilting Rose
A wilting rose,
A broken heart,
A lost bouquet,
Loneliness overtakes the sweet smell,
The smell of his cologne,
The brightness of colors,
The happiness that passed,
Oh, why, has it left,
Why does it never last?
Izabelle McCammant, Grade 7
East Marshall Middle School, IA

Rosa Parks
Rosa Parks
Was an African American…
Who wanted equal rights
On the bus?
In 1955,
Arrested for not giving up her seat
Why?
Because she believed in equal rights,
Between all races.
Skylar Hedges, Grade 8
Morton Magnet Middle School, NE

A Heart
A heart tends to be tossed around
Without a worry or a care
Until it's broken
Beyond repair
You think there's no hope
For you again
But who knows what time
And a friend
Can mend
Amelia Reiswig, Grade 9
Goodrich High School, ND

What I Would Cook for My Teacher
Finger food salad,
Eyeball stew,
Bat brain sandwiches,
Rattlesnake venom soda,
Toenail clippings pie.
Taylor Shimitz, Grade 7
Whittier Middle School, SD

My Self Portrait
My hair is like gold
My eyes are like an endless hole
My fingers are like lightning
My mouth is like a shy mouse
My heart beats like pure determination
My skin is as tan as wheat
Skylar Chapin, Grade 7
Whittier Middle School, SD

The Essence of the Weeping Willow
The young, imaginative girl enclosed by a shelter of branches,
Inhaling the acute scent of the weeping tree's flowers.
Her sanctuary provided a utopia of unicorns
where fairies flew and bunnies bounced.
A palace, she was the reigning princess of her kingdom.
But before she could travel any farther in her fantasy,
a call came from her mother.
Reality restored,
but every day this cycle repeated.
The girl and time grew with the tree
as the weeping tree floated away from her mind…
But not forgotten.
Years later the same tree, larger and more dazzling than ever,
became visited by the girl again.
She caressed the jagged bark, once again inhaled the flowers.
The wind created a rhapsody of noises and songs that spoke,
"Welcome Back."
Marissa Galardi, Grade 7
Lourdes Central Catholic School, NE

Nevada
6-0 is our goal, 4-0 is our record
Nevada is our opponent, with a record of 4-1.

We are the tremendous terrifying Tigers, they are the cowering Cubs
I have the ball and I'm running down the sideline, trying to get to the end zone.

At the half, the score is 8-3; we're up, we kickoff and the momentum suddenly turns;
He had bright red hair that lit up like fire, he was running down the sideline.

We all held our breath, like a swimmer before he comes up for air
It looked like he was going to score; his foot landed on the line
The ref blew his whistle, we all could breathe
Like a swimmer bursting to the surface for air.

Another score for us, and it is 16-3
I felt great with two touchdowns
We had the game. It was over; we won.
Austin Barrientos, Grade 8
Gilbert Middle School, IA

My Life as a Cell Phone
I am no fortunate cellular calling device.
I get extremely tired and sore.
I must hear all your boring conversations.
You constantly punch me and cram me into your pocket.
My antennae is sore, catching all that reception.
My speaker wears out, asking politely for a command all the time.
Must I always go to the post office to send your messages?
I always play games for you, who insists that we play until you win.
Quit pushing my buttons all the time!
I keep track of all your friends and where they live. Use a phone book!
For once, can you just use my cousin, Telly Phone?
As you can see, I am no fortunate cellular calling device.
Sophie Glaubius, Grade 7
Wisner-Pilger Jr-Sr High School, NE

Moving On

One is gone, two is gone, now three?
Why is this happening to me
Serious sorrow surrounds my room
Half my life just went away in a big boom

I cry out to my Lord up high
Should I go where no living human has gone?
Should I seek for the unknown
I need to be shown

Stupid secrets kept from me
This disease is breaking up our family tree
I cry out to you oh Lord take me,
So I can be in harmony

It's time to move on so wipe your tears
No more need for pain and fears
Earth is my home that's were I'll stay,
Until I reach heaven's great gateway.

Gabi Howard, Grade 8
Carroll Middle School, IA

Bedtime

When I was young,
Going to bed was scary.
I would lie in bed
Tired and anything but merry.

I always wanted the door open;
If it was shut, they'd be trapped with me.
What if they got hungry in the middle of the night?
I could only wait and see.

I couldn't have any fingers or toes
Hanging out of the bed.
They could eat them
Or maybe my head.

Then I grew up
And realized they were gone,
But I still sleep with the door open
And my light on.

Emily Weber, Grade 8
Gilbert Middle School, IA

Treasure

Below the ground
Down by the river
Following the map
Beyond the forest
Against all odds, you find the X
Under the earth
Inside the chest, you see gems and coins
Unlike the others, you found a treasure chest

Jade Bolin, Grade 7
Whittier Middle School, SD

Me and You Apart

Me and you apart is like eating Skittles without tasting the rainbow,
Like eating a peanut butter and jelly sandwich without the bread,
Like eating cereal without the milk.

Me and you apart is like wearing shoes without socks,
Like bleeding without blood,
Like a body without bones.

Me and you apart is like baking brownies without an oven,
Like swimming in an empty pool,
Like living while you're dead.

Me and you apart is like breathing without lungs,
Like speaking with no voice,
Like walking without legs to keep you held up.

Me and you apart is like holding a pencil without fingers,
Like turning the page in a book with no pages to be turned,
Like riding a bike with no wheels.

Me and you apart is like walking on clouds,
Like eating once a year,
Like reading chapter 4 in a book with no chapters.

Me and you apart would be nearly impossible.
Our never-ending love is indescribable.

Meranda Schmaltz, Grade 8
Rugby High School, ND

Staying Strong

Before the grass is green
It is not yet spring
The leaves have already fallen
But there are no birds callin'

Frozen rain falls to the ground
It floats gently all around
All animals are asleep
And do not make a peep

This peaceful place is silent
And there is no violence
This place is so gentle
And every object is plentiful

This wonderland is like a desert
Full of frost and sleeping balls of feathers
This place is the Arctic
Cold and sometimes dark

But soon to come is Spring
To turn everything green
Unlike the Arctic, winter doesn't stay long
But until winter comes back, this place will stay strong.

Keegan Webber, Grade 8
Carroll Middle School, IA

High Merit Poems – Grades 7, 8, and 9

Here Now Gone…That Fast!*

He was here, now he is gone. Yes we expected it, but I didn't want to believe it. Heart broken, pillow filled with tears, heart racing, and not understanding why. Questioned faces, looking at me like I should have already been expecting it to happen, but for some reason I'm still heart broken.
He left April 5, 2012.

It had only been one day and he is still always and forever missed.
It seems like you can still hear that laugh that just lights up the whole room. We repeat the same words every Sunday night.
I would say "Bye Papa, I LOVE you; I'll see you next week."
And he would say back "I LOVE you too and I'll see you next week."
You never know what you have until it's gone. You laugh to keep from crying.
Bleeding on the inside, crying on the out, no one really knows what your life is all about. A week later he's gone!
No last hug, no last kiss, no last bye. No last…

I want to be happy and keep a smile on my face,
Because now he's in a better place.
There's no more pain, no more tears he has to shed,

All he has to do is lay at rest, peacefully.
Gone off this world, yes

But forever in our hearts!
I know for a fact that he doesn't want us to be sad, or morn and cry,

But he wants us to be happy and he wants us to know that we will all meet again when the time is right.
If he's happy I'm happy, because I know one day, we will see each other again and we will join hands in my father's house.
I cry no more tears of sadness, but I yet cry tears of joy.
So, not again until the end…

Na'Tori McNealey, Grade 7
West Middle School, KS
*R.I.P Papa, you're truly missed.

Dreamers

This is for the billionaire dreamers whose days are wasted away by lack of focusing.
Whose minds are running wild, even though they have a mountain of work piled high
Thinking that maybe one day they will become the next billionaire with all the fancy stuff
But in reality everyone knows it's just a bluff.
Keep dreaming
This is for the basketball dreamers who believe that they are a spitting image of T-Rob.
Even though they can't shoot a basketball to save their lives, they still try and impress their wives.
They wish their name would be on the back of the jersey that every child wants to wear.
And when they are practicing every time they mess up they try not to sear.
Keep dreaming
This is for the rock star dreamers who sing in the shower,
Even though they want their song to be sung on every music tower.
Without working towards their goal,
They want it to be handed to them in a silver bowl.
Wanting to be the next Miley Cyrus or Justin Bieber.
Keep dreaming
This is for the movie star dreamer who wants the new car
So they can drive a million miles away.
But they sit by the mirror in fear of thinking about their career.
Trying to get their heads together
So they can go out there and face the weather, keep dreaming.

Angela Faherty, Brynlee Robbins, and Cheyenne Ford, Grade 8
Tonganoxie Middle School, KS

Serenity

It's the color of serenity, as waves curl onto shore,
And light winds travel through the trees, ousted my open door.
It is the supple touch of cotton, and scent of morning dew.
A new start of the misbegotten, the shade that is sky blue.

it is a rain upon the street, with sidewalks damp and still.
The puddles splashed upon my feet, are sprays of sky blue chills.

I taste sky blue in sweet, crisp drinks, at any time of year;
I feel the sky blue skating rinks, on the ice, so smooth and clear.

I amble along the oceanfront; my toes in sky blue sand,
And find a seashell, worn and blunt, that's washed upon the land.

This hue is in the slick, smooth stones, enduring years of wear.
It is a feeling of it's own; there's nothing to compare.

I've yet to eye another shade as peaceful, pure or true
As the color of serenity; the color of sky blue.

Lydia Heydlauff, Grade 8
Gilbert Middle School, IA

Track of Anger

I was angry
I had to end it
The taunting had gone too far
I had to, I told myself

The good part of me was saying no
The bad was saying yes
I couldn't decide
The first berm coming up I got to make a decision

I got an idea
Pull the clutch in, let him pass
Follow behind get close to him
The rider turns, and I go straight

Boom!
I smash into the rider
We both hit the dirt
Revenge has gotten the best of me.

Gage Hendrix, Grade 8
Tonganoxie Middle School, KS

Fred the Flaming Ferret

Fred the Flaming Ferret fled to France
where he fought the flames of chance
one day Fred found he was on fire
the fire frightened him so
that it made him fly with fright
Fred the Flaming Ferret went home in the night
frightened by the fear of fire

Jared Pohlmann, Grade 9
Deshler High School, NE

I Wish

I wish I had a heart full of life,
I wish I had someone to like,
I wish I had someone who liked me the same,
I wish I had such great beauty like no other.
I wish I had a place of peace to go and stay.
I wish I had a wonderful life full of laughter and bliss.
I wish I had my own life where I could stay.
I wish I had a magic wand
To make all my wishes
Come true and worries go away.

Emily Lambrecht, Grade 8
Zion Lutheran School, NE

The Light

When all the light has been stolen away,
but the darkness refuses to come.
The people will be praying,
begging for guidance.
It will not come in a miracle,
but in a whisper.
Most will listen and follow.
Those who don't will be lost forever,
trapped inside this limbo until days end,
wishing for the day when the light had shown.

Tia Crail, Grade 8
Jefferson County North Elementary/Middle School, KS

I'll Wait for You

Time ticks away.
You're sitting in a chair.
Waiting for me.
You think of everything.
You think of everything we will do together.
But time is slow.
It is like a turtle trying to complete a marathon.
But yet you remain faithful to me.
Reminding me that
"I'll wait for you."

Mikayla Matteson, Grade 7
Dallas Center-Grimes Middle School, IA

Rosa Parks

Rebellious against segregation
Once helped Martin Luther King, Jr.
Started a boycott
Always respected the people she knew

Parks died October 24, 2005
Arrested for not giving up her seat
Raymond Parks was her husband
Known as a civil rights activist
She was born on February 4, 1913 in Tuskegee, Alabama

K'Lyn White, Grade 8
Morton Magnet Middle School, NE

High Merit Poems – Grades 7, 8, and 9

Football
On the field
Under pressure,
Through the air, the ball is flying,
Until it is in his hands
Between people, swerving
Across the line
TOUCHDOWN!

Josh Stirler, Grade 7
Whittier Middle School, SD

Planes
Around the world
Across the sky
Above the earth
Beyond the clouds
Until we stop
Aboard the plane
Whoosh!

Brendan Hansen, Grade 7
Whittier Middle School, SD

Swish!
Off a rebound,
Past the ref,
Beside the free throw line,
Between the players,
Beyond the elbow,
Underneath the basket,
SWISH!

Skylar Moen, Grade 7
Whittier Middle School, SD

Hunting
H ot or cold depending on the season
U nless you have a heated blind
N ot for the faint of heart
T urkeys gobble in the distance
I ntelligent deer hide in the woods
N atural instincts kick in
G reat shot, time for pictures

Kohl Prose, Grade 7
Olpe Jr/Sr High School, KS

My Mommy
You are my sky,
Speckled with clouds and stars,
So kind to safely hold Yin and Yang,
Endless with happiness and love,
Beautiful but sometimes dark and sad,
That's you mommy, my mom and my world

Kieran Wilson, Grade 7
Frontenac High School, KS

Winter's First Snowfall
Everyone is sitting in their classes
taking notes or doing homework.
We try to pay attention, but for some reason
it's an extremely hard task today.
Silence engulfs the school like a slithering snake;
no one is in the hallways or even talking
because, without realizing, we are all waiting —
Waiting for something.

The students who are lucky enough to sit by the window see it first:
small white specks sprinkled through the crisp air.
They are miniature ballerinas,
twirling and waltzing before delicately landing on the frozen ground.
It comes faster and faster;
everyone is out of their seats.
Teachers don't even try to make us return to our desks.
Our school fills with cheers
and then awed whispers as we are struck by the beauty of
winter's first snowfall.

Kyla Brandenberg, Grade 8
Gilbert Middle School, IA

It Sees You
Black is death, it has no boundaries.
It is night and day, the difference between life and death.
He's been everywhere; he has seen everything.
If walls could talk they would say, I don't know ask black.

It looks like a new sleek car. It smells like a new sleek car.
It is a robber staling, and methodically thinking. What they see, think, and even look like.

Black has no sound; he creeps along quietly, slowly, evilly.
Black is a ninja sneaking along. How you feel when you get yelled at, when people tease you.
It is not an external pain, it is within you.

You do not taste black, black tastes you.
Black is a black hole; it eats you up without any thought, chewing, chomping, crushing you.
We can look at it, and look at it, and still see nothing.
This so-called color can sense fear, and when it does, it strikes.
It is a shark; when it senses fear it attacks. Black is everywhere, and in everything.
You don't see it, but it sees you.

Jackson Breen, Grade 8
Gilbert Middle School, IA

The Singing of the Family
I hear the graceful singing of the family,
Those of the children, each one singing proud in the sun soft and smooth.
The mother singing as she puts the sleepy child to bed for the night,
The father singing his song as he readies for work, or leaves off work,
The grandparents singing stories to their grandchildren as wondrous tales,
The brother singing as he does school work, the sister singing as she relaxes,
The aunt's song, the uncle on his way in the morning, or at lunch or sunset,
The delightful singing of the mother, sweet and soft, calming for all.

Tristan Hobbs, Grade 7
French Middle School, KS

Unfavorable Crawlers

Eight long, agile legs swiftly scrambling
The dark abdomen is splashed with a red symbol
Venom flowing through miniscule veins.

Fangs, sharp like needles
When pricked, you're left with a rash.
Burning, itching, stinging, hurting
Carefully I stay away.

Long, lengthy legs crawl quickly, leaving little trace
The eerie feeling lurk around me
Goose bumps cascade my body
I turn around, left with an eerie feeling

I spot it on the blood red wall
I act swiftly, a sly fox hunting its prey.
Moving effortlessly with lanky legs
The lights go off
The darkness overpowers me

Crawling away, leaving me frightened.
Creeping along the corridor, I'm terrorized

I hear its leg nimbly running —
Like a grandfather clock
Tick, click, tick, click.

Michelle Lang, Grade 8
Gilbert Middle School, IA

The Blank Paper

It's time to try
To start working, I see
It's time to start writing
On the blank paper in front of me

My pencil is at the ready
My hand is so steady
But as hard as I try, I see
Nothing on the blank paper in front of me

The wheels in my head aren't turning
And my stomach starts churning
Because not a mark I see
On the blank paper in front of me

My eraser is worn
My paper is torn
But still nothing is written
On the blank paper in front of me

A light bulb pops on in my head
It goes away, the feeling I had started to dread
I begin to birth the amazing poem
On the no longer blank paper in front of me

Melissa Miller, Grade 8
Carroll Middle School, IA

Overrated

Eighth grade relationships are overrated:
They are unneeded train rides.
They won't matter in the future,
Yet people worry about them so much.
They are as pointless as endless complaints;
In eighth grade, dating relationships
Don't mean anything.
Two teenagers say they are in love
When really they are only involved
For the social status it earns them.

The "lovers" end up splitting;
Rumors ruin the relationship.
The relationships are like ticking time bombs
Just waiting to explode.
When they explode, nothing happens,
Showing that it wasn't true love.
Eighth grade relationships are overrated.

Sam Campbell, Grade 8
Gilbert Middle School, IA

The Squirrel

The fluffy orange squirrel leaps to the
Next post connecting the power lines
Like a tiger pouncing on its prey.
The speedy sly squirrel is determined
To get home to his extended family.

As he finds a shorter way,
He begins to wonder which way?
Slipping through the power box,
The squirrel does his best
To not touch a thing,
But he does connect with a thin smooth wire.
~ A sharp shock! ~

Though he lives no more,
Gilbert Middle School turns into a dark alley
And students leave school two hours early.

Aaron Rinehart, Grade 8
Gilbert Middle School, IA

Death

Death
Why does it happen
No one
Knows
Just the thought if it
Happening
Makes everyone
Scared
But life can't last
Forever
So cherish it while you can

Emily Pantle, Grade 8
Jefferson County North Elementary/Middle School, KS

Similes

The sky is blue like the ocean
Animals like humans
Living a life of love and hate
Every day hoping to find food
Some do, some aren't so lucky
They whimper like a baby waiting for food
God waiting on them
One by one they go up
Some go down
Ascending and descending

Kaden Henry, Grade 7
Wisner-Pilger Jr-Sr High School, NE

Rosa Parks

Rosa Parks
Was born in 1913
She wouldn't give up her seat
Because it wasn't really needed
They arrested her right there
For not knowing her place
After she was released
There needed to be a change
No one would ride the bus
They walked through sun, fog, and rain.

Sarah Drake, Grade 8
Morton Magnet Middle School, NE

Burning

The soft brim of rays
Swings to the horizon
Mimicking light.
It dances to shore
Waves its sweet petals
Onto the marshy greens.
Quickening its pace
Time runs short.
Pushing its heart to warm the waters
Is all that it longs for.

Mackenzie Thomas, Grade 9
Seaman High School, KS

Stay Strong, and Believe

Long ago, in 1940
Jews were scared
And ready to scurry.
They kept strong,
And did not give up.
Germans were undefeated,
But Jews still live on.
Some are living,
To tell their story
TODAY!

Taje'Nae Abram, Grade 8
Morton Magnet Middle School, NE

Wrestling Is...

a lot of hard work.
determination to succeed.
beating a person straight up.
not relying on anyone else.
six minutes on the mat pushing yourself as hard as you can.
a competition of strength, conditioning, and outsmarting your opponent.
being humble, yet confident.
like no other sport.

Tate Cullers, Grade 8
Chadron Middle School, NE

Adrenaline

The jet black curtains
Are a cloak of invisibility
Hiding the knots in my stomach
From the audience's wondering eyes.

The jet black curtains
Are opening faster than I wish
Revealing the oversized jury
Judging my every move.

The jet black curtains
Are my source of adrenaline
The only thing stopping me
From breathing steadily and easily.

The jet black curtains
Are looming like lanky shadows
Posing just one question
Will all go as planned?

Nick Day, Grade 8
Gilbert Middle School, IA

Loving God

When I rebel against thee,
You accept me
With your forgiving heart.

When I hurt thee,
You take me
With your healing hand.

When I refuse to look at thee,
You watch my way
With your caring eye.

When I use harsh words at thee,
You ease me
With your peaceful words.

Holy, son of God
When I hate thee,
You love me back.

Kingsy Devadass, Grade 9
Olathe South Sr High School, KS

Life Is Complicated

Life is complicated
And so is death,
It brings you down
Without any breath

Life is complicated
Like ripping steel,
It's your choice
To be open or conceal

Life is complicated
Getting around,
The many things
That brings you down

Life is complicated
Of the things you desire,
It is not easy
To get what you admire

Jonathan Reyes, Grade 8
Perry Middle School, IA

Finding a Cure

There are many types: brain, lung, skin.
When the cells divide
It devours your body from the outside in.
Finding a cure? People have already tried.

Anyone can have it,
But most people don't.
It can change your life forever,
Or end it altogether.

Boys can have it, so can girls,
The elderly, children, and middle-aged.
There are treatment centers everywhere,
With lots of people who really care.

Many organizations are trying to end it,
But scientists can't even comprehend it.
As you can see, this is something I fear;
Hopefully one day we will find a cure.

Riley Loonan, Grade 8
Gilbert Middle School, IA

To Be Human

Sometimes sadness takes over
Like an angry swarm of ants.
Sometimes it takes us down
Down, down;
Almost too far to walk again.
But the love from family brings us high up again.
To feel love is like you're floating high
Above your head.
That's how we, the people, survive
Time and hardship again.
Anger makes us go crazy
Like floating wasps.
But only love and sadness combined
Take it away.
Without love, anger and sadness
We would not have become who we are:
Humans

Hunter Belgarde, Grade 8
Rugby High School, ND

Sports

Volleyball, Football, Basketball, Wrestling, Cross Country and Track
You pass, kick, and dribble the ball.
You tackle and run and hope not to fall.

It can be easy and it could be hard.
And sometimes you can even get a par.

There are many different sports to do.
HMMM?
But most of the time, you just have to choose.
And sometimes you'll even lose.

If you have pride,
You just might make it to the other side.

You hear the fans screaming for you, WHOO!
So take first place, just for your crew.

Brinley Linton, Grade 8
Thayer Central High School, NE

Duck Season

We wake up in the morning with sleepy eyes,
And then we jump in our waders and say our goodbyes.
We get out of the truck with our big gloomy eyes
And then we hear the ducks calling to our surprise.
We get to our spot and spread the decoys
As we sit down I comprehended a peculiar noise.
It turns out it was just the mallards in our majestic decoys.
As the sun rises the ducks fly around
They fly by our decoys and we pump out a round.
Then we see ten beautiful ducks fall to the frosty ground.
As we clean up the decoys and we get in the truck
Looks like this year we will have astonishing luck.

Cody Ruden, Grade 8
Jefferson Middle School, IA

The Obstacle

I am running and running,
and there are things in the way.
I have to learn how to deal with it,
so I jump, thinking it's all over.

Sometimes I miss and fall,
but I have to get right back up and keep on going.
It may end, until my next try,
all the sudden, I begin to ask myself "Why?"

My answer is "Because I have to,"
or just "Because I want to."
It seems like it's only me,
until I hear the crowd.

Some people think you can run around it,
but I know you can't.
It's something you have to overcome,
even though it can be horrifying.

Maddy Jans, Grade 8
Perry Middle School, IA

Flags

It stands tall and strong
Patriots who are proud,
Join together to sing aloud,
Their national anthem

Some don't know it
Others don't show it,
But they just follow along
Quiet, but respectful

During the World Cup,
There are flags, flags, and lots of flags!
The winner is known to be #1
That's why everyone wants to win it, and when they do,

In the country, they celebrate all around,
Cheerful, joyful, and crying tears of happiness
Their name goes down in history,
And so does their flag that led them to victory

Ian Velasco, Grade 8
Perry Middle School, IA

Lake Buchanan

Sunny, majestic
The first Saturday of Spring Break
Right at midday
People laughing, boat motors gurgling
Fish jumping, children fishing, people skiing
Swimming, camping
Spring Break
Pumped up and energized

Jude Faulkender, Grade 8
St Francis Middle/High School, KS

High Merit Poems – Grades 7, 8, and 9

Marines

We stand tall
We are brave
We are superheroes for the brave

We are everywhere
Protecting our country
Fighting for freedom
And liberty

We train for hours on end
Learning how to defend
The people of America

We go around
Looking for trouble
Completing our objectives
Were always on the double

Fighting for freedom and liberty
The few, the proud, the Marines
Race Brant, Grade 8
Perry Middle School, IA

My Hat!

Swirling and twirling goes the wind,
And there goes my hat
But wait I forgot,
In a pouch up in my hat
I had a handful of money
Turning around I saw a cat
That mischievous
Little cat, had my hat
It ran like a horse,
I searched and ran
Inspecting every little space
My face turning red
My hair swirling snakes
I plopped down and
There on my buttocks
Was a pool of money
I laughed with joy,
Kissed the money,
Skipping through the halls of
Glory!

Ivana Xiong, Grade 7
Arrowhead Middle School, KS

Nature

N ature is —
A mazing
T ough
U nique
R ough
E ssential

Chase Litchfield, Grade 7
Blessed Sacrament School, NE

Nowhere to Run

We're in a plane crash
We all made it out alive
And yet, we haven't
Made it out of
The greater, larger problem
Nowhere to run to

Running won't help
Triangles? Maybe, if
Someone starts to look
For us out here
The fear is slowly, silently stalking us
Nowhere to run to

I have been trained
But I forget my training
And uncertainty starts to creep
Like a snake into my
Secure cocoon of safety
Nowhere to run to

The old and young go
They're better off now
We're still not found
Robby White, Grade 8
Gilbert Middle School, IA

Soccer

Warming up for today
Getting ready for the game
We need to win
We are a team no one can tame.

We're warming up, passing the ball
We are jogging and stretching
The goalie it getting ready too
He is diving and catching.

We line up in our formation
The game is about to start.
I hear the referee blow his whistle,
Lace up my shoes I got at Wal-Mart.

We score a goal, they score one too
Feeling tired, my mouth is dry
But they get the ball, they might score.
He shoots, he misses, it's a tie.

We didn't win, I didn't score
Next time it might be the same.
I might get injured, I might not play.
But I will never quit this amazing game.

Jeffrey Gutierrez, Grade 8
Perry Middle School, IA

She Is

She's a gentle breeze
Flowing like an ocean wave
An effortless grace

She's a warrior
Demanding your attention
Silent but so strong

She's just a rhythm
Slow, fast, running with the beat
Following the sound

That girl is precise
A ticking clock, passing time
An exact science

She's like a beacon
A star shining in the dusk
Her smile a light

The stage is her home
A place she belongs and owns
Like a lock and key

She is a dancer
Her sport vital to her life
Doing it for love

Jordan Longabaugh, Grade 8
Sabetha Middle School, KS

Cry

Please let
Your love show.
Please don't leave me.
Please don't go.
Please be kind.

Please tell it to me straight,
I can take it
Please be honest.
Please just wait.
Please stop hiding it.

Please stop making
This feeling hurt so.
Please remember, not so long ago
Please stop lying, to yourself.
Please remind me, of myself.

Please just go back,
To the way it was.
Please try.
Please attempt.
Please cry.

Ana Michele, Grade 8
Dallas Center-Grimes Middle School, IA

I Heard That, America

I hear American singing the many
Ballads I hear,
Those of entrepreneurs, singing
As they risk money to make more,
The working class singing as they break their
Backs for mediocre payments,
The immigrants singing as they
Go through hardships searching for a dream,
The jobless singing carefree, yet
Depressing blues, as they lose their hope,
The frontline infantry singing as they
Become martyrs for our great nation,
The panhandlers singing as they beg
For even a morsel of hope for the future,
Each the chorus to what him or her
Deserves, and nothing else.
The day which belongs to the citizens,
The night to the thugs, formidable, lost souls.
Singing with open mouths, their robust, yet frail
Strong, yet weak, melodious, yet discordant songs.

John Martin, Grade 7
French Middle School, KS

Love

Look around — it's all you see,
everywhere it's happening;
love your neighbor, love yourself,
love your family, love everyone else;
love your pets, love your home
even if you love to roam;
love your life, love to smile,
love to laugh, love to cry,
love to say hello, love to say goodbye,
love to kiss, love to hug,
love to catch little bugs;
love to remember, love to forget,
love to hide, love to seek,
love to cover your eyes and peek;
love to have fun, love to run,
love to wake up, love to go to bed
and have little fairies dance in your head;
love to kiss the stars goodnight,
love to forgive and love to fight,
love to love because that's just right.

Claire Boeke, Grade 7
St Mary's Immaculate Conception Catholic School, IA

I Am

I am fantastically different
I wonder if you feel the same way I do
I hear screaming in my head
I see you walking past me like I'm not here
I want you to listen to what I have to say
I am fantastically different

I pretend to act like I'm not sad
I feel that's you're never there to help me
I touch you shoulder and ask if everything is okay
I worry about what will happen next. Is it good or bad?
I cry because you're not there for me when I need you most
I am fantastically different

I understand that we get in fights at times
I say forgive and forget, let's put it all behind
I dream that we'll be close again
I try to talk things out, but it never works
I hope we can forget about this and laugh about it in the future.
I am fantastically different

Amparo Menendez, Grade 8
Perry Middle School, IA

I Am

I am who I am
I wonder what people think of me
I hear people talking around me
I see shadows as I walk outside
I want to know what people think of themselves
I am who I am

I pretend that my grandma is still here
I feel someone touch my shoulder
I touch my sweater
I worry about my baby brother
I cry for my grandma to come back
I am who I am

I understand what's happening at school
I say what I think
I dream about me winning the lottery
I try my hardest in school
I hope to see my grandma just one more time
I am who I am

Amber Laws, Grade 8
Perry Middle School, IA

Poems

Writing poems is something I dread,
words get stuck in my head,
I try to think of a rhyme for wrath,
I would rather do ten pages of math,
but I have to admit when I'm done,
writing poems is kind of fun.

Braden Burr, Grade 7
St Mary's Immaculate Conception Catholic School, IA

Summer

The days are long like waiting for your birthday,
Water more valuable than gold;
The temperature is like the desert.
Ice cubes saying "Get me out of this heat!"
Parents preparing you for school and tests,
Summer will end soon as you blink...R...I...N...G!!!

Lucas Coble, Grade 7
Olpe Jr/Sr High School, KS

The Sky
It is blue and white
Like a sea of floating clouds
Blowing in the wind.
Taryn Zweygardt, Grade 7
St Francis Middle/High School, KS

The Valley of Death
The valley of death
Black, barren, empty, a wasteland
There is no one there
Melissa Graf, Grade 8
Isaac Newton Christian Academy, IA

Pepsi
Pepsi is awesome!
My savior of life—gem blue!
It's reviving pep!
Ty Kral, Grade 7
Graettinger-Terril Middle School, IA

Nails
Designing with love
Painting and styling with care
Colors all around
Hannah Stafford, Grade 8
St Francis Middle/High School, KS

Sleep
Dozing off slowly
The darkness takes over me
Morning alarm…Beep!
Kattie Jenik, Grade 8
St Francis Middle/High School, KS

Reading
To read is so fun,
It's where you learn and explore.
So let's just all read!
Jesse Osnes, Grade 7
Faith Christian School of Kearney, NE

Water
Water is so cool
It's important for you, too
It is H_2O
Joe Ferguson, Grade 7
Graettinger-Terril Middle School, IA

DiDi
DiDi is my dog
She loves to play on the farm
When we're together
Rebecca Noah, Grade 7
Graettinger-Terril Middle School, IA

Grades 4-5-6 Top Ten Winners

List of Top Ten Winners for Grades 4-6; listed alphabetically

Ashutosh S. Bhown, Grade 5
Duveneck Elementary School, CA

Ashley Chou, Grade 5
Bowen School, MA

Valerie Ho, Grade 5
Dingeman Elementary School, CA

Sierra Kolodjski, Grade 4
East Bethel Community School, MN

Layla Razek, Grade 6
The Study School, QC

Niyati Shah, Grade 6
CrossRoads Middle School, SC

Michael Shragher, Grade 5
Our Lady of Mount Carmel School, PA

Crista Thyvelikakath, Grade 5
White Eagle Elementary School, IL

Olivia Wagner, Grade 6
Jefferson Middle School, PA

Madelyn Wolf, Grade 6
Mount Nittany Middle School, PA

All Top Ten Poems can be read at www.poeticpower.com

Note: The Top Ten poems were finalized through an online voting system. Creative Communication's judges first picked out the top poems. These poems were then posted online. The final step involved thousands of students and teachers who registered as the online judges and voted for the Top Ten poems. We hope you enjoy these selections.

A Bad Day
How my day
Went bad
It was quite sad
I tripped on
The way.

To my dismay
I felt like
A fool
Which was not cool.

I hurt my
Knee while I
Was at P.E.
I got hit in
The face
By a ball
All I wanted
To do was fall.
Brandon Otto, Grade 5
Aurora Elementary School, NE

Carnival
swish, swish
yeah cotton candy
slurp, slurp
can I get another ice cream
pop, pop
pops the corn
yum, yum
down goes the popcorn
chu-ching, chu-ching
money goes in
slurp, slurp
now a pop
aah, aah
the roller coaster riders scream
nooo
slurp, slurp
down goes the slushy
groan, groan
oh, did I have to eat that hot dog
Alyssa Andress, Grade 4
Hettinger Elementary School, ND

Football
F ootball is tough and rough
O nly you should be expected
O ffense and defense are the bomb
T OUCHDOWN the Iowa Hawkeyes score.
B oom, oh boy that was a big hit.
A lways be undefeated.
L ots of people cheering in the crowd.
L ook, Iowa scores again!!!
Beau Miller, Grade 4
River Valley Elementary School, IA

Little Prairie Farm
On a small little farm
Grass, wheat and grain grow.
While the wind brushes through the grain,
The cattle and bison feed.
As the farmer tends his crop,
The barn doors are open
While the farmhands oil the tractor,
I play in the tall prairie grasses
And the deer prance around me.
How I love my home
Our little farm on the prairie.
Cecilia Garcia, Grade 4
Holy Cross Catholic School, KS

Red
Red is a Mustang.
Red is bloody.
Red is a coat.
Red is a tape measure.
Red is scissors.
Red tastes like apples.
Red smells like candles.
Red sounds like a mallet.
Red feels like a guppy.
Red looks like fire.
Red makes me feel excited.
Caleb Bookout, Grade 4
Ellinwood Grade School, KS

Blue
Blue is the sea.
Blue is the rain.
Blue is the Kansas flag.
Blue is the afternoon sky.
Blue is the tears in the eye.
Blue tastes like a blueberry.
Blue smells like water.
Blue sounds like a weeping cry.
Blue feels like wetness.
Blue looks like dark with a shape.
Blue makes me feel happy.
Ryan Niles, Grade 4
Ellinwood Grade School, KS

Puzzles
Puzzles, puzzles what do I see?
The picture on the box is a mystery.
Puzzles, puzzles a whole new universe,
Unto which one can be so diverse.
Puzzles, puzzles what do I see?
A hidden world,
That's twirled and swirled.
Puzzles, puzzles what do I see?
The picture on the box is a mystery.
Noma Kreegar, Grade 5
Ponca Elementary School, NE

Softball Game
1st base, 2nd base, 3rd base, homerun
Wow, we made it
Pitcher and catcher
They're the bomb
Get up to the mound
See the numbers one by one
Just hope they don't
Hit a homerun
Pitch the ball
Hear the booming "Crack"
Think "Oh no"
Wait a minute
She caught the ball
We won the game
Now shake hands
Say good game
Think in your head
What a great game
We did our best
Time to leave
I can't wait until next week
Bailey Tjossem, Grade 5
South O'Brien Elementary School, IA

River Valley
Lush green trees
Swaying in the wind

A rainbow of flowers
Their faces to the sun

The river
Giggling all the way

Silver little fish
Flitting through the water

Big bald eagles
Watching ever intently

Wind
Brushing past everyone

A lone human
Watching, waiting
Until nightfall
Carin Mellick, Grade 6
Ponca Elementary School, NE

The First Time
I still remember the first day we met.
We were too shy to say much at all.
It's funny to think back to that time,
Because now we're having a ball!
Alexes Baeza, Grade 4
South Tama County Elementary School, IA

The Black Girl*
I am a black girl who is sad.
I hear a white girl talking to me.
I see a white girl facing me.
I wonder if the law will change back.
I am a black girl who is sad.

I pretend that when I walk into school I don't hear people yelling at me.
I feel the sweat in my hands when I walk into school.
I touch the new notebook in my hands.
I worry that one of these days I might have to leave this white school.
I cry tears of joy that I am in this white school.
I am a black girl who is sad.

I understand that white people don't want me in this school.
I say I want to stay at this school.
I dream someday we can all be friends.
I try to tell them we are all the same.
I hope we can be friends.
I am a black girl who is sad.

Clarissa Rosenberger, Grade 4
South Tama County Elementary School, IA
*Written from the perspective of a child in the 1960s. We are thankful attitudes have changed.

Segregation*
I am a black elementary student.
I hear people yelling at me.
I see a lot of white people yelling at me.
I wonder if segregation will ever stop.

I am a black elementary student.
I pretend I like going to school.
I feel mad and sad.
I touch the ground.
I worry that someone will hurt me.
I cry that segregation will never end.
I am a black elementary student.

I understand this is the way it has to be.
I say that segregation should end.
I dream that it will stop.
I try to be friends with the white students.
I hope it will stop.
I am a black elementary student.

Bryce Timm, Grade 4
South Tama County Elementary School, IA
*Written from the perspective of a child in the 1960s. We are thankful attitudes have changed.

Hearts
Hearts to me mean love, passion, kindness, and caring.
I see hearts almost everyday,
knowing they are something other than a shape.
Hearts can mean many different things.
Like happy Valentine's Day!
Or just plain saying hi.

Kaylee Petty, Grade 4
River Valley Elementary School, IA

Wind
Dancing in my hair,
Swirling me around as it races through the sky.
Teasing leaves and tossing them around amusingly.
That is the wind's favorite game.
A light breeze kisses my face as a smile is drawn from below.
A silent pleasure is what I call…wind.

Sara Divingnzzo, Grade 6
Crossroads Park Elementary School, IA

Nature
Squirrel
Furry, animal,
Running, playing, hunting,
Brown, red, crunchy, food,
Feeding, falling, hitting,
Eating, circular,
Acorns
Kaleigh DeGeldere, Grade 5
Central Middle School, ND

The Pencil
I got a pencil with a stencil
That was very sticky and really icky.
It had hair but my dad said,
That wasn't fair because
He was bald and never solved
The mystery how the pencil
With the stencil got hair.
Wyatt Pokorny, Grade 5
Ponca Elementary School, NE

Winning
To win, be confident
Never give up and run away from it.
To be a champion,
Always have your game face on.
Even when the referees make a bad call,
Be sure to stand up proud and tall.
Joel Watchorn, Grade 6
Ponca Elementary School, NE

The Scared Scarecrow
The scarecrow was in the field.
It had a helmet and a shield.
It is scared by a crow.
It is protected by an arrow and a bow.
It is all out there alone.
Its spine is hay not a long bone.
Kelby Krueger, Grade 5
Ponca Elementary School, NE

Clean
Sanitizer
shiny, clear
slimy and smushy
it goes all over
goo
Cherise Rolf, Grade 5
Central Middle School, ND

Midnight Cardinal
Bird in the spring night
The moon is shining brightly
Sleep gentle cardinal
Colten Burnham, Grade 4
River Valley Elementary School, IA

The Super Market
My mom made me get ready
We loaded into the car
There were strange yellow triangles, red octagons
And occasionally a green rectangle
We stopped in front of a giant house
With people coming out with food in strange buckets
We unloaded the car and my mom said,
"Welcome to the Super Market."
We walked around the Super Market and saw a lot of food
So I took some of my favorite candy
And some of my favorite soda
I thought it wouldn't hurt to mix them
But my soda was possessed and it rocketed into the air
With such a force it knocked down all the soda and candy off the shelf
It caused a hurricane of foam like a rushing river
It swiped 13 people off their feet and 2 really big men
They took mom away and said
"You have the right to remain silent."
Adam Merical, Grade 5
Ponca Elementary School, NE

Germany
Where can you go to see the Wall of Berlin and grab a quick snack?
In Germany!
If you want to learn more, read till the end and the fun will begin now.
I am from busy roads and buildings always filled with noise and chaos.
I am from Oktoberfest that is crowed with people.
I am from wonderful pools with water slides and sparkling lights.
I am from the Wall of Berlin that fell when the Cold War ended.
I am from delicious foods that my face is always in.
I am from the Alps that highways and railroads run through.
I am from wonderful festivals that have awesome rides.
I am from Legoland, a world of imagination.
I am from hikes by the river walks where we have family time.
I am from wonderful zoos where powerful lions SNUZZ!
I am from Germany, where my family and friends will always be
Along with my good childhood memories.
Curtney Dawson, Grade 4
Westwood Elementary School, KS

A Friend...
A lways gives you a forgiving soul. **B** elieves in me.
C alls you just to say "Hello." **D** rains your sadness away.
E ncourages you to do your best. **F** orgives you easily.
G ives you strength. **H** umors you when needed.
I ntimidates you in a good way. **J** okes to turn your frown upside down.
K eeps you company. **L** oves you for who you are.
M ocks you in a joke. **N** ever lets you down.
O bviously applauds you. **P** leases you as best they can.
Q uick to say you're sorry. **R** eveals the truth to you.
S atisfies you. **T** hey're always there for you.
U ses their manners. **V** ery kind.
W ishes all your dreams come true. **X** -tremely cautious when you're angry.
Y ells your name to cheer you on. **Z** aps you when you're down.
Caitlin Woods, Grade 5
Westwood Elementary School, KS

Candy

Candy is so sweet.
It's an amazing treat,
There are many kinds from which to choose.

There's caramel, chocolate, and vanilla,
and so many more.
Candy tastes so sweet.

It can taste tangy or sour,
Some look like a flower.
Candy tastes so sweet.

You can chew or suck on them.
Some can sparkle like a gem.
Candy is my favorite treat to eat.

We get yelled at for ingesting too much candy,
But it tastes so dandy.
Candy is so sweet.

Kimberly Axelson, Grade 6
Canistota Public School, SD

The Sights of Nature

The sights of nature
There's about a billion beautiful sights of nature
There's cliffs with granite that are really high
With rocks in the side and caves in the dirt
With all different kinds of colors
It's a sight of nature

The sights of nature
The water in the ocean sparkles in the sun
The waves go ragged like an unfolded blanket
In the moon it shines dim like a flashlight running out of batteries
It's a sight of nature

The sights of nature
The most beautiful of all is the trees in the fall
With all the different colors like red, green, yellow, and orange
It looks like the sunset and sunrise that comes in the sky
The trees that you can climb and cut down for a bon fire
It's a sight of nature

Walter Messerlie, Grade 6
Ponca Elementary School, NE

I Am

I am a shy girl who likes zebras
I wonder how my life will turn out
I hear noises that aren't really there
I see me flying on a zebra over the ocean
I want to live my life before it passes
I am a shy girl who likes zebras

I feel indestructible
I touch the clouds the sun and the stars
I worry that my life wont turn out how I planned
I cry when people make fun of me
I am a shy girl who likes zebras

I understand that people cant always be perfect
I say to never give up
I dream that I am in a candy land exploring with my friends
I try to be the best I can
I hope that I will be a very successful
I am a shy girl who likes zebras

Desirae Arbuckle, Grade 5
Lake Mills Elementary School, IA

Football

Football is really fun,
Your defense tries not to get outdone.

Learning the basics is where you start.
You may not be the best, but just do your part.

Running around trying to get a sack on the quarterback,
When you hit him, you might hear a bone crack.

For a while he will be in pain,
But that's all right because that's the name of the game.

Playing with your friends is a real blast,
Unfortunately the time goes by really fast.

Planning on winning it all is your main goal.
But you have to want to win it with your whole soul.

Football is an amazing sport.

Scott Jolley, Grade 6
Canistota Public School, SD

Tornados

Tornados are in Kansas history,
Because we are in tornado alley!
Some days we have sunny days,
But sometimes the clouds are gray!
Everyone loves funnel cakes,
But nobody likes this funnel today.
Sometimes they go ripping through the heartland
so watch out for those nasty things!

Meg Friday, Grade 4
Holy Cross Catholic School, KS

Nebraska

I hear Nebraska singing,
I see the blue agate blinging,
I know where Kool-Aid was made,
I saw the Niobrara ocean fade.
I see the corn grow,
I heard the Western Meadowlark crow,
I know Nebraska is the fifteenth largest state,
I know that Nebraska is totally great.

Lorianne Laird, Grade 6
St Philip Neri School, NE

Mall
Go grab my wallet
Down the stairs
Into the car
Through the streets
Toward the mall
Into the parking lot
To Aeropostale
Among all the clothes
Toward the counter
With my wallet
Through the other stores
Down the escalator
Past the candy machines
Around the swivel doors
Outside at last
Without my friends
Under the sky
To my house
In my Ferrari
Up the street, into my house
Under my covers
Sarah Krehbiel, Grade 5
Omaha Christian Academy, NE

Mirror on the Wall
Hey, remember me?
I'm the one who makes
you hate yourself…
You know the one that
says "You're not beautiful"
"Go hide under a rock"
Yeah, that's me, I'm the mirror
I make you feel self-conscious,
at least I show you the truth
In my image, you're never
"Perfect," it's my job
to make you hate yourself
while showing the truth
I'm not to blame it's you
not me, it's not my fault
you don't have ANY Confidence
It's not my fault that you
hate your image, It's yours…
That's right, yours
so go ahead and hate me
I don't mind, it's my job…
Jasmina Gracanin, Grade 6
Urbandale Middle School, IA

Very Sad Day
I was very sad when my cousin Jessica died
during a heart transplant
but they failed to do it
and she is dead and I miss her.
Abigail Dominguez, Grade 5
Central Middle School, ND

Red
Red is sweatshirts in the winter
Red is Nebraska Huskers
Red is leaves in the fall
Red is Santa's suit
Red smells like cherry pie
Red taste like fruit punch
Red sounds like birds
Red looks like stop signs
Red feels like soft silk
Red makes me happy
Red is my dad's favorite color
Jazzmine Wortman, Grade 4
River Valley Elementary School, IA

My Dear Aunt Julie
I love you here
I love you there
I'll always remember what you'd wear

I miss you dearly
I love you really
You always look through me clearly

You told me to always exercise
You never told me any lies
I always hated our good-byes
Faith Walton, Grade 5
O'Neill Elementary School, NE

Nathaniel Sidak
Nathaniel
Annoying, funny; troublemaker
Big brother of Autumn
Who loves family, playing; games
Who feels sad about going to school
Who needs family, friends; football
Who fears sharks, 2012; my cat Riso
Who'd like to see Florida with friends
Who dreams of becoming a Navy SEAL
A student of Mrs. Sellers
Nate S.
Nathaniel Sidak, Grade 5
O'Neill Elementary School, NE

The Sad Tear
One day a tear was sad
It's weird to have a tear cry
But it was!
Oh that poor old tear was sad as his friend,
The pouting lip!
His other friend the eye said,
"I need you so that I can cry."
But the tear said, "I'm already crying!"
Oh, still so sad that tear won't stop crying.
Brooklyn Bacon, Grade 5
Ponca Elementary School, NE

Whitney
Whitney was a black lab
On her stomach she had a scab

She had silky black fur
And never had to say brrr

She was really husky and long
And also amazingly strong

She barked but didn't bite
When she wrestled, it looked like a fight

Whitney didn't like mice
Her life she sacrificed

Whitney was a glorious mammal
She was my favorite animal.
Gunner Labenz, Grade 6
Wisner-Pilger Middle School, NE

True Beauty
You're beautiful no matter what they say
You're beautiful in every way

Don't let anyone stop you now
Reach your goal and take a bow

You're on your way to the top
Keep on going, don't ever stop

Everyone is different, never the same
Everyone is different, beauty's just a game

Feeling good inside is what counts
Not wearing makeup by the ounce

Everyone is beautiful in a different way
So it pays to be careful of what you say
Alexis Heller, Grade 6
Wisner-Pilger Middle School, NE

South Dakota
S torybook land
O ahe Dam
U niversity of South Dakota
T rails of Lewis and Clark
H ot springs

D acotah Prairie Museum
A berdeen
K eystone
O riginal 1880 town
T erry Redlin Art Center
A rt Galleries
Megan Titus, Grade 4
Roncalli Elementary School, SD

Nature

No one can create you
No can stop you
You're always there
You always share
Nature

You're green
Never mean
You're always kind
And one of a kind
Nature

You make the Earth pretty
Never a pity
You keep us healthy
You keep our hearts wealthy
Nature
Nishita Gaba, Grade 4
Centennial Elementary School, ND

Useless Things

An arrow without a bow.
A buck without a doe.

Bees without a hive.
Numbers without a five.
A miner without coal.
A stew without a bowl.

Gold without a price.
Monopoly without dice.
A robber without a gun.
Cinnamon without a bun.

A ship without a bow.
A bell without a cow.
A bed without a sheet.
A drum without a beat.
Collin Lorenz, Grade 5
O'Neill Elementary School, NE

The Potatoes

The rice grass goes,
Where the toasted hills are,
Where the butter roses grow,
Where the chocolate river flows,
Where the ice cream bridge never melts,
Where the cab and carriage goes,
Where the potatoes live.
They came out squished.
The grapes squished the potatoes.
The tomatoes began to scream.
The orphans ate the cream.
Poor potatoes.
Marco Diaz, Grade 5
Crestview Elementary School, KS

Taya

At the hospital one day,
Mom had you, Tay.

I was out of town,
When mom called with the countdown.

I went to the store,
When I opened the door.

There it was through the fog,
The amazing frog.

It was then I knew it was for you,
I knew it would make you say, "Goo-goo."

As I got closer to the hospital,
I got excited a little.

As I walked through the door,
The excitement got more and more.

The first time I saw you, Tay,
It made my whole day.
Whitney Watson, Grade 5
O'Neill Elementary School, NE

Wasabi Peas

I hate them despise them
They were created by the devil

My taste buds quiver and tingle
As I place one on my tongue

They look so innocent
So sweet and tasty
Yet something evil
Is waiting to come out of its shell

Every once in a while
You run into people like that, too

Wasabi peas are like
Raging fireballs
Plummeting to Earth

With their snowy white coating
And their pea green inside
You might think you were
Dealing with an angel
But really, just the opposite
Cambria Raines, Grade 5
Indian Hills Elementary School, KS

Shine

The stars shine so bright
in the gleaming night
the moon is in its place
up up in outer space
it's so very bright
in the midnight
looks so blue blue blue
shining gleaming shimmering
the moon
Tessa Francis, Grade 5
Aurora Elementary School, NE

The Farming Dream

I've always had a dream
About living on a farm.
I'd raise a cow for cream,
He would not cause any harm.

I'd have a lot of dogs,
I would want to raise some hogs.
My fields would have some corn,
I would have a sheep with horns.
Rylee Karella, Grade 6
St Paul's Lutheran School, NE

Cheetah

On a rock or stalking
In the grass, eating
Through a dead animal or
By a river caring for her cubs
Until they've all gotten drinks
Past the grass
Into the dirt she runs
Except she stops when she's tired
With the rock she ends up again.
Collin Hammond, Grade 4
Central Kansas Christian Academy, KS

Children

C reative
H appy
I ndividual
L ove
D rive parents crazy
R ide bikes
E nergetic
N ice
Ben Whitaker, Grade 5
Hawthorne Elementary School, IA

Worm

Wiggly, wild, wet, worms
Jumping joyfully in rain
Squirming muddy pools.
Andrew Harman, Grade 4
Alpha Omega Academy, IA

Running

Running makes me feel amazing.
I feel free and refreshed.
After that I drink a lot
of water.

Running is so great
I really think I will
Go to track when I
Get older.

You can be young
or old. You just
have to love
running.
Josie Heyd, Grade 6
Canistota Public School, SD

Fishing

Fishing is my favorite thing,
We go fishing in the Spring.

I like to fish with my dad,
When we lose a fish, he gets mad.

We go fishing at dawn,
When I catch a fish, I say, "Fish on."

We have to measure it to keep it,
If it's too small, I sometimes have a fit.

I have a pink fishing pole,
Catching some walleye is my goal.
Skylar Bultje, Grade 4
Canistota Public School, SD

Tomorrow

A wonderful sunset is coming,
A time that is enchanting,
Vivid and bright,
It will light up the night,
As the harvest moon appears,
It washes away the tears.

Soon it grows dark,
You no longer hear the singing lark,
For it has flown to its nest,
I miss him so,
For he was no pest,
Soon it will start over,
A brand new day.
Brynn Honeyman, Grade 5
Hettinger Elementary School, ND

Oreo

Oreo is my cat
He likes to chase a rat.
Oreo is really smart
He also is a fast as a dart.

Oreo is black and white
He is quite a sight!
Oreo isn't very big,
But he eats like a pig.

Oreo would eat anything he caught
He wasn't even taught.
He runs all around
And doesn't make a sound.

Oreo is always hurrying
To catch a mouse that is scurrying.
Oreo is my favorite pet,
He has been ever since we met.
Trey Ortman, Grade 4
Canistota Public School, SD

I Am a U.S. Marshall

I am a U.S. Marshall
I hear a lot of screaming
I see blacks as human beings
I wonder if this screaming will stop
I am a U.S. Marshall

I pretend that nobody is ever mad
I feel sorry for blacks
I know they are nice people
I worry that there will be a war
I cry for freedom
I am a U.S. Marshall

I understand why people are yelling
I say segregation is wrong
I dream that everyone will be treated fairly
I try to treat blacks like me
I hope that everyone will be free
I am a U.S. Marshall
Logan Plowman, Grade 4
South Tama County Elementary School, IA

Football

Beside me is the quarterback
Beyond me is the end zone
In a moment the quarterback yells, "Hike!"
Beneath me is the turf
Behind me is a linebacker
Against the Bears
Nearly getting a touchdown
Like a cheetah I run into the end zone
Christopher Schenk, Grade 4
Central Kansas Christian Academy, KS

Weather Goes by too Fast

Here comes the snow
Let's watch it go
Weather goes by too fast
Here comes the Sun
Time for some fun
Oh no, not the wind, time to go in
Weather goes by too fast
Hurray, autumn leaves, a nice fall breeze
Not a freeze
Weather goes by too fast
Yes, weather goes by too fast
Ally Dobesh, Grade 4
Rohwer Elementary School, NE

Useless Things

A Dalmatian without spots
A kitchen without pots

Chuy without Munoz
A foot without toes

A baby without a fit
Aaron without DeWitt

A king without a cape
A torn paper without tape
Aaron DeWitt, Grade 5
O'Neill Elementary School, NE

Color, Color Everywhere

Red, yellow, green, and blue
These are the colors of rainbow stew.

Look in the sky after a storm,
You might see a rainbow form.

You can find blue in the sky,
And white in the clouds up high.

Rain or shine, colors abound
Open your eyes and look around.
Dylan Daly, Grade 5
St Paul's Lutheran School, NE

Spring

The flowers are blooming
and what a nice fragrance they have.
The buzzing of the bees, the chirping
of birds, snow melting, the wonderful
signs of Spring!
The season to wear raincoats,
the season to look for boats.
Spring is a very colorful season,
and it all starts on March 20th.
Brianna Bamberger, Grade 5
South Union Elementary School, IA

High Merit Poems – Grades 4, 5, and 6

Skiing, Skiing, Skiing
Skiing, skiing, skiing
The best sport of all.

I like it when I go fast,
I like it when I fall.

The sun shines so bright,
My sight goes so white.

I feel the wind blowing,
It makes me feel like I'm floating.

I hear the snow slushing,
When people passed fast by.

I smell the fresh air,
All and everywhere.

Ski ski skiing,
I love this sport.
Laine SaBell, Grade 5
Aurora Elementary School, NE

Baby Brother
I remember when you were born.
You were cute and you were crying.
When I saw you I felt like crying
Knowing that somebody was going
To make my life happy.

I was the one who named you
And I knew it was an
Excellent name for you.

I remember when you were a
Month or two and now I
See you much bigger.
Also I remember when
you opened your eyes
They looked blue because they
Were so black.

Whatever happens to you
I'll always be your big sister.
Stephanie Gonzalez, Grade 5
O'Neill Elementary School, NE

Sports
S ports can be a fantastic exercise. Some
P eople play sports for fun while
O ther people play as professionals. The
R ookies are great too. My favorite
T eam is the Steelers. It's important to
S upport your favorite team.
Harley Cormany, Grade 4
Canistota Public School, SD

I Like to Read
I like to read
In quiet places,
And in my mind I picture new faces.

In my house or in my car,
Whether distance near or far,
Outside with a chilly breeze,
Or on the branch of a tall tree,
Wherever it may be,
I like to read.

Books that are thick,
Books that are thin,
Once I pick,
Let the reading begin!

Books with heroes, who do great acts,
Books with fiction and/or facts!

I can go most anywhere,
With my favorite book right there.

Sometimes I may have to grovel,
So I can read my newest novel.
I like to read!
Hannah Jones, Grade 6
Belle Fourche Middle School, SD

Softball
Softball is very fun,
You play it in the sun,
　You catch it
　In your mitt
Then you run and run.

The score is 0-4,
You hope your team will score,
　The ball is hit
　Into your mitt
The crowd lets out a roar.

The score is tied 10-10,
The ball is hit right past Ben,
　Sally picked it up,
　Izzy said, "Yep,"
And she threw it to their first baseman Ken.

It is the last inning,
And our team is winning!
　Our teammate hit the ball,
　The ump make a bad call,
But out team was grinning.

We had won the game!
Gabriella Weidenbach, Grade 6
Canistota Public School, SD

Blue
Blue is like the sky.
Blue is cool.
Blue is a car.
Blue is a flower.
Blue tastes like a blue berry.
Blue smells like paint.
Blue sounds like music.
Blue feels like smoothness.
Blue looks like the sky.
Blue makes me smile.
Ivan Briseno, Grade 4
Ellinwood Grade School, KS

A Poem Is Like a Baby
A poem is like a baby,
Crying with emotions,
Lines flowing like drool,
Strolling stanzas,
Precious ideas
In naps,
Inspiring words
Crawl on paper,
Similes and metaphors
Are loving babies
Dexter Pierson, Grade 5
Indian Hills Elementary School, KS

Lucy
Oh, Lucy Goosie
You're so sweet
That when I see you in the window
I drop my backpack at my feet.

When I walked into the room
I saw something more
There were toys all over
I couldn't even see the floor!
Caitlyn Kaml, Grade 5
Central Middle School, ND

Lava Lamp
Lava lamp, your red drops flowing,
like cherries glowing in the sunlight.
Like red diamond earrings, sitting
nearly perfect, in the sun.
Your blue water glowing,
like a clear blue lake on a hot sunny day.
The cherries falling in the lake.
Make a splish, splash noise,
just like the lava in the blue water.
Victoria Pliler, Grade 5
South Union Elementary School, IA

The Happy White Teenager*
I am a happy white teenager.
I hear giggling and talking.
I see them holding hands and getting along.
I wonder if the blacks are mean.
I am a happy white teenager.

I pretend to hate her cause I am not allowed to talk to her.
I feel kindness when I look in her eyes.
I touch her friendly hand.
I worry that my mom will get mad.
I cry when I leave my best friend.
I am a happy white teenager.

I understand how she feels.
I say that I am going to be nice to her.
I dream that the blacks and whites will get along.
I try not to let go of my friend.
I hope that we all will be friends.
I am a happy white teenager.

Haylie Prugh, Grade 4
South Tama County Elementary School, IA
Written from the perspective of a child in the 1960s. We are thankful attitudes have changed.

I Am an African American*
I am an African American girl.
I hear the water running.
I see myself in the mirror.
I wonder if the white girl next to me will like me.
I am an African American girl.

I pretend that the white girl next to me will like me.
I feel that the white girl next to me is my friend.
I touch my lips with my lip balm.
I worry that the girl next to me may hurt me.
I cry that one day I will make a difference.
I am an African American.

I understand why we can't be equal.
I say we all should all be equal.
I dream that blacks and white work together.
I try to stay strong to be equal.
I hope that one day blacks can go where whites go.
I am African American.

Julie Matta, Grade 4
South Tama County Elementary School, IA
Written from the perspective of a child in the 1960s. We are thankful attitudes have changed.

The Bottomless Pit
The bottomless pit,
Full of darkness and emptiness,
Hopeless and meaningless once you fall,
What foolishness to play by the
bottomless pit, now prepare for
a life of stillness.

Kailyn DiCesare, Grade 5
Martensdale-St Mary's Elementary School, IA

Georgia
Welcome to Georgia where peaches grow.
I am from Georgia where trees like the Live Oak grow.
I am from Georgia where Coca-Cola was made.
I am from Georgia where the True Hearts grow.
I am from where you will love to play outside.
Georgia will live in my heart forever.

Armani Roberts, Grade 4
Westwood Elementary School, KS

High Merit Poems – Grades 4, 5, and 6

I Am Myself
I am a blonde, hilarious girl
I wonder if I will ever be as good as my brother at basketball
I hear the crowd cheering now
I see the scoreboard running out of time
I want my own basketball
I am a blonde, hilarious girl

I pretend to be funny
I feel warm when I am actually embarrassed
I touch the hearts of many people
I worry that people take me seriously
I cry when they do
I am a blonde, hilarious girl

I understand I won't be as good as everyone else
I say "I don't care"
I dream I will be the first woman president
I try my best to reach that goal
I hope it will come true
I am a blonde, hilarious girl

Elisabeth Heagel, Grade 5
Lake Mills Elementary School, IA

Baseball
Baseball is my favorite sport,
You don't play it on a court.

You play it in the great outdoors,
If you hit the ball, the crowd roars.

The pitcher is an important part,
He throws the baseball like a dart.

The catcher is important too,
When he catches the ball, the crowd goes "Woo hoo!"

When the outfielder goes to catch the ball,
He hopes he doesn't trip and fall.

You get excited when you are the batter,
When you hit the ball, there is a loud clatter.

All in all baseball is fun to play,
I like to play it every day.

Preston Haynes, Grade 4
Canistota Public School, SD

The American Flag
It stands for freedom. It's the home of the brave.
It shows people we're American.
When they see us they start running.
It shows people we're not afraid to fight for our freedom.
It shows that we love our country a lot.

Leah Norton, Grade 6
Roncalli Elementary School, SD

Special Days
Christmas has gone by,
I'm asking why it has gone so fast,
here comes New Year's,
hope that doesn't fly.
Now comes Valentine's,
forgot the chocolate this time.
Must be Easter, I can tell by the bunny all happy and hoppy.
Summer already,
time to get packed with swimming trunks and goggles,
this time it will last.

Fernando Escamilla, Grade 5
Central Middle School, ND

Spelling Bee
I made it into the Dixon County Spelling Bee
I didn't know what the words would be
I was honestly scared to death
I'm sure everyone could hear my breath
When kids didn't get in, they were dramatic
Because most of them missed the word ecstatic
There were only three fifth graders there
One big kid looked like a big scary bear
I hope I make it into the Spelling Bee next year
Because now…I…have no fear!

Kortney Fethkenher, Grade 5
Ponca Elementary School, NE

Always Together
A lways together.

F orever or never.
A lways play together.
L eaves fall forever.
L aughs throughout the year.

D ays are getting shorter.
A utumn leaves falling from the trees.
Y es, it is fall, my favorite part of the year.

Jayda Cammack, Grade 5
Enning-Union Center Elementary School, SD

The Ear Who Went Away
One day my ear started talking
The next thing I knew it started walking
Then I said, "Come back I can't hear!"
But he just said, "You have another ear."
That day I went and talked to my nurse
But she said she's heard it before, it's a family curse
So now all I can do is wish for an ear
And hope that soon I will hear
Now I won't have to clean half of the wax
These may or may not be very true facts

Morgan Swick, Grade 5
Ponca Elementary School, NE

Summer
Summer
Sunny, warm
Bright, peaceful, flowers
Butterflies flying around
Love
Stormi Washburn, Grade 5
Hawthorne Elementary School, IA

My Favorite Dish
Steak
Meaty, juicy
Chomping, chewing, munching
Steak is my favorite.
Steak
Randy Sharp, Grade 4
Ellinwood Grade School, KS

My Favorite Dish
Pomegranates
Sweet, tasty
Chomping, licking, sucking
The best food ever.
Pomegranates
Nayeli Mendez, Grade 4
Ellinwood Grade School, KS

Basketball
Basketball
Working hard
Sweaty, running, playing
I love playing basketball
Fun
Bryanna Abston, Grade 5
Hawthorne Elementary School, IA

Cats
Cats, little balls of fur
Curiosity blooming everywhere
Calmly finding love,
Which is not so hard to come by,
When you are a cat.
Logan Grose, Grade 5
Broken Arrow Elementary School, KS

L.A. Noire
L.A.
Surprising, epic
Detecting, spying, arresting
Always awesome to play
Noire
Trevor McDaniel, Grade 5
Hawthorne Elementary School, IA

Meghan
Meghan
Friendly, active, creative, awesome
Sister of Trinity
Lover of volleyball, turtles and penguins
Who feels tired after volleyball, happy when school is over, sad when volleyball is over
Who fears spiders, snakes, and bad grades
Who would like to meet a famous person, be rich, own a mansion
Resident of Lake Mills
Fails
Meghan Fails, Grade 5
Lake Mills Elementary School, IA

Where I Am From…New York
Welcome to New York where the city never sleeps.
I am from New York City where the Super Bowl champs, the Giants, play football.
I am from where the Twin Towers got crushed and many great lives were lost.
I am from Central Park where playgrounds have merry-go-rounds.
I am from New York City where there are a lot of buildings.
I am from Yankee Stadium where the World Champions, Yankees, play baseball.
I am from Times Square where the New Year's Eve ball drops every year.
I am from the Atlantic Ocean shore where the Statue of Liberty welcomes people to America.
I am from Queens where my family lives.
Matthew Harley, Grade 4
Westwood Elementary School, KS

I Am From…Mississippi
Hi, I am from the Magnolia State where there are lots of cool animals.
I am from where there are alligators and snakes.
I am from where the cornfields grow.
I am from the pumpkin patches that are as pretty as flowers.
I am from rivers and lakes.
I am from snow as thin as paper.
I am from playing baseball in the summer.
I am from a small state but it's where my heart will always be.
Anyah Winters, Grade 4
Westwood Elementary School, KS

The Sky
The sky sits above me.
I watch it as it waits for forever to pass.
I watch it as it brags to all of us who wait for the same fate,
but eventually disappear into one of the world's many mysteries.
The sky stays.
I watch it as it provokes us to try and escape from the world it covers up.
I watch it as it sits so high above us, fearless, because nothing can reach it.
And as I sit there and wait I realize that the sky envies the ground.
Brittney Wilson, Grade 5
Indian Hills Elementary School, KS

Cars
Cars cars
they're so fun!
Until you crash them
one by one!
Treyton Blaser, Grade 5
Lake Mills Elementary School, IA

Running Wild
Running wild on the prairie
where no one can tell you what to do
running in the grass
running wild is the best.
Tristin Lopez, Grade 5
Central Middle School, ND

My Family

My grandma is kind,
She makes cookies and great meals.
She never gets mad.

My grandpa hunts deer,
And constantly make me laugh.
He loves the outdoors.

My mom is helpful.
She is kind and supportive.
She always loves me.

My dad is caring.
He plays sports and games with me.
He's competitive.

My brothers are fun,
We do bicker quite often,
But, we're still buddies.

My family's sweet.
They love me and I know that.
I'll love them always.
Andrew Weber, Grade 6
Canistota Public School, SD

What A Puzzle

A poem is like a puzzle
Words fitting together
Piece by piece
Ideas different
From any other

Lines connect
With similes and metaphors
Combined with imagination
And inspiration
That make
The perfect picture

Thoughts flow
Onto the paper
As your mind opens up
And fills with the colors
Of nature

Poems take time
But when put together
You have completed
The masterpiece
Nadia Jackson, Grade 5
Indian Hills Elementary School, KS

The Wind

The wind
The jumps
The pistons
The gas
The roar of the exhaust
The clutch
The motor
The frame
The shifter
The chain
The sprocket
The tires
The air filter
The air
Levi Krohn, Grade 6
Ponca Elementary School, NE

Useless Things

Students without a teacher
A church without a preacher
An apple without a core
A dresser without a drawer

A foot without a shoe
An actor without a cue
A pencil without lead
A bolt without a thread

A train without a track
A hiker without a pack
Police without a town
A bride without a gown
Heydon Strope, Grade 5
O'Neill Elementary School, NE

Christmas

Christmas is white
Like the snow falling down
Like Santa's white beard
And an Angel's wings.

Christmas is green
Like the shimmering lights
The decorated evergreens
And the wrapping paper.

Christmas is red
Like Santa's hat
The warm fire place
And the color of the stockings.
Jami Oyster, Grade 5
East Mills Community School, IA

I Am

I am a nice person who loves baking
I wonder if I actually will be a baker
I hear people yelling for cupcakes
I see people lining up at my bakery
I want to open my own bakery
I am a nice person who loves baking
I pretend I already have a bakery
I feel good when I bake
I touch baking tools
I worry people might not like my baking
I cry when I can't eat my cupcakes
I am a nice person who likes baking
I understand baking takes practice
I say baking a cake is awesome
I dream of opening my own bakery
I try to make good cakes
I hope to be a baker my whole life
I am a nice person who loves baking
Raven Budach, Grade 5
Lake Mills Elementary School, IA

Teacher

Hey, Dad.
You're my teacher —
Teach me to be wise.
Teach me to drive the tractor,
Mow the lawn.
Teach me inappropriate jokes
And let me watch *Family Guy*.
You teach me to be easygoing,
To have common sense.
How to summon a horse,
How to hold a cat,
How to hold a chicken.
Hey, Dad,
How does that tube work
And why do you smell like cat food?
Dad, you're like a teacher at home,
A sunny summer day.
Zoe Burkholder, Grade 5
Indian Hills Elementary School, KS

Love Is…

Love is comfort.
Love is shame.
Love is joyful.
Love is pain.
Love is mysterious.
Love is vain.
Love is a word with
no exact meaning.
Love is a word that
threatens every
human being.
Taylor Oberg, Grade 5
Ruth Hill Elementary School, NE

The Black Boy Reading a Book*

I'm a black boy reading a book.
I hear the teacher talking, and the kids reading.
I see the words in my book. I see the furniture in front of me.
I wonder when segregation will end?
I'm a black boy reading a book.

I pretend I'm sitting in a white school.
I feel the pages in my book.
I touch the pages in my book.
I worry about the future.
I cry out to my teacher that it's not fair.
I'm a black boy reading a book.

I understand that they don't like me.
I say I want it to be fair.
I dream I'm reading with a white boy.
I try to make it better.
I hope segregation will end.
I'm a black boy reading a book.

Garrett Arp, Grade 4
South Tama County Elementary School, IA
*Written from the perspective of a child in the 1960s. We are thankful attitudes have changed.

I Am a Nice White Girl*

I am a nice white girl.
I hear kids talking about working together.
I see black and white children.
I wonder where these children's mom and dad are.
I am a nice white girl.

I pretend we will all work together.
I feel sad for the black girls.
I touch the words on the wall.
I worry about all children.
I cry because she is worried about my mom.
I am a nice white girl.

I understand we all should work together.
I say let's all be friends, black and white.
I dream I could have fun with the black girls.
I try to be kind to all.
I hope to be friends with all girls.
I am a nice white girl.

Logan Dvorak, Grade 4
South Tama County Elementary School, IA
*Written from the perspective of a child in the 1960s. We are thankful attitudes have changed.

I Want to Bake!

I want to bake!
I want to bake a big cake!
I want to bake a big cake for a snake!
I want to bake a big cake for a snake to take!
I want to bake a big cake for a snake to take and a pancake!
Wait! That's a mistake!

Samara McDermid, Grade 4
Louis L'Amour Elementary School, ND

Love

Love is so strong it pulls people together
Love is when two people bond together forever
Without it the world would fall apart
Love is a strong and powerful feeling
Mankind can never break love apart
No matter how hard they try

Samantha Munoz, Grade 4
Hettinger Elementary School, ND

The World
The world as I see it
as beautiful fields
with waves of grass
the dirt is clean and soft
with dusty winds
that are lovely to the eye
and I end this poem
with the most lovely thing
the world.

Liam Sheeley, Grade 4
Broken Arrow Elementary School, KS

Winter
Winter, winter, winter,
There is a very good reason
Why I like this season.
It may be cold and wet,
But it's the best season yet.
Even though you might freeze,
At least there are no bees.
And that's the reason
I love this season!

Hannah Feil, Grade 6
Langdon Area Elementary School, ND

A Precious Flower
Life is a flower.
It blooms and blossoms,
It grows and sometimes,
Droops.
It needs to be taken care of,
Loved.
Because a flower,
And a life,
Is too precious to lose.

Emily Persinger, Grade 6
Ponca Elementary School, NE

Reverse Psychology
Before I even sat down
My brother formed a big frown
He started to cry
I wanted to die
He stopped and laughed at my breakdown

Alec Estes, Grade 6
Wisner-Pilger Middle School, NE

Love
Love is pink
It sounds like harp music
It smells like perfume
It tastes like chocolate cake
It looks like a heart
Love feels warm

John Lim, Grade 5
Omaha Christian Academy, NE

World's Embrace
The smile on your face,
Makes the whole world embrace.

When you stand,
You hold out your helping hand.
Everyone stares in awe,
As you stand there proud and tall.

When you walk across the land,
You hold out your helping hand.
Leaving everyone in awe.

Because,
You are the best of all.

Lauren Anderson, Grade 6
Crossroads Park Elementary School, IA

What Is Green?
Green is the kiwi that I eat.
Green is the grass under my feet.
Green is the coat I like to wear,
as I am playing in the cold air.
It is a feeling called envy,
when you see me under a tree.

Green is the apple that I like to eat.
Green are the leaves blowing with ease.
Green is a snake I see.
Green is when I think of stuff happy.
Green is slimy, it is not fake.
Green is the moss in the lake.

Jaika Purk, Grade 4
South Tama County Elementary School, IA

Seasons
Winter
White, cold,
Playing, cleaning, resting,
Outside, friends, family, home,
Running, sleeping, eating,
Cool, joyful,
Spring

Liberty Komanetz, Grade 5
Central Middle School, ND

Spartans
We are the men who fought
We are the ones to rot
We are so ever tough
We are 300 buff
We are only but faint memories
We are waiting for the Persians' battle call
We are ready to charge with no fear
We are Sparta.

Diego Reynoso, Grade 6
Wisner-Pilger Middle School, NE

Summer
Put down those books
come and look
It's summer
Let's go to the pool
you guys are cool
It's summer
Let's get some ice cream
Let's play on the softball team
It's summer
Let's go to that party
we can't be tardy
It's summer
Let's get on that boat
don't need a coat
It's summer
Put on those shorts
Let's go out for those sports
It's summer
You know summer doesn't last
so let's have a blast
It's summer

Victoria Davis, Grade 6
South Central School, SD

Kevin
K ind
E nergetic
V aluable
I nteresting
N ice

M arvelous
I mportant
C urious
H appy
A wesome
E xcellent
L oud

D aring
I ntelligent
G ood
G iving
I mpressive
N aughty
S mart

Kevin Diggins, Grade 5
Algona Middle/High School, IA

Gone
It happened a long time ago,
the wind picked up and it took me.
My mom got nervous, my dad got mad,
it took me away with all my dreams.

Logan Ferguson, Grade 5
Central Middle School, ND

I Am a Black Girl with a White Friend
I am a black girl with a white friend
I hear white people talking about black people
I see people yelling and screaming
I wonder if this will be the end
I am a black girl with a white friend

I pretend that we will have peace
I feel my little heart breaking
I touch my dad's U.S. uniform
I worry about the world being like this
I cry out to God and tell him to help
I am a black girl with a white friend

I understand that we have to be strong
I say my prayers
I dream there will be peace among us
I try to be courageous
I hope there will be peace
I am a black girl with a white friend

Lara Lasley, Grade 4
South Tama County Elementary School, IA

Fishing
Fishing is a fun
thing to do;
it takes strength, muscle,
and all you ever knew;
it is wonderful
in the breezy air,
all you need is a
soda, snack, and
a fold-up-chair;
and then you have
to wait and wait;
later, it gets cold
and very late;
then it's time
to go home;
it's just you
and no fish —
you are alone

Jesus Morales, Grade 6
St Mary's Immaculate Conception Catholic School, IA

Snow
Snow is cooling, freezing, and whitening.
Snow is the taste of hardened water.
Snow smells like liquid water, and flakey whiteness.
Snow makes me feel cold.
Snow is the sound of chattering teeth, and shivering bodies.
Snow is tasty, watery, and freezing.
Snow is white flakey water.
Snow is the dandruff in hair.
Snow is a ground white crayon.

Isaak Fischer, Grade 4
Ellinwood Grade School, KS

Jump Roping
J umping and jumping with a rope
U sing a song a riddle or a poem
M aking a sound with the stomp of your feet
P ounding and pounding with some sort of beat

R esponse of people thinking it's cool
O r sometimes they do competitions at school
P eople doing it more and more
I n the outdoors on the floor
N ow knowing that trying will make you so good
G oing with people to jump rope like they should.

Ashley Nordhues, Grade 4
Wakefield School, KS

Blue Is All Around
Blue is the vein that flows through my body.
Blue is a majestic mountain in the morning light.
Blue is a ribbon I excitedly win at softball.
Blue is a new robin egg protected by a nest.
Blue tastes like the iciness of raspberry slushy.
Blue smells like the niceness of violets in my Grandma's yard.
Blue sounds like a conversation of blue jays in pine trees.
Blue feels like the softness of my oldest jeans.
Blue makes me feel like the luckiest kid in the world.
Blue is the reason I'm me.
Blue is my favorite color you see.

Meg Mogensen, Grade 5
Covington Elementary School, NE

Thank You, School
Thank you, books, for helping me to learn about the moon.
Thank you, teacher, for instructing me in this big classroom.
Thank you, counselor, you help me with my problems.
Thank you, pencil, for helping to write my definitions.
Thank you, notebook, for keeping my notes to learn in my desk.
Thank you, desk, because you hold my handy white board.
Thank you, white board, because you can make music.
Thank you, floor, because I can go and get the marker.
Thank you, marker, for coloring pictures in art.
Thank you, gym, for letting me exercise and play.
Thank you, office, for the principal to help me.

Carlos Campos, Grade 5
Covington Elementary School, NE

Lightning
Lightning is shocking, amazing, and booming.
Lightning is the taste of shocked ribs.
Lightning smells like fire in the field.
Lightning makes me feel special.
Lightning is the sound of trains running and trees breaking.
Lightning is cool to see, sunny, and lights up my day.
Lightning is the sun.
Lightning is nature's light.
Lightning is matches lighting a mountain.

Tyler Knop, Grade 4
Ellinwood Grade School, KS

A Scared Little Kid*

I hear my teacher talking and reading.
I see the teacher and kids looking at me.
I wonder if the kids are mad or angry.
I am a scared little kid.

I pretend that nobody is there.
I feel sorry for blacks.
I touch the sole of my shoe.
I worry something will hurt me.
I cry inside, "Why did this happen?"
I am a scared little kid.

I understand what the blacks feel.
I say we should be equal.
I dream we were all equal.
I try to think about others.
I hope and wish we were all free.
I am a scared little kid.

Wesley Upah, Grade 4
South Tama County Elementary School, IA
*Written from the perspective of a child in the 1960s. We are thankful attitudes have changed.

Mad*

I am a mad teenager.
I hear yelling and screaming.
I see teenagers running at cars with me.
I wonder if they will come back.
I am a mad teenager.

I pretend they will not come back.
I feel mad there are blacks here.
I feel the meanness of my soul.
I worry they will come back.
I cry, "Do not come back!"

I understand they might come back.
I say, "Do not come back."
I dream that I will be happy.
I try to run after the car.
I hope they will leave us alone.

Megan Jordan, Grade 4
South Tama County Elementary School, IA
*Written from the perspective of a child in the 1960s. We are thankful attitudes have changed.

Georgia

Welcome to Georgia where the peaches and dogwood grow.
I am from the Appalachian Mountains where rivers run cold.
I am from a place where snow is very rare.
I am from where the snow may only come as often as once every three or four years.
I am from the clay state where sleeping outside is cool.
I am from the place where dolls are born in hospitals from cabbages.
I am from beautiful sunsets looking out my back door.
I am from country horseback rides through rivers and back again.
I am from Georgia where my heart will always lie with the mountains and rivers of my childhood memories.

Sarah Elizabeth Pinson, Grade 4
Westwood Elementary School, KS

Leo
Even as a puppy, her optic nerve never
developed. So she has always been
70% blind. My mom roared
as loud as a train "I don't
want another
dog,
because we
already have three
of them!" She said we don't
need another dog, especially one that's
70% blind, but we talked her into
it. So after we got her, my dad
trained her to do all
sorts of cool
tricks.
The coolest
trick that she learned
was the puppy push-ups;
she can do them as fast as a
Lamborghini. She is now a therapist
she is the best, the best therapist you can get.
Donovan Deathe, Grade 6
Nieman Elementary School, KS

The Cupcake
So delicious it looked
Not like something you cooked
With its bright white frosting, flavored cream cheese
It stares at me and pleads
Oh please, oh please, eat me!
I look right and left
To make sure no one could see my theft
And grabbed it as quick as I could
When I took my first bite
I was filled with delight
For it tasted oh so good
Soon I was down to my last bite
I wish I could say that I wasn't
But I was finished in not too long
Sure, I felt bad
But then I wasn't so sad
For a new cupcake was what I'd make
Fortunately, I knew how to bake
From then on and there, I knew one thing
Next time I eat the last cupcake
More ingredients I'll bring!
Nicole Feltman, Grade 5
South O'Brien Elementary School, IA

Bees
B uzzing
E ntirely mean
E vil
S tingers
Clayton Boeke, Grade 6
St Mary's Immaculate Conception Catholic School, IA

Happiness Is
Happiness is that:
Jesus died for me,
and the beautiful flowers
on a Red Bud tree.

The smell of the
grill outside,
and the headstand
in the pool I've tried.

And being with my family,
that is what makes me happy!
Marissa Wonders, Grade 6
Collins-Maxwell Middle and High School, IA

Heat of the Game
The pounding of the ball echoed in the gym,
Their team was faster, bigger, and stronger,
But no, not better, not never.
You could hear the excitement of the crowd,
Feel the heat of the game,
Inside and out.
The basketball player was a cheetah,
As she moved down the court.
She came to the hoop, stretching her long legs.
Up with a lead,
She made the score,
And victory was all hers.
Jessica Buckles, Grade 6
Ponca Elementary School, NE

Mallori
Mallori
Loving, caring, creative, smart
Sibling of Masen
Enjoys playing saxophone, and playing all sports
Who feels happy and sad
Who needs love and care
Who gives laughter and love
Who fears snakes and spiders
Who would like to see the world
Omaha
Dinklage
Mallori Dinklage, Grade 5
Omaha Christian Academy, NE

Military
Men and women brave and strong
Risking their lives to protect our country.
Air Force, Marines, National Guard, Navy and Coast Guard,
All protecting our land form bad guys.
From the Civil War to Iraq War they are protecting us,
So next time you see any branch of the military,
You should say thanks.
Dallas Miller, Grade 6
Canistota Public School, SD

High Merit Poems – Grades 4, 5, and 6

The Poet Knight
A poet is like a knight
Riding the lines of imagination,
Colorful poems,
Attacking dreadfulness
With his pencil
Using stanzas of creativity
To light the darkness
Of the world
The lines as beautiful
As a princess
And fierce as a dragon
Shooting fireballs
Of thought

The poet makes people
Happy, wonderful, and kind
With his poems of creation
He makes the plants grow taller,
The world more beautiful
And touches the hearts
Of his kingdom
Trey Bohlender, Grade 5
Indian Hills Elementary School, KS

Seasons
Summer
Many hot summer hours,
Spent working with garden flowers.
A long handled spade,
Keeps me looking for the shade.
Fall
Leaves turning red, yellow, and brown
Blowing all over town.
Frosty mornings are telling us when,
School is about to begin.
Winter
Snow is falling lightly all around,
Making a white blanket for the ground.
Children bundled up ready to play,
While Santa Claus is on his way.
Spring
Birds are chirping a new melody,
Legs of baby calves are a bit wobbly.
Longer days give me time to play,
School is almost over…HOORAY!
Fallon Budmayr, Grade 6
Belle Fourche Middle School, SD

Sarah
S wims like a fish
A rtistic like a painter
R ides like a rodeo star
A s fun as a carnival
H orseback rider.
Sarah VanBeek, Grade 4
River Valley Elementary School, IA

Ten Little Lines
One line will be a fence-post
Two can make a pallet fork
Three, a nice cattle shed
Four, a square bale
Five, a mailbox
Six, Bang! a gun
Seven, a water tank
Eight, a cliff will make
Nine, a rock pile
Ten, a smashed pickup without wheels
Loyal Johnson, Grade 5
Omaha Christian Academy, NE

Catilyn Ten Eyck
Catilyn Ten Eyck
Awesome, talented, and tall
Daughter of Annette and Richard
Who loves horses, dolphins, and music
Who feels happy about riding horses
Who needs family, hugs, and water
Who fears bugs, spiders, and snakes
Who'd like to see Blake Shelton
Who dreams of being a teacher
A student of O'Neill Elementary School
Catilyn Ten Eyck, Grade 5
O'Neill Elementary School, NE

Assassin
He rustles, hits, throws bombs.
He does this all to save his mom.
He will be betrayed by his friend.
He will fight until the end.
He was trained to do this
But did not know it would be so soon.
So he will set off to be an assassin.
But not just any assassin,
He is Noah and he is a master assassin
For his country.
Noah Johnson, Grade 5
Westwood Elementary School, KS

Basketball
B is for Basketball being so fun to play
A is for our Awesome super head coach
S is for Smiling after winning a game
K is for being a Key player
E is for having an Elite team
T is for the best basketball Team
B is for the Best Canistota Hawks boys
A is for Attempting to dunk the ball
L is for Loving the game
L is for Losing, which we try never to do
Tristan Pierce, Grade 5
Canistota Public School, SD

Basketball
Basketball is so fun,
you get to jump, dribble, and run,
you get to compete,
with all the other elite,
you have to try your best,
to beat the rest,
if you get a foul it doesn't matter,
but you might hear a lot of chatter,
you don't have to be tall,
to play basketball,
even if you're losing,
keep on cruising,
always try your best,
never let it rest,
cause the best never rest.
Jade Burr, Grade 6
Belle Fourche Middle School, SD

Dogs
Brown dogs,
Yellow dogs,
Fat dogs,
Skinny dogs,
Mean dogs,
Nice dogs,
Weird dogs,
Nerd dogs,
Popular dogs,
Dumb dogs,
Smart dogs,
Hairy dogs,
Hot dogs,
Whatever they may be…
DOGS RULE!!!
Dallas Dunn, Grade 5
Aurora Elementary School, NE

Time Goes On
A goes to B
As B goes to C.
Changing as
Time goes on.
Like a minute
In time
One will
Not matter,
If it
Gets lost,
Until it's
Gone forever
When you
Need it
Most.
Brooke Crawford, Grade 5
Indian Hills Elementary School, KS

The Black Man*

I am a mad black man.
I hear people yelling to blacks.
I see whites getting rocks to hit us.
I wonder if whites feel sorry for us.
I am a mad black man.

I pretend it is equal.
I feel like I am not real.
I touch my soul.
I worry if whites are going to hit us.
I cry for our kids and our lives.
I am a mad black man.

I understand that whites have no sympathy.
I say we should all be equal.
I dream that we are equal as whites.
I try to stop whites from hitting us.
I hope we can be equal.
I am a mad black man.

Monse Nunez, Grade 4
South Tama County Elementary School, IA
*Written from the perspective of a child in the 1960s. We are thankful attitudes have changed.

On the Rugged Shore

My bare feet touch the rocks that line the deserted beaches. Up and down, all I can see are the magnificent ocean and the massive rocks. Seagulls swarm the beaches as if they own them; they fly overhead, watching. I sit down on the rough rock surface. My legs swing freely over the freezing, salty Pacific Ocean. The back of my legs brush something hard; I look down and the tens, even hundreds of still, pink starfish clinging to the rocks are pounded once more by the powerful ocean. I look out at the never-ending Pacific, rolling with waves led by white foam that sits on the brink of each wave and leads them into the rocks, crashing against them with such force and spraying fishy water on everything near. I am awed by the vast ocean, spreading out in every direction. As I look out once more at the wonderful sea, I can almost feel the life of the many creatures below. An old lighthouse on a rock island sits, just visible over the horizon. It is the only thing visible on the ferocious ocean. A gentle mist comes clearly down from the dreary clouds that hang overhead; the blinding sun is hidden in the blanket of clouds. I take a deep breath and all of the sights, the smells, and the many wonders of the Oregon Coast seep into my lungs.

Sophia Bone, Grade 6
Southwest Middle School, KS

I Am From…Kansas

I am from the Sunflower State with the Meadowlark chirping.
I am from the Tallgrass Prairie where eleven thousand acres of land lay.
I am from hiking on field trips down to the lake shore and finding shells.
I am from the Rolling Hills Zoo looking at and watching animals.
I am from horseback riding in Kansas City and playing with the other animals.
I am from boating in Milford Lake, swimming and fishing too.
I am from visiting the Kansas Cosmosphere and Space Center.
I am from the acres of Flint Hills and acres of Rolling Hills.
I am from the Wheat State where the wheat grows taller and taller.
I am from Kansas where I will stay most of my life and even if I move I will come back for pure delight.

Paris Souza, Grade 4
Westwood Elementary School, KS

Because of Segregation*

A Sad Childhood
I am a sad black child.
I hear people making fun of me and saying mean things.
I see signs that say "No Negroes Allowed."
I wonder why they don't like me.
I am a sad black child.

Why Me
I pretend that I am one of them.
I feel mad because they make fun of me.
I touch signs saying "No Negroes."
I worry that people might chase me.
I am a sad black child.

Why Can't I Be One of Them?
I understand I am not one of them.
I say, "Who cares what color I am? I am still one of them."
I dream that segregation will end.
I try to believe, but it is too hard.
I hope this will stop.
I am a sad black child.

Kaitlyn Riha, Grade 4
South Tama County Elementary School, IA
Written from the perspective of a child in the 1960s. We are thankful attitudes have changed.

I Need Civil Rights*

I am a sad black girl.
I hear the loud heater.
I see my fellow black friends.
I wonder why whites act better than blacks.
I am a sad black girl.

I pretend that whites are no better than me.
I feel sad that I'm treated with little respect.
I touch my old ripped textbook.
I worry that we'll never be treated as well as whites.
I cry out to my friend, "I want civil rights."
I am a sad black girl.

I understand that whites think they are better than us.
I say that we need civil rights.
I dream I will be treated better.
I try to stop segregation.
I hope for segregation to be over.

I am a sad black girl.

Rylee Campbell, Grade 4
South Tama County Elementary School, IA
Written from the perspective of a child in the 1960s. We are thankful attitudes have changed.

School Days of Segregation*
I am a scared colored teenager.
I hear screaming and yelling.
I see rude signs and guns.
I wonder what they feel like doing to me?
I am a scared colored teenager.

I pretend I am in a school with white boys and girls, too.
I feel heartbroken, ain't I like you? Who cares about the color?
I touch my book, I hesitate and feel the voices of people yelling.
I worry it will get worse and worse if someone doesn't stop it.
I cry because I'm separated from my family.
I am a scared colored teenager.

I understand they think I'm black and hideous.
I say that we will be able to have freedom someday.
I dream of walking into a store with a white friend.
I try to ignore people by walking straight in school.
I hope to be able to be released like my dreams someday.
I am a scared colored teenager.

Callie Frakes, Grade 4
South Tama County Elementary School, IA
*Written from the perspective of a child in the 1960s. We are thankful attitudes have changed.

Us*
I am a young black child.
I hear people yelling and scratching at me.
I see a white child. She's my friend.
I wonder if they hate me as much as they show.
I am a young black child.

I pretend that hate doesn't bother me.
I feel sorry for them screaming at me because I'm black.
I touch her white hand.
I worry she won't be my friend anymore.
I cry when her mom yells at her because of me.
I am a young black child.

I understand her mom doesn't want her near me.
I say to her, "She's my friend, not my enemy."
I dream we can have school together.
I try to make her mother like me, and understand I'm ok.
I hope someday we can have equal rights.
I am a young black child.

Kara McCollister, Grade 4
South Tama County Elementary School, IA
*Written from the perspective of a child in the 1960s. We are thankful attitudes have changed.

Nature Through Dorothy's Window
Yellow, red, brown, and blue
Mother nature's beauty through and through
Yellow finch and cardinals too.
Squirrels that chase and play
Flash of blue from the jay
Help to pass the time away.

Kristie Criddle, Grade 6
Ponca Elementary School, NE

A Marine
A marine, a marine is what I'd like to be,
Marine that got to see, see again his family,
Feel a mother's hug and know that he is loved,
Though he won't forget what happens in war,
He will forever be so much more…
More than when I became a marine.

Elija Perales, Grade 6
Ponca Elementary School, NE

High Merit Poems – Grades 4, 5, and 6

Ode to Summer

Summer.
A time for gardening.
Handling the hose.
Sidetracking into a water balloon fight
In the middle of July.
Watching the exploding fireworks.
Having a bonfire in the middle of the night.
Being exhausted.
Taking a nap.
Summer is like a holiday.
A special time for enjoying.
Summer is identical to the sun.
They both make you feel warm and fuzzy.
Taking part in catch with dad in the backyard.
Mom is saying, "Don't break a window."
Flying onto the lawnmower excited to cut the green grass.
Smelling the green grass when I'm done.
Leaping on my ATV and feeling the breeze on my face.
Now, it is dim and I feel exhausted.
Then, it is August and I'm getting ready for school.
The holiday is over.

Zach Pregler, Grade 6
Thomas Jefferson Middle School, IA

Poetry Is Like the Sky

Poetry is like the sky,
each verse connecting...
like stars in a constellation
Painting a picture of vivid colors
Telling a tale of heaven and hell
Releasing the emotions
with every stroke of the pen
the words glowing, soaring, storming
Creating a mysterious imagery of vast dreams,
Each idea flowing smoothly like the wind...
Poetry is everywhere calming
expressing silently,
with every wondrous, hazy stanza
Stretching and striking the world
with every beautiful, exploding choice
Like lightning,
booming, blasting,
being heard.
Poetry is like...
the sky,
reaching for the stars

Sydney Houser, Grade 5
Indian Hills Elementary School, KS

Junction City, Kansas

I am from Junction City, Kansas, where my heart belongs.
I am from where movies are 3D!
I am from where we grow the wheat we eat.
I am from where my mom is and who I love with all my heart.

Julian Pagan, Grade 4
Westwood Elementary School, KS

Texas!

Welcome to Texas the hot state.
I am from the Lone Star State.
I am from where the longhorns roam.
I am from where the Alamo was once happening.
I am from the where the bluebonnets grow.
I am from Medina Lake.
I am from where the armadillo is the official state animal.
I am from Texas where my true home will always be.

Juliana Adan-Kruzic, Grade 4
Westwood Elementary School, KS

Lightning

Lightning is terrifying, amazing, and daring.
Lightning is the taste of an electric barbecue.
Lightning makes me feel worried about fire.
Lightning is the sound of thunder and drums.
Lightning is dangerous, deadly, and beautiful.
Lightning is friction.
Lightning is a reflection.
Lightning is a nightmare.

Cole Kubick, Grade 4
Ellinwood Grade School, KS

Kansas

Welcome to Kansas where I am from.
I am from where the American Indians once roamed.
I am from where there are lots of artists.
I am from where buffalo and cattle drives once roamed.
I am from where the sunflowers grow.
I am from where the deer and antelope play.
You should come to visit Kansas.
It is the most wonderful place to be.

Tyler Roberts, Grade 4
Westwood Elementary School, KS

Fishing

F un for everyone
I ncredible fight they give you
S uper fun
H ard to find the fish
I ncredible kinds of fish
N ever know what is going to be on the other end
G reat when eating them

Derek Ludovissy, Grade 6
St Mary's Immaculate Conception Catholic School, IA

Fishing

F un for all ages
I nteresting kinds of fish
S ecret fishing holes
H ard
I ce fishing
N ot as easy as you think
G ood to eat

Mitchell Breitbach, Grade 6
St Mary's Immaculate Conception Catholic School, IA

Yellow

Yellow looks like the sun shining down on Earth.
Yellow tastes like fresh bananas right off the tree.
Yellow sounds like cheerful yellows birds flying to a tree.
Yellow feels like happiness when I wake up ready for school.
Yellow smells like sweet honey on my bagel.
Yellow looks like gold out of the mine.
Yellow tastes like sweet pineapple freshly cut.

Thomas Anderson, Grade 4
East Mills Community School, IA

The Deer

I was sitting on a hill one day.
Then all of a sudden here came a deer.
I got my gun.
Then I shot at the deer.
And hit it straight in the heart.
The deer dropped straight in the path.
I was really happy because that was my first deer.

Michael Logue, Grade 5
Ponca Elementary School, NE

Shinouski

My monster is smelly.
He likes to eat jelly.

He is very pokey.
His pet frog is croaky.

He has an eye on his head.
He likes to use thread.

He has two buck teeth.
His friend's name is Keith.

He has sharp claws.
They fit in his jaws.

He wears gauze.
On each of his paws.

He has spikes on his tail.
He has shiny scales.

He has warts.
He works at the courts.

He likes thunder.
He likes to plunder.

His name is Shinouski.
He likes to say "Ouski!"

Taryn Robl, Grade 4
Ellinwood Grade School, KS

Jackzilla

He is green
And also a teen.

We ride bikes
And take hikes.

He's two inches from the ground
And his weight is about a pound.

He doesn't really think he matters
Just because he makes platters.

He's really rad
And always mad.

He thinks he's big and bad
But, he's really small and mad.

His best friend is Cheesy.
Cheesy is very wheezy.

He's very colorful
But, not dull.

His dad is Godzilla
They have a chinchilla.

He's neither hairy
Nor scary.

Faith Ringering, Grade 4
Ellinwood Grade School, KS

Poetry Is Like Grass

Poetry is like grass,
Creativity overflows with
Plentiful, slick words.
Pastures and fields filled with soil,
Planting roots
That grow to be words, lines,
And eventually poems.
Solely, a word is weak, but together
They create descriptive, flowing stanzas.
Sometimes we look at it and want to find
The roots, the deeper meaning,
We want to look PAST the dirt.
Some are long, some are short,
Some are dead, while others are joyful.
They need fertilizer and imagination
To grow into emotional poems.
Poetry grows everywhere,
Enjoy it.
Write it.
And next time you look at it,
Look past the dirt.

Michael Allison, Grade 5
Indian Hills Elementary School, KS

High Merit Poems – Grades 4, 5, and 6

My Flute
My flute is very delightful and fun,
I even play it outside in the sun.

I've learned all the notes to play my flute,
If I hit a wrong one, it's a hoot!

I love to hear the flute sound,
My instrument is the favorite one I found.

I love playing a song,
Especially when the song is quite long.

I play my flute with all my might,
Hearing the beautiful music is a delight.

I play my flute a ton
Until I get tired and want to be done.

My grandma loves to hear me play
Each and every day!

At contests there's always a large crowd,
My mom says, "Good job! I am proud!"
Lauren Wells, Grade 5
Canistota Public School, SD

Green
Green is the color of grass.
Green is the color of our math book
Green is the color of my sister's bag
Green smells like fresh grass
Green sounds like nice spring
Green looks like grass in the summer
Green feels like slimy swamp water
Green makes me feel happy
Green is my favorite color
Kendra Pry, Grade 4
River Valley Elementary School, IA

The Magic Wand
I got a magic wand
Because I had a special bond
With the wizard that could do anything.

I made the toothpaste talk,
The shampoo bottle walk,
I made the TV eat,
And the books grow feet.

My magic wand is fun,
But now I have to run,
Because my neighbors are mad,
Because I did things with my wand
That I shouldn't had
Taylor Lamprecht, Grade 5
Ponca Elementary School, NE

Every Kid's Dreams
While every kid is in school,
They wish they were at the pool,
Taking a walk in the park,
Climbing a tree,
Trying not to scrape their knee.
When the bell rings,
Everyone sings,
School's out!
They all scream and shout,
But when they get home,
They all know,
They will do all these things,
That is every kid's dream.
Kelsey Fields, Grade 6
Ponca Elementary School, NE

The Lonely Cloud
One little cloud
So friendly, so sweet
But so lonely.
The other clouds moved
North, South, East, and West
But this one little cloud
Stayed in one spot.
I thought he would move one day
But every day I went to school.
Then there he was
Even though he was alone in the sky
He is not alone in the world
Because I was his friend.
Kora Eslinger, Grade 5
Ponca Elementary School, NE

South Dakota
S unny
O pen range
U nending land
T -Rex found here
H omestead

D ams for electricity
A ntelope in the field
K illdeer is a bird
O utdoor fun
T ravel in a car
A lways free
Kaleb Norton, Grade 4
Roncalli Elementary School, SD

Trucks
Peterbilt, Kenworth
Driving, working, hauling
Rolling down the highway
Semi
Mason DeFoe, Grade 4
Hettinger Elementary School, ND

Animals
A dorable to humans
N ature's work of art that we love
I ntelligent creatures
M ammals
A wesome as can be
L oving to their babies
S pecial in every way
Tanner Hofer, Grade 5
Canistota Public School, SD

Wrestling
Wrestling
Quick, intense
Grappling, shooting, sweating
Winning matches through the season
Sprinting, learning, battling
Career, strength
Lifestyle
Kyle Burwick, Grade 5
Hettinger Elementary School, ND

Pokemon
Pokemon
Awesome, fun
Battling, attacking, learning
Hoan, Joato Dulist Kingdom Battlecity
Dueling, playing, drawing
Cool, hard
Yu-gi-oh
Cole Thierstein, Grade 5
Omaha Christian Academy, NE

Sunsets
Sunsets
Bright and colorful
Illuminating, color breaking, quiet
Splashing gorgeous colors around
Giving, moving, running
Brightly, lively
Sunsets
Janette Schraft, Grade 5
East Mills Community School, IA

My Life
Now, I see
My life as,
A big blob
But soon
When I get older
Hopefully,
It will all make sense
Alexa VanDyke, Grade 6
Ponca Elementary School, NE

Desperate*
I am a desperate black student.
I hear whites yelling, screaming, and people wanting to hurt me.
I see people wanting to kill me, whispering, and pointing at me.
I wonder if this yelling, screaming, and this unfairness will stop.
I am a desperate black student.

I pretend that people aren't yelling at me and there will be world peace.
I feel sad that I am getting made fun of.
I touch my friends' hands, hoping they'll feel better.
I worry that this unfairness will never end.
I cry at people, "PLEASE, STOP!"
I am a desperate black student.

I understand that I am not being treated right.
I say that we should treat others the way we want to be treated.
I dream that I will be free someday.
I try to cooperate with people and be fair.
I hope that in the future things will be equal.
I am a desperate black student.

Nate Drummer, Grade 4
South Tama County Elementary School, IA
Written from the perspective of a child in the 1960s. We are thankful attitudes have changed.

The Feel of Segregation*
I am a black girl looking in a mirror.
I hear sinks going on and off.
I see myself in the mirror.
I wonder what segregation was like.
I am a black girl looking in a mirror.

I pretend I am not bullied.
I feel the water rushing through my hands.
I am touching my face.
I worry that a person will hit me.
I cry because white people get nicer things.
I am a black girl looking in a mirror.

I understand that segregation is wrong.
I say nothing.
I dream that this will end.
I try not to be mean to white people.
I hope this will end.
I am a black girl looking in a mirror.

Ryley Jurgensen, Grade 4
South Tama County Elementary School, IA
Written from the perspective of a child in the 1960s. We are thankful attitudes have changed.

I Am From...Iowa
Welcome! Would you like to take a journey to where the fun is? The fun begins in the state of Iowa.
I am from the big farms of Iowa where corn is grown.
I am from the Hawk Eye state, that's Iowa's nickname.
I am from the big countryside where you can do many things like horseback riding.
I am from the campgrounds where you can go hunting and fishing.
I am from Iowa where I wish I could be.

Cole Miller, Grade 4
Westwood Elementary School, KS

High Merit Poems – Grades 4, 5, and 6

Please Get Out of My Way

Oh please, oh please,
I'm on my knees.
Please get out of my way.
I've been waiting since May,
Not trying to stay,
Oh please get out of my way.

Oh no! Oh no!
Look at the time.
It's already a quarter to nine.
I don't want to be late on my very first time.
I've tried to be patient.
I've tried to be kind.
But there's no way I'll get there just right on time.
Oh please, get out of my way.

Oh please, oh please,
I've had enough
I'm tired of waiting and sitting here bored.
Please move out of my way.

Thank you! Thank you!
You've brightened my day.
You've finally moved out of my way.
Audrey Glad, Grade 6
Crossroads Park Elementary School, IA

Foster Care

All of the time you feel all alone
Knowing you don't have a place to call home

Wanting and hoping for a mom and a dad
Longing for one that will make you feel glad

They come put your stuff in a trash bag
You have that feeling that makes you want to gag

When you get split, you feel far apart
You don't have a brother, you don't have a heart

You would do anything to have him back
But instead you only have a half-filled garbage sack

Your new family is okay
But all you can do is live day-by-day

As I watch the rain
I try to demolish our pain

I now have a new mother
But I'll remember you as my brother
Nate Welsh, Grade 5
O'Neill Elementary School, NE

Four Wheelers

Four wheelers are fun to ride
Especially in the mud outside.
If it is slippery, you might slide,
Be careful so you don't collide.

It's fun riding in the hills
It gives me lots of thrills.
You have to be careful of the trees,
Otherwise, riding four wheelers is a breeze.

When it gets dark, you need to get home,
You might want to roam,
But it's best to get home and park my four wheeler in the shed,
Then I will eat my supper and go to bed.
Austin Parry, Grade 6
Canistota Public School, SD

Friendship

Friendship is good to have
friends will always share
even in very hard times
you can count on friends to care

Even though you tell them to leave
no matter what, they will always be there
even when things are difficult
they will always be supportive and fair

Friendship is good to have
friends will always share
through greatly depressed times
we'll always be the perfect pair
Katelyn Amfahr, Grade 5
Martensdale-St Mary's Elementary School, IA

Horses at Night

A big full moon looks down
Onto my tiny town.
I make not a sound.
My heart starts to pound.
I see without a shadow of a doubt
A herd of wild horses on the lookout
Their leader is amazingly bold.
He's faster than wind is what I'm told.
They majestically stand.
The big black horse is in command.
They come in colors of gold, brown, white, and black.
Wild animals do not dare to attack.
I stand silent so they do not fright.
I watch them run in the black of night.
Lydia Saxton, Grade 5
Lake Mills Elementary School, IA

Cheetah
Fast and lean cheetah
Predator to the gazelle
Lives in Africa
Kaylie Hole, Grade 4
Humboldt Elementary Charter School, KS

Fishing
I caught a big bass
It was the biggest bass ever
So, I got a trophy
Jackson Aikins, Grade 4
Humboldt Elementary Charter School, KS

Pepper
The pepper was hot
I need a drink of water
No peppers for me!
Colten Fritch, Grade 4
Humboldt Elementary Charter School, KS

Bears
Big, fat bears do roar
During fall hunting season
They are furry, cute
Solomon Shahan, Grade 6
Roncalli Elementary School, SD

Fishing
Fishing's really fun
I cast the line and catch fish
Then I release it.
Reagan Montgomery, Grade 4
Canistota Public School, SD

Nature
More than just beauty
Infinitely puzzling
And mysterious
Morgan Hunt, Grade 4
Broken Arrow Elementary School, KS

The Rainforest
Dew glistens on plants,
Leaves sway on trees with a breeze.
Rainforest mornings.
Adelle Remke, Grade 4
Broken Arrow Elementary School, KS

My Tree
My tree is my soul
It is getting chopped down
It is very sad
Joslyn Ebert, Grade 4
Hettinger Elementary School, ND

Four Delicate Seasons
Winter's faint cries of the winds scaring the deepest soul,
Blowing many towering drifts like Hawaii's waves,
With bitterness in the beast-like weather,
Exterminating nature's beauty and god's creation,
Birds chirping, wolves singing…gone, as fast as lightning.

Spring brings back our fellow friends from the south with new and annual crops,
Lilliputian or voluminous creatures will revive themselves from hibernation,
Varieties of different species mating forming clones of its ancestors,
Morning dew waiting patiently on the freshly cut grass,
Its superior presentation will take breaths away from any creature.

Summer's decalescent weather makes you cry in pain and fear,
Little precipitation brings mortality to any suffering plant,
Sweat oozes down your face like St. Helen's lava running down its side,
Burning up a vast forest with fire and death creeping up onto many trees,
Scorching your red feet as you pace across the ocean's sand.

Fall brings bareness to nature's forest with leaves that are crumbled from their way down,
Cooler breezes tell the animals to prepare for their relaxing slumber,
Sounds of leaves crunching under big, hunting boots is loud like thunder,
Distant roars of the bullets frighten and surprise a peaceful herd,
Food will become scarce—new weather awaits with more prey.
Hannah Surat, Grade 6
Kimball School, SD

Yellow Is…
Yellow is a bunch of blonde girls walking yellow labs.
Yellow is a Golden Retriever playing happily in my back yard.
Yellow is a pile of sticky notes on the teacher's messy desk.
Yellow is the New York taxi that rushes back and forth from one stop to another.
Yellow tastes like the tart lemons that zap your taste buds.
Yellow smells like my Mom's precious golden roses basking in the spring sun.
Yellow sounds like a school bus roaring down the dirt road.
Yellow feels like the warmth of the sun on my face at the beach.
Yellow makes me feel like freshly squeezed lemonade on a hot summer day.
Yellow is my star that twinkles goodnight in the cloudless sky.
Emma Jo Hawkins, Grade 5
Covington Elementary School, NE

Where I Am From…Kansas
I am from Kansas and the Flint Hills.
I am from Junction City where my adventures happen.
I am from Eagle Days, the place where I learn new things about eagles.
I am from Milford Nature Center, the place I play games.
I am from snowy winters, where I have snowball fights and make snowmen.
I am from weddings I like to attend.
I am from Milford Lake, where I like to fish.
I am from hot summer days in the pool.
I am from time to relax on the porch.
I am from wonderful Fourth of July.
I am from a place I spend time with my cousins.
I am from the Sunflower State and I want you to come here today.
Please come to my state of Kansas and check it out.
Nicole Figueroa, Grade 4
Westwood Elementary School, KS

A Friend…

A ccepts me for who I am. **B** elieves in me.
C alls to check on me. **D** oesn't gossip about me.
E xciting. **F** riendly.
G ood to have laughs with. **H** elps me when I'm stuck.
I s there in case I need help. **J** okes with me.
K eeps my secrets. **L** ies about nothing.
M isses me when I am gone. **N** otices when I am sad.
O nly one who knows about me. **P** uts everyone first.
Q uits when it's really hard. **R** eminds me of their family.
S ticks around with me. **T** reats me good.
U ses technology. **V** isits every now and then.
W ill work hard. **X** -tra fun.
Y ou are always there for me. **Z** esty.

Alesha Helm, Grade 5
Westwood Elementary School, KS

Tree Kangaroo

T wo strong legs made for jumping and climbing
R ed, black, brown to gold colors great for hiding
E xciting to see in different ways
E ndangered, yes, 2000 left in the wild today

K een senses of sight and smell
A mazing at jumping thirty feet to a tree
N o fur on its nose but is everywhere else you see
G reat at eating fruit and leaves
A wful at swimming but great for the trees
R ain forests of Australia, New Guinea, and the Foya mountains
O mnivores they are, they eat mainly plants and bugs
O pposite from most kangaroos, they live in trees

Hazel Youngquist, Grade 5
Perry-Lecompton Middle School, KS

Blue Is my Favorite Color

Blue is the nail polish painted on my nails.
Blue is a shiny diamond on your finger on your wedding day.
Blue is a bright star blinking in the night sky.
Blue tastes like a juicy delicious blueberry.
Blue smells like a beautiful blooming lily flower.
Blue sounds like a wave coming from the ocean.
Blue feels like my favorite blue jeans.
Blue makes me feel like a bird flying in the air filled with happiness.
Blue is a sweet lollipop in your mouth.

Jackie Laurel, Grade 5
Covington Elementary School, NE

Lego Brick

What is a Lego Brick?
Is it small, is it big, is it colorful or is it dull?
Well, this is what I think…
It is a marvelous creation
That you can build with, create with and have fun with.
When you create things with Legos
You can build anything you can imagine.

Mathew Richard, Grade 5
Westwood Elementary School, KS

A Poem Is Like Lightning

A poem is like lightning
striking someone's mind
with ideas…
as the pen hits paper
penetrating into the mind,
the wind carrying emotion to the pursuer
Bright, flowing,
that's what poetry is
sparking our creativity,
every stanza a flair of lightning
igniting our minds
our feelings now being heard,
expression changing as we see the exotic light
Powerful, fierce, burning…
every lyric creating a blazing notion
lighting up the night sky with its glow,
the poet making the clouds of
fear disappear,
scorching excruciating thought
flashing as though never seen,
but leaving a scar of tranquility.

Nia Jackson, Grade 5
Indian Hills Elementary School, KS

Nature

Fragile
Delicate
Tender
Begging for great care
Nature   Pure
Pristine   Fresh
Sheer Beauty   Nature
Intricate   Detailed
Patterns   Elaborately Unique
Nature   Silent
Speaking   Unheard
Needs to be Heard   Nature
Perceive   Listen
Hear
Understand the message
Nature
Act
Do
Work
Stand Up
Nature

Madi Grenstiner, Grade 6
Wall Elementary School, SD

What Is Light Blue?

Light blue is the sky endless and free.
Like the ocean roaring and the salty great sea.
It's the color of sadness deep inside, but for me
Light blue is a color that represents me!

Tony Carrera, Grade 4
South Tama County Elementary School, IA

Me

I am a farm boy with hair follicles
I wonder if I will be famous
I hear the crowd when I score a touchdown
I see the football in the air
I want to be a marine when I grow up
I am farm boy with hair follicles

I pretend I will never die
I feel a football in my hand
I touch people's hearts
I worry my brother will die in the marines
I cry when family members die
I am a farm boy with hair follicles

I understand my mom will never be the same
I say my parents never crashed
I dream my mom and dad were never in a motorcycle crash
I try to do my best in school and at home
I hope my mom will get better
I am a farm boy with hair follicles

Hunter Tritch, Grade 5
Lake Mills Elementary School, IA

Baseball

I am an enthusiastic guy who loves baseball
I wonder what I will be like when I'm old
I hear the sound of a baseball hitting a baseball bat
I see the pitch when it's a strike
I want to be in the MLB
I am an enthusiastic guy who loves baseball

I pretend I'm the best baseball player ever
I feel the baseball in my hand when I throw it
I touch the ball when I bunt
I worry that I will drop the ball when I try to catch it
I cry when I get hit by the pitch
I am an enthusiastic guy who loves baseball

I understand when the ump makes a bad call
I say "Let's go, team," when I'm in the dugout
I dream I will hit lots of home runs
I try to hit a home run when I'm up to bat
I hope I'll be in the MLB
I am an enthusiastic guy who loves baseball

Cael Boehmer, Grade 5
Lake Mills Elementary School, IA

Rodeo

R iding on bulls
O r riding bareback
D eath is at every moment
E very second counts
O h, every day is always thrilling

Beau Austin, Grade 4
Enning-Union Center Elementary School, SD

Invisible

First day of school, learning the rules,
She's trying to find her way.
Each day is the same, they're playing their games
While she sits alone, far away.
Because everything is the same, when you're invisible.

The recess bell rings, she runs to a swing,
And sits there, on her own.
Nobody comes near, so they just can't hear,
Her crying to go home.
Because you're always all alone, when you're invisible.

Each day at two, back of the room,
She sits there, tucked away.
A question is asked, but she's the one they pass,
Though she knows the answer anyway.
Because every day is the same, when you're invisible.

End of the day, she's on her way,
When a girl by her side smiles and waves.
They talk on the way home, then some more by phone,
And a friendship is started that way.
Because sometime you're okay, though you're invisible

You don't really have to be invisible.

Amanda Trout, Grade 6
Independence Middle School, KS

Questions

Some puzzle people,
Others are annoying,
It depends on what you ask,
Not always getting answers.

Why can both good or bad things happen,
Sometimes, when you ask, it makes people angry,
You say, "I just asked a question,"
You wonder.

Your parents tell you to leave them alone,
That makes everything hard,
Being quiet isn't really that easy,
Getting in trouble is even harder.

Consequences are even less fun,
They are there for a reason, though,
They keep you out of trouble,
You will never learn.

People think you ask really dumb things,
You honestly don't know,
What does this mean or what is it;
Why does everything have to be so complicated?

Drakkar O'Neal, Grade 5
Kimball School, SD

High Merit Poems – Grades 4, 5, and 6

Transportation in Time
Old transportation was much different from today's
People traveled in much more weird ways
Sometimes they would use horses to get from place to place
And oh! how it slowed their pace
Transportation today has improved by miles
Many fast moving vehicles have so many dials!
Some people travel in colorful cars,
And some even use spaceships to travel to the stars!
Sophie Kramper, Grade 6
Ponca Elementary School, NE

Spring
Spring is a time
for new beginnings,
it's for flowers,
Easter, and everything;
there is no
more cold weather,
I think it would be better
if Spring would stay forever!
Haley Heitman, Grade 6
St Mary's Immaculate Conception Catholic School, IA

Green
Green is a leaf on tall trees.
Green is money out of a ATM.
Green is a four leaf clover in spring.
Green is like leprechauns on St. Patrick's Day.
Green tastes like a watery grape inside my mouth.
Green smells like a hard and minty mint.
Green feels like the murky water from the Missouri River.
Green is the bright color of Mother Nature.
Isaac Chavez, Grade 5
Covington Elementary School, NE

Marines
M is for the **M**en and women who serve their country
A is for being **A**rmed and ready
R is for the **R**espect that they deserve
I is for the **I**ntelligent marines who do their best
N is for the **N**ation's protectors of the sea
E is for the **E**xperts in the Marine Corps
S is for the **S**uccessful soldiers of the USA
Dominique Krinke, Grade 5
Canistota Public School, SD

My Dog
My dog is like the sun
His eyes are like the sunshine
His ears are like a mountain
His fur is silky and fresh
His heart holds love and joy that is blue as the sky
He lives in a house in Omaha and eats
Puppy Chow
Christina Wells, Grade 5
Omaha Christian Academy, NE

My House
My house is where I stay,
I'm there almost every day.

My house is the color of blue,
There is white trim too.

It is the place where I play games,
It is where my brother and sister call me names.

My house is sometimes a mess,
I could help clean, I guess.

My house is sometimes loud,
Especially when there's a crowd.

My house is where I eat,
When I'm at the table, I take a seat.

My house is where I sleep,
The fire alarms wake me when they beep.

My house gives me protection,
When I'm there, I feel no rejection.

My house is filled with love,
A love that comes from above.
Carson Roshone, Grade 6
Canistota Public School, SD

The Apple Trees
The apple trees,
They hold so many graceful memories,
In the beautiful autumns,
I would pick the big, juicy, ripe apples.

I would take them back to the farmhouse,
And lather them in icy cold water,
Then, I would bring the lathered apples to my dad and Grandpa,
So they could slice them into chips and dry them.

After they dried the beautiful crisp chips,
The aroma would lead itself to the dinner table,
And when dinner came around,
CRUNCH! I bit into the mouthwatering apple chip.

But now, those days are over,
The tree has died, and with it, the annual tradition,
We now use it for a place to remember our past dogs,
I know they have gone somewhere special.

A place that fits their personality,
A place where we all go someday,
That place will give something to everyone,
Even the apple tree.
Grace Sinclair, Grade 5
Kimball School, SD

My Saxophone

My saxophone sounds the best of all,
You could hear me play through the wall.

I play very loud,
It makes my mom proud.

ABCDEFG,
Who plays these notes? Me!

My saxophone is so loud,
You could hear it in a crowd.

When I play, I make beautiful noise,
And guess who gets jealous, the rest of the boys!

Before I play, I get the reed wet,
And after that I'm all set!

I am better than you, I bet,
It's a good thing you haven't heard me play yet.

In the concert we are playing a song,
That makes my lips hurt because it is very long.

That instrument is my saxophone, you see,
The instrument that makes me fill up with glee.

Caleb Nugteren, Grade 5
Canistota Public School, SD

Walking on a Rainbow

Walking down a colorful, tricky path,
Some things can be fun, but others can be bad,
It can be hard with lots of labor,
Others can be as easy as pie.

Fun, cool, in the sky, all day you climb up and up,
Creating dreams and hopes and wonderful times,
Playing and running in your youth,
Laying in the sun and daydreaming all day.

Big adventures and little missions on the way,
Learning in places all over the world,
From laughs and giggles and smiles, too,
The fun side of your rainbow.

But sometimes, the dark clouds roll around,
It makes things gloomy, sad and broken,
Breaks your heart and the tears rush down,
Crumpled dreams; it's too late to do.

Your voice crackles; the memories fade away,
On the horizon, the dark clouds roll in,
The bright sun wraps you up and cuddles you,
You're on the high rainbow in the sky, now.

Morgan Kunzweiler, Grade 5
Kimball School, SD

In Heaven's Hands

In your hands I humbly rest
I will make myself more than a guest
I follow my Shepherd
Who healed the lepers
In Heaven's Hands I give myself to you

In your calm valley of peace I quietly lie
I do not worry what should happen when I die
For I know that thou art near
And thou dost not provide fear
So, in Heaven's Hands I will come to you

In the spitting fire
I shall then admire
The glory of your love
I shall forever remain in Heaven's Hands
To be with my Lord

Faith Maddox, Grade 6
Cair Paravel Latin School, KS

Ring-tailed Lemur

R ings of black and white on their tails
I t stink-fights
N o lemurs are left behind
G ray or tan fur on their bodies

T ail is longer than their bodies
A larm calls
I t sunbathes
L ives on the island of Madagascar
E ats fruit, leaves and flowers
D oes gas out competitors

L emur means ghost
E ats fruit specially so all the juice goes in their mouth
M ates in April
U nquestionably adorable
R eproduces from August to November

Jolie Hirsch, Grade 5
Perry-Lecompton Middle School, KS

Halloween

Halloween is orange
Like the scary and silly jack-o-lanterns,
The bright orange glow of the harvest moon,
The eerie color of the lights that people put up on their houses.

Halloween is black like the mysterious black cat,
The wicked witch flying on her broom at night,
And the creepy vampires ready to approach unlucky victims.

Halloween is purple like the little princesses going trick-or-treating,
The tasty little Nerds candies I get from trick-or-treating,
And the decorations that people put up everywhere possible.

Emma Seipold, Grade 4
East Mills Community School, IA

High Merit Poems – Grades 4, 5, and 6

I Miss My Family, I Miss My Home
I am beautiful, I am free,
I live high above the trees.

I miss my family, I miss my home,
and during most days I roam alone.

I have beautiful white wings, and beautiful blue eyes,
and curly golden hair that no one can despise.

There is two things I miss the most,
I miss my family, I miss my home.

I dream of the day we meet again,
my parents, my sisters, my brothers, my friends.

I am an angel flying with glee,
over the rainbows, over the trees.

There is still two things I miss the most,
I miss my family, I miss my home.
Katerina Marlow, Grade 6
Belle Fourche Middle School, SD

Uncle Teddy
My Uncle Teddy is funny and sweet,
He sometimes reminds me of a puppet from Sesame Street

When he was younger he was a Marine,
When he was there he was a working machine

In his family, Teddy is the middle child,
He has such a great sense of style

Teddy has an awesome life,
Because he has the coolest wife

Her name is Katie,
And she is really quite a lady

He thinks he is the man at Ping-Pong,
But I dominate him like King Kong

My Uncle Teddy means a lot to me,
Now that he is in our family tree.
Amaya Dinslage, Grade 5
O'Neill Elementary School, NE

Junction City, Kansas
I am from Junction City, Kansas where I will always live.
I am from concerts in the park where I have fun.
I am from McDonald's where I eat and play.
I am from Spin City where I skate and bowl.
I am from buying dresses that I like a lot.
Brytni Johnson, Grade 4
Westwood Elementary School, KS

Happiness
Happiness is a time
When you aren't
Feeling other emotions,
You just want
To let
Go

You don't think
About anything else.
You are
Free

No one will
Stand in your
Way.
Callie Haupert, Grade 6
Collins-Maxwell Middle and High School, IA

Snow
snow tickled the ground,
not wanting to let go of the clouds
frost hugged a pole,
a long lost friend
the snow jumped and parachuted from a tree
to land delicately on the ground
crackling pops of the fire,
soothe me of stiffness
hot chocolate slips and slides down my throat
sending spicy hot chills down my back
clouds, spitting snow and swallowing the sun
boots by the fire, warmed for a ski ride

when all is done, the fire lights again,
warming those who are near.
Paige Morris, Grade 5
Pinedale Elementary School, SD

I Am
I'm
An evergreen
Tree, my bark is brown,
My bark is rough, I will always
Be green, but never soft, I live in
The Black Hills, and stand tall all day,
Birds land on my branches and if they build
A nest I know they will stay, I'm not just a tree I am
More, I don't just stand and watch the eagle soar, and don't
Just stand around bored, I am a proud tree, with responsibility
Do you know what I am; I'm the South Dakota State Tree.
The
Black
Hills
Spruce
Preston Eisenbraun, Grade 6
Wall Elementary School, SD

Track

Track is a very competitive sport,
It's great to have your team's support.

My brother and sister both run,
They say competing is really fun.

My brother loves to run around the track,
He runs quickly, so he's not at the back of the pack.

My sister loves this unique sport,
She is very competitive as her rivals report.

I hope to run in track and be fast,
I think that would be a blast.

Jordan Ferguson, Grade 6
Canistota Public School, SD

Ode to Madison

She is a best friend
Always there for you
Always looking after you
Her tan, white, and black fur is soft and silky
Her personality is a luminous star
Glowing in the dark, peaceful night
She's like an alert watchdog
Barking at neighbors with a low, growly tone in her voice
She only knows sit, shake, high five, and lay down,
But that's fine with me
Whenever I take Madison on a walk
She makes sure
That I am not too far away from her
Madison is a lifelong, loving companion

Brianna Fry, Grade 6
Jefferson Middle School, IA

Summer Time

In the summer, I watch butterflies
Until I pin them
Under my net.
Flitter, flutter, flippity, flop.
Hop, Hop, Hop.
I let them go, and they fly to the sky.

On days when the blazing sun shows no mercy,
I go on my slip 'n' slide
With water that chills to the bone!
Or, I have a water war to stay cool.
And…I could always go to the pool.
But on days when it rains,
It feels like I have pains.

Jacob Kram, Grade 6
Langdon Area Elementary School, ND

What Blue Means to Me

Blue is your beautiful big eyes.
Blue is a blue jay flying over me on a hot day.
Blue is a whale I see on vacation when I go on a boat ride.
Blue is cool water in a big, deep pool.
Blue tastes like sour, tasty blue raspberry Jolly Ranchers.
Blue smells like blueberry pie on Thanksgiving.
Blue sounds like your lovely emotional whispers in my ear.
Blue feels like fluffy cotton candy at a circus.
Blue makes me feel depressed on a rainy day.
Blue is the jewel of the sea that I see hiding in you.

Keilah Luna, Grade 5
Covington Elementary School, NE

How I See Yellow

Yellow is a rain coat on a rainy day.
Yellow is a spicy yellow pepper.
Yellow is a bumblebee buzzing around the park.
Yellow is a sunflower in my backyard.
Yellow tastes like a juicy fresh mango.
Yellow smells like buttery popcorn right out of the microwave.
Yellow sounds like little chicks running around a farm.
Yellow feels like the hot sand on the beach.
Yellow makes me feel like playing outside the whole afternoon.
Yellow is the color of the sun when it wakes me up in the morning.

Maira Muñoz, Grade 5
Covington Elementary School, NE

Kansas

I am from Kansas where yellow sunflowers grow.
I am from the state that I will always know.
I am from swimming in the pool.
I am from learning at Westwood School.
I am from going to the skating ring.
I am from going to the movies.
I am from camping in the sun.
I am from going to Worlds of Fun.
I am from Kansas!

Gianna Redding, Grade 4
Westwood Elementary School, KS

The End

You're done.
Feeling bad for what you did.
So put down the gun,
And just go home, kid.
Don't just stand there like
A boulder.
You did what you could.
As a loving, caring…
Soldier

Nash Kennedy, Grade 6
Collins-Maxwell Middle and High School, IA

Softball

I like to play softball,
But I don't like dodge ball.

My dad is the coach for us,
When he tells us to do something, it's a must!

Last year I played on two teams,
When we score a point, our team screams.

We took first in a tournament last year,
Before we started, we had no fear.

Softball is my favorite sport,
We don't play it on a court.

Softball is really fun to play,
We could do it every day.

Reagen Miller, Grade 4
Canistota Public School, SD

My Family

My family includes five sisters and one adopted brother,
I love each and every one like no other.
All of them have graduated except for two,
We are united through and through.

Watching movies together is our favorite thing to do,
We watch action movies and scary ones too.
While watching movies, popcorn is a real treat,
That is what my family likes to eat.

We also like to play outside,
Getting on our bikes and going for a ride.
We play kickball in the yard,
But have to be careful not to kick it hard.

My family is very important you see,
They mean the world to me.

Jordan Lee, Grade 6
Canistota Public School, SD

Dancing Across the Nation

When I was little I danced like a ballerina, a great pro;
when spinning across the floor, you should have seen me go!
Racing around the room,
those admiring were watching my dancing skills bloom.
I was a butterfly in the wind,
my audience watching me spin.
I was like a speck of dust twirling in the air,
my skin so fair and my long, long hair.
I couldn't control it, I just let it flow;
even when I am old, dancing will make me glow.
This truly is a great sensation and
I will always have the moxie to dance across the nation.

Hannah Piros, Grade 5
Buckner Performing Arts Magnet School, KS

Nature

Nature is all around us,
With animals big and small.
Grazing on some of the grass,
Or living in trees that are short and tall.

With all the birds singing,
While they are siting in a tree.
Nature is an amazing thing,
But trees and animals are all some people see.

Nature is all around us,
With animals big and small.
If you are like most people,
You would know that somebody must have made it all.

Samual Brickett, Grade 6
Ponca Elementary School, NE

A Poem Is Like a Flower

A poem is like a flower,
ready to bloom into colorful stanzas.
The tall stem is a simile,
and petals its metaphors.
Turning the flower into a garden.
It grows as you add more lines,
getting stronger as the words rain onto the paper.
Inspiriting yet delicate.
Ideas are the leaves,
creative and bright.
Flowing like a flower has roots,
to be there so it doesn't fall down.
A poem is like a flower,
free from weeds.

Katie Mans, Grade 5
Indian Hills Elementary School, KS

Poetry

Poetry is like living on a page.
You can write your feelings.
And your thoughts.
Poetry brings comfort.
It is like sitting on a cloud.
Poetry can be your soul and your expressions.
Like a passage to your heart.
When I am sad,
Poetry is something that makes me glad.

Aubrie Waldemar, Grade 5
Aurora Elementary School, NE

There Once Was a Man Who Was Lonely

There once was a man who was lonely.
He thought, "Am I the one and only?"
He wanted someone
To have some fun.
So he wouldn't be quite so lonely.

MacKenzie Said, Grade 4
Briggs Elementary School, IA

I Am

I am an athletic girl who loves basketball
I wonder if I will ever be in the WNBA
I hear a voice in my head telling me you can do it
I see my brothers cheering me on
I want to be able to break any of my school's records in basketball
I am an athletic girl who loves basketball

I pretend that I will make all my shots
I feel pressure on me while shooting free throws
I touch the leather of the basketball
I worry that I'll miss a shot with everybody watching
I cry when we lose championships
I am an athletic girl who loves basketball

I understand someday, somebody will be better than me
I say you can do anything if you put your mind to it
I dream one day I'll be hanging on the rims
I try to work on all different kinds of skills
I hope one day I'll be really good at basketball
I am an athletic girl who loves basketball

Kristyn Throne, Grade 5
Lake Mills Elementary School, IA

I Am a Sporty Girl Who Loves Polar Bears

I am a sporty girl who loves polar bears
I wonder if I will ever own a polar bear
I hear basketballs dribbling
I see polar bears swimming
I want to achieve all of my goals in sports
I am a sporty girl who loves polar bears

I pretend I'm a professional sports player
I feel my hand touching a polar bears soft white fur
I touch the inside of my softball glove while I catch a pop fly
I worry if a polar bear gets hurt
I cry if I get struck out in a softball game
I am a sporty girl who loves polar bears

I understand I probably won't get a polar bear
I say I'll achieve all of my goals in sports
I dream that I own a polar bear
I try to beg my parents for a polar bear
I hope I'll be a professional sports player
I am a sporty girl who loves polar bears

Kendall Kirschbaum, Grade 5
Lake Mills Elementary School, IA

Bullying

I am a smart girl who gets bullied
I wonder if the bullying will stop
I hear kids making fun of me
I see all sorts of kids being bullied
I want the bullies to stop
I am a smart girl who gets bullied

I pretend that the bullies are not around me
I feel them laughing when they bully me
I touch God when I feel low
I worry that they won't stop
I cry because it hurts
I am a smart girl who gets bullied

I understand how they feel
I say to just leave me alone
I dream of a happy place
I try to not let it bother me
I hope to live a happy life
I am a smart girl who gets bullied

Madison Kopp, Grade 5
Lake Mills Elementary School, IA

I Am

I am a fifth grade boy with the nickname Kibbles.
I wonder how I got that name.
I hear it from my sisters and friends.
I see it on cat food bags.
I want a new nickname, instead of Kibbles.
I am a fifth grade boy with the nickname Kibbles.

I pretend I'm the best Vikings player in history.
I feel the laces on the football.
I touch the grass with my cleats.
I worry if I'll ever get on the team.
I cry when I get injured or if my career ends.
I am a fifth grade boy with the nickname Kibbles.

I understand what a life well spent is.
I say "What a life well spent!"
I dream I will never die.
I try to stay as healthy as I can to live a long time.
I hope I have a life well spent.
I am a fifth grade boy with the nickname Kibbles.

Tommy Kaktis, Grade 5
Lake Mills Elementary School, IA

Hoven

Hoven is a town with a fun-filled pool
People from everywhere think it's cool
There is a cathedral in the town
It's in the color of brown
My grandma and grandpa went to that school

Jacob Goebel, Grade 4
Roncalli Elementary School, SD

Pictures

Pictures are like stories,
Stories without words.
Words that can teach you,
Teach you new things.
Things that you never knew.

Morgan Ekhoff, Grade 5
Aurora Elementary School, NE

High Merit Poems – Grades 4, 5, and 6

Crocheting
I like to crochet with yarn
But I don't do it in a barn

I use colors blue and white
The white is sparkling bright

I use a crocheting hook
Following the directions from a book

Pulling yarn through loops makes stitches
From single to double it switches

I go back and forth, up and down
Crocheting, I think, is a noun

It takes effort to make a huge blanket
Although mine is not complete yet!
Bailey Ahlman, Grade 6
Wisner-Pilger Middle School, NE

What Is Summer?
Vacation time
Relaxing
Getting school supplies
Sleeping in late
Going swimming
Going tubing
Going boating
Picking wild flowers
Chasing butterflies
Catching fireflies at night
Staying at friends' houses
Going places
Staying up late
Splashing in the pool

That's Summer!
Dezirae Drake, Grade 4
East Mills Community School, IA

Football
A wesome. **B** elieve in yourself.
C atch. **D** rive the other team to the ground.
E very day it's game time. **F** un.
G et in position. **H** ike the ball.
I love football. **J** ump.
K ick the ball. **L** inebacker.
M iddle linebacker. **N** ice job.
O utside linebacker. **P** unt.
Q uarterback. **R** un hard.
S core. **T** ackle.
U nderpass the ball. **V** ictory.
W in. **X** -back.
Y ou are good. **Z** ero to twelve.
Frank Archer, Grade 5
Westwood Elementary School, KS

The No Rule Game
Adventure is always out there.
You just need to know where.
It can be right outside your door.
Or under the boards in your floor.
Adventure has no specific name.
And there are no rules in the game.
In an adventure you must not be weak.
Or you will be the one to seek.
Remember to stay strong.
Because this journey may be long.
And once you start this chase.
You will have no hiding place.
Natalie Callaghan, Grade 6
Dakota Valley Middle School, SD

Where's Waldo
Where's Waldo?
Up there.
No he's not—I was just there.

Where's Waldo?
Down there.
No he's not—I was just there.

Where's Waldo?
Not here.
That's not true,
I am Waldo!
Jacob Mayes, Grade 5
Aurora Elementary School, NE

Rain Drops Falling
Some are small
Some are tall
Some are loud
Others don't make a sound.
Little drops of water fall on my head
Sometimes I can't go to bed.
They are a sight to see
Sometimes I think this can't be.
I love when they hit the ground
I think they could hurt when they pound.
Don't you hear the sound when they burst
Doesn't it really need to come first.
Lexi Gill, Grade 6
Ponca Elementary School, NE

Red Deer
I see the deer with the doe.
I smell the fresh droppings of the deer.
I hear the roar of the stag.
I feel me shaking when I pull the trigger —
   is it dead or alive?
I taste the victory when I kill it.
Logan Hammeke, Grade 4
Central Kansas Christian Academy, KS

Useless Things
Bristles without a brush
A teacher without a, "Hush."
Inches without rulers
Ice without coolers.

A bathtub without water
A teeter without a totter
A pen without ink
A faucet without a sink.

A microwave without heat
A bed without a sheet
Freckles without a face
A carpenter without a tool case.

A sentence without punctuation
A diploma without a graduation
Glasses without a lens
Kids without friends.
Claire Morrow, Grade 5
O'Neill Elementary School, NE

Useless Things
A radio without sound.
A homeless dog without a pound.
A library without any books.
A model without any looks.

A dog without a bark.
A firework without a spark.
A boat without an oar.
An apple without a core.

A kernel without a pop.
A janitor without a mop.
A Harry without a Potter.
A pool without water.

A man without a dog.
A farmer without a hog.
A farm without a hen.
A start without an end.
Olivia Grass, Grade 5
O'Neill Elementary School, NE

Softball
S ummer is when it's time
O utstanding players are on the team
F avorite sport to me
T he team is very helpful
B est friends with my team mates
A wesome sportsmanship
L aughing and playing
L ove softball forever
Sydney Zahnley, Grade 4
River Valley Elementary School, IA

My Horse Tee
I have a horse named Tee.
He has a special bond with me.

Tee is very handsome and tall,
When I ride, he won't let me fall.

He has never ever kicked,
With him I will never get ticked.

Tee is a large, brown quarter horse,
When I show him, he knows every course.

His mane isn't soft to the touch,
But I still love him very much.
Payton Ortman, Grade 4
Canistota Public School, SD

World Peace
What if we don't have to scream or shout
If we have nothing to argue about
If we don't make fun of the short or stout
That's World Peace

What if there is nothing on the floor
If someone helps, or opens your door
If nobody's left with a really bad sore
That's World Peace

And what if there were only nice words
Or if there was nobody clashing swords
Or if nobody's sitting around being bored
That's World Peace
Molly Lenz, Grade 5
South O'Brien Elementary School, IA

The Deer
The skies are clear,
The birds are chirping,
I see a big deer,
Then it disappears.
The next day,
I see it again,
But this time it blows in the wind.
So just some good advice,
Don't ever think twice,
When that deer blows,
You might never know where it goes.
I may have trouble,
But you could be different.
Just to let you know, don't ever let it go.
Rianna McGee, Grade 5
Crestview Elementary School, KS

Basketball
Onto the court
Past the defender
Into my hands
To my teammate
Beside the goal
Toward the basket
Off the backboard
Through the hoop
Malachi Williams, Grade 5
Central Kansas Christian Academy, KS

Seasons
Seasons come and seasons go
While the wind will suddenly blow
Summer, spring, winter, fall.
In summer you can play softball.
In the spring you can smell the flowers.
In the fall you will get some hail showers.
Don't forget most of all
Winter is where the snow will fall.
Kaitlyn Beach, Grade 5
Ponca Elementary School, NE

The Lake
One fine spring day
In Lake Sam
My dad and I went fishing
We brought all kinds of bait
We sat there all day and
Didn't catch anything
He said
Well son we lost our luck.
Garrett Anderson, Grade 5
Ponca Elementary School, NE

Dads
Dads will always make you laugh,
Even when they help you with math.
Dads will love you,
With all their heart.
Because they know,
You are really smart.
They will always love you,
And of course you will too.
Kaitlyn Kastning, Grade 5
Ponca Elementary School, NE

What Is White?
White is a cloud.
White is vanilla ice cream.
White is a dove.
White is when the angels sing.
White can be milk and cream.
White can sometimes not be seen.
Ariel Carmer, Grade 4
South Tama County Elementary School, IA

Trees
They are in full blossom,
During the spring.
Shading the possum,
From that scary thing.

The sun is burning
The tree that's yearning,
For a nice rain shower.
To bring back beautiful flowers.

Now it is the beginning of fall,
The green leaves are dying.
While I'm hearing the bird's last call,
They leave for the South, flying.

The storm blows
Its enormous nose
While the tree tips,
Then slowly dips.
Elizabeth Holzkamm, Grade 6
Hettinger Elementary School, ND

Basketball
Basketball is the sport
I most like to play,
I usually shoot hoops
several times a day.

I play ball with my brother
with my travel team guys,
It's a fun game to play,
You get lots of exercise.

I like to rebound
Make a fast break,
Draw a foul on the shot
Count the point that I make.

Whether you are old or young
If you're short or tall,
You can have a great time
Playing a game of basketball.
Jeremy Nissen, Grade 5
Aurora Elementary School, NE

Victory
Bump! Spike! Set!
As I watched the ball go over the net,
I anxiously waited upon my knees,
To finally win this game with ease.
We were down six to nothing,
Until we came a-huffing and puffing.
That game was one we won't forget,
And also one to not regret.
Molly McDermott, Grade 6
Crossroads Park Elementary School, IA

I Am a U.S. Marine

I am a U.S. Marine
I hear gunshots
I see people avoiding me
I wonder why white people don't like me
I am a U.S. Marine

I pretend to see everybody as equal
I feel the pain of people being mean to me
I touch people's hearts by serving as a U.S. Marine
I worry that they will kill me
I cry tears of anger
I am a U.S. Marine

I understand the pain of segregation
I say courageous words
I dream that people would be equal
I try to be friends with white people
I hope the world will be a better place
I am a U.S. Marine

Joe Burnes, Grade 4
South Tama County Elementary School, IA

I Am a Little Black Girl

I am a little black girl
I hear everybody screaming at me
I see everyone yelling
I wonder if they will kill me
I am a little black girl

I pretend everyone is happy
I feel everybody's pain and how we need to change it
I touch my pain inside and it hurts
I worry if the world will ever change
I cry when I can't go to school with everyone else
I am a little black girl

I understand why I can't go to school
I say if I could change the world I would
I dream the world will be a better place
I try to keep my tears in but I can't
I hope the world will be a better place someday
I am a little black girl

Jessica Nachazel, Grade 4
South Tama County Elementary School, IA

God

In God we trust
Up in the sky, God is there.
With God, I have good dreams.
Near the rock, God is waiting.
During the day I hear Him talking to me.
Without him, I don't know where I would be.
Above me He's in Heaven.
Along every cross I see Him.

Heaven Wornkey, Grade 4
Central Kansas Christian Academy, KS

My School Family

Jorge is my bro he's like the best one ever!
He always got my back and
I always have his, he always cheers me up when I'm sad
And his hair looks like a porcupine.
Well, that's enough about him back to the subject
Lyssa is my sis she's always there for me when I need help.
She is like the best sis ever, ad she's hilarious.
She is as fast as a cheetah, but not faster than me.
If we talk after school, we would be laughing 24/7.
Josey is my big sis, she is awesome.
There's always something to talk about on the phone.
She always helps me when I need certain stuff.
And she's really nice!
George R. is my little brother
He is as funny as a clown.
He always wants to be my messenger for some weird reason.
Best people in my life
I'm always gong to be with them
Because they mean the world to Me!

Edward Zepeda-Perez, Grade 6
Nieman Elementary School, KS

Baseball

Baseball is very fun,
You play it in the summer sun.
Even though you might get out,
You should never start to pout.

Baseball is my favorite sport,
Even though I am a little short.
I have a whole lot of fun,
Even if the game is not won.

Bases are out on the field,
A bat is what you wield.
Pitching, batting, and running everywhere.
If you make an exciting play, people might stare.

Sitting in the dugout are people in matching outfits.
Players are putting on their baseball mitts.
You better not upset the ump,
Or you might have to sit on your rump.

Joseph Nugteren, Grade 6
Canistota Public School, SD

New Baby Brother

I walk into the room. I see mom
holding him! I sit down, dad brings him
over as I hold my arms out. He places
him in my arms. He felt so tiny and as his
baby blue eyes looked at me. I smile, he holds
my hand tight, and he feels so soft and
smells like a baby. Then I leave and kiss him
by Gage, I say.

Mackenzie Jo Franks, Grade 6
Logan View Public School, NE

Poetry Is Like Fire

Poetry is like fire.
The subjects are uncontrollable.
When the pen touches paper,
Colorful sparks head in every direction.
Emotions glow as the paper
Blazes with ideas.
The artistic words hit you like a spark.
The expressive ideas heat you up,
You always want to learn more.
Feelings in poetry are like
Trick candles on a cake,
No matter how hard you try
They won't blow out.
Poetry always has unique words,
They're so expressive they will soon burn you,
And you will never stop repeating them.

Caitlynn McLeod, Grade 5
Indian Hills Elementary School, KS

The True Me

Madison
Friendly, fun-loving, funny, and athletic
Sister of Kayline, Skye, and Christian
Lover of volleyball, chocolate, and Justin Bieber
Who feels funny with her friends.
    hyper when she eats chocolate.
    happy when we win in volleyball.
Who fears alligators because they could eat me.
    snakes because they are so disgusting.
    sharks because they are so BIG!
Who would like to see Michael Jackson.
    my mom play *Just Dance 3*.
    the end of cancer.
Resident of Emmons
Volk.

Madison Volk, Grade 5
Lake Mills Elementary School, IA

Phoenix

The Phoenix rises again and again,
with a new life ahead of him.
We are like the Phoenix rising once more,
with a new life ahead of us.

When we move to a new place,
we have a new start and a new life
as we introduce ourselves to new family and friends.

When we graduate high school and college we will
get a job and new beginnings.
Everyone is a Phoenix either a strong and wise Phoenix
or a young and naive Phoenix.

So soar proudly with your new, fresh, start.

Gabbie Velder, Grade 6
Belle Fourche Middle School, SD

Easter!

Easter is very bright
The eggs are all colorful,
With joy and fun.
The bunny comes
and hides the eggs.
When I wake up I think
Of an Easter egg hunt.
Have flowers everywhere with beauty.
How fun it is to see the joy of everyone.
I go outside, it is so bright.
This is why Easter is so great!

Kodi Fees, Grade 5
Enning-Union Center Elementary School, SD

Rainbows

The ground is wet
but, the storm is not over yet.

Let the rain fall and let it pass,
so we can see the dewdrops glistening off the grass.

Now a rainbow crosses the sky,
while the birds begin to fly by.

Then the rainbow disappears,
and leaves me nothing but tears.

Abiagil Ericksaon, Grade 6
Belle Fourche Middle School, SD

Khobe Aka Wildman

Khobe
Inventive, athletic; ornery
Nephew of Lance
Who loves family, animals; summer
Who feels happy about going to Colorado
Who needs family, Bella Bear; food
Who fears homework, hair brushes; boredom
Who'd like to see the Smurf movie
Who dreams of going to an amusement park
A student of life
Aka Wildman

Khobe Sommersted-Simmons, Grade 5
O'Neill Elementary School, NE

Maria Grace

Maria, Maria, Maria Grace,
So little, so small, when they found the trace,
They found a trace of Cystic Fibrosis,
And found out she was diagnosed.
All we told her was "Maria, Maria it's okay
A cure is on the way, and when it comes you will say,
Thank you, thank you, thank you much,
for blessing my heart, and keeping me safe
from dying at a young age."

Anna Thompson, Grade 5
Central Middle School, ND

High Merit Poems – Grades 4, 5, and 6

Ode to Friends
Secrets whispered
heart to heart
our giggles
filling the room,
our smiles
brightening the halls

The melody of
pencil lead on paper,
as our notes are passed

The clicking sound of
buttons,
as our messages are sent

The smooth and silky fabric
kissing our fingers
as our clothes are exchanged

Our exposed tears
hitting the floor
like rain on a rooftop

But that's okay,
because in friendship,
there are no secrets…
Maddie Perreard, Grade 6
Jefferson Middle School, IA

Useless Things
Winter without snow
Cookies without dough
A person without a name
A problem without blame

A mouth without spit
A peach without a pit
Colors without eyes
Shoes without ties

A snowman without a hat
A baseball without a bat
School without a class
Windows without glass

A word without a meaning
A mop without cleaning
Books without words
Nests without birds

Food without taste
Trash cans without waste
A secret without a friend
A story without an end
Julia Emme, Grade 5
O'Neill Elementary School, NE

Volcano Eruption
The volcano is sitting idle,
until a loud rumble and a loud boom!
Crash! crack!
The lava spills out of the volcano,
like an overfilled cup.
And it slowly goes towards the water.
It hits and you hear, SSSSSST as it slowly
disappears beneath the ocean surface.
Gage Simmer, Grade 5
South Union Elementary School, IA

Sun Sun
Sun sun…big and blazing,
You're big and yellow.
Sun sun…big and round,
Sun sun…
I see you with your big rays.
Sun sun…with your big heat waves.
You're what warms the earth.
Sun sun…
Kylee Moline, Grade 6
Langdon Area Elementary School, ND

Love
Love is like a heart,
Big and juicy beating constantly.
A diamond you never want to let go of.
Love is happiness and joy.
Love is warm and cozy,
Something you want to be in at night.
In love.
Samantha Blackburn, Grade 5
Algona Middle/High School, IA

Art
Art
Colorful, beautiful
Designing, coloring, thinking
Looking for inspiring ideas
Painting, laughing, crying
Expressive, talent
Art
Natalie Ann Bushey, Grade 5
Westwood Elementary School, KS

Martin Luther King, Junior
Martin Luther King, Junior
Courageous, legendary
Believing, dreaming, speaking
He made history forever
Loving, caring, freeing
Brilliant, historical
Hero
Myndi Weidenbach, Grade 5
Canistota Public School, SD

Chickens
I have a chicken named Spike,
He is such a delight.
He is black and white with a rose comb,
He has a funny tone!
When he wants to squeak,
He opens his beak
And out comes a little tweet tweet!
He likes to peck the brown ground
And see what he has found.
I love my chicken named Spike!
Ashley Ratzlaff, Grade 6
Langdon Area Elementary School, ND

Baby Bird
Off the nest
In the tree
Into the air to learn
Like their parents
Toward the teacher
Within its head it's very frightened
Underneath the wings the wind carries it
Behind the tail it never looks
Near the tree it is now coming
After the flight it goes again.
Evan Hammond, Grade 4
Central Kansas Christian Academy, KS

The Artist
Listen to the paint swish,
I wish to be an artist.

Look at all those colors,
Making a beautiful painting,
I wish to be an artist.

Look at the final,
So great and grand,
I wish to be an artist!
Samantha Zimmerman, Grade 6
Ponca Elementary School, NE

Earthquake
E arth starts shaking.
A hhhhhhh!
R unning away from buildings.
T sunami about to come.
H elp! It says in the ground.
Q uickly away from water
U p on the roof
A ll of us are safe for now.
K im runs away form the water
E arth stops shaking now.
Carlé Stahl, Grade 5
Logan View Public School, NE

The Wind
The wind is all I ever feel
Just whistling through my window.
The small croak of the frog
In the smog.
Quietly waiting for some love,
Every night sleeping in peace
With the misery of the blues.
Never once do you hear
A cat in a hamster sphere.
Julia SanGrait, Grade 5
Central Middle School, ND

Boxes
Boxes boxes all over
Styrofoam peanuts overflowing
Rooms are empty nothing on the walls
When I finally realized we're moving
Boxes boxes unloading
Boxes boxes overflowing
When I come in my new room
Guess what I see
Boxes boxes...
Emma Webb, Grade 5
Ponca Elementary School, NE

The Talking Grape
Once there was a talking grape.
That was very odd shape.
It was square and squishy.
All of a sudden it said,
"Hi, my name is Bob."
"Will you be my friend?"
I could make you a drink or raisins.
I could be your friend that's at the
End
Graci Tangeman, Grade 5
Ponca Elementary School, NE

There Once Was a Man with the Flu
There once was a man with the flu.
He sneezed. His nose he blew.
He did so well
That it started to swell.
He didn't know what to do.
Brendon Koch, Grade 4
Briggs Elementary School, IA

Crazy
Crazy is green.
It sounds like a man.
It smells like a dead fish.
It tastes very bitter.
It looks like a dumb dinosaur.
Crazy feels like a rough rock.
Noah Krehbiel, Grade 5
Omaha Christian Academy, NE

Thunderstorm
Flash!
Flash!
Goes the lightning
Boom!
Boom!
Goes the thunder
Splash!
Splash!
Goes the rain
Swoosh!
Swoosh!
Goes the wind
Bing!
Bang!
Bing!
Bang!
Goes the hail
Crack!
Crack!
Goes the trees
Megan Lien, Grade 6
Hettinger Elementary School, ND

The Seasons
When you see
Kids playing in the playground
You know the school year and
Fall is on its way

You can see
The snowflakes falling from
The sky you know winter
Is here

When you play
In the rain you know
That the flowers and rainbows
Are on their way with...
SPRING

When you sign the summer
Rec forms you know summer
Is on its way for softball,
Baseball and summer vacation.
Mackenzie Crosgrove, Grade 6
Ponca Elementary School, NE

Alone
The lonely girl
Sang a song
But never got what she wanted
Her brothers teased her,
Her father left her
And all she had was her mother.
Brianna Bracey, Grade 5
Central Middle School, ND

Waves
Waves, waves, you are so blue,
I see them best from Honolulu.
Waves, waves, you are so true,
Tell me how the fish see you.
Waves, waves, every now and then,
It seems as if you're trying to bend.
Waves, oh waves, I miss you.
Kathryn Brinegar, Grade 6
Langdon Area Elementary School, ND

Snow
Snow
Wet cold
Falling covering blowing
Snowmen snowballs fireballs lava
Warming spreading burning
Hot red
Magma
Grace Pafford, Grade 4
Central Kansas Christian Academy, KS

Sports
Hockey
cold, icy,
shooting, scoring, celebrating,
trophies, victory, home run, bat,
hitting, throwing, finishing,
warm, active,
Baseball
Matthew Suda, Grade 5
Central Middle School, ND

Candy and Cupcakes
Candy
Delicious, sugary
Eating, chewing, swallowing
Chocolate, caramel, frosting, sprinkles
Baking, smelling, smiling
Fancy, messy
Cupcakes
Jase Lehfeldt, Grade 5
Central Middle School, ND

Elements
When there is a fire burning
I shall swim in it,
If a fire is strong,
I will drink it
When the fire is gone
I shall fill another bucket full
For everyone to enjoy
Zachary Nelson, Grade 6
Ponca Elementary School, NE

High Merit Poems – Grades 4, 5, and 6

My Sister
My sister is a whiny baby,
Every day she has to cry.
She gets whatever she wants,
We don't know why.
Chanler Braman, Grade 5
Algona Middle/High School, IA

What Might I Be?
In the water deep and blue
Something warm and fun too,
Fish, dolphins, and the anemone,
Can you guess what I might be?
Anna Ramaker, Grade 5
Lake Mills Elementary School, IA

Leaves Birds, and Apples
Leaves turn red and brown
Birds fly south for the winter
Honey crisp apples
Alec Brown, Grade 4
Rohwer Elementary School, NE

My Little Kittens
My little kittens are cute
Kittens are very fluffy too
I brush my kittens
Tymber Kaufman, Grade 4
Humboldt Elementary Charter School, KS

Bees
Bees buzz in your ear
Bees are a thing of nature
Bees live in a hive
Morgan Cole, Grade 4
Humboldt Elementary Charter School, KS

Ducks
Ducks are really lame
Duck hunting is a cool sport
I hunt with my Dad
Gunner Elder, Grade 4
Humboldt Elementary Charter School, KS

Vets
Vets are very kind
They love animals a lot
Vets can help your pets
Kilea Heslop, Grade 4
Humboldt Elementary Charter School, KS

Snow
Snow is really white
Snow in the winter time
Snow falls gently down
Winter Lohmann, Grade 4
Humboldt Elementary Charter School, KS

God's Plans
Cancer drowns our hearts with its thick cover of sorrow,
We never know what's going to happen when we wake up tomorrow,
But even though we never know, we keep our heads held high,
We make sure God knows how we feel,
We ask God to steer the wheel to the right path,
And even when we think He's not listening He always is.

God has a plan to carry through,
He never tells it to me and you,
Instead God takes our hands and walks us through,
Making sure we understand everything, me and you.

Sometimes you feel the pain gnawing at your heart,
Those tears flow like a river right from the start,
Your mind is wondering why He has done this to you,
But you have to remember God is holding your hand and walking you through.

Maybe God has in His plans to let you live 'til you're ninety-two,
Or bring you to his kingdom when you're only two.
All you have to do is let God steer you through
The highway of life.
Chandra Spangler, Grade 5
O'Neill Elementary School, NE

I Am
I am a girl who loves cats!
I wonder if cheetahs really do run fast.
I hear a swoosh.
I see a flying cat.
I want a puppy.
I am a girl who loves cats!

I pretend that I am a kitty sometimes.
I feel happy when people don't get hurt.
I touch kitties.
I worry about kitties, because sometimes I find a dead cat.
I cry when a kitty dies.
I am a girl who loves cats!

I understand that there's no such thing as a flying kitty, unless it's an angel.
I say that kitties are cute.
I dream of kitties sliding down the rainbow.
I try to get one of my kitties to trust me.
I hope that none of my cats ever die.
I am a girl who loves cats!
Aubrey Smit, Grade 5
Lake Mills Elementary School, IA

Fat Cat
Once there was a mommy cat.
The cat was really fat.
She was so fat but then they figured out why.
But then in a joyful mood the cat started to cry.
Then the kittens were born, and the mom was not as thick and that was that.
Ashley Nordhues, Grade 4
Wakefield School, KS

The Lake with the Talking Fish
I went to a big shiny lake
Full of magic talking fish
I said there's no such thing
But I was wrong I had one on my line
They are really mean
Ow, he said, you caught me
I let him go
All of a sudden, crash, boom, bang
It must have been strong because it hit me with his fin
Then like lightning it was gone

Cody Martin, Grade 5
Ponca Elementary School, NE

Kansas the Heartland
The golden wheat rest on plains,
Where clouds send sweet spring rains.
The meadowlarks chirp all day,
And buffalo graze and play.
The box turtles munch and eat,
Where the cottonwood trees grow strong and neat.
The sunflowers stand proud and tall,
Where children play and bounce a ball.
Kansas is the true Heartland,
The home of the farmers where the flag stands grand.

Helen Yong, Grade 4
Holy Cross Catholic School, KS

Red Roses
Red is a heart that makes you feel good.
Red is a fox that creeps up on you.
Red is a sunset going down.
Red is slippers dragging across the soft floor.
Red tastes like juicy seedless watermelon.
Red smells like a strong, spicy huge pepper.
Red sounds like cardinals chirping in the woods.
Red feels like crunchy leaves in my yard.
Red makes me feel like when I am in love.
Red is my feeling that I feel for you.

Kaitlin Hofmeister, Grade 5
Covington Elementary School, NE

Red
Red is an angry bird flying above my head.
Red is like a red-tailed hawk soaring in the sky.
Red is a first-aid kit when someone gets hurt.
Red is a red Hawaiian Punch slurping in your mouth.
Red tastes like a tasty raspberry that I eat outside.
Red smells like a fizzy can of cherry soda.
Red sounds like a fire truck roaring down the road.
Red feels like a hard fireman helmet.
Red makes me feel like the kid who has good grades.
Red is a Manchester United uniform.

Michael Lomeli, Grade 5
Covington Elementary School, NE

Orange
Orange is a strip of color from the rainbow.
Orange is a cold, refreshing can of Fanta.
Orange is a construction vest in the night.
Orange is a building block from the toy box.
Orange tastes like jiggling Jello in a Chinese restaurant.
Orange smells like a fragrance in the janitor's closet.
Orange sounds like an annoying cat meowing.
Orange feels like a bumpy basketball.
Orange makes me feel like a joyful and playful person.
Orange is a smoothie nice and cold on a hot summer day.

Brittney Edwardson, Grade 5
Covington Elementary School, NE

White
White is snow falling down from the sky.
White is water from the cool ocean.
White is a cloud full with fluffiness.
White is a paper getting ready to be written on.
White tastes like cake sweet and soft.
White smells like the inside of a tasty crunchy coconut.
White sounds like the music from a wedding.
White feels like lamb's skin.
White makes me feel like a dove flying in the sky.
White is as clean as shiny diamonds.

Yasmin Sarceño, Grade 5
Covington Elementary School, NE

Blue
Blue is a powdery blue butterfly.
Blue is a chirping blue jay taking a bath in a pond.
Blue is a crystal clear blue sky with fluffy white cotton balls.
Blue is warm and buttery blueberry pancakes.
Blue tastes like soft and chewy cotton candy.
Blue smells like delicious and messy blueberry pie.
Blue sounds like wild waves crashing on the sand.
Blue feels like fresh blue bells in a small garden.
Blue makes me feel like a sad and boring rainy day.
Blue is a sparkle in a beautiful eye.

Emely Alvarez, Grade 5
Covington Elementary School, NE

True Story
This is no lie I'm telling you,
this whole story is completely true,
I walked into this dark tomb,
and that is how I found my doom;
a mummy came to life, I swear,
chasing me around giving me a big scare,
I ran up and down side to side,
trying to find a place to hide;
he caught me and drowned me in his swimming pool,
and that is why I can't go to school

Elayna Simon, Grade 6
St Mary's Immaculate Conception Catholic School, IA

I'm Going to School*

I am a happy black student.
I hear people yelling for me not to go to school.
I see white kids ignoring me, and adults yelling at me.
I wonder if the white kids will ever like me.
I am a happy black student.

I pretend this is not happening.
I feel the anger of the white student.
I touch the schoolbook that I never had.
I worry if this can get worse.
I cry about the white kids not letting me play.
I am a happy black student.

I understand why the white people don't like me.
I say we all can get along.
I dream this can get better.
I try to make this a better place.
I hope all this will get better.
I am a happy black student.

Mitchell Knock, Grade 4
South Tama County Elementary School, IA
Written from the perspective of a child in the 1960s. We are thankful attitudes have changed.

I Am a Soldier

I am a soldier
I hear a war going on around me
I see people fighting each other
I wonder about how my family is doing
I am a soldier

I pretend I'm at home and that there was never any wars or fights at all
I feel encouraged to fight in this war and win
I touch my heart and think of my family waiting for me to come home and I give them big bear hugs
I worry that something is wrong with my family and I'm not there to help them
I cry because I'm here and not with my family
I am a soldier

I understand I'm here to help the world be a better place
I say I'll be home soon
I dream I'm at home safe and sound
I try to get home safely
I hope my family's okay
I am a soldier

Brianna Morrison, Grade 4
South Tama County Elementary School, IA

Where I Am From…Philippines

I am from the 7,000 islands of beauty where happiness never ends.
I am from the tropical islands where summer never ends.
I am from white sand beaches and palm trees.
I am from a place where Mango trees are familiar sights.
I am from the Flower Festival where there is lots of food.
I am from where every song and dance will bring a smile to everyone's face.
I am from the Philippines where my heart will always be and where good childhood memories were made.

Erin Ganuelas, Grade 4
Westwood Elementary School, KS

Summer

As the wind blows in my face,
The sand tickles my toes.
Which brings laughter of joy,
That everyone knows.

The cold of the water,
Sprayed onto me by a friend,
Starts a water balloon fight,
That sends everyone wet in the end.

The 4th of July! The 4th of July!
Fireworks light the sky,
For the celebration of freedom,
That sends a tear to my eye.

When summer is over,
School starts,
And all we have left over,
Is the joy in our hearts.
Sarah Seymour, Grade 5
J Sterling Morton Elementary School, NE

Soccer

Soccer is my favorite sport,
I get so tired I could drink four quarts,
I like to play on sunny days,
Although I get hot from the sun's rays.

Winning is satisfying to me,
Although having fun is my priority,
I get excited when my team scores a goal,
So does my team as a whole.

The forward is my favorite position,
To score a goal is my mission,
But when I am a defender,
I try to protect the goalie from offenders.

I like to play soccer in all seasons,
And I love soccer for many reasons,
Soccer is my favorite sport,
And if you do not like it, I may retort.
Dylan Burns, Grade 6
Belle Fourche Middle School, SD

I Found It

I found it, I found it
I finally found my phone,
I looked everywhere
under the couch
under my bed,
in the drawers
on the book shelf,
I found it in the dishwasher.
Madison Bogert, Grade 5
Grafton Central Middle School, ND

May

I like the sunlight.
I like to fly my kite.
I will go to the bay.
Then I get back in the month of May.
Then the sun will be bright.
Matthew Lesser, Grade 4
Wakefield School, KS

Earthquakes

Quaking foundation
Mother Earth is annoyed
Run to a shelter
Crumbling towns all around
Watch out for the aftershocks
Kelby, Grade 4
Hettinger Elementary School, ND

Leaves

Falling all over
Whisping away in the wind
Changing in autumn
They fly everywhere all day
They are like fragile paper
Jesse Qualls, Grade 6
Hettinger Elementary School, ND

Trees

Cultivating, impelling, reposing
Trees
Exquisitely
Sprouting
Around the world
Pamula Melton, Grade 4
Hettinger Elementary School, ND

Birds

Soaring through the air
Gracefully flying strongly
Singing in the trees
Then jumping into the breeze
Only with courage, no fear.
Sarah Corradi, Grade 6
Hettinger Elementary School, ND

Horse

Galloping, trotting, riding
Horse
Marvelously
Playing
In the pasture
Madelyn Larson, Grade 4
Hettinger Elementary School, ND

Stream

Weaves its way through the marsh
It survives our winters, even harsh
It may all seem a bit much
But for Mr. Raccoon it's all just lunch

It's what their world rotates around
It's crystal water filters through the ground
The sun shines down to the bottom
It's even more pretty in the autumn
Mack Buckmier, Grade 5
Hettinger Elementary School, ND

Winter

Winter is cold.
The snow is white and sunshiny gold.
Everything is covered with snow.
The snow is a beautiful sight.
Be careful not to get frostbite.
It's fun to play in the snow.
The snow amount can be very vast.
The frigid winds loudly blow the snow past.
Winter is very surprising.
Dalton Bynum, Grade 6
Canistota Public School, SD

Rain

Rain is dripping, dropping, and bursting.
Rain is the taste of water.
Rain smells like flowers and sugar.
Rain makes me feel wonderful.
Rain is the sound of drops and dribbles.
Rain is cold, wet, and beautiful.
Rain is God's tears.
Rain is nature's bath.
Rain is my shower.
Macy Phillips, Grade 4
Ellinwood Grade School, KS

Tammie

My mother will always help me
Whatever the problem may be
She makes excellent food
Even in a bad mood
And we always laugh, tee hee!
Maci Batenhorst, Grade 6
Wisner-Pilger Middle School, NE

Purple

Purple is the color of K-State
Purple is the color of my room
Purple is the color of my bed spread
Purple is the color of my slippers
Purple is the color of my pillow
Purple is the color of my flower bed
Sage Martinz, Grade 5
Central Kansas Christian Academy, KS

Washington, D.C.

W hen will we see the White House?
A fter we see the Washington Monument,
S ee all the lights at night,
H ouse of Representatives is located here;
I n the Smithsonian, people learn new facts,
N eat to take a tour at night,
G o to the hot and humid city.
T o Washington's National Zoo we go,
O oohhh, how cute the pandas are!
N ation's capital

D istrict of
C olumbia

Trenton Liermann, Grade 6
Wisner-Pilger Middle School, NE

Howler Monkey

H owls to scare things
O pens its mouth to howl
W eighs 20 to 25 pounds
L ives in South America and Central America
E nemies are harpy eagle, bats, and other birds
R eally long tail

M ammal it is
O n the tree branches it lives
N eeds not to be extinct
K een sense of sight
E ats fruits, flowers, figs and nuts
Y ells really loud

Kampbell Kilburn, Grade 5
Perry-Lecompton Middle School, KS

Miles Apart

There I sat waiting and waiting, wondering and wondering.
Would I see her again? Would she ever come back?
For she is going away and away.
My heart is hurt, my head is confused.
Why, why does she have to go?
We are close at heart but will be miles apart.
She is like my other half, I can't live without her.
She is my best friend and she is moving,
She is leaving me, she will be miles apart from me.
I have to go; I have to tell her goodbye.
I start running, running to say "I'll miss you." I'm too late.
She is gone. "I'll miss you" I say to the air.
For we are miles apart, forever and always.

Graci Thompson, Grade 6
Valley Center Intermediate School, KS

Flowers

The flowers smell good.
They make me run all day.
I love the flowers!

Tyler Davidson, Grade 5
Martensdale-St Mary's Elementary School, IA

I Am

I am a girl who loves nature and animals
I wonder how the sky got its color
I hear birds singing in the sky
I see the sun shining so bright
I want to see the sun rise at dawn
I am a girl who loves nature and animals

I pretend I am flying with birds
I feel the air pressing against me
I touch the grass on the ground
I worry something might not shine as much as the others
I cry when I see an animal hurt
I am a girl who loves nature and animals

I understand everything is not perfect
I say to dream big and be proud
I dream of being a girl who lives outdoors
I try to do my best
I hope I could become nature someday
I am a girl who loves nature and animals

Autumn Kopp, Grade 5
Lake Mills Elementary School, IA

Frogs

Frogs enjoy being jumpy,
But they are slimy and bumpy.
Frogs like being leapy,
And they're often not sleepy.
Frogs and toads are kinds of amphibians,
Along with newts, salamanders and caecilians.
Frogs will eat various types of bugs,
But they will surely refuse to eat any slugs.
A frog loves basking on a green lily pad,
When this is done, they're not very sad.
Some kinds of frogs can be blue, green or red,
They might be pretty but are poisonous instead.
Frogs like to croak loudly in the night,
They're peaceful and they do not fight.
When frogs are first born, they come out of eggs,
They're kind of like fish because they don't have legs.
You may not know that frogs' skin absorbs water,
They need to do this when the temperature's hotter.
Some frogs shed their skin everyday,
Then they eat it and it goes away!

Sarah Graves, Grade 6
Belle Fourche Middle School, SD

Birds Chirp!

Birds,
Chirp, chirp,
Flying fast,
Noisy at the feeder,
Falcon

Christian Husted, Grade 5
Martensdale-St Mary's Elementary School, IA

Scared Black Girl*
I am a scared black girl.
I hear screaming, angry voices.
I see security men helping.
I wonder when they will stop screaming.
I am a scared black girl.

I pretend that I'm a black girl.
I feel scared that the people are going to hurt me.
I touch my bookcase down the stairs.
I worry that I will not get through the people.
I cry because people might kick me.
I am a scared black girl.

I understand that I will get through the people that are yelling at me.
I say I feel bad for the people that are yelling at me.
I dream that I will get home.
I try to not cry.
I hope the people that are helping me don't leave me.
I am a scared black girl.

Tara Brown, Grade 4
South Tama County Elementary School, IA
*Written from the perspective of a child in the 1960s. We are thankful attitudes have changed.

A Happy White Child*
I am a happy white child.
I hear laughing and happiness.
I see white and black children.
I wonder if my parents are mad.
I am a happy white child.

I pretend I had a bad day.
I feel happy to play with everyone.
I touch the heart of a friend.
I worry I will get pulled out of school.
I cry that I won't get to be friends with blacks.
I am a happy white child.

I understand how blacks feel.
I say "Hi" to people.
I dream to stay like this forever.
I try to make my parents happy.
I hope I make lots of friends.
I am a happy white child.

Maisie Lacina, Grade 4
South Tama County Elementary School, IA
*Written from the perspective of a child in the 1960s. We are thankful attitudes have changed.

Sports
Sports like baseball and football are fun
I play with all my friends
Football I'm a QB and baseball I'm a pitcher
My dad and I play in the yard
Sometimes I play with my sister
I like to play sports like football and baseball

Evan Anderson, Grade 5
Ponca Elementary School, NE

A Shooting Star
One day I saw two shooting stars,
When I looked up again
I saw a constellation as some moving cars.
Then my mom called me inside
But I had to get one more view
The last time I looked up I saw a picture of Mars!

Hailey Zimmerman, Grade 5
Ponca Elementary School, NE

High Merit Poems – Grades 4, 5, and 6

My Nephews
My nephews can be crazy
They can be funny or lazy

With the dogs they love to run free
Even though they are both peewees

They are so very cute,
And they are quite a hoot

Blaine goes out to check his calf
I like it when he smiles and laughs

Stockton rolls on the floor
Baby Stockton I adore

They are four and almost one
They are my brother's two sons.
Sutton Bellar, Grade 6
Wisner-Pilger Middle School, NE

Penguin and Otter
The penguin jumped out of the water
He saw his friend Otter
Otter said, Hello
Penguin said, You look a bit yellow
Penguin said, Why are you a yellow fellow?
I know I look funny
But I went to see Dr. Bunny
For my cold
But then he told
I needed some rash cream
The cream is called beam
The reason it is called beam
Is because it is the color of a bean
That is why I look yellow
Hey wake up sleepy fellow
Penguin said, So why are you so yellow?
I will tell you later when you play cello
Olivia Eifert, Grade 5
Ponca Elementary School, NE

Hiking with Nature
I love hiking with nature,
The trees are always with me,
The leaves are always with me,
The animals are always with me,
When the leaves crack,
I know they're with me,
When the trees sway,
I know they're with me,
When the animals gaze,
I know they're with me.
That's why I hike,
I hike with nature.
Logan Kingsbury, Grade 6
Ponca Elementary School, NE

South Dakota
S ioux Falls Zoo
O utrageous customs
U niversity of South Dakota
T on of cool towns
H ot and way different food

D eadwood's casinos
A lot of forests
K imball trackers
O utdoor sports
T rains in Aberdeen
A pplebee's
Jared Loecker, Grade 4
Roncalli Elementary School, SD

The Beautiful Valley
As walking through the valley
The sharp grass
The ice cold river.
As walking through the valley
Fruity smelling flowers,
The hot campfire sun.
The wind blows harder than
On a cold winter day.
As walking through the valley
Looking at the scenery
More beautiful than the city.
Brianna Scott, Grade 6
Ponca Elementary School, NE

Lego Master
L ong
E xciting
G ames
O bjects

M onthly magazine
A mazing
S ets
T ower
E ntertaining
R iches
Seth Winget, Grade 4
Ellinwood Grade School, KS

Box Turtles
The box turtle is our state reptile.
It is a tad faster than a snail.
On the shell it looks like a soccer ball.
The tail is smaller than a snail.
The box turtle is slow.
It can go as long as it doesn't snow.
It can live in a house.
It can be the size of a mouse.
Jacobe Tramp, Grade 4
Holy Cross Catholic School, KS

What Is Blue?
Blue is the sky
When the clouds aren't high.
Blue is water
That waves in the wind.
Blue can be socks
That we wear.
Blue can be a cover
Of a book that we read.
Blue can be lollipops.
Blue can be the Earth
Which we live in.
Angel Aguilera, Grade 4
South Tama County Elementary School, IA

Brown
Brown is dirt.
Brown is squishy.
Brown is crayon.
Brown is hair.
Brown smells like leather.
Brown tastes like cinnamon.
Brown sounds like low voices
Brown looks like mud.
Brown feels like rough skin.
Brown makes me feel awesome.
Brown is the most awesomest
Sawyer Cockburn, Grade 4
River Valley Elementary School, IA

Costa Rica
C olorful plants and animals,
O h! So many activities to do,
S it down by the beach or
T ake a tour through an exotic forest,
A nd you have to try the zip-lining, too!

R esting is an option
I n this perfect place;
C an't you see the sunset glow?
A fter all this, you'll never want to leave!
Lauren Jacobsen, Grade 6
Wisner-Pilger Middle School, NE

Kansas Animals
I am the heartland
Great and wide
I am the land where bison roam
In gentle strokes the meadow lark flies
From dawn to dusk my creatures
Roam from grain to grain
From hay bale to hay bale
And light to light
I am the heartland
Great and wide
Joseph Walter, Grade 4
Holy Cross Catholic School, KS

There Once Was a Girl on the Floor
There once was a girl on the floor
Who rolled into a hard cold door.
She bumped into a beam.
It started to seem
That she wanted to do it once more.
Melodee Kovinchick, Grade 4
Briggs Elementary School, IA

Aberdeen
Aberdeen is quite the fun place.
It's in SD and there is lots of space.
It's one fun city,
And it sure is pretty!
In the town once a year, there is a race.
Erica Carda, Grade 4
Roncalli Elementary School, SD

Volleyball
A lways ready to play
B e on time to practice
C oncentrate on the ball
D odge to get it over
E njoy the sport volleyball
Mikayla Simmons, Grade 5
Lake Mills Elementary School, IA

Football
Who: Hines Ward
What: hit a person hard
When: on Friday night at 8:00
Where: on a football field
Why: He was big and awesome
Isaac Beeson, Grade 4
River Valley Elementary School, IA

Basketball
I feel sweat on the ball.
I taste water in my mouth.
I hear, "Go! Go! Score!"
I smell fun on the court.
I see we won the game!
Kelsi Dalton, Grade 4
Central Kansas Christian Academy, KS

Snow
Snow is so fun and bright.
To play in it, you don't need light.
So light and fluffy,
So pretty and white,
Go and play tonight.
Katie Samples, Grade 6
Andrew Community School, IA

Kansas
Did you know Kansas was named after a Native American tribe?
The Kansas Indians live here many years ago and the state of Kansas was named after them.
I am from where sunflowers grow.
I am from where the Monument Rocks are found.
I am from where Native American tribes live.
I am from where wheat grows.
I am from camping at Milford Lake.
I am from Kansas where I've always lived and I will never leave this great state.
Devin Searles, Grade 4
Westwood Elementary School, KS

Kansas
I am from a farm where horses, cows, sheep, cats and dogs play.
I am from a family with three brothers, a mom and dad.
I am from a big house with a runway outside for my grandpa's airplanes.
I am from a family with a lot of aunts who have babies.
I am from a small town where tornados come around and destroy most buildings.
I am from a town where helpfulness and forgiveness comes around.
I am from Chapman, Kansas, my true home.
Merci Clark, Grade 4
Westwood Elementary School, KS

I Am From…Kansas
I am from the Sunflower Sate where sunflowers grow up to ten feet tall.
I am from Kansas where catfish weigh up to six hundred and fifty pounds.
I am from the Rolling Hills Zoo where many different animals like to play.
I am from many pumpkin patches where pumpkins can grow very big.
I am from Dodge City where the Boot Hill Museum is close to the cemetery.
I am from Junction City where most of my adventures started.
Michael Gerebics, Grade 4
Westwood Elementary School, KS

Black
Black is the color of deadly darkness that you are afraid to enter.
Black is the color of sorrow.
Black is the color of fear eating at you from the inside out.
Black is the color of a deadly black widow spider piercing its fangs into you.
Black is the color of death.
Black is the color of forbidden happiness that can never be.
Maggie Hillman, Grade 6
Central Kansas Christian Academy, KS

Austin
Austin
Half-monkey, hardheaded, booming
A member of the monkey family
Who loves monkeys, amphibians, reptiles
Who feels passionate about fishing
Who needs turtles, frogs, lizards
Who fears nothing, nothing, nothing
Who'd like to see a Komodo dragon
Who dreams of owning a reptile farm
A student of nature
Psychowits
Austin Dow, Grade 5
O'Neill Elementary School, NE

Black
Black is zebra stripes.
Black is midnight.
Black is snakes.
Black is crows.
Black is deadly.
Black tastes like licorice.
Black smells like smoke
Black sounds like bats.
Black feels like fur.
Black looks like the midnight sky.
Black makes me dizzy.
Hunter Smyth, Grade 4
Ellinwood Grade School, KS

High Merit Poems – Grades 4, 5, and 6

Start to Finish
I start the race,
my heart beating.
I can feel it and hear it.
I reach the finish of the race
and come in first place!
Addison Cronk, Grade 4
South Tama County Elementary School, IA

Play Time
When the moon is round and bright
I howl and howl all through the night
But don't be scared and run away
I'm calling out, "who wants to play?"
Then we play and play until the light
Hudson Schweers, Grade 6
Ponca Elementary School, NE

Dance
D rove crazy by music
A wesome people do cool routines
N ight time is when I get to dance
C oocoo for the really cute clothes
E xciting dances that people do
Kendall Fitch, Grade 4
River Valley Elementary School, IA

Basketball Player
Who: A Basketball Player
What: practiced for a game
When: every afternoon
Where: at her house
Why: she wanted to be good
Reagan Bahrke, Grade 4
River Valley Elementary School, IA

Volleyball
R eady to play
S tay in the game
T his makes me happy
U se your legs and call it out
V olleyball is what I got and I got game
Lyv Arispe, Grade 5
Lake Mills Elementary School, IA

Dog
Dog,
Dog,
Running around town,
Why do you run around?
I wonder if you ran away?
Casie McIntosh, Grade 5
Aurora Elementary School, NE

The Eastern North American Tree
Whoosh! Straight to the sky 50 feet high
Up goes the Autumn Flame Red Maple
It's colorful wavy, and red like a cherry
Sometimes it's like a roaring bonfire
And sometimes it's like a flying fairy
Different colors every time you plant a new one
Some leaves drop like butterflies fluttering in the air
Some float in the air like a pretty feather floating in the sky
Some change colors from pink to red, like mood rings
Bark solid, brown, hard, rough, plain, and dark — tough like alligators skin —
The mysterious Eastern North American tree — a tree on fire
Paisley Godfrey, Grade 6
Wall Elementary School, SD

I Am From…Kansas
Welcome to Kansas. This is where I live. I was born here.
I am from out in the farm, where it is a wheat producing state.
I am from Milford Lake, where it is a man-made lake.
I am from the Junction City pool, where it is a great place to swim.
I am from Westwood Elementary, where it is a good place to learn and grin.
I am from Vertical Heart Church, where it is a great place to worship God.
I am from the Manhattan Zoo, where kids come there a lot.
I am from the Rolling Hills Zoo, where the rolling hills of Kansas are near.
I am from the Junction City High School, where Blue Jay fans cheer.
I am from Kansas, where it is a paradise, and it is like a demo of heaven.
Jordan Duncan, Grade 4
Westwood Elementary School, KS

Silver and Ice
Silver is like a shiny wedding ring for a happy girl.
Silver is like the magnets that pick up my heart.
Silver is like a ring that helps me know my feelings.
Silver is like a water fountain that can get you wet from head to toe.
Silver tastes like the fresh spring water that cools you down when you drink it.
Silver smells like the wet spring grass that's freshly grown.
Silver sounds like the laughter of children when they're happy.
Silver feels like the soft, pretty bunny fur as he hops away.
Silver makes me feel sweet like a bowl of chocolate chip ice cream.
Silver is the color of my eyes when I'm happy.
Sami Coffin, Grade 5
Covington Elementary School, NE

Blue
Blue is the sky strongly and elegantly shining.
Blue is how snow appears in the darkness of night.
Blue is sapphire sparkling in the bright and beautiful sun.
Blue is the ocean gleaming with life.
Blue tastes like blueberries that are sweet with a pinch of sourness.
Blue smells like the fresh smell of the flower indigo.
Blue sounds like bluebirds chirping softly on a gray morning.
Blue feels like the fabric of my crisp blue jeans.
Blue makes me feel like sadness cutting like an open wound.
Blue is the deep midnight sky with stars sparkling like diamonds in the sky.
Sydney Comstock, Grade 5
Covington Elementary School, NE

Softball

Softball is so much fun!
I love to play it in the sun.

Make sure you wear a hat,
And don't forget to bring your bat.

We hit the ball,
Hoping it goes to the outfield wall.

Make sure you run to the base,
Don't trip over your shoelace.

Make sure you wear your gear
Then you will have no fear.

Playing softball might be hard
Unless you practice in your yard.

If your team wins the game,
You may hear someone in the crowd call your name.

I won't forget to say "good game,"
I hope the others do the same.

Hannah Parry, Grade 4
Canistota Public School, SD

Nature's Beauty

A fresh breath fills your soul,
Glancing around you don't believe your eyes,
Noticing how beautiful nature is,
Animals—only worrying about survival,
While new vegetation timidly sprouts from the ground.

Birds, deer, snakes—few of nature's creatures,
Some life threatening some harmless,
Giving a scare to cheering you up,
All trying to survive in this world,
All unique in different ways.

Leaves turning shades of burnt orange to soft brown,
Snow melting turning into green grass,
Animals being born at a special time of the year,
Animals starting hibernation when snow starts falling,
These are all factors that changes nature's beauty.

The sun lighting up the sky at daylight to stars at night,
Clouds make precipitation fall of disasters come about,
All shaping and changing nature's beauty,
These are all magical creations of God that affect nature,
Nature is a mystery and that is the way it is.

Darissa Overweg, Grade 6
Kimball School, SD

Oregon

Are you looking for the best place to go for a vacation?
Oregon is that place, with its mountains, seacoast and forests.
I am from where there are tall volcanos!
I am from where the land is not flat.
I am from where there are pretty waterfalls.
I am from where the trees are tall.
I am from Oregon and its rugged coastline.
I am from all of these wonderful things about Oregon
And I hope to go back someday.

Levi Davis, Grade 4
Westwood Elementary School, KS

Oh What a Beautiful Sight to Have Seen

The sky so blue the grass so green
Oh what a beautiful sight to have seen
The earth so many colors red, blue, purple, and green
Oh what a beautiful sight to have seen
The mountains so grey and white and the trees so brown and green
Oh what a beautiful sight to have seen
What would we be without colors boring is what I would say
So beautiful with red, blue, purple, and green
Oh what a beautiful sight to have seen

Jay Brockhaus, Grade 6
Ponca Elementary School, NE

Nothing More

I could not ask for anything more,
Ocean water, sparkling seas, beautiful flowers, and silver trees.
It's all in our world,
All year round,
It's all so beautiful,
Everything,
Right outside my window,
And even if I try,
I could not ask for anything more.

Abby Schweers, Grade 6
Ponca Elementary School, NE

Oh So Beautiful

The open skies, the smell of pies,
Oh so beautiful!
The land where wheat grows, where the smells flow,
Oh so beautiful!
Buffalo and bison feed,
Farmers growing many more seeds,
Miles and miles of beautiful plains,
Rows and rows and wheat and grain,
Oh so beautiful!

Sierra Garcia, Grade 4
Holy Cross Catholic School, KS

High Merit Poems – Grades 4, 5, and 6

Football

F ootball is fun to play with my friend Brady
O n a sunny day.
O utside we go to
T ackle each other and run to the end zone. We have fun together
B ut we always try out hardest
A nd do our best. We
L earn how to play well; we
L augh and have a great time.

Colter Lacey, Grade 4
Canistota Public School, SD

Duluth

The tall boat goes under the bridge,
we sit and view from the ridge.
As we walk on the boardwalk,
we listen to people talk.
We chatted with the old man in the elevator;
as he gets off, he says, "See you later!"
Daddy and I enjoy the sunset from the balcony;
finally, we fall asleep…Z…Z…Z…

Autumn Ormiston, Grade 6
Langdon Area Elementary School, ND

The Magic of Snowflakes

I wish snow could become whatever you wish it to be.
Finally something in this world would be free.
Fine objects would fall from the sky.
You could see them coming way up high.
You would know they would be for you.
For all the good things you do.
But if all these fine things fell from the sky…
The price of a snowflake would be high!

Emilee Pauley, Grade 6
Wall Elementary School, SD

Danielle

D orky
A ctive
N ice
I ntelligent
E xcited
L over of dogs
L ikes ice cream
E nergetic

Danielle Miller, Grade 6
St Mary's Immaculate Conception Catholic School, IA

Football

Football is green
It taste like dirt
It sounds like pads cracking
It smells like fresh cut grass
It looks like dirt slinging
It makes me feel happy

Tristan Mammen, Grade 4
River Valley Elementary School, IA

Track

Track is my favorite,
I run every day;
it's my favorite thing to do,
it makes me want to play,
it makes me feel fast —
even when I'm last;
it's my favorite thing to do;
What about you?

Blake Smith, Grade 6
St Mary's Immaculate Conception Catholic School, IA

Earth

Earth, Earth, beautiful Earth,
We have to protect it or we'll have no Earth.
Earth, Earth, sensitive Earth,
Trash cans were built so we wouldn't pollute,
Earth, Earth, only Earth,
How are we to live if we have no Earth?
Earth, Earth, huge Earth,
It is huge so it could support us but we have to support our Earth.

Emma Beach, Grade 6
Ponca Elementary School, NE

Past and Present

The computers flash on,
Hear the typewriters click, click, click.
The gigantic combine swoops up the corn,
The slaves' hands are covered in dirt.
The cell phones receive a new text message,
The man is tired from running.
From past to the present most things are different,
Besides the knowledge of mankind.

Braeden Maise, Grade 6
Ponca Elementary School, NE

How Wise

How wise we are depends on
How we think before we do.
How wise we are depends on
How you are always prepared.
How wise we are depends on
How many questions we ask.
How wise we are depends on
How many times we choose to take the right path.

Zachary Statema, Grade 6
Ponca Elementary School, NE

Citizen Soldier

I want to go to college
And serve as a soldier
I know it will be hard when I am older
I will feel proud when this is done
Because then I will know
I have won

Sam Thompson, Grade 6
Ponca Elementary School, NE

Page 187

Trees
How beautiful are the trees
Although they hold nasty bees
Their leaves make me sneeze
But they bring a big breeze
The wind blows through my hair
It sounds like a bear
It makes a big gust
And moves lots of dust
Justice Anderson, Grade 6
Hettinger Elementary School, ND

Ghost
My room is messy
and mom said I had to clean it
and I said no
because there is a ghost under my bed
and she did not believe me
so she went to clean it
and there to her surprise was the ghost
so my room never got cleaned again
Alyssa Otto, Grade 5
Central Middle School, ND

Wagon
I look out my window,
and while I look,
I see a wagon,
red-striped,
with some black,
and some white,
filled with water,
under the light.
Cassie Monson, Grade 5
Central Middle School, ND

Deer
Around the trees
Through the grass
Within a mile away from me
Near my house
With a scratch on its back
Toward home it turns
Before it left
Among its herd
Christian Arndt, Grade 4
Central Kansas Christian Academy, KS

I Hear Nebraska Sing
I hear Nebraska sing.
I see the meadowlark's wing.
What history we've made,
like our ice-cold Kool-Aid.
The state flower's a goldenrod.
Nebraska, a true gift from God!
Zeus Sobetski, Grade 6
St Philip Neri School, NE

Wolves
They have bushy tails.
They howl on top of mountains
Beautiful creatures.
Mario Blaine Leon, Grade 4
Ellinwood Grade School, KS

Index

Abbas, Maggi ... 33
Abernathy, Mandy ... 67
Abram, Taje'Nae ... 127
Abston, Bryanna ... 144
Adams, April ... 19
Adan-Kruzic, Juliana ... 157
Adrian, Angelina ... 92
Aguilera, Angel ... 183
Ahlman, Bailey ... 171
Aikins, Jackson ... 162
Albert, Tyler ... 47
Alefteras, Spencer ... 84
Alexander, Sara ... 26
Alfaro, Neyda ... 90
Alholinna, Alexis ... 24
Allison, Michael ... 158
Alvarez, Emely ... 178
Amfahr, Katelyn ... 161
Ammon, Aaron ... 26
Anderegg, Rachel ... 69
Andersen, Molly ... 76
Anderson, AnnMarie ... 88
Anderson, Carter ... 107
Anderson, Evan ... 182
Anderson, Garrett ... 172
Anderson, Justice ... 188
Anderson, Lauren ... 147
Anderson, Patricia ... 11
Anderson, Thomas ... 158
Andress, Alyssa ... 134
Andrew, Luke ... 21
Andrews, Stephanie ... 85
Ansley, Jonathan ... 120
Ansong, Daniel ... 18
Anthony, Jeremiah ... 33
Arandus, Maddie ... 89
Arbuckle, Desirae ... 137
Archer, Frank ... 171
Arispe, Lyv ... 185
Armitage, Siri ... 8
Arndt, Christian ... 188
Arp, Garrett ... 146
Auer, Amanda ... 79
Ausdemore, Alex ... 66
Austin, Beau ... 164
Axelson, Kimberly ... 137
Backer, Kayla ... 32
Bacon, Brooklyn ... 138
Baeza, Alexes ... 134
Bahrke, Reagan ... 185
Bailey, Dakotah ... 47
Baker, Adam ... 96

Bakula, Jack ... 103
Baldridge, Tyrel ... 17
Bamberger, Brianna ... 140
Bandel, Kyla ... 53
Bane, Jordan ... 74
Barnard, Makenzie ... 40
Barnes, Marcus ... 75
Barrientos, Austin ... 121
Bartek-Miller, Clarice ... 49
Bartels, Leah ... 92
Barth, Jared ... 45
Batenhorst, Maci ... 180
Bates, Gabriel ... 36
Bates, Sammi ... 106
Battles, Julianna ... 69
Bauer, Tamilyn ... 13
Baumhover, Brittany ... 27
Beach, Emma ... 187
Beach, Kaitlyn ... 172
Beeson, Isaac ... 184
Behrens, Brittany ... 120
Beikman, Mariah ... 114
Belgarde, Hunter ... 128
Bellar, Sutton ... 183
Bendig, Miranda ... 95
Benitez, Gracely ... 91
Bennett, Vincent ... 14
Benvin, Victoria ... 26
Bertels, Mikayla ... 58
Birzer, Connor ... 31
Bishop-Martinez, Devon ... 27
Blackburn, Samantha ... 175
Blankartz, Joseph ... 89
Blaser, Treyton ... 144
Bluestone, Jr., Marc ... 53
Blum, Ryan ... 96
Bock, Macie ... 80
Boehmer, Cael ... 164
Boeke, Claire ... 130
Boeke, Clayton ... 150
Bogert, Madison ... 180
Bohlender, Trey ... 151
Bolin, Jade ... 122
Bollinger, Maddy ... 68
Bolsinger, Tyler ... 93
Bone, Sophia ... 152
Bookout, Caleb ... 134
Bormann, Layne ... 87
Borslien, Felicia ... 96
Bouska, Kayla ... 30
Bowers, Lea ... 20
Boyes, Kim ... 54

Boyle, Tanner ... 19
Braaton, Katie ... 42
Bracelin, Cade ... 59
Bracey, Brianna ... 176
Brackenbury, Madison ... 68
Braman, Chanler ... 177
Brandenberg, Kyla ... 125
Brant, Race ... 129
Braun, Lindsay ... 60
Breen, Jackson ... 125
Breitbach, Belle ... 84
Breitbach, Mitchell ... 157
Bretey, Micaela ... 105
Brickell, Jake ... 45
Brickett, Samual ... 169
Bridges, Alissa ... 99
Bries, Logan ... 81
Briganti, Mary ... 55
Briggs, Jarrod ... 48
Brightwell-Kelley, Joseph ... 27
Briles, Beau ... 57
Brinegar, Kathryn ... 176
Briseno, Ivan ... 141
Broadway, LaTeya ... 114
Brockhaus, Jay ... 186
Brodrick, Isaac ... 79
Brown, Alec ... 177
Brown, Shayla ... 84
Brown, Tara ... 182
Bruggeman, Tori ... 32
Brugger, Joseph ... 97
Bruha, Maddie ... 40
Buck, Dan ... 88
Buckles, Jessica ... 150
Buckley, Katie ... 98
Buckmier, Mack ... 180
Budach, Raven ... 145
Budmayr, Fallon ... 151
Bultje, Skylar ... 140
Burkholder, Zoe ... 145
Burnes, Joe ... 173
Burnham, Colten ... 136
Burns, Dylan ... 180
Burr, Braden ... 130
Burr, Jade ... 151
Burton, Kaitlyn ... 29
Burwick, Kyle ... 159
Bush, Emmalea ... 78
Bushey, Natalie Ann ... 175
Buske, Callie ... 21
Buskirk, Megan ... 12
Bynum, Dalton ... 180

Calease, Maddie	92	
Call, Selina	78	
Callaghan, Natalie	171	
Calovich, Zachary	75	
Cammack, Jayda	143	
Campbell, Morgan	155	
Campbell, Rylee	153	
Campbell, Sam	126	
Campos, Carlos	148	
Cannon, Andrew	73	
Caraccilo, Zachary	89	
Carda, Erica	184	
Carl, Mary-Elizabeth	91	
Carlson, Spencer	105	
Carmer, Ariel	172	
Carper, Emma	108	
Carrera, Tony	163	
Carter, Hanna	31	
Carter, Kiersten	115	
Carter, Tavia	31	
Cassaw, Clayton	94	
Castro, Cleanna	77	
Catches, Kevin	41	
Chandler, Tressa	35	
Chapin, Skylar	121	
Charboneau, Brittany	32	
Chavez, Isaac	165	
Choat, Evey	25	
Choi, Daisy	26	
Christensen, Ben	74	
Christiansen, Jacia	43	
Church, Jakob	70	
Churchill, Murphy	52	
Clark, Isaac	108	
Clark, Mackenzie	8	
Clark, Megan	10	
Clark, Merci	184	
Clinton, Haley	69	
Coble, Josh	56	
Coble, Lucas	130	
Cockburn, Sawyer	183	
Coffin, Sami	185	
Colarossi, Madelaine	28	
Cole, Grace	116	
Cole, Jordan	59	
Cole, Morgan	177	
Collings, Matthew	18	
Comstock, Sydney	185	
Conrad, Madie	44	
Cooklin, Kalyn	63	
Copperstone, Weston	107	
Cormany, Harley	141	
Corradi, Sarah	180	
Cote, Dominic	50	
Counter, Kaitlyn	8	
Coverdale, Hannah	23	
Craig, Jordan	18	
Crail, Tia	124	
Cravens, Quinton	60
Crawford, Brooke	151
Criddle, Kristie	154
Cronk, Addison	185
Crooms, Carah	83
Crosgrove, Mackenzie	176
Crow, Aly	116
Crum, Josh	62
Culek, Elisabeth	61
Cullers, Tate	127
Cunningham, Madeline	102
Cunningham, Talia	102
Dade, Hannah	72
Dalton, Kelsi	184
Daly, Dylan	140
Danze, William	107
Davidson, Tyler	181
Davis, Levi	186
Davis, Victoria	147
Dawson, Curtney	136
Day, Nick	127
Deathe, Donovan	150
Debus, Kylie	72
DeFoe, Mason	159
DeGeldere, Kaleigh	136
Den Burger, Rendi	11
Deng, Linda	98
Denney, Brandon	68
Derrickson, Hailey	119
Devadass, Kingsy	127
DeVlaminck, Zane	61
DeWitt, Aaron	140
Dial, Zac	116
Diaz, Marco	139
DiCesare, Kailyn	142
Diggins, Kevin	147
Dinklage, Mallori	150
Dinslage, Amaya	167
Divingnzzo, Sara	135
Dixon, Brittanie	36
Dobesh, Ally	140
Dobson, Rebecca	109
Doescher, Toni	85
Dominguez, Abigail	138
Doser, Brianna	64
Dougherty, Liam	100
Dow, Austin	184
Drake, Dezirae	171
Drake, Sarah	127
Draper, Savhannah	26
Drinkard, Tamara	40
Drosdal, Mykal	110
Drummer, Nate	160
Dudgeon, Bryanna	13
Duncan, Jordan	185
Dunn, Dallas	151
Dunn, Ethan	156
Dvorak, Emily	57
Dvorak, Logan	146
Dvorak, Reilly	43
Easter, Nick	66
Ebert, Joslyn	162
Eckholm, Annika	33
Edwards, Tyler	15
Edwardson, Brittney	178
Eickhoff, Elizabeth	28
Eifert, Olivia	183
Eischeid, Rose	71
Eisenbraun, Preston	167
Ekhoff, Morgan	170
Elder, Gunner	177
Elfers, Emily	59
Ellensohn, Leah	9
Elliott, Madison	70
Elshere, Carter	74
Emme, Julia	175
Emo, Andrew	94
Ericksaon, Abiagil	174
Erlendson, Emily	74
Escamilla, Fernando	143
Eslinger, Kora	159
Esposti, Ethan	12
Estes, Alec	147
Fabre, Carl	113
Faherty, Angela	123
Fahrenholz, Tanisha	14
Fails, Meghan	144
Falconer, Mallory	23
Fangmeier, Colton	87
Fangmeier, Rachael	13
Faulkender, Jude	128
Fees, Kodi	174
Feil, Hannah	147
Feltman, Nicole	150
Felts, Cassie	76
Ferguson, Joe	131
Ferguson, Jordan	168
Ferguson, Logan	147
Fernandez, Aby	92
Ferris, Emily	61
Fethkenher, Kortney	143
Fields, Kelsey	159
Figueroa, Nicole	162
Firoz, Humza	112
Fischer, Alexandra	72
Fischer, Isaak	148
Fitch, Kendall	185
Fleener, Austin	78
Florer, Ashley	117
Folkens, Brady	25
Fool Bull, Kim	96
Ford, Cheyenne	123
Fordyce, Jack	82
Foster, Aubrey	107
Frakes, Callie	154
Francis, Tessa	139

Index

Francis-Ramirez, Tomi 98
Franks, Mackenzie Jo 173
Fraser, Lorraina 81
Frederick, David 34
Freestone, Shelby 89
Frey, Zach 15
Friday, Meg 137
Friedlein, Trevor 117
Friesen, Caryn 17
Frink, Danielle 113
Fritch, Colten 162
Froehle, Sydney 80
Fry, Brianna 168
Funke, Maggie 116
Gaba, Nishita 139
Galardi, Marissa 121
Gallus, Timothy 64
Gammon, Natalie 44
Ganuelas, Erin 179
Garcia, Brian 100
Garcia, Cecilia 134
Garcia, Gil 80
Garcia, Sierra 186
Garrett, Jayden 74
Garriott, Reece 113
Garvis, Ben 44
Gates, Anna 42
Gepson, Corey 119
Gerebics, Michael 184
Gerving, Katy 11
Gill, Lexi 171
Gilmore, Ashtyn 112
Glad, Audrey 161
Glammeier, Kassie 46
Glaubius, Sophie 121
Godfrey, Paisley 185
Godfrey, Winter 88
Goebel, Jacob 170
Goldring, Taylor 76
Gonzalez, Kendra 42
Gonzalez, Stephanie 141
Gormley, Joshua 118
Gould, Adrianna 93
Graber, Austin 115
Gracanin, Jasmina 138
Graf, Melissa 131
Grannes, Macy 119
Grass, Olivia 171
Graves, Sarah 181
Gray, Vanessa 30
Greiner, Nick 115
Grenstiner, Madi 163
Gress, Alex 48
Gress, Victoria 119
Groesbeck, Caroline 55
Grose, Logan 144
Grush-Wolf, Whitney 82
Guerra, Hunter 79

Guinn, Kason 66
Gurath, Emera 104
Gutierrez, Jeffrey 129
Hack, Morgan 36
Haddican, Sam 104
Haefke, Ryan 31
Hageman, Chandler 81
Hager, Hunter 77
Hajek-Jones, Emma 87
Hall, Selena 99
Halverson, Hailee 27
Hamilton, Courtney 37
Hammeke, Logan 171
Hammond, Collin 139
Hammond, Evan 175
Hampton, Conner 28
Hansen, Bonnie 54
Hansen, Brendan 125
Hansen, Kailey 40
Hanson, Krystal 36
Hardenberger, Clayton 31
Hardy, Noah 66
Harley, Matthew 144
Harman, Andrew 139
Harman, Rachelle 28
Harms, Broderick 45
Harpenau, Madison 11
Harris, Carol Eve 59
Harris, Devlin 9
Harris, Nate 78
Harris, Sara 66
Hart, Cameron 103
Harter, Reed 95
Harwood, Sonya 114
Haselhorst, Rodger 32
Hastings, Mikaela 41
Haupert, Callie 167
Hawk, Rylee 76
Hawkins, Emma Jo 162
Hay, Justin 67
Hayes, Kelsey 31
Haynes, Preston 143
Headrick, Darrell 12
Heagel, Elisabeth 143
Hedges, Skylar 121
Hefel, Crystal 89
Hegstrom, Victoria 86
Heidlebaugh, Shea 109
Heineken, Jacob 59
Heitman, Haley 165
Heller, Alexis 138
Hellyer, McKayla 86
Helm, Alesha 163
Henderson, Kayla 14
Hendrix, Gage 124
Henry, Abbigail 68
Henry, Kaden 127
Herling, Desiree 11

Heslop, Kilea 177
Heyd, Josie 140
Heydlauff, Lydia 124
Hickman, River 155
Higgins, Keely 24
Hill, Joel 102
Hillman, Maggie 184
Hinsley, Ben 86
Hintz, Ben 27
Hintz, Kylea 42
Hintz, Mariah 82
Hirsch, Jolie 166
Hoard, Chris 64
Hobbs, Tristan 125
Hobrock, Lane 118
Hockenberry, Emma 54
Hofer, Tanner 159
Hoffman, Tommy 80
Hofmeister, Kaitlin 178
Hole, Kaylie 162
Holmstrom, Morgan 84
Holzkamm, Elizabeth 172
Honeyman, Brynn 140
Houser, Sydney 157
Houtcooper, Angela 89
Howard, Bailey 90
Howard, Gabi 122
Howe, Alyssa 58
Huang, Jenny 80
Huettl, Alexis 43
Huff, Melissa 16
Hughes, Allison 64
Hulme, Rachel 51
Hummel, Kirsten 15
Humpal, Katelynn 101
Hunt, Morgan 162
Hunter, Christina 77
Hurt, Tara 36
Husted, Christian 181
Hyer, Josh 91
Iben, Maddie 47
Ihle, Kristy 103
Ijaz, Omair 84
Isom, Katerina 24
Iverson, Madison 10
Jabben, Natalie 120
Jackson, Autum 29
Jackson, Nadia 145
Jackson, Nia 163
Jacobs, Megan 52
Jacobsen, Karissa 86
Jacobsen, Lauren 183
Jaeger, Laura 21
Jahner, Kaitlin 156
Jamison, Hannah 68
Jans, Maddy 128
Janvrin, Bryleigh 108
Jarecke, Jarrett 40

Jenik, Kattie	131	Klumpe, Jessica	99	Lee, Journey	87
Jenkins, Jesse	54	Kneip, Dustan	30	Lee, Samantha	156
Jensen, Alexia	79	Knight, Isabelle	91	Lehfeldt, Jase	176
Jensen, Garret	108	Knight, Isabelle	108	Lehmann, Brenna	51
Jensen, Stepheny	59	Knock, Mitchell	179	Lehr, Nathanael	99
Jensen, Willow	47	Knop, Tyler	148	Lenox, Emily	48
Jesse, Genevieve	36	Koch, Brendon	176	Lenz, Molly	172
Johnson, Allie	119	Koelzer, Jacob	107	Leon, Mario Blaine	188
Johnson, Anna	22	Koenig, Emily	120	Lesser, Matthew	180
Johnson, Brytni	167	Koenigsfeld, Meghan	61	Lethcoe, Brenda	94
Johnson, Kaleb	40	Koestner, Emma	69	Lickiss, Sabrina	76
Johnson, Loyal	151	Koger, Josh	63	Lien, Megan	176
Johnson, Nicole	12	Kohn, Megan	107	Liermann, Trenton	181
Johnson, Noah	151	Koley, Laura	48	Lim, John	147
Johnson, Paul-Michael	100	Komanetz, Liberty	147	Lingo, Joshua	41
Johnson, Rachel	10	Kopp, Autumn	181	Linn, Jacob	67
Johnston, Lizzy	78	Kopp, Madison	170	Linn, Kassandra	73
Jolley, Scott	137	Kovinchick, Melodee	184	Linton, Brinley	128
Jones, Echo	117	Kral, Ty	131	Lipman, Dani	106
Jones, Hannah	141	Kram, Jacob	168	Litchfield, Chase	129
Jones, Kelsey	86	Kramer, Grace	110	Livermore, Megan	9
Jones, Sarah	107	Kramer, Jenna	93	Livermore, Patrick	29
Jordan, Megan	149	Kramper, Sophie	165	Livingston, Leo	14
Juarez, Samuel	87	Krapfl, Collin	69	Loecker, Jared	183
June, Dayton	24	Kratz, Margaret	119	Loeffler, Cheyanne	18
Jurgensen, Ryley	160	Kreegar, Noma	134	Logue, Michael	158
Kaiser, Therese	91	Krehbiel, Noah	176	Lohmann, Winter	177
Kaktis, Tommy	170	Krehbiel, Sarah	138	Lomeli, Michael	178
Kalcevic, Kyleigh	76	Krinke, Dominique	165	Longabaugh, Jordan	129
Kaml, Caitlyn	141	Krohn, Levi	145	Longie, Trevor	112
Karella, Rylee	139	Krueger, Kelby	136	Loonan, Riley	127
Kastning, Kaitlyn	172	Kubick, Cole	157	Lopez, Tristin	144
Kaufman, Tymber	177	Kubik, Kacey	110	Lorenz, Collin	139
Kelby	180	Kucera, Kassidy	79	Lorenz, Heaven	62
Keigley, Lucas	75	Kunzweiler, Morgan	166	Lott, Lyric	92
Kelly, Bailey	20	Labenz, Gunner	138	Lovvorn, Megan	10
Kelly, Vanessa	33	Lacey, Colter	187	Lowery, Genevieve	63
Kemp, Kristen	81	Lacina, Maisie	182	Lucas, Taviar	75
Kennedy, Nash	168	Laird, Lorianne	137	Ludovissy, Derek	157
Kent, Kassie	75	Lakha, Arria	26	Luna, Keilah	168
Kenyon, Haileigh	65	Lambrecht, Emily	124	Lund, Nathan	67
Kerner, Matthew	120	Lampe, Bethany	16	Macke, Zachary	79
Kessenich, Hannah	35	Lamphier-Meier, Margaret	107	Maddox, Faith	166
Kessler, Annie	87	Lamprecht, Taylor	159	Maddox, Wade	34
Kilburn, Kampbell	181	Landenberger, JR	113	Madsen, Clay	90
Kim, Nulee	22	Lang, Michelle	126	Mahlmeister, Madison	99
Kimrey, Brody	74	Lansing, Blake	42	Maise, Braeden	187
King, Matt	34	Larson, Madelyn	180	Mammen, Tristan	187
Kingsbury, Logan	183	Lasley, Lara	148	Mander, Caitlin	57
Kinney, Abby	45	Lathrum, Taylor	43	Manders, Gabrielle J.	85
Kinzer, Mariah	80	Laurel, Jackie	163	Mans, Katie	169
Kirch, Madison	25	Lawrence, Stephanie	88	Marlow, Katerina	167
Kirschbaum, Kendall	170	Laws, Amber	130	Martin, Alyssa	11
Kirwan, Alec	48	Lazio, Hannah	85	Martin, Cody	178
Klahr, Chelsea	72	Lazio, Hannah	88	Martin, John	130
Klein, Gillian	60	Lazio, Taylor	60	Martin, Steven	102
Klein, Michelle	8	Lee, Duana	77	Martinz, Sage	180
Klick, Kiley	16	Lee, Jordan	169	Masching, Ethan	102

Index

Matta, Julie 142	Mogensen, Meg 148	Olnes, Devyn 114
Matteson, Mikayla 124	Mogensen, Trey 16	Olvera, Joe 47
Matthews, Spencer 73	Moline, Kylee 175	Ormiston, Autumn 187
Mauch, Zack 61	Moller, Trevor 77	Orth, Ashlee 53
Mayes, Jacob 171	Monson, Cassie 188	Ortman, Payton 172
Maynard, Emily 19	Montgomery, Jonah 48	Ortman, Trey 140
Mazour, Wyatt 56	Montgomery, Reagan 162	Osnes, Jesse 131
McAfee, Carissa 58	Moody, Abbie 65	Ott, Krista 114
McCammant, Izabelle 121	Morales, Daniel 156	Otto, Alyssa 188
McCance, Joe 49	Morales, Jesus 148	Otto, Brandon 134
McCollister, Kara 154	Morgan, Ciara 62	Overweg, Darissa 186
McCord, JR 43	Morris, Paige 167	Owen, Allison 35
McCoy, Natasha 73	Morrison, Brianna 179	Owens, Salem 60
McCullough, Sierra 117	Morrison, Kamryn 156	Oyster, Jami 145
McDaniel, Trevor 144	Morrow, Claire 171	Pacheco, Justin 97
McDermid, Samara 146	Morrow, Jasmine 71	Pafford, Grace 176
McDermott, Molly 172	Morse, Georgia 109	Pagan, Julian 157
McElmeel, Maggie Jo 22	Morton, Sydney 56	Palafox, Michelle 9
McGee, Rianna 172	Mueller, Kara 78	Pantle, Emily 126
McGivern, John 21	Mullen, Brianna 53	Parr, Vivian 52
McGrew, Maddie 32	Mumm, Madison 74	Parry, Austin 161
McGuire, Christopher 70	Munoz, Samantha 146	Parry, Hannah 186
McGuire, Molly 110	Muñoz, Maira 168	Passero, Kiya 65
McIntire, Rebecca 20	Myers, Kayla 44	Patterson, Hannah 120
McIntosh, Casie 185	Nachazel, Jessica 173	Pauley, Emilee 187
McLaughlin, Mark 86	Nakazono, Daniel 50	Paz, Richie 101
McLeod, Caitlynn 174	Nawara, Brianna 23	Peil, Alxis 108
McNealey, Na'Tori 123	Neidig, Hailey 103	Penne, Kaylee 25
Mead, Kourtney 105	Nelson, Audrey 81	Pentecost, Dakota 29
Mejia, Cindy 68	Nelson, Erik 66	Perales, Elija 154
Melendrez, Henry 95	Nelson, Hannah 70	Perez, Cinthia 63
Mellick, Carin 134	Nelson, Zachary 176	Perreard, Maddie 175
Melton, Pamula 180	Neuhalfen, Kyle 65	Persinger, Emily 147
Mendez, Nayeli 144	Nguyen, Ajia 46	Peter, Caitlin 36
Menendez, Amparo 130	Nicholson, Jena 22	Peterson, Alyssa 83
Mennecke, Jonathan 115	Nickel, Isacc 103	Peterson, Grant 99
Merical, Adam 136	Nicolaisen, Sabrina 63	Petrich, Joshua 66
Messerlie, Walter 137	Niederle, Megan 47	Petty, Kaylee 135
Metivier, Casadi 156	Nieves, Jeremiah 155	Pfeiler, Meggan 119
Metzger, Andrew 90	Niles, Ryan 134	Phillips, Macy 180
Meyer, Allissa 88	Nissen, Jeremy 172	Pierce, Josh 67
Meyer, Rachel 61	Noah, Austin 45	Pierce, Tristan 151
Meysenburg, Molly 92	Noah, Rebecca 131	Pierson, Dexter 141
Michele, Ana 129	Noll, Avery 66	Pile, Tiffani 44
Miller, Anna 156	Noll, Josie 114	Pinson, Sarah Elizabeth 149
Miller, Beau 134	Nordhues, Ashley 148	Piros, Hannah 169
Miller, Cole 160	Nordhues, Ashley 177	Pistello, Rachel 88
Miller, Dallas 150	Norton, Kaleb 159	Pliler, Victoria 141
Miller, Danielle 187	Norton, Leah 143	Plowman, Logan 140
Miller, Joel 113	Novotney, Tyler 41	Pohlmann, Jared 124
Miller, Melissa 126	Nowlan, Noni 84	Pokojski, William 36
Miller, Reagen 169	Nuese, Kayla 32	Pokorny, Wyatt 136
Mills, Emily 91	Nugteren, Caleb 166	Porter, Zach 17
Mills, Mikka 22	Nugteren, Joseph 173	Powell, Shelby 22
Miser, Jocie 8	Nunez, Monse 152	Pregler, Zach 157
Mockler, Emma 106	O'Neal, Drakkar 164	Prescott, Austin 34
Mockler, Sarah 109	Oberg, Taylor 145	Price, Tyson 74
Moen, Skylar 125	Oligmueller, Jayda 118	Prose, Kohl 125

Prugh, Haylie	142	Rowlands, Kennedi	71	Sidak, Nathaniel	138
Pry, Kendra	159	Ruden, Cody	128	Siegner, Ashley	54
Purk, Jaika	147	Rupard, Cheyenne	47	Siess, Devon	51
Qualls, Jesse	180	Rush, Ann	29	Sigler, Brianna	120
Quigley, Colten	35	Rush, Logan	156	Simmer, Gage	175
Rahman, Shoilee	46	Russell, Athena	98	Simmons, Mikayla	184
Raines, Cambria	139	Russell, Laura	33	Simmons, Nathan	48
Ramaker, Anna	177	Ryan, Katelyn	109	Simon, Alex	63
Ramirez, Sebastian	44	SaBell, Laine	141	Simon, Elayna	178
Ramos, Josh	27	Said, MacKenzie	169	Simon, Rylee	51
Rants, Sydney	88	Salmeron, Almudena	14	Simpson, Mary Ann	12
Rasmussen, Devin	100	Salter, Noah	52	Sinclair, Grace	165
Ratzlaff, Ashley	175	Salyers, Madeline	62	Sloan, Seth	94
Rector, Cameo	104	Samples, Katie	184	Smit, Aubrey	177
Redding, Gianna	168	Sampson, Trae	110	Smith, Blake	187
Redeker, Dylan	100	SanGrait, Julia	176	Smith, Jordan	94
Redmond, Brianna	13	Santiago, Beverly	30	Smith, Kylee	116
Reed, Dallas	45	Sarceño, Yasmin	178	Smothers, Darien	91
Reed, Kayla	59	Savick, Korbin	90	Smothers, Krisondra	16
Reichert, Amanda	82	Saxton, Lydia	161	Smyth, Hunter	184
Reiners, James	113	Sayaloune, Naleka	85	Snyder, Brett	93
Reiswig, Amelia	121	Schaal, Hunter	60	Snyder, Madison	64
Remke, Adelle	162	Schany, Beau	100	Sobetski, Zeus	188
Reth, Mikaela	83	Schave, Carey	82	Sommersted-Simmons, Khobe	174
Reuter, Ashley	94	Scheller, Maranda	59	Soto, Daniella	62
Reyes, Jonathan	127	Schelling, Hannah	67	Soukup, Kristan	90
Reynoso, Diego	147	Schenk, Christopher	140	Souza, Paris	152
Rheinschmidt, Grant	45	Schmaltz, Ashley	118	Spangler, Chandra	177
Rice, Kyle	117	Schmaltz, Meranda	122	Spencer, Andrea	61
Richard, Mathew	163	Schmid, Katie	118	Springer, Alexandria	51
Riesberg, Rylie	100	Schmidt, Sammie	69	Stack, Jayden	81
Riha, Kaitlyn	153	Schnell, Sydnee	29	Staebler, Jaderial	82
Riley, Meghan	109	Schoettger, Jenna	41	Stafford, Hannah	131
Riley, Sean	105	Schraft, Janette	159	Stahl, Carlé	175
Rinehart, Aaron	126	Schroeder, Samantha	97	Stahr, Isaac	57
Ringering, Faith	158	Schultz, Molly	84	Stammer, Dennis	21
Riniker, Bryce	71	Schultz, Trevor	64	Stamper, Mariah	12
Rioux, Abby	94	Schulz, Helena	116	Stanley, Nicklas	58
Robbins, Brynlee	123	Schwager, Sydney	22	Stanwix, Jamie	58
Roberts, Armani	142	Schwarte, Delaney	49	Starman, Macey	86
Roberts, Ashlynne	19	Schweers, Abby	186	Starsnic, Samantha	49
Roberts, Tyler	157	Schweers, Hudson	185	Statema, Zachary	187
Robertson, Quintin	56	Scott, Brianna	183	Staton, Virginia	53
Robl, Taryn	158	Searles, Devin	184	Steele, Nate	54
Roder, Sara	15	Seipold, Emma	166	Steffen, Sarah	73
Rodriguez, Giovanna	156	Seppanen, Amalia	74	Steffens, Travis	112
Roes, Brooke	70	Seymour, Sarah	180	Steinlage, Sydney	60
Rogers, Makayla	113	Shahan, Solomon	162	Stellingwerf, Karlyn	30
Rogers, Taylor	89	Shanno, Cody	95	Stephens Jr., Terence	52
Rogers, Travis	40	Sharp, Randy	144	Stirler, Josh	125
Roldan, Bladimir	43	Shaw, Misty	77	Stokes, Tristyn	97
Rolf, Cherise	136	Sheeley, Liam	147	Stoysich, Ashlynn	85
Romine, Nicole	26	Shelton, McKinna	92	Strader, Connor	30
Rosales, Wendy	54	Shepherd, Shaundra	87	Strathman, Michaela	36
Rosas-Kirkman, Maryha	101	Sheridan, Kristin	114	Strope, Heydon	145
Rosenberger, Clarissa	135	Sherlock, Kylie	120	Struck, Bradley	97
Roshone, Carson	165	Shield, Levi	95	Stuart, Ashton	51
Rote, Alexandra	53	Shimitz, Taylor	121	Stueck, MacKenize	111

Index

Sturgeon, Chance	112
Suda, Matthew	176
Sullivan, Haiden	45
Sullivan, Rachel	113
Sunderman, Jacob	24
Surat, Hannah	162
Swanson, Peter	33
Swartout, Justis	25
Swick, Morgan	143
Talent, Faith	40
Tangeman, Graci	176
Tanking, Trent	17
Taylor, McKayla	80
Taylor, McKenzie	51
Taylor, Simon	118
Taylor, Skyelar	108
Tegarden, Lane	52
Ten Eyck, Catilyn	151
Terpstra, Holden	71
Terry, Ian	110
Thelen, Tacy	13
Thierstein, Cole	159
Thies, Tony	19
Thomas, Jaugger	86
Thomas, Mackenzie	49
Thomas, Mackenzie	127
Thompson, Adam	22
Thompson, Anna	174
Thompson, Graci	181
Thompson, Hannah	107
Thompson, Katie	56
Thompson, Sam	187
Thooft, Justin	93
Throne, Kristyn	170
Tiefenthaler, Shaela	42
Tift, Kristy	116
Tilden, Triana	75
Tilton, Lindsay	64
Tilton, Zach	75
Timberland, Sean	65
Timm, Bryce	135
Titus, Megan	138
Tjossem, Bailey	134
Tompkins, Sophia	117
Torster, Kara	54
Tramp, Jacobe	183
Trisler, Justin	9
Tritch, Hunter	164
Trout, Amanda	164
True, Kyler	59
Trujillo, Chris	67
Two Bulls, Tasia Rae	86
Upah, Wesley	149
Van Allen, Trey	89
Van Hull, Hailey	111
VanBeek, Sarah	151
Vandenberg, Quinn	62
Vanderfeen, Madeline	102
Vanderpool, Adeline	101
VanDyke, Alexa	159
Vasquez, Cheyenne	97
Velasco, Ian	128
Velder, Gabbie	174
Verdoni, Nico	111
Vesely, Rose	14
Vesely, Shelby	102
Villa, Yaretzi	55
Vinogradov, Sam	51
Vinogradov, Sam	118
Virus, Trelby	9
Volk, Madison	174
von Behren, David	13
Von Ehwegen, Kort	119
Vonnahme, Heather	102
Wachendorf, Katelyn	96
Wagner, Sydney	64
Waldemar, Aubrie	169
Walker, Riley	41
Walter, Joseph	183
Walters, Lezlie	99
Walton, Faith	138
Wangerin, Taylor	106
Warren, Virgil	113
Warwick, Dylan	100
Washburn, Stormi	144
Watchorn, Joel	136
Waters, Kaleb	53
Watkins, Austin	23
Watson, Hannah	85
Watson, Whitney	139
Weaver, Paul	67
Webb, Emma	176
Webb, Tagan	66
Webber, Keegan	122
Weber, Andrew	145
Weber, Emily	122
Webster, Brittany-Ann	156
Wegener, Brooke	101
Weidenbach, Gabriella	141
Weidenbach, Myndi	175
Weir, Alexandra	78
Weir, Sara	61
Welch, Gage	101
Wells, Christina	165
Wells, Lauren	159
Welsh, Nate	161
Welu, Angel	90
West, Devany	24
Wetta, Sophia	106
Whitaker, Ben	139
White, Jessup	35
White, K'Lyn	124
White, Philip	120
White, Robby	129
White, Sophie	116
White, Zach	60
Whitmer, Laura	15
Whitney, Cole	91
Whitt, Kassidy	103
Wickham, Stephanie	34
Widdowson, Natasha	104
Wilkey, Ronald	19
Wilkinson, Cameron	56
Willenborg, Jackie	93
Williams, Allyssa	104
Williams, Bernadette	47
Williams, Destiny	85
Williams, Jacob	25
Williams, Jenna	116
Williams, Malachi	172
Williams, Tyler	70
Willis, Andres	93
Wilson, Bralyn	110
Wilson, Brandon	88
Wilson, Brittney	144
Wilson, Chase	34
Wilson, Kavi	73
Wilson, Kieran	125
Wilson, Logan Donald	110
Wingert, Molly	113
Winget, Seth	183
Winters, Anyah	144
Wistuba, Amanda	72
Wolf, Emily	24
Wolf, Marie	104
Wolff, Hannah	40
Wolters, Michelle	21
Wolverton, LeAnna	54
Wonders, Marissa	150
Woods, Caitlin	136
Wornkey, Heaven	173
Wortman, Jazzmine	138
Wright, Angela	56
Xiong, Ivana	129
Yong, Helen	178
Youde, Nate	8
Young, Jessica	95
Young, Olivia	92
Youngquist, Hazel	163
Zaccardi, Heather	117
Zahnley, Sydney	171
Zellmer, Kristine	97
Zepeda-Perez, Edward	173
Zheng, Anna	18
Zimmerman, Hailey	182
Zimmerman, Samantha	175
Zimmerman, Tyler	90
Zweygardt, Taryn	131

Author Autograph Page

Author Autograph Page

Author Autograph Page

Author Autograph Page

Author Autograph Page

Author Autograph Page

Author Autograph Page

Author Autograph Page

Author Autograph Page

Author Autograph Page

Author Autograph Page

Author Autograph Page